The King is Dead, Long live the Queen

Volume 1 to 4

By
Julia Phillips

About the Author

Julia Phillips is a middle-aged trans-woman, born and raised in Essex, England and has led a closeted life up until the events detailed within this volume. Her life was turned upside-down at the end of the Covid lockdown in the most fundamental of ways, due to a profound heartbreak leading to a failed suicide attempt. She began a journal the day after this attempt, to help her navigate this crucible, to break down and then to resolve the myriad of thoughts and feelings she was going through at the time.

These pages are a transcript of all four volumes, covering the days and weeks that immediately followed, as she began to try and rebuild her life…

As a true account of real events, names and a few specific details have necessarily been adjusted to protect the parties involved.

The King is Dead, Long live the Queen - Volume 1 to 4

Author: Julia Phillips

Copyright © 2025 Julia Phillips

The right of Julia Phillips to be identified as author of this work has been asserted by the author in accordance with section 77 and 78 of the Copyright, Designs and Patents Act 1988.

First Published in 2025

ISBN 978-1-83538-523-4 (Paperback)
   978-1-83538-524-1 (E-Book)

Book Cover Design and Book Layout by:
   White Magic Studios
   www.whitemagicstudios.co.uk

Published by:
   Maple Publishers
   Fairbourne Drive, Atterbury,
   Milton Keynes,
   MK10 9RG, UK
   www.maplepublishers.com

A CIP catalogue record for this title is available from the British Library.

All rights reserved. No part of this book may be reproduced or translated in any form or by any means, electronic or mechanical, including photocopying, recording or by any information storage and retrieval system without written permission from the author.

The views expressed in this work are solely those of the author and do not necessarily reflect the publisher's opinions, and the publisher, as a result of this, disclaims any responsibility for them.

Contents

Book	Section	Pages
The King is Dead... Long live the Queen	**Volume 1 - (April 4th to April 24th)**	**0 – 113**
	About the Author / disclaimer	02
	Copyright	03
	Contents	04-05
	Foreword and Dedication	06
	Black and white photo: Journal 1, a very dark place to begin	06
	Photo: Another pack of playing cards ruined	15
	Illustration: The Grand Gender Experiment	20
	Illustration: Some kind of future?	24
	Illustration: I like being Julia	40
	Illustration: Fingers crossed...	52
	Illustration: Must sleep now	69
	Illustration: For Love. A good deal. The very best	89
	Illustration: I am worried for you	98
	Illustration: The train of change	112
	Illustration: Fin. End of part 1	113

Book	Section	Pages
If the Shoe fits	**Volume 2 – (April 25th to June 27th)**	**114 – 361**
	Dedication	115
	Forward	116-118
	An interlude: I feel sorry for the scriptwriter!	119
	Illustration: I like drawing flowers	126
	Illustration: Validation, my heart soared!	127
	Illustration: Night mum x.	136
	Illustration: The Whirlpool of Grief	189
	Illustrations: Gender scales	240-241
	Illustration: Smile, a simple philosophy of life	250
	Illustration: Life is good again, at last	292
	Illustration: This is my dream	296
	Illustration: Happiness is a nice pair of undies	321
	Illustration: A good set of goals	331
	Illustration: Wedding dress	347
	Photo: Ruby Wedding	356
	Photo: Journal 2	361

Book	Section	Pages
Skirting the Issue	**Volume 3 – (June 28th to August 25th)**	**362-547**
	Dedication	363
	Forward	365
	Interlude: A truly rubbish restaurant!	366
	Illustration: Travel	373
	Illustration: And then, Eve	397
	Photo: The last of love	399
	Photos: The three most important pages of my life	404-406
	Photos: A perfect spot for mum	436-437
	Photo: So beautiful, but I can't appreciate it	449
	Photo: Last night at the pool bar	453
	Illustration: Sketch of the last photo of Eve	478
	Illustration: Here lies Adam	482
	Illustration: Appreciation	487
	Illustration: Gender jigsaw	489
	Photo: Horses	498
	Illustration: Broken heart	503
	Illustration & Photo: I've written a book!	516-517
	Illustration: I hate it when she shuts me out	532
	Illustration: Clapperboard	546
	Photo: Journals 1 to 3	547

Book	Section	Pages
I am Julia!	**Volume 4 – (August 26th to November 5th)**	**548-695**
	Dedication	549
	Forward	550
	Interlude: "Dysphoria's Freak Show!"	552
	Illustration: Sweet dreams	567
	Illustration: Cream tea	571
	Illustration: The flowers over there are pretty…	575
	Pho to: Wow, that's a tight fit	597
	Illustration: Sore feet	599
	Photo: Mogs	609
	Illustration: Frog	614
	Illustration: How to make housework is enjoyable	639
	Illustration: 12 hours of bliss	648
	Photo: The end?	679
	A conclusion, of sorts… October 4th 2022	681
	Epilogue: May 10th, 2024	685
	Photo: Bye to my little furry man	688
	Photo: All four journals	695

Forward & Dedication

This diary belongs to: Miss Julia Phillips

...and is dedicated to the loving memory of Adam, a man who fought to be, but ultimately was overwhelmed. He passed away at the end of 2020 when his reason for existence was taken away from him, and his 50-year gender identity struggle ended. He exists now only as an acceptable face to society, to enable his true self, Julia, to fit in and be successful as a human being.

This journal will detail Julia's rise and the protracted death throes of Adam as he is slowly turned into someone else. Someone who desperately needs to find a reason to go on, someone true and authentic now that Adam's life as he knew and loved it, is over.

A very dark place to begin...

April 4th, 2021

'J-Day' + 1...

Dear Diary...

Where to begin? With the truth of my situation, I suppose. I am in Hell.

My life was built on being Eve's boyfriend, part of a couple, in a loving, all-be-it largely platonic relationship. That life, I have recently found out, has been a lie for at least the last 5 years.

I am no longer a boyfriend. So, there is now no longer any need to deny who I am and force myself to be male. You see, I have also recently found out that I have been living a lie for the past 50 years too. But we shall come to this in more detail later, for now, I am recording my current situation — there is a lot to unpack here, and it is easy to get side-tracked.

When Eve and I got together, I decided that I would become the best Man, Boyfriend, Soul Mate, Partner, even Husband (if she wanted, she did not), I could possibly be. I decided that I could define myself in this role for love, for Eve, for us as a couple and also, for me.

I have been that man. A man named Adam, very successfully (I thought) for 15 years. But for Eve, I have not been her boyfriend for around a third of it...

It came to a head at the end of 2020, when after a year of utter despair at the loss of my mum during lockdown, I decided to try to close the distance I felt had grown between Eve and I over the previous 12 months. I declared my intentions to her in her Christmas Card. Hoping we could work together and rebuild the wonderful life we once had. Mum's passing resulted in me going to a dark place, becoming emotionally distant because I was so raw. And this meant I was withdrawn and needed Eve more than ever.

She wasn't really there for me in the way that I needed.

She tried. She could see I was hurting. But Eve had already stepped away from us as a couple. She had spent a lot of time prior to this, way before lockdown, thinking of herself as an individual, not my girlfriend and had moved on.

I knew things were not going well, I had attributed this to being so grief stricken and wrapped up in my own little emotional turmoil. By Christmas, I was ready to make things better...

*It did **NOT** go well.*

Things got worse in December through January when she decided she wanted to sleep apart. She began sleeping on the sofa. I have never been so lonely. I still am, and I think I will now always be lonely. I felt and still feel utterly rejected.

Adam's world was built on being part of a couple. Without this, he is nothing.

Late March 2021. I cannot take it anymore and have a breakdown. I confronted Eve in tears, desperate for my love to be returned. Eve can't though. SHE DOESN'T LOVE ME, at least not in that way, not anymore. She hasn't for years and explains that she is not the same, naive and innocent girl of 21 she was when we first got together, now that she is 35. She entered into our relationship believing she could deal with my gender issues, but as the years went by, while I was falling deeper and deeper in love with her, she matured and realised that she just couldn't. I only just found out. For Eve, it was gradual, but for me, it was sudden and profound.

My whole life collapsed.
Adam was mortally wounded, he died shortly after.

The man he was, the man built for the sole purpose of making Eve, the woman he loves, as happy as possible. The man who existed only to be her boyfriend, ceased to exist the moment Eve said the thought of him as her brother. At this point his reason for living vanished and with his core being gone – he no longer existed as a real person.

In 2020, I lost Mum.

In 2020, I began to realise I had lost Eve too. My love, my life, my one true soul mate.

In 2021, I lost her for real.

In 2021, I lost Adam as well, part of my soul was fatally wounded.

Grief is utter shit.

I AM JULIA

How else can I carry on?

I still love Eve, more than I love life itself. I went out to kill myself, but it didn't happen – I am still at the very brink though. She has driven me to the edge and (unintentionally), completely ripped out Adam's heart. He has no reason to continue and if he were ALL there was, he would have physically died too. As it happens though, I am more than Adam. I am Julia too. Julia who is now, for the first time, released and is at last driving the ship. Julia saved my life on that day. Julia is the reason I did not kill myself. Julia has hope, hope that she can now blossom. As Julia, I can continue...

You see, although I am one person, despite being physically male, I have been, at my core, of indeterminate gender. At least this is how I have always thought of myself. When I am dressed as a male, my name is Adam. I fit into society and am able to function and be accepted as a male. To the extent I am reasonably successful by most standards.

But recent events have compelled me to face that inside, I am not some strange genderless mixture.

I am actually female.

I have struggled with this for my entire life. I realised I was not "a boy" incredibly young, maybe 4 or 5 years old – it's one of my very earliest memories, feeling like I was not very much like other boys and that I was, in fact, a **LOT** like girls. 1970's, with two very conservative parents meant I was not able to deal with or come to terms with my nature. And family, friends or society were never going to even comprehend, let alone accept someone like me.

Things began to improve, little by little from a societal point of view in the 80's. But for me, I was dealing with something utterly earth shattering – puberty. Puberty was an inescapable nightmare for me and in terms of my body, an irreversible disaster that, in more recent, enlightened times, would have been completely avoidable.

> I watched my own body decide for me who I was going to be. It was stealthy and deliberate. For the first time in my life, I could not handle it. I needed help, my female nature was being physically assaulted, inch-by-inch, day-by-day. She was turned into a man against her will.

I fled screaming in panic from this nightmare, not physically, but mentally, although it manifested itself in my behaviour – dysphoria running rampant. I needed help. And help came in the form of a psychotherapist named Jane. She helped me come to terms with who I am, encouraged me to accept my female side and nurture it enough to heal. Julia was born from these sessions, and it took years for me to find a balance. I did it by spending regular time expressing myself as her and I slowly came back from a place of trauma to a place where I could live with the ramifications of my body choosing a side. But it was never true acceptance, just a detached logical approach to making the best of a bad lot.

I developed a daily routine, I lived as Adam, but by night, in bed, I slept as Julia. In a pretty nightie, curled up for 8 hours of female bliss. It keeps me stable, even today and along with the occasional longer sessions where I dress completely as Julia in day clothes, I am on an even keel and can release the stress of having to keep a male countenance.

It was about balance. Both sides of my nature are expressed, all be it less so as Julia, because Julia is forever trapped in the body of a big, very male, man. Julia is unlikely to be able to function successfully in society as a female. Puberty destroyed all hope in me of life as a physical woman.

There are days, weeks and sometimes months at a time when this is all I want. To live 24/7 as Julia, be physically female, a woman in every possible way and be happy. But this is not very realistic and equally there *were* days when I loved being Adam. My time as Adam, with Eve are by far the best days of my life. I finally came to terms with Adam as me (an enormous and profound step) and lived to be him, for the sake of our relationship, for Eve's love. Life was good, the very best. I miss those days so much and I was trying to get them back over Christmas 2020 – too little, too late.

Balance is an interesting concept. I knew asking Eve to sleep with her boyfriend wearing a nightie was a big ask. But I do not have a choice, I must express my *entire* nature and as Julia cannot successfully exist outside of the house due to my physicality, being her whilst we were both asleep was the only way to fit a large amount of time into our lives with as little impact as possible. At first, although awkward, we made it work. But in the end, the sight of her boyfriend as a woman proved too much for Eve and she slowly fell out of love with me.

It is no one's fault. Eve's reaction is as a normal, heterosexual female and she dealt with the situation as best as she could for as long as she could. As her boyfriend, Julia was unacceptable ultimately. By turning her romantic love into a sibling love, I became her sister when I was Julia, and we could stay together as siblings and great friends. But <u>not</u> as boyfriend and girlfriend. Our romantic relationship fizzled out and she began to think of herself as an individual rather than as part of a couple.

This wasn't understood by me at all and caused me massive confusion, hurt and heartache when it began to manifest itself. Culminating in two of the most painful holiday experiences I have ever had. We typically go on car rallies together across Europe within a group of great friends. At least I thought we were together. Eve had a couple of great holidays, on her own, abandoning me to drive the car while she rode in other cars on the rally. I felt lost and confused – my holidays were ruined.

I wish we had talked this through five plus years ago, but in truth, I think it's likely we would have ended up where we are today. I cannot change who I am, equally Eve can't be romantically involved with even 50% of a woman it seems. We were doomed as lovers – it felt like hard work for me to be honest. I am, more or less, asexual and do not find either gender physically attractive. I love Eve, so much, enough to deny a fundamental part of me and throw myself into being a man for her, but we have both learned that sex without attraction is not as enjoyable or as fulfilling as it should be. Who knows, maybe now that I am Julia at my core things will change? Wishful thinking maybe, I am never going to fit into a so-called "normal" sexual pigeonhole. As much as I wanted to be a man for Eve in all ways, I failed at this utterly – I'm now sure this is what drove her away (although I wish I'd recognised this at the time) and what ultimately killed Adam. He is a shell now, and he has lost everything – I cannot *be* him anymore. I am only Julia; she is all that is left of me.

I love Eve as much as ever; she will always be everything to me. But she doesn't love me anymore. Adam is broken and his heart is shattered, to the extent he cannot go on. I am Julia because I have to be, being Julia means that Adam can take the time he needs to heal, if he can, but he will <u>never</u> be the same again.

I wear Adam as a mask, in order to continue. The only way to survive is to become something new, Julia is all I am, Julia is my life from now on.

> *I will be Julia more than Adam. Each day will be spent as a woman. Adam will be put on to function in society, but I will spend 50% or more of the rest of my life living completely as a woman.*

This sounds like a manifesto, or maybe a solemn vow, but the truth is, I am Julia already. She is who I am all the time, and now that I know & have faced up to who I fundamentally am, there is no way back. There is nothing left to go back to.

Eve seems fine with this. I am not sure how fine, she keeps telling me that she relates to me as a sibling, so how I am dressed doesn't matter. I do not think she realises that something profound has shifted in me, but as the days roll on and not only do I embrace being Julia, but grow her into a real person as I, after 50 long years, finally explore my female nature as fully as I can, I think she will realise. She is one of the most intelligent people I know and inevitably our life together will change. I hope for the better, it can't feel any worse...

As much as she realises that she has hurt me deeply, as a hetero person who is at home with her gender, she can never comprehend just how fundamentally. She has not only taken her love from me, but by doing so, has destroyed Adam's self-worth completely. To the extent that I feel like I have switched genders. He has no reason to be. I am Julia and (I hope) Adam is on life support, but he has lost everything, including his very identity. Julia is a safe place; she is one step away from the pain – oh so much pain.

So, dear Diary, this is where I am at this moment in time. I am currently expressing myself truly, as Julia, dressed in a skirt and blouse, lingerie, make-up, jewellery and heels and have been since around 7:30pm. As I woke up in my nightie as usual and did not change out of it until after 7:30am I will be spending more than 50% of the day in a skirt, as a woman. This has been my life since I began to come to terms with the situation. Eve says I should "own" this. She doesn't realise that Adam has gone, and "this" is who I am now. She thinks this is good for me, it is helping and that it is giving me a welcome respite from dealing with the grief and the pain she felt she had to inflict on me, and she is right. It <u>is</u> good for me, and I <u>am</u> getting some much-needed calm and relief from the stress and hurt of a broken heart. But Adam will never fully come back. He can't exist without Eve. Eve is his reason for being, she is the meaning of his life and without Eve at this pivotal point in his psyche, he has lost the very lynchpin that held him together. There is nothing for Adam in this world, he no longer exists.

I can't express who I am as Adam anymore. He is broken, likely beyond repair. So, my life has flipped. Julia is real, she is who I am. Adam is 'dressing up' now to express what little is left of my male side. He is no more than a necessary façade, a disguise to function, and hopefully, maintain the balance, as well as my prison sentence. He is not a real person anymore; I'm beginning to suspect he never truly was...

I am Julia.

**The King is indeed dead.
Long live the Queen.**

Another pack of playing cards ruined...

April 5th, 2021

Easter Monday

15 hours in a skirt, most of my day spent as me. I wore Adam's clothes to leave the house and accompany Eve to the horses. We also exchanged the blind for her bedroom for a shorter one to fit inside the window reveal from our local DIY store and then installed it. It is nice and cosy in there now. Eve is happy, so I am happy for her – that is just how it works.

We watched Crocodile Dundee again together and later, after pizza, I took off my disguise and dressed more comfortably. Overall, today has been a good day. I love spending time with Eve. I am trying to appreciate every moment because part of me thinks that they may be our last (irrational, we still have time, at least in the short-term anyway), so I am as best I can, making the most of every second together and not taking the time for granted.

It's stupid, but I feel every second we are apart. Even when she is just in the room next door. When we are apart, I am truly alone.

Adam, although automatic, is feeling more and more like a mask. He is just not who I am anymore – to let him take over again is too painful, it's impossible and the more I am Julia, the more real she becomes. I wear him like a disguise to function and I despise every second I spend looking like him; I always have to a greater or lesser degree, but never more so than now. I've denied who I truly am my whole life, but I've now had to face it head on. I am, and always have been, Julia but she was kept locked up tightly in a box, a box named Adam, tucked away from the world – the world that hates her. The box is gone, and its contents laid bare, after 50 years, she is blinking at the unfamiliar light, nervous and full of wonder. I hope that this fundamental shift will not affect my life in the public realm. I hope that 50 years of inhabiting Adam's face will make the change automatic and convincing – this <u>must</u> work, or everything will unravel.

Spending time as Adam is hard work though, working and living in his shoes is a raw experience, his agony is always *just* below the surface, and I cycle through great highs and lows as his pain tries to break through. Thankfully, my time hiding behind his face is limited. I can't be him for long anymore, it is far too exhausting fighting his emotions. I only wear him because I must, he is a chain society firmly locked around my ankle from the day I was born and then puberty wired it directly into the mains.

The future...

At the moment, Adam has no future. Rather dramatically I have declared him dead as I can't see him recovering from this. But now that I am Julia, I have hope and I wonder if his pain will diminish over time? If what little is left of him does survive, he will not be the same. But I hope that time will lessen his agony enough for him to be close to an equal part of my psyche again. Balance is a goal worth striving for, already I can feel that being Julia full time may leave a hole in my well-being. I am Julia now, but this is a necessity, unlike being Adam, it was not chosen.

I have always been both male and female. My male side is stricken and riddled with pain, so my female side has had to step forward. But I am beginning to realise that, just as I need to express myself as a woman, I might also need to do the same as a man.

Being Adam 24/7 literally drives me crazy. I have tried denying my female side in the past and it <u>always</u> goes very badly. I am currently, for the first time in my life, Julia 24/7. Adam is on sick leave and can't express himself in any way other than raw, excruciating pain. If the situation remains as it is, based upon my previous experiences of it being the other way around, I am beginning to think it could end badly too. In the past, if the circumstances were right, Julia could come forward when she needed to. Adam can't come forward at all now, he is in too much pain and has nothing to live for. This may well affect me in the long term. I am unable to achieve balance. But perhaps I no longer need to? I think I was Julia all along and the stress of maintaining Adam's façade is why I needed to spend time as me. Only the dysphoria when I am in Adam's shoes is now through the roof. The chain of conformity locked around my ankle and wired into the mains? Recent events have welded the breakers wide open – having my heart broken and then confronting who I truly am shocked Adam out of existence, and the power is still turned up to eleven.

Eve is working tomorrow; she is up early and will be gone before me. I am unlikely to see her until after work and in my room, as I write this, I am missing her company already. Tomorrow will be hard. Another of the endless day's disguised as Adam but hopefully my time shackled in trousers will zip by. I really look forward to shedding my mask in the evenings and tomorrow I shall see my love too when she gets home.

My number one concern is not scaring Eve away. I love her and have to be with her. Being Julia, all the time may be too much for her to deal with. Afterall, my female side is likely to have been the root of this crisis in the first place. Eve thinks that I am asking her permission to get changed, but I am actually making sure I haven't overstepped the mark, and she is still OK with this. Her happiness is, as it always was, paramount to me, more so than my own – I love her and would do anything for her, even if it ultimately hurt me.

But I can't be Adam for her anymore, his whole life was built on being Eve's boyfriend – he was destroyed when he realised his sole reason for being was invalidated. As Adam, there is no hope, he will go insane through the pain or worse, do something really stupid to make the pain stop.

I know this because he has tried already – I became Julia because I had to. She is all I have left of who I am. Julia is new, unexplored, ready to blossom, and has hope. She loves Eve just as much as Adam, but she is not Eve's boyfriend, so is not invested entirely in that role. I think I can live like this. I can grow and survive while I hope Adam's pain lessens, he is not a real person, he never really was, not even the male side of my nature. Just an expertly crafted layer to hide who I am, even from myself. This is how he now feels to me; a raw mass of pain and emotion – there is no logic, reason, or sense, he is raving at how his entire life has been taken away. I cannot live in his world like this, so, even though Julia is socially unacceptable, she is who I fundamentally am, and now I've faced up to this, I have to be her, I have to be *me*.

But most of all, I have to be with Eve. I can't scare her away. Our lives must continue together somehow, so I can't do anything too scary, and I am worried that she won't be able to deal with me like this. I can see she is emotionally exhausted, and this scares the hell out of me. If she cannot deal – because she has built and is comfortable with an independent life, she could just bail out and leave.

At this point, I believe Julia becomes the same as Adam. Neither version of me can live without Eve in our lives in some way – I love her and I'm sure I always will.

I can live as Eve's sister and her (hopefully best) friend as Adam once was. I can live with her in the house and share parts of our lives together, as a sibling. It is NOT the same as being her boyfriend, but it will have to be enough – I <u>must</u> make this work. Somehow...

I am going to stumble, I am going to have some dark times, but if Eve and I are in each other's lives, in whatever form that takes. <u>I can live</u>.

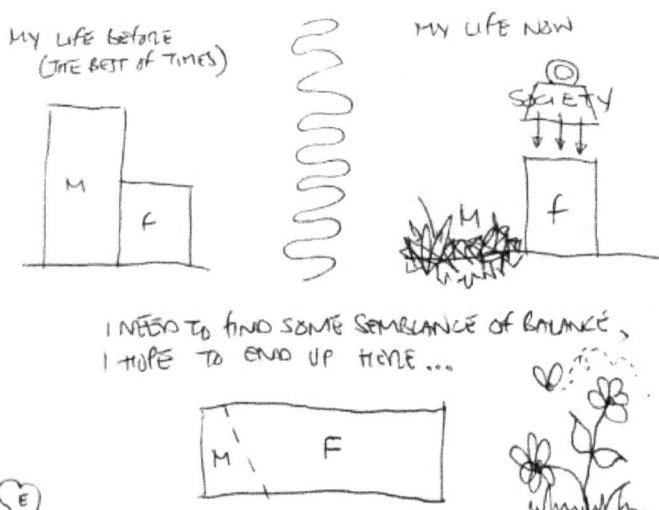

Tuesday, 6th April

Today was horrible.

Eve left early for work; I have not seen her other than a bleary eyed "good morning" all day. It is 7:20pm as I write this, and she is stuck at work. She will come home late, tired, and likely go straight to bed. I am feeling very lonely at the moment. I now have to face the evening alone and it is very upsetting.

Eve's life, other than the stress of seeing me in pain, goes on as normal. We do normal things together and have fun if we can. We spent a wonderful Saturday/Sunday at her mum and dad's place, Eve's sister and her girlfriend were there too. It was lovely, but wearing Adam's face all the time was trying. Still, overall, it was great. These high points keep me going, but they are few and far between and when they come along, I have to be in the right frame of mind to firstly recognise them and then appreciate them.

I was late leaving the house this morning. I just didn't want to look like Adam. I wasn't sure I could face work and the stresses it causes in my current state, but I had no choice. I stuck it out to the last possible moment and ended up being 10 minutes late. I worked until 6pm though, so no time lost.

Adam's emotions were very close to the surface today, I wasn't pleasant company and snapped at my brother when he pushed one of my many 'wrong buttons' and tried my patience. He doesn't know what I am going through, there was no excuse for my reaction. I am sure he is puzzled by my very short fuse; I should apologise – I will do so tomorrow.

I lost myself in my drawing work and when interrupted I had no patience for anyone, let alone some of the idiot 3rd parties I have to deal with. Note to self: "be professional". I have put up with morons in my work life before, I can do it again. Adam is good at his job, so I can be equally so when I am channelling him. Don't let his agony influence work – but when I am wearing him, he is very close to the surface and his raw emotions try to break through. Loosing myself in a drawing, calms what little there is left of him down, it gives him a logical and creative task to do, but this is why I was tetchy when interrupted. This is really hard - I am exhausted.

On top of this I couldn't drop the façade immediately when I got home. Mogs, bins, other stuff to do – life got in the way – this meant I wore Adam's face for longer than I would have liked. I decided to trade dinner for some much-needed time in a skirt. I am always less hungry as Julia, and I could stand to lose some weight. I think this may be a good thing to work on, a project for Julia. It is good to have a goal. I think I can reduce my calorie intake by simply not clearing my plate at dinner. Once I have dealt with the last of my Birthday treats and Easter Eggs that is! Actually, not clearing my plate is quite a difficult thing to do, I'm brainwashed into it, as a lot of my generation are, due to some nebulous, un-named group of supposed "starving Africans" my mum would bring up at every mealtime when I was a kid. Thanks mum, it's no wonder I love my food too much...

I am feeling better. Adam is hung up in the closet, I am Julia in full once more. I have decided to have a lazy night, I am in my nightie early, instead of going for a full outfit. I need the extra comfort and with no company, I plan an early night, so I am writing this entry ahead of my usual routine. I am going to curl up in my nightie, snuggle in bed and watch some Veronica Mars on TV. Sounds like some good medicine, I need some after today.

I am not sure how I am going to deal with my work trip and night away later this week. I will pack an outfit of real clothes and spend some time as me in the hotel room – this will help I think, it's about as much as I can do. I am missing our phone calls when I stay away. They dried up over the years and now

I know why. Eve has all the time in the world to chat to folks in another language but can't spare me 10 minutes when I am stuck in a hotel room halfway across the country. Now that I think about it, this is a big clue as to her feelings for me. It hurt then; it hurts even more now. She is the single most important thing in my life, but I am less important to her than a language learning experience, one of hundreds. I am not angry, I should be, I feel abandoned. But I love her too much and would forgive her anything. I am simply not a priority to her in the same way she is to me. It hurts, but it is not meant maliciously. It just is.

Adam cannot deal with this, as Julia I can rationalise things as I am in a calmer place and in less pain. But regardless of how I am expressing my gender, hidden, or truly, I still love Eve desperately. She defines Adam though; she does not define Julia. So as Julia I can function, and this will give time I hope to heal my male side somewhat. With a bit of luck, enough to restore some of the balance at least. If not, then at some point I may well lose my sanity, I think. Trying to live without my female side drove me to the edge in the past. Trying to do the same but without my male side could quite possibly do the same. If true, this means that the current solution is temporary, recovery is not a foregone conclusion. I don't think I can exist with a piece of who I am missing, just like I couldn't exist with me denying the rest of me in the past. Adam recovers, or potentially all is lost. He won't come back fully; I know this is not going to happen. He wasn't real and is just too damaged. But there is hope he can heal enough to restore the balance. Julia is driving now.

Balance is everything, without it I have no future. I am working on restoring the balance. It is going to be a long, hard road and until Adam's pain subsides, I have yet to take my first step.

Wednesday, April 7th.

I'm freezing. The whole house is cold, and I am on my own. I HATE sleeping by myself, I miss Eve's company and just being close to her. I need her touch, a hug, her warmth, even the smile on her face. Actually, *especially* the smile on her face. She is less than 2m away from me, in her room, but it might as well be a billion miles.

I love her with every fibre of my being. After 15 years, my love has deepened and now it is consuming me, eating me alive. I think I am obsessed with her; this is not a good place to be, and it scares me witless. I cannot live without her in my life. I can't just switch my love off.

Why didn't she talk to me when she realised, she couldn't deal with me as Julia? I would have found a way; Eve is more important to me than my personal wellbeing. She is my whole world, and my entire life was built around the concept of "us", including defining, for the first time in my life, who I am.

Instead of being at the mercy of my indeterminate gender. ***I took control and CHOSE to be a man***. This is a critically important point, I was *fully* aware of what I was doing, it was a conscious decision, I did it for Eve, for us, and for me. Our life together was amazing and my love for her grew to the point where it became fundamental to my being.

When she said she didn't love me and that our relationship was over, she destroyed the man I became utterly.

For the first time in my life, I was in charge of my gender and that life was astonishingly good. I no longer have control over who I am anymore. The construct that was Adam has died, so instead of being able to choose who I am, I have had to become Julia, me. A switch has been thrown in my soul and it was done TO me, I had no say in the matter. I am Julia because

Adam was taken away from me. I am not in control of who I am anymore, and my life is totally in flux.

Becoming Julia saved me. But to engage with life again, I think I need to be able to choose once more. At the moment there is no choice. This is because Julia is highly unlikely to be able to function in society, *I must choose to live as Adam in order for my life to continue*. But this option is not there anymore. I can't inhabit his face like I used to. I am stuck as Julia, me, as a woman, in a layby trying to fix who I am. But my life is the road and as Julia, the fuel tank is empty – Adam has gone for petrol, I do not know when or if, he will return. Maybe he is lost? I think though he was mowed down by the traffic…

My love for Eve was my core, so Adam's pain is all consuming.

I want to get angry, to vent, and to scream until I am blue in the face. But it is not Eve's fault – she can't help the way she feels about me, just as I can't help the way I feel about her. My anger has no focus, so it cannot come out. I want to scream from the pain, from the loss of who I am, from the loss of my life as I knew it and most of all, from the loss of Eve's love. I am so desperately unhappy, I have never felt so sad, I burst into tears randomly and I have never been so lonely.

I miss her terribly and she is only 6 feet from me.

How can she be so close, and yet be completely in another universe?

How can she live in the same house as me when I am like this? This must be unpleasant for her, seeing me in agony, seeing me as a woman **all** the time. How can she stand to look at the pathetic shell I have become?

I worry that it is only a matter of time until she walks away. She isn't invested in me, that much is clear, so why should she stay? Why should she put up with this misery? She alluded to falling out of love with me because she couldn't be in a relationship with a part-time woman. But now, she is living and sharing her home with a woman full time. When she realises this, I think it may be too much for her.

If she leaves me, I will die.

Adam is on critical life support – his whole life is shattered, and he has no reason to carry on. The man I was, he was defined by his relationship with Eve. Without it, he no longer exists.

Julia is new, unexplored and a welcome relief from the agony Adam is going through. But I don't think I can fully exist in society as a woman, I desperately want to, but I don't think I can stay as a woman for ever. At some point I think I must choose to throw the gender switch in my head back to male – although I have absolutely no idea how. Julia, trapped forever in Adam's body, is I think ultimately untenable. But the switch is fully welded in the female position, the lever is broken off so there is nothing to grip onto and the male position is burned out completely.

Eve makes it possible to continue. I think we can continue to live together and have a life, all-be-it more separately. This is emphatically NOT what I want. But it will have to do. It is the best of a set of options as that are ALL awful. The fact that these options include becoming physically female, and/or suicide shows how desperate I am. The extreme options are the result of Eve leaving me – I can't live without her in my life somehow, I love her too much. And if me being here causes her too much pain I will gladly remove myself permanently from her and take the problem away. This feels like a rational option to me, and the fact that it does, scares the hell out of me. But I am clinging on by my fingernails – the pain is just unbearable.

So, I will live as Julia, be true to myself, and will try to heal at least some of Adam. I will strive to put myself in a position where Eve and I can stay together and share some of our separate lives. This means building a life for ME, once I work out exactly who I am...

It is not a great option to be honest, at least it is nowhere near what we had. But it will do, and it will enable me to carry on. However, I can't lose Eve, I can only do this if she is with me and in my life. So, I CAN'T scare her away and she can never see the true depth of the agony she has caused me. Other folks can live with the loss of a relationship. Other folks get to choose who they are. Other folks are not defined by their relationship at a fundamental level.

Other folks are not me...

I am in hell. I don't know who I am. All I know is my love for Eve and the despair at her stepping away from me. My love is keeping me alive; my identity is in flux; my life is in ruins. But if she is with me, I have hope. Hope that I can continue. And hope that there is a future.

It is 8:25am, I am late for work for the second day running. Time to adopt an *acceptable* face. Time to disguise myself as Adam. I hope that today will be better than yesterday, at least I have an evening with Eve to look forward to.

7:55pm, I am dressed comfortably. Eve is in the bath, she worked 21 hours straight yesterday and understandably is very tired. My evening with her has been lovely so far. She told me all about her day and it was like it used to be for a while. I love listening to her talk, even if it is something, I have little intertest in (which it wasn't, I was hanging on every word). I am appreciating every moment with her as I have this feeling that at some point, there will not be any more. I am making memories to look back on just in case the absolute worst happens – I hope not, but I am being prepared. Eve seems happy and content with the status quo. I don't understand how this is possible. How can she not see I am broken? Is my disguise as Adam <u>that</u> good? Or is she only seeing what she wants to see?

She truly has moved on. I am alone. Rudderless, directionless, with no purpose or reason to try to bear the pain. And she doesn't see, or worse, does not care. I am lost.

But I still hang on every word. I cherish every moment and I miss her terribly, even when we are together. Her life goes on despite my pain, it is not in any way as earth shattering to her as it is to me. I truly am lost.

I noticed something odd tonight too. I had a small moment of clarity. I was sitting on the sofa listening intently to Eve's account of her epic workday and I was suddenly very aware of my posture and position. I was mirroring Eve (which happens a <u>lot</u> anyway), but I was not sitting as Adam would. My body language gave my true gender away and it was entirely subconscious. I sat and was comfortable as a woman. Legs up on the sofa, knees together and my hand tucked between my thighs. I <u>know</u> my gender has shifted, but this was the first physical manifestation on a subconscious level. At least the first that I have noticed. Up to now, Julia's persona is something I adopt, or lately something I default to. But it is a conscious decision, to dress in a skirt, do my make-up, put on a bra and some nice heels. I am comfortable and it is a safe space to express myself in my female role.

It is a place of calm and a place to relax. Julia comes to the surface, and I am released from the agony of Adam. But this evening, despite still being in Adam's personae, Julia exerted herself and manifested in my body language. I am stronger than

I thought, nourishing my female nature is having an effect. I am a stronger woman than I was, and I imposed myself through the mask of Adam. In a detached kind of way, I find this interesting and wonder if I am filling the void left by Adam's departure?

My day as Adam was crap. Maybe I just couldn't maintain the deception any longer?

I am wearing my new bra. I took the time to measure myself a week or two ago properly. I can't believe I have never done this before! To date, working out my sizes has always been a matter of awkward trial and error. The bra is still not quite the right size, but the band is now 100% spot on. The underwire is correct, but the cup fabric is a bit baggy (likely wishful thinking when I chose it). Overall, a much better fit and a vast improvement. I think I am a 50C, the 50D I am wearing is about 80% right. Wow, that is big…

Just for the record, here are my sizes:

Underwear

Bra	50C
Knickers	20-22
Stockings	XL

Clothes

Skirt	24-26
Dress	28
Blouse	28
Shoes	10½

I am a very odd-shaped woman and being 6'-2" tall doesn't help. So, I don't think I will ever be able to "pass" in public as myself. I can see why Eve has had an issue with this in the past. I am not a convincing woman, despite being more female inside than a lot of other women. **Fuck you, puberty!**

On the plus side, I am getting better at make-up. Wearing it every day is really nice. And, dare I say it, every now and then I do it well enough to be just a little bit pretty. I love looking like this. I love the artistry and the expression. I would like to explore this further, and I am thinking of a nice mirror, or maybe a dressing table to sit at and do my make-up. I've never had a dressing table; I think I am going to buy one. It's an important part of who I am and needs a dedicated space, a place where my identity is recognised and can manifest properly. Plus, as someone entirely self-taught, I need the practice!

Eve is home safe, my crap day hiding as Adam is finished and I am relaxed as Julia again. Tonight, I am feeling OK. I was down earlier, but now I am feeling better.

I need to pack an overnight bag for tomorrow's work trip to Barnstaple and then on into Bristol (via Gloucester) on Friday. But not yet, for the time being at least, I am relaxing.

Tomorrow's entry will be from a hotel room. I hope I can chat with Eve tomorrow night. She hasn't wanted to when I've been away previously, but I need it now.

8am, Thursday 8th April

My bag is packed. Another emotional morning. I detest waking up alone, cold and sad. I took an extra-long shower to wash away my tears – I broke down again. Eve is so close, but so far – it is maddening and with no hope of a reconciliation I am utterly lost.

There are times when I feel violated. Becoming Julia fully was not a choice, it was forced on me, she is all I have left. Adam's reason to exist was taken away and he ceased to be. I know this is all in my head, and I have **absolutely** no frame of reference, but I feel like I have been raped. Forced to become a woman as Adam died. Wow, that's dramatic...

This is the *most* extreme view of course, the above implies malicious intent – there was none – this was not done to me deliberately, but it WAS done to me. There was a loss of power, or agency, I was helpless, unable to resist as my male façade was destroyed and my soul stripped bare, raw, and exposed. A fundamental and unfathomably painful change. I am in hell; it is no wonder I am in agony. My life, and who I was, has been taken away from me – I am incredibly lucky to be left with a safe place (Julia) and the tiniest hope that I can continue to share my life with Eve, even though we are now separated. I hate this. I hate the fact it was inflicted on me. I hate not knowing who I am. I hate that I can't get angry, there is no one at fault. I hate the fact that I missed this situation gradually happening over years, building to a crisis. I hate that I have missed so many opportunities to discuss it with Eve before and maybe, just maybe avoided getting to this devastating point. Or at least, been able to manage it better.

I hate feeling so powerless. I hate feeling like a victim. I hate being so pathetic.

Today is going to be hard. I don't want to stay away tonight. I need to be close to Eve.

I am about to put on my disguise. I hate that this is all that the man I once was, is now reduced to. My life is a sham. I am miserable. Julia will get me through this. But I am having a bad day again.

    Take a deep breath, I am ready. I will face the day...

It is 9pm as I write this, I am in a hotel room in Bristol and have just had a wonderful chat with Eve.

This morning was awful. I lost it again and broke down in tears with Eve. The hug was amazing and very much needed. But most importantly of all, I began to explain what I am going through to her. She will never fully understand, how can she? But she knows that I am Julia 24/7 now, regardless of what clothes I have on. She knows that I am not just heartbroken, I am also lost. I don't know who I am anymore. Talking to her really helped. I was VERY low this morning and even though I was still crying as I left the house and drove away, I was able to face the day, so I am in a better place than I was in earlier this morning, when I donned Adam's disguise.

My survey of Gloucester was postponed, so even though my breakdown put me an hour late leaving the house, I ended up being 2 hours early for the handover in Barnstaple. I stopped for a break mid-journey in Leigh Delamere Services (not very nice) on the M4 and had a phone chat with Eve. We are both on each other's minds today and it was good for her to hear I was in a better place than I was earlier. Me? It is always good to hear her voice. Well, apart from that one time, when she broke my heart...

The hotel is, well, a hotel. Nothing to write home about, so I won't.

I am dressed in my gold, satin high-necked blouse (my current favourite) and my all-time favourite below the knee, A-line black skirt. I love this skirt, it's so old and has been worn so many times, but it still looks good, despite the lining being stretched to the point it is shredded in places. At some point, and not too far away I think, I'm going to have to cut the remnants of the satin lining out and will have to wear a slip. Shame – lined skirts seem to be out of fashion at the moment and are hard to come by outside of formal wear (even more so in larger sizes). Full lingerie, jewellery, and lipstick. No other make-up sadly, need to have Adam's face for tomorrow and don't want to run the risk of make-up traces.

The call with Eve tonight was exactly what I needed. We talked for over an hour and had lots to say. It was genuinely nice and equally welcome. Additionally, one of our good friends has put details up online and in a WhatsApp group of a European rally, over a long weekend in September. It is in our diaries, and it is great (finally) to have something to look forward to. We also pencilled in Fully Charged Live, we are both up for it.

The day started off really badly, but ended up as good as it could, given I am so far from Eve.

Despite everything, today has been a good day.

Friday, 9th April

I am alone in a hotel room. Despite being 200 miles away from my love, oddly I am not as upset as I was this time yesterday. There is no logic to my emotional state.

Today will (I hope) go pretty well. At least yesterday's handover bodes well for the three more I lined up for today. We shall see...

The clock in my room is an hour behind, it is reading 7:06am as I write this, but it is actually 8:06am – it hasn't been adjusted to British Summertime! Thankfully I am not relying on it as I need to put my glasses on to see it and I don't to read my phone on the bedside table next to me.

I will get up and adopt Adam's face shortly. I may well be at the first site early.

Legacy. This is something I have been thinking about a lot recently. The only thing I have achieved in my life, the only thing that matters, is to love and be loved. And this is enough to justify my existence. Professionally, most of what I do is transient and meaningless. My Public Sector work has much more worth, and it will outlast me and, in some small way, have a positive effect on potentially thousands of lives. This is good. But it will not be remembered, my role in this will be forgotten. The mass Covid vaccine centres I designed will save lives. This is also good. But no one will know my involvement. Despite being very good at it, my professional legacy is, and will remain, unrecognised.

Eve doesn't want kids, I am ambivalent. But my personal line of DNA ends with me. My family line continues through my brother, niece, and nephews though, so this is also OK. Eve brings so much light into my life and the world. Her own personal line of DNA ends with her, and her sister is gay. So, her family line will also end. **The world is a much poorer place**

because of this. But it does mean that we are not going to damage the world beyond our lifespans. Humans consume and damage the world. By ensuring we do not make further generations of humans we end the circle of destruction our very existence creates. This is a good legacy. But it is hard to take any satisfaction from it without love. I think, overall, my nett contribution to this world will be positive. But this, and indeed I, will be forgotten ultimately. I have not achieved anything that will be remembered and nothing of me will survive beyond my years, other than the memories of others and these will die with them eventually. My legacy is to break the cycle of damage my potential progeny will cause to the world. Some would say this is the single most important thing anyone can do. Others will vehemently disagree. Either way the only thing I have found in this world that truly matters is love. Love enables me to take joy in the moments that make up my life. Love and joy; they are what makes life worth living.

I love Eve. But she doesn't love me.

I am finding it hard to take joy in the moment and this renders my life meaningless.

I hope that my love for Eve will be enough. I hope that the immense pain I am feeling will subside. I hope I can redefine who I am. I hope my male side can recover somewhat. I hope I can re-achieve balance between my genders or come to terms with being female. I hope to find joy again.

Hope. It is all I have.

Saturday April 10th

A nice lie in this morning. I was tired after yesterday's driving and Eve woke me around 9:30am as she had the Farrier coming to the horses this morning. Eve's sister would be there too, it sounded like it might be fun, so I asked If I could join them.

I put on Adam's face, and we drove to the horses. It was very cold, but dry and our friends in the next-door livery were there when we arrived having their horses attended to. It was so nice to see and chat with them again. The Farrier is a nice chap, and we had a long conversation too. Eve's sister then arrived, and we headed over to the field so he could trim 2 of the horses' hooves. Sheez it was cold out there! But nice to get out and do something "normal" again.

We sat in the tack room for a bit afterwards. Trying to both warm and catch up, just Eve, her sister, and me. It was lovely and I tried to take joy in the moment and make a good memory. <u>My love for Eve was enough and I was successful.</u> But I still feel like Julia wearing a disguise. Adam is gone. Julia has a good memory. Julia has some joy in her life. Julia smiled today. The first genuine smile she has had in weeks. I was happy for a while as Julia, even if the world only saw Adam.

Today has been a good day. Today my hope, for a time, allowed my love to turn into joy. Today being a woman was worthwhile and felt real. Today, I had a glimpse of a life that may be, a life that has value, a life that is possible, a life that is worth living. A life containing love and joy.

I can live like this. I also think that some of Adam may be able to come back. I don't think I will ever <u>be</u> Adam again though. At least not like I was. But Julia can love and find joy, so I can continue. My life as Julia can blossom, and I can have substance. I think I can be happy, and I think I can make the pretence of looking like Adam work.

For the first time in weeks, I really liked, even enjoyed being a woman today.

I was happy as Julia, and I liked who I was.

This gender switch was forced on me and I think I have been fighting it ever since. Julia is a safe haven, I had to become her when the artifice of Adam was shattered and because I had nowhere else to go. Unlike when I chose to be Adam for our relationship and for Eve, I resented it. I need to be in charge of who I am, and I was until Eve said those fateful 5 words – **I don't love you anymore**. At that point Adam couldn't continue – I had to become Julia, or I would no longer exist and not existing ends up with *literally not existing*, if you know what I mean. The man I was? He's gone for good, so I inhabited the woman that has always been a fundamental part of me.

And today, I liked myself. I smiled. I took joy. I love Eve still and yet, I am Julia. Today I saw that I can continue. I can be Julia, I can like who I am and as Eve said to me, I can "own" this.

It was not my choice to become a woman, but today I liked who I am, today I saw a future.

I think today I took my first step on the road.
It is not a road to recovery.
It's the road to my future. I liked being Julia today.
I liked taking my first step...
A good day indeed.

Mundane stuff happened too. The three of us had lunch at McD's, we chatted and had a nice time. Eve took her sister back to the stables to collect her car and I took one of my cars to my local tyre place to have a puncture fixed. 248 miles covered; nearside front tyre picked up a nail. Unbelievable. But only £27.00 to fix and at least it was repairable.

This evening, after we had both washed our cars, I removed my disguise and relaxed in my blue blouse and my long, tan skirt. My new bra and knickers arrived earlier, and they are an excellent fit. Very, very comfy. As the bra has no under-wire, I have decided to try to sleep in one tonight. I hope it works out as I love wearing a bra. I love feeling cupped and supported, almost like being hugged. But the under-wires, after a time, jab me in the boob under my arm, so I cannot sleep in one without it ultimately hurting me. At least, I've had painful experiences in the past after I had unintentionally dozed off. The correct size, a good fit and no under-wires should be much better for long-term wear. Fingers crossed.

I have also taken to sleeping in my make-up. I adore wearing make-up and am wearing it daily now in the evenings. Because I wash my face before applying it, I am clean at bedtime, so I don't cleanse it off until the morning. The mascara is 100% waterproof, so my bedding (mostly) survives, and I am not going all out with my make-up often. I wear it as any other woman does. A little to add pretty-ness, subtle, just mascara and lipstick to complete my outfit, accentuate what I can and make me feel good about my face. It's enough to just tip the balance over to female in terms of how I look. I will never be beautiful in a classic female sense, I'd love to be, but I can and do look much less masculine, with just these two make-up items. I love wearing make-up and I intend to get better at it.

So, it's now 11pm, I am in bed in one of my long, satin nighties, bra and matching knickers, painted toenails, hoop earrings, lipstick, and mascara. I am relaxed, comfortable, and satisfied with a good day.

I still miss Eve dreadfully, but she is only 6' away and we had fun today. I liked being her sister today. I liked who I have become. My life will never be the same, but it looks like it can contain love and joy after all. I am looking to the future at last and I am beginning to see a life now, I didn't before. I can make this work.

I like being Julia.

Sunday, April 11th.

Another nice lie in. Eve had to go feed the horses, so I had an extra-long time in my nightie. I finally showered and changed around 10:30am and was back in a dress from 7pm - 15½ hours living openly as a woman.

I feel differently about my situation today. I have some optimism back and even though I am still Julia all the time and am beginning to suspect that I will always be Julia now, dressing and being dressed as my true self not only feels natural and comfortable as always, but I am actually starting to enjoy my time and feel that expressing who I am like this <u>is</u> doing me good.

Putting on Adam's clothes feels like work. I am emphatically <u>NOT</u> comfortable looking like him, but today was OK. When Eve returned, I threw my disguise on, and we headed over to see dad. We also met his new lady friend for the first time. I have been dreading this moment, but it was alright in the end. She is lovely and it was so good to see dad happy at last. I broke the ice by going in for a warm hug straight away – it dispersed any tension and set the meeting up in a very positive way. We had a nice lunch and chatted for a good few hours. It was nice and not weird in any way. I think mum would have liked her. They are very different, but I think mum would've liked how she makes dad happy. I do.

We went in Eve's car, I forget how much I love these little sportscars, regardless of my mood, a drive with the hood down on a sunny day will always put a smile on my face.

At home, Eve and I re-watched Michael Jackson's Moonwalker. It is a great film; he was such an immense talent. What a show man. Eve is such a fangirl! She loved every moment and I love to see her so happy. I lost my disguise halfway through and made myself comfortable in my black skater dress. I don't look too bad in it to be honest; I think it suits me, although a little low cut to be 100% decent. A girl needs to think about her modesty...

Eve helped me cut my own hair afterwards, it looks nice, layered and when loose, feminine. I like it a <u>lot</u>. I also helped Eve re-pierce her ears. She doesn't wear earrings, but for work, every now and then, she is required to. Each time is painful and awkward for her as the holes would've closed up somewhat in between. After her recent work, her ears were sore, so she opened them up again tonight and used Savlon to calm them down while she relaxed in the bath.

It has just gone 11pm, I am in bed. Earrings, make-up, nail polish, knickers, nightie and now, a pseudo woman's hair style. A good day.

Work again tomorrow. Let's see what the week brings...

Monday, April 12th

I woke up desperately sad again. Eve and I have been sleeping apart since late December and every morning, without fail, I wake up cold and lonely. It's a slap in the face to remind me just how miserable and in pain I am. I can't get used to this; it hurts too much.

Yesterday, and indeed the whole weekend was good. I began to see that there could be (fleeting) moments of joy in my future and that I may not be miserable for the rest of my life. Nothing has changed though. The brief moments of happiness over the weekend were had by Julia, even though she looked like Adam. I am Julia. I cannot see me being able to be Adam in any way other than as a disguise any time soon. But I think I am getting better at looking like him. And more importantly, I am beginning to like the woman I now am. When I drop the pretence of being Adam and express myself fully as a female, I like it. I like feeling calmer. I like feeling more relaxed and I can feel myself fully inhabiting my female nature – <u>I like it a lot</u>. I like who I am becoming. And in some small way, this makes the loss of Adam, someone I also liked being VERY much, easier to bear.

We have some things in the diary to look forward to at last. I hope they come to fruition, but I think the European tour will be EXTREMELY hard for me and quite upsetting. The last two trips have been very painful for me. It was where I began to realise things were not great between Eve and I. I thought we were a couple and really close. But Eve already, it seems, was thinking of herself as an individual. She kept ditching me. The first trip she spent more time as a passenger in someone else's car than with me. The second time she decided practicing her language skills was far more important than her boyfriend. I realise now that as far as she was concerned, I wasn't her boyfriend anymore. But I didn't know this at the time – it massively hurt me. I was confused and abandoned. My holidays were utterly ruined and even though the trip was brilliantly conceived, put together and run, I came home more stressed than when we started. This was the beginning of the end I see now. I went on holiday as a couple. Eve did not. And we came home with me wondering what the hell had just happened?

Now that I know what is going on with Eve, I don't think this is going to help. We are emphatically NOT going to be a couple when we do the tour later in the year. It doesn't matter how much I want to go with her and be with her and share every moment happily with her. I know that she will do her own thing and I will be left to try to do the same. But it is NOT the same, not at all. She can enjoy every moment as an individual. I will not. Nothing has any meaning without sharing it with Eve. Despite everything, I still love her desperately. Knowing this now makes me worried for the holiday. It feels like it is ruined before we even go, to the extent I am seriously considering not going at all. I **really** want to go. I really want to see all my great friends again. I really want to relax and have a great time (and boy do I need it). But I think there is a very real chance it will be unbearable. To go with Eve, but not go **with** her. To see her having a great time with our (my) friends without me. And to feel rejected, lonely, and miserable whist "putting on a happy face", on top of my "Adam face", surrounded by others, some of the most important friends in my life, also having a great time.

I am not sure I can do this. It was incredibly painful the last 2 times, I can see this trip just cementing the status quo between Eve and I and, upsettingly, I can see me not being able to cope.

So, I am sad again today. It is 7:40am on a Monday and my week is awful already. I hate this.

Yesterday I had hope and something to look forward to. Today I am desperately unhappy and have managed to ruin the trip before we have even signed up for it. I am a fool and I seem to be sabotaging myself. This is hell. I hate feeling this way.

I just want Eve back! But this simple thing, the thing that makes life worth living, is just too much for her.

The momentous first step I took over the weekend, I think I may have just undone it.

I really am a fool.

I have no idea who I am. I have no idea where my life is going. I am in desperate pain, and I am miserable. I still love Eve, more than ever. She doesn't love me anymore. This is overwhelming, a perfect storm. My life as Adam is over. My life as Julia is empty without Eve. I exist, but I am not actually living.

A new working week beckons. Soon I will need to look like Adam again. I will play the part to perfection and to all intents and purposes, be who the world demands to see. But inside, I am Julia, and I am broken.

I have lost my hope again this morning. I will find it again, I <u>must</u>. But it is so hard.

Hopefully, I will feel better later. I will see Eve this evening and I always feel better when I am with her. But today, as I write this, I am not in a good place again.

Let's see what today brings. It may be a good day after all. Who knows? It has happened before; I have started the day in a pit of despair but ended it in a reasonable place. We shall see…

I go on because I must. I will find hope again because I must. Things will get better because they must, but for the moment, I am sad. Regardless, I go on…

10:45pm – what a totally shit day.

I went to work as planned. I sat at my desk, and I was busy. But distracted. Eve was on my mind all day. My colleagues and I gathered around mid-day for a company meeting. My mask slipped. I was not present, and it showed. For the first time my pain was evident, and people noticed...

After the meeting, I asked my brother for 5 minutes, so he suggested I join him and my nephew on a trip to the station, as he had a survey to do in London. We dropped him off, then parked up and I broke down. I told him EVERYTHING. He was supportive and upset for me. He thinks that staying with Eve is non-productive. Typical of him to try to fix things, even when they are beyond repair. Concerningly, he tried to paint Eve as a bad person. This is emphatically not the case, but all he can see is his brother in immense pain and literally holding on by his fingernails. I told him who I am now and how I came to have nothing but Julia left. I don't think he understood – how could he? When we were a lot younger, I told him about me, but like dad, I don't think it ever truly registered – he is very much like dad in a lot of ways – cut from the same cloth and neither of them has ever wanted to meet the real me. He will process what he can and ignore what he can't. But he cares for me, and this means a lot. I also hope he begins to understand what a strain I am under and tries to give me some respite at work. I need this, but circumstances may not allow. I suppose it will be what it will be, and I'll have to roll with the punches as always...

Afterwards, I drove home. Eve was surprised to see me, and I broke down again. I cried and emptied my heart to her again and it took its toll. I am putting her through hell too and I hate myself for doing this. But I can't help it. Every now and then the façade cracks and I fall apart once more. She held my hand and listened. I cried myself out and just appreciated being with her. Even if we were both in tears. I need her so much and worry that I am driving her away. I still love her, and I can't switch it off – I wish I could.

We had a nice evening, despite everything. We watched "The Mask" again – a great film, but I was too sad to be swept away by it. Some parts got through to me, and I enjoyed it, but most of all, I enjoyed sharing it with Eve. I got changed early today, around 6pm. 15 hours living as a woman. I am beginning to really like the woman I am becoming. I think that if anything good comes from this it is likely to be a fuller and truer understanding of who I actually am. All this time spent exploring my female side is wonderful, a gift even, and I think that Julia is a good, worthwhile person. At least I like looking in the mirror and seeing her face, even when it is hidden behind Adam's disguise. I said to Eve earlier that I am wearing make-up 24/7 now, it's just that some of the time my mascara is invisible. Most importantly of all, although I had no choice but to become Julia, I am beginning to really like who I am as her. This is a really positive step. It shows some acceptance, and it shows that I am no longer, at least in this regard, a victim of circumstance. I am Julia and I like being her. This has got to be a good sign.

So, today started off really badly, then got much, much worse. But I am OK now. I have regained some lost ground. I have managed to find a positive in the mess my life has become. I hope tomorrow will be better.

Tuesday, April 13th.

A better morning. I was so tired yesterday, emotionally exhausted, that I fell asleep writing this journal. I woke up still completely dressed, in every way bar heels. Bra, knickers, tights, skirt, blouse, make-up, earrings, everything. And when I awoke, not only was I comfortable, but I was warm and toasty in bed too. Not waking up cold I think gave me a much-needed boost. Today I am feeling OK.

Eve on the other hand was rudely awoken by her phone. Her sister had a puncture and called for her help. In the meantime, I got ready for work. And you know what? It was OK today. I put on Adam's face, and it didn't feel like such a hard slog. My workday felt less stressful, and I left for home in fair spirits.

...and then dad rang.

It was so good to talk to him. Finally. My brother had let him know yesterday and he rang me while I was driving. I had to pull over and we had quite probably the most touching, frank, and open conversation we have ever had. It was so special. We were both blubbering messes, but it didn't matter. It was heartfelt and we spoke about mum as well as the crap I am wading through. We have so much in common right now. He has had such a terrible year and the last thing I wanted was to pile my worries and pain onto his already overflowing plate. Despite begging him not to, my brother told him straightaway and part of me resents it. He meant well, but I desperately wanted to keep this from dad, show him some stability and spare him any more anguish. But I am so glad I could finally talk to him. My whole life, he has been aloof and on a pedestal. Such a role model – I have strived every day to make him proud, to be someone he approved of and not this strange, indeterminately gendered mess of a human being. After 50 years of hiding who I am from the world, I am bloody good at it. A mistress of deception in every way. Today we spoke as equals, for the very first time. What we are both going through has levelled the playing field and he IS proud of me. More importantly, for the first time in 50 years he spoke to Julia. I am still Julia and although I am sure he didn't comprehend, he wasn't talking to his son, the boy who just wanted to make his dad, the man he looked up to, proud and consequently would never show him who he truly is. Today, he spoke to me. Today the walls and the masquerade fell for a time. Today, we were not only father and child, but for the first-time we were equals. He opened up and shared his pain over losing mum and I did the same. I shared my agony at losing Eve with him. For the first time he spoke to his daughter, Julia and it was a beautiful moment. It was painful, it was a revelation. I will cherish this moment for ever. After 50 years, <u>today my dad and I met for the first time.</u>

So special. I hate you bro for giving him my pain. But I love you too, for giving me my dad.

You cannot know what this means to me.

I composed myself and drove the rest of the way home. I can't be a mess again for Eve, it's not fair on her and truly, for once I am in a good place.

The evening turned out to be a revelation too. I walked in the door with red eyes and a tear-streaked face and Eve was immediately worried for me again. But I told her I was having a good day, that I had just spoken to dad, and it was amazing, but <u>very</u> emotional. I think that she could see I was not going to break down again and that today was not going to be "yesterday – part 2". Eve told me about her day, her sister and her tyre, a very amusing tale of her sister bursting for a wee on the roadside and fabricating a makeshift cubicle using car doors and clothes as curtains! And then, she suggested we go out for dinner...

It's been months. The lockdown began to lift this week, so we booked a table (outside) at a local pub, and we had a lovely meal out. It was a simple thing, but astonishing nevertheless. And then, much to my amazement, Eve said she had been working on a project since January and showed me her new website she has built. It's brilliant! Really, really good and sooo much work has gone into it. I am so proud of her. I am so pleased I was in a good enough headspace she felt she could share it with me. This is why I love her so much. She is a genius and despite knowing her so well, she can floor me with stuff like this. It came out of the blue and my jaw dropped. Amazing.

I started writing this when we got home. I am now on my third pen, lots to say and rubbish pens, wow. I have not spent so much time in a skirt today, probably less than 50% for the first time in weeks. But I have decided to sleep fully clothed again tonight. Undies, skirt, and a blouse. A little lipstick and some earrings. Waking up like this set me on the path to a great day. I want some more of this. Today I was happy. Today was amazing. Today was special. I will remember this day forever.

Wednesday April 14th

My plan worked! Although not as well as yesterday. I was OK this morning. Not great, but not so bad either - and that describes my entire day pretty much. It was OK, and so was I.

I woke up as I always do, as Julia. Today, like yesterday, I was Julia in every way, to the max, and this is a nice way to start the day. But I suspect it will be a case of diminishing returns, so I will try to save this trick for the days when I really need it. Still, I was completely dressed in every way until 6:30 and my morning shower. After which I put on some fresh knickers, a bra, and my nightie up until 8:10ish. I then swapped nice clothes for horrid ones and faced the day in the way the world demands. But it was OK. I had a good start this morning. Home around 5:45pm and after dinner, back in comfy clothes, make-up, and heels by 7pm. So, a good 13 hours fully lived as a woman. I am really liking this. I am enjoying exploring me as a full female. I am enjoying my time in skirts more and more. I like who I am becoming. I like not having to deal directly with the pain. I am beginning to like ME again. This <u>has</u> to be a good thing.

Eve is hurting today physically. After lockdown the local gym opened upon Monday, and she was there, her muscles are giving her grief consequently. We had a nice evening. I helped proof-read her website (very impressive) and then we watched an episode of Death in Paradise. It's nice to watch something together that we both enjoy. Eve had a bath to soothe her aching muscles and then we both retired around 11pm.

I am about to change for bed. A solid 8 hours in my nightie again is always wonderful. I hope it will be enough to give me a good start again tomorrow. Fingers crossed...

Thursday, April 15th

Not too bad this morning. I am definitely not in the same mood as yesterday or Tuesday, but I am nowhere near the despair of Monday. I slept in full lingerie, make-up, earrings, and my nightie, so a bit of a half-way house – this I think explains my mood somewhat. Also, for the first time in ages, Tara, one of our cats, has come to see me. She is curled in a fuzzy ball between my ankles. Cute!

The day will begin shortly, I have weekly site progress meeting today and I think the programme has slipped (bloody Covid) – this will not go down well with the Client, but it is what it is, and we will work with the cards we are dealt.

But before all this, I had a nice heart to heart with Eve for about an hour. I sat on the floor of her room in my nightie, next to her bed and we chatted away, clearing the air, and saying how we are doing. It turns out all the while I was having an upsetting time as Eve slowly distanced herself from me over the 2 or 3 years leading up to the crisis at Christmas - she was equally distressed as she knew the way she was feeling would devastate me, so she couldn't say anything. She was stuck and felt trapped by not wanting to hurt me. The irony is that over the past few weeks, Eve and I are closer than we have been for years. It is mind-blowing to me that her ending our relationship has actually brought us closer together.

As well as this, from my side of the fence, I reiterated that I am liking the person (Julia) that I am becoming. I am Julia, all the time, but I am also, for the first time in my life, exploring who she is. I have done a little of this over the years, mainly in my late teens / early twenties and again in my mid-thirties, but my personal circumstances, living with parents etc, limited my opportunities and the time available. Julia was a relief from the dysphoria and stress of having to live as Adam – very welcome, much needed and necessary. But I haven't <u>lived</u> as her. She was never a fully fleshed out, real person and so this is uncharted territory. I am discovering things about me, as her, that are wonderful, interesting, fascinating, and well, just nice. Example: Make-up – I <u>really</u> like wearing it. I never thought I would. My attitude was as the stereotypical woman supposedly has, it's nice, but daily, a chore. But guess what? It's not at all! I am wearing make-up daily for around 8 hours or so. Sure, I am putting it on in the evening and sleeping in it, which is weird. But Adam's face is not acceptable wearing make-up so I can only do so when the disguise comes off. I like putting it on. Even the minimal mascara and lipstick I wear most days – it is rare I do a full face... I have an "evening look", but the phrase "all dressed up and nowhere to go" seems to sum things up, so I only do this when I feel I want to take things up a notch or two. For fun. I wear make-up as most women do. Simple, sensible, enhancing and, dare I say it, well, pretty. I can go to town with my make-up to try and achieve 'beautiful', I have yet to succeed and likely never will, but it is fun. 'Pretty' however, I think I can do to some extent. And I can't tell you how much I love looking in the mirror and seeing someone I like staring back at me. I am at the point where, to me, I look strange without it. My true face gleefully accepts the make-up and the girl in the mirror looking back at me with pretty eyes is nice. She is someone I like and someone I like being. Putting on make-up completes my outfit and is good for me. I like it and I like me for liking it – if you know what I mean? Furthermore, I also like finding this out about myself. The journey of discovery is fascinating and compelling. I want to play with make-up, become more skilled and investigate this part of myself further. For the first time in my life, I am Julia fully, one gender, and every moment I spend as her is a moment of discovery and wonder. There is a purity in who I am that has always been absent in my life.

14 hours today in a skirt. 14 hours expressing who I am fully. 14 hours exploring this neglected side of me, this important, key part of my being. For the first time I am free to develop into someone who is true to myself. And although this wasn't my decision, I like who I am like this. My wardrobe has expanded, and my clothes are functional, not just fun, or an escape. They help express who I am for hours and hours at a time. I am supremely comfortable and there is no novelty, just nice clothes that I like to wear. I feel like I have taken a little bit of control over who I am again, I don't have a choice, but like Eve said some time ago, I am owning it. Furthermore, I can see me liking who I am more and more as Julia continues to blossom into a real person. This is so good for me, and I find the journey I am on immensely gratifying. I want more! And guess what? I can have as much as I can! An all you can eat buffet of authenticity. This is a revelation, and I feel that for the first time ever, I'm free from having to be Adam all the time. The fact is, I am not Adam anymore. *Some* of his nature may come back, I am fairly convinced of this now. But I will never <u>be</u> him again. I am something new. Something untainted by the world, someone who will be much more fully formed, someone who can live, love, and take joy in her life. Someone I really like. And after decades of subterfuge, someone genuine at last.

14 hours in a skirt today. But it's been more or less 12 hours plus in a skirt every day – over 50% of my time spent in a skirt or a dress. I am living as a woman now, although in private. And I like it. It is good for me, and I can feel things ever so slowly getting better.

Friday April 16th

Wow, 4 days in a row where I am OK first thing in the morning. Is this how it is now? I really hope so. But I am nervous, I am waiting for the hammer to fall... I want this to continue, mornings can be truly awful, but I know I am a long way from being out of the woods, so at some point I am sure to have a bad day again. Today thankfully, is <u>not</u> that day.

Last night I felt I needed to be a bit more girly. My make-up was its usual understated, simple look – I came very close to doing my full face, but in the end, I went for sexy undies. Black satin and lace, full matching set, bra, knickers, and suspenders, with lace topped silky stockings. I can feel what I am wearing, and it feels great to know I have ramped things up in a secret way, entirely for my own benefit. My favourite skirt, my current favourite blouse and some nice heels completed my outfit. Playful, sexy, and really pretty on the inside – kinda sums up who I am at the moment.

Getting back to last night's ramblings, I am liking looking in the mirror, seeing Julia, not Adam looking back at me through my eyes. Enhancing my face with make-up to make more of her and liking what I see. Liking the honest expression of who I am. Liking being comfortable with myself. It validates me at a fundamental level and anything remotely male jars me terribly and takes me out of the moment. It's a total immersion and I really love it, I love inhabiting the new, child-like person, who is full of wonder and eager to experience <u>everything</u>. Sadly, it is unlikely she could every truly exist out in the world, but at home, I can explore who I am and manifest myself fully in this way, like I never have before. I feel free. I feel real. And I like it and who I am in ways previously unknown. I want and need more! I want to experience <u>everything</u> female, all the female stereotypes, from wearing a spectacular wedding dress to a humble working waitress uniform as well as all the myriad of combinations in between. This kind of thing will definitely scare Eve, but for me it is fun and exploration. Previously it was just fantasy, but now, I <u>could</u> actually experience some of this. At least in theory and within the confines of my room. I want to know, I want to feel, I want to experience. I want to have fun and play. I want it all, and after 50 years, it seems I can finally have some more.

So, I think that I may buy some unusual clothes, just for me. Just to have the experience. Just to explore and grow who I am. For fun and because I can. A wedding dress is at the top of the list, but I don't have the fortune. Something more realistic then, Nurse, Maid, Waitress, Bikini, Swimsuit, Corset something along these lines. Something a little more extreme, but practical. Something only a woman would experience as real clothes, not a costume. Just to get a genuine insight into a stereotypical, exclusively female gender role. Something that, when I look in the mirror, could <u>not</u> be Adam in <u>any</u> way. A 100% expression of my female nature.

Validation. It's important. I crave it. The above is a small part of validating who I am, but it goes much further than merely manifesting a stereotype – I am a real person and to be treated as a real person validates me. It's little things, like Eve recognising that I have spent time on my appearance. She said I looked nice a couple of days ago and it means the world to me. It's hard for her, I get it, but if she could acknowledge me as a female, just in conversation, in a minor way, it would be earth-shattering for me. It would make everything I am going through valid and real. Something like "Here she is" when I emerge after I have changed, or "Hey girl" as a greeting, or just calling me Julia. Female pronouns, or using my name, really small stuff, but astonishingly potent. Incredibly meaningful, I want this. But it is not who Eve is and it makes me wonder just how comfortable she really is with the situation. So, I have to keep talking to her, I must give her the space to come to terms with this fundamental shift in me and I have to reassure her that if I go too far, she <u>must</u> tell me. I won't push this, I want it badly, but other than letting her know it is important to me, she needs to be comfortable and come to it in her own time, or not at all if she can't. Hopefully she will, hopefully this can happen...

Enough writing for now – time to face the day. Nearly the weekend, yay!

So, today was alright. Work is what it is and to be honest, none of it has any meaning anymore, I am just going through the motions. It is just a stressful means to an end. Financial stability. But we knocked off a bit early, so I went to see dad around 4:30pm. As I arrived, two of my aunts were leaving. It was great to see them both again after all this time. We chatted for a while and hugged – nice.

Dad and I talked; we didn't plumb the same emotional depths as before but there is a new understanding there. We built some new garden furniture together and then headed to the pub for some dinner – east end pie and mash, yum!

Home at 8pm, in a dress by quarter past. Just made it in time, will be just over 50% female attired today.

Eve was in the bath when I got home, relaxing. Had a brief chat through the door, but our daily catch up is yet to happen. Soon...

We sat for an hour or so catching up on our days, then a relatively early night.

I decided to ramp up my outfit for a short while, but then started falling asleep when my bedside light switched itself off. So, I got changed for bed in the dark, I look like a rainbow! Black knickers, blue bra, and a red nightie! Mad, but oh so comfy – I slept like a log.

A good day.

Saturday, April 17th

Woke up late, nice lie in. It is 10:30am as I write this, and I am in the process of getting up. We are going to see Eve's mum and dad today, so I am going to face being in Adam's skin for longer than I would like. But it'll be worth it. We always have a good time when we get together.

I had a weird dream last night, not sure if I should tell Eve, normally I share dreams if I can remember them, and she likes to hear of them, but this one is a bit close to home as it involved me telling her parents who I am. So, it may not go over very well. Basically, we all go on holiday together to Las Vegas (of all places, no idea why, I've no desire whatsoever to holiday there) and stay in one of the huge hotels. Somehow, I end up locked out of our room and am lost in the maze of floors and corridors – I have forgotten our room number, they all look the same (I wasn't paying attention when we checked in) and had to be rescued by Eve's mum. I am wandering around the packed hotel, trying to hide from folks because I am dressed only in a lady's swimsuit, shaved legs, painted nails, and full make-up. Eventually, Eve's mum finds me and takes me back to the room. She isn't phased by my appearance at all – I am female – the embarrassment is from being lost and from being in such a public place in only my swimwear. All very odd. Despite the dream, I am in a fair mood today and am looking forward to the weekend.

Well, Larry cat buggered off, so we were late leaving the house, then, as we were packing the car, his sister, Tara cat escaped too! She thought it was great fun until she realised, we were not messing around. One cat in, the other one will have to spend the night outside – daft mogs.

The drive up was a chore, Eve drove thankfully. We chatted about my frustrations trying to catch her up learning a new language and I am sorry to say I was a bit tetchy. I am missing being in a skirt and Larry cat escaping had stressed Eve out. Plus, every idiot in the world was on the road today.

Things improved when we arrived at Eve's folks' place. I helped her dad finish building a new BBQ and then we took it for its inaugural test run. We were joined by their neighbours. They are great company and good fun. The BBQ was excellent (as always), and we ended up chatting well into the night. By this time though I had been out of a dress for some time and putting on a show as Adam was beginning to take its toll. I went a bit splat, exhausted by the effort of maintaining Adam's persona.

Nice to finally be in my bed in my nightie. But I am on my own again. Eve is on the sofa-bed in the room next door. I really hope not, but I think tomorrow will be hard.

Sunday, April 18th

I woke up alone, in a strange bed, without my make-up or earrings. It was bound to affect me, and it has. I am a bit down today, not badly, but I am not in as good a place as I have been.

I can hear everyone else up already, downstairs, chatting and busying themselves with the morning. I will join them soon; I will put on my disguise and hide my mood. My pain. And it will be alright. I will have some fun today. I always do with Eve's family – they are good folks and fantastic company. But my relationship status with Eve makes me feel at odds with them. After 15 years, they are <u>my</u> family too and I love them. But now that relationship is being questioned. As Eve's best friend, they are her family, not mine. Eve says she loves me like a bother (even though I am now her sister), so I suppose that means they are my family still? Just not in the same "in laws" way. It's a really odd place to be to be honest. I feel a little uncomfortable, a little ill-at-ease. It's very subtle, but it's there all the same and I really don't like it at all. Something has shifted, just a little bit, and now I don't feel quite as at home as I used to. It's upsetting my mood this morning. But I know that when I join them downstairs, they will be the same, welcoming folks they always are, and I will be happier for the day. This is all in my head, it'll be all right.

It was nice sitting in the garden, in the sunshine for a few hours earlier. I just enjoyed and appreciated the moments and made some good memories. All too soon it was time to head home. Eve drove again and we had a meaningful conversation for most of the journey. We have said it all before, so it, like this diary, was a bit repetitive, but it was honest and deep – these talks mean a lot. Eve expanded upon why she took so long to tell me, she knew it would hurt me badly, so put it off for so long to protect me. But it was making her miserable, she had to do something and ultimately, she had no choice but to hurt me. I don't think she could possibly have known just how devastating it would be for me though. How could she have known that it would not only break my heart, but also destroy the man I was utterly and force me to take refuge in whatever I had left? No one could have known this, not even me. I am worried for her; this has taken a toll I can tell. More importantly, I really hope this hasn't affected things between her and my family too much. She is not the "bad guy" here and I have driven this point home with both my dad and my brother over and over, but somehow, I get the feeling that it will be awkward, like they are looking for a scapegoat. My brother moving so fast to protect the Company hasn't helped either. Show some god-damned sensitivity! When he told me I just wanted to drop everything and storm out. But I didn't, I am "being professional" as I mentioned previously in this journal. What he is doing needed to be done, but his timing really sucks. I told him what was going on for some support and because I had to, my mask slipped. But I am truly regretting it now. If things become awkward between Eve and them it's another wedge between us and this is the absolute LAST thing I want, I am holding on by my fingernails here, to whatever I can salvage from the last 15 years, and to my very sanity. I need some time and some space to get to grips with things, but instead of this, he has moved like a sprinter out of the blocks to protect the Company from a completely non-existent threat. I am actually nervous about the next time we all get together. I <u>really</u> hope it is OK, it <u>has</u> to be, if Eve doesn't feel welcome, then this really is the <u>first</u> major wedge that splits us apart. It is also why my mood at Eve's parents place was so difficult for me, they have done this 100% correctly, made me feel welcome and included, but it was still a bit awkward for me. If my family do not do the same for Eve, then it is likely she will never see them again, the awkwardness I felt will be multiplied up – and if this happens, then some of the tiny amount of hope I have left is extinguished as others, who have no say in our relationship at all, come between us. I want and need support, not meddling and bad feeling towards the woman I love.

Eve suggested I might want to take myself off for a weekend or two, in much the same way she does for herself. She travels to immerse herself fully in a foreign culture and the idea is that I immerse myself fully as a woman. Literally spend every moment as Julia in every possible way. I would rent a cottage and arrive with provisions, then spend the weekend living full time as a female. Exploring who I am now in a safe and fulfilling way. Do something purely for me. Although I <u>really</u> like the idea, I am not so keen on spending so much time away from Eve. Sure, she has been away on trips before and I have been on my own, going to work and minding the cats. But this is different. This is me CHOOSING to spend time apart. I am <u>not</u> comfortable with this at the moment. I like the idea of doing something for me. I like the idea of spending a large amount of time exploring who I am and truly living as Julia all the time. But I know I will miss Eve dreadfully; how can I dedicate the time to exploring myself if all I can think of is how lonely I am? I still love her, and I haven't <u>chosen</u> to spend time away from her since we first got together. So, this is a <u>huge</u> step for me. I am sure that the very moment she can, Eve will be on a plane to somewhere in Europe, to "be a European" again. She loves it and loves being completely self-reliant, emersed in a different culture. So, I shouldn't have any issues with me doing the same. But I am not sure I am ready just yet, we shall see... Maybe I am scared? Maybe that's what I am worried about? What if I want to stay and live fully as a woman for the rest of my life? What if I like myself so much as a woman, I end up not *wanting* to step back over the line? It's a moot point at the moment, there is nothing over the line to step back to, but from where I am now, I can see this is a very real possibility, even if it is a totally impractical one. If I felt full gender reassignment would be remotely successful I would gladly do so. I like being female in my head, so it stands to reason I will like being female in body too. I like expressing myself in a fully female manner and I can see myself being happy if I could be a woman physically and function as such in society. I like being Julia and Adam's disguise is <u>really</u> hard work. He needs to come back; I can't go day-after-day pretending to be him. It's exhausting. He has to feel comfortable and natural again, or I am facing a long and painful transition into the world's biggest woman. I am just too big to fit in as a woman, so I have to be able to choose to be Adam again. Somehow. I hope it will happen, I think I have made some progress, but I have a ways to go yet and, in the meantime, being Julia is nice, so I may well do as Eve suggests. Take some time to be me completely, for an entire weekend or two. Explore who I now am in depth and see just who this lady called Julia actually is. I want to know, and I think it will be fun finding out.

Lastly, as mentioned, I am worried for Eve. I said that if she needed to talk to her sister, she had my permission to tell her about me. Given her own situation she may well have somewhat of an understanding, or some insight she could share with her. But it will change my relationship with her and likely her girlfriend too. So, I said that she needs to be aware that doing so has consequences, but that if she needed to, she could, it's not a betrayal, she has my permission.

Monday, April 19th.

Not so good this morning, I do not want to face the day. The world is cold, and I don't feel welcome – I just don't fit anymore. Eve is awake, I can hear her, but I don't want to go to her, I will only upset her and ruin her day too. But I need her company right now, so I may well end up being a selfish git anyway. I am trying not to, but I may not have a choice.

Speaking of choices, Eve, when she eventually goes away to Europe is choosing to do something exclusively for her. But she is also choosing to do something <u>without me.</u> This hurts. I <u>need</u> to be able to do the same, but <u>I don't want to.</u> I want to share my life with Eve, I want to share everything with her, and I want her to want to reciprocate in kind. Her not wanting to do the same is painful for me and at times impossible for me to deal with. Cumulatively all these missed events in her life add up. Ditching me on holiday is a stab in the heart. Doing it more than once, plus going on trips by herself, for herself, without me is just awful for me. And then finally, choosing to sleep on an uncomfortable sofa, as it is preferable to sleeping in a comfy bed with me is unbearable. I love her so much, but I have been completely rejected. It bloody hurts.

So, choosing to do things for me, like taking a long weekend and literally living as a woman in every way, is something I would very much like to do. But choosing to spend time away from Eve is really very difficult, after all, time is the most precious thing any of us have. So, I am quite sure that at the end of the weekend, it'll be a hollow victory. Time spent away from Eve is lost time I could have spent with her – QED. That said, I think this is a necessary step on the road to re-building myself. I don't want to be apart from her, but somehow, I must. I must <u>choose</u> to do this. I can't continue to live solely for the concept of "us", I need to start living my life for "me". But I don't want to. I love being part of a couple. I love the life we built together and most of all I love Eve, and who I am as a consequence.

Change is an inevitable part of life.

At the moment?

I fucking HATE it.

I don't want things to change, it sounds petulant, and the truth of the matter is they already have. But it hurts and I confess, today I am struggling again.

I knew it was too good to last. I am down today. Maybe I will feel better as the day progresses? I hope so. I need to. Positive outlook, I can do this. Is this a Monday thing? Weird.

8:55pm. I have had a nice evening and an OK day. I am about to go to bed early, have a brutal 3:30am start tomorrow, need to be in Swansea for 9am...

I have just had a <u>VERY</u> dark thought though. So dark, I don't want to write it down. I trust Eve and I know with absolute certainty that she wouldn't do this to me. But I am in such turmoil at the moment, random paranoid shit pops unwanted into my head. If I write it down, then I am acknowledging it. But if I don't get it out, onto paper, I will obsess over it. I must get it out of my head, so I *am* going to write it down. But it <u>can't</u> be real, she wouldn't do this to me, I am <u>SURE.</u>

Is Eve having an affair with my mate Steve?

Fuck, there is a fair amount of coincidental evidence. Spending a lot of time in his car instead of mine on the first rally. Always going to his hometown (it is lovely, and we both feel at home there, plus she knows it well), but it IS where he lives. Even throwing herself into learning his language could be seen as a way to get closer to him. It CAN'T be true. He is my mate, and she is <u>everything</u> to me. This would be a betrayal on <u>EVERY</u> level. So, I <u>won't</u> believe it. I can't.

Go away random paranoid thought, just go away. I do not need a little devil sitting on my shoulder whispering the evillest things in my ear on top of everything else.

At some point, Eve may well fall in love. But not him, and not now. If this is true then it has been going on behind my back for <u>years</u> and although I get completely that the heart does what it wants and love just happens, even at the worst possible time. This would be unforgivable. So, it is NOT true, it can't be.

She may not love me romantically anymore, but Eve still cares about me. She has caused me enough pain, surely this isn't waiting around the corner to finish me off? I hate myself; how could I possibly think this? I am shocked at myself; I am not as progressed as I thought. This is a setback and no mistake. To even think it means my faith in her is rattled and that shows how vulnerable I am right now.

> RANDOM DARK THOUGHT – YOU ARE UTTER BOLLOCKS – FUCK OFF.

So, putting this aside, how am I doing? Well, to be honest I am not so sure. The man I was is gone. What little is left of him is very, very broken, and utterly lost. Me? I am now a woman. In my mind, I am 100% female and I used to be able to step to and fro over the gender line in my head. I have always been, more or less, a 50 / 50 split, male / female, but now I find myself stuck on the female side. There is no male side left, nothing. Just agony. For the first time in my life, I am 100% a single gender, it is just that that gender is the opposite of the body I inhabit. It's a scary place to be, but as the days roll on, I am liking who I am now. I am enjoying the calm when I express myself fully. It feels natural, comfortable, and genuine. When I dress as a man it feels uncomfortable, awkward, false, hard work and I constantly feel ill-at-ease. Dysphoria. I am exhausted maintaining the pretence. I desperately want to feel at home dressed as a man again. If I could just re-inhabit this life, even a little, then it wouldn't be so hard. It feels like I am putting on a show and I am having to work my socks off, err, quite literally, just to keep going. On the flip side I can't get enough of expressing myself as a female. I love it, everything about it, even the stuff most women supposedly consider a chore. In terms of hours, I am now living as a woman. I spend more than 50% of everyday living as a female and have done so for weeks. Furthermore, even the time spent locked in trousers is spent as a woman in mind.

So, I think I will book a little cottage somewhere and spend a long weekend living every moment fully as a female. Exploring who I am and taking my life to the next level. This has been 50 years in the making. Time to embrace who I am, it is long overdue.

My male side needs to come back. I have to be a man in the eyes of the world, so I need to be able to be this man in the same easy manner I used to. Hopefully, all he needs is time and space? To go out as him, interact as him and find some joy as him? I am trying to do so, but every joyous moment I have is being had by a woman hiding behind a man's face.

Time and space to heal and grow.

Must sleep now, awfully long day ahead tomorrow...

Tuesday, April 20th.

3:30am! Ouch, brutal. Mega busy day today, out the door at 4am, then drive to Neath, near Swansea for 9 o'clock. Then onto Gorseinon for 10:30am. After this, I drive into Swansea itself for a survey at mid-day. This wraps up my work in Wales, so I head back into England to Bedminster, Bristol, then finally my hotel in Filton. Ready for another survey, first thing in the morning in Cribbs Causeway, Bristol. Finally, I can then drive home.

A very long day. To say I am tired is an understatement, but it is coming up to 5pm now and I am in my hotel room about to get changed. Be right back…

OK, that's much better. I cannot physically make the 50% threshold today, but I am grateful for whatever time I can get.

So, I had a <u>lot</u> of time driving today, alone with my thoughts. It occurs to me that the single biggest change in Eve and my relationship I have, is the same issue I have struggled with most, prior to what I am now calling "J-Day" (the day I became Julia completely, the day I went out to end it all, in more pain than I ever thought possible, my lowest ebb and the day what was left of Adam gave up the fight and did not come home – the day before I started this journal). It boils down to this…

I <u>want</u> to share my whole life with Eve, because I love her, and she is all I have.

Eve <u>doesn't</u> want to share her whole life with me, because she doesn't love me and wants to be independent. She wants some privacy.

It's a bit of a conundrum and no mistake. Eve believes the solution is for me to move to the same position she is in. I need to find and do things <u>for myself.</u> She is now a closed, and locked book to me, but I am still an open book to her. I can't just switch off my love, I want and need someone to share my life with.

I think companionship and friendship is the most I can hope for from her in the future, and even this may be a stretch – she wants to leave me and our life together behind. It will <u>have</u> to be enough. But to her I will always be an open book, I think the difference is whether she wants to read it.

There is a very real parallel here. This journal is literally and open book of my life. It is available for Eve to read, all day, at home and if she wants to, she is **VERY** welcome to. Indeed, I **WANT** her to. But she says she doesn't want to. I respect that. There is a fair amount of mad and scary stuff in here. Although we talk all the time and I have shared everything I am going through with her, reading some of the darker stuff would be hard for her. She will come face-to-face with what she has (unintentionally) done to me. So, I get it. She can't face the pain I am still in, the utter turmoil my life has become. It would make it hard for her to continue as she is. Not wishing to hurt me resulted in this happening all at once, instead of over time. Not reading this diary is not facing the scale and depth of how much damage has been done.

This book is a brutally honest record, in black and white, of the damage caused.

And it is a painful read in places.

It is also a book about who I am now, my faltering steps to heal and become a person again. So, amongst the negatives, there is hope. And although I don't want her to truly face what I am going through – I wouldn't want that for anyone, least of all my love, I <u>really</u> want her to see the wonder of the person I am becoming and most importantly, the hope.

I have never written a diary before, but I look back at these pages and I am proud of what is there. It is sooo personal, I truly have never read anything quite like it. I wonder if it could, or even should be published? I think others may also find it fascinating. I am a pretty unique person, I suppose we all are, we deal with some fundamental issues at a major crisis points in our lives, but I don't think I've ever read anything quite this deep, or different. I mean, how much more drama could there be? Hubris. Although I am proud of my words and most of all my honesty, I am no writer. This is very much a first attempt and one driven by necessity. I am writing this for me, it is part of the very important process of dealing with my bizarre situation and trying to make some sort of sense of who I now am. What makes this book compelling is also the reason it is likely impossible to publish. My only true audience beyond myself is Eve. And through her own choices, she is very unlikely to read it.

Such a shame.

Just done a count up, I have handwritten so many pages! Wow, just wow. But sheesh, my handwriting really sucks! I'll need to type this up if it is ever to be read by someone other than me...

Wednesday, April 21st

Boom! It had to happen; I am not in a good place this morning. I should have seen it coming, a long, hard day, too long spent channelling Adam, and an early night in a hotel room on the other side of the country to Eve. And most of all, no chat with her last night. I feel so down today, it's unbearable. I am so lonely, and this is my life from now on. I sat on the loo in floods of tears as I realised that no one could possibly love me. A fat, ugly, 50-year-old bloke with a receding hairline and poor eyesight. And that's the best bits! Scratch the surface and what do you find? Inside, this huge man is actually a woman. How? How could such an incongruous combination exist? How could <u>anyone</u> love me? Eight billion people on this planet and not one of them could love me. I am going to be alone and desperately unhappy for the rest of my life. I see this now. It is inevitable. My one shot at true happiness has gone.

Eve doesn't love me.

Shit. I am crying again.

I shared myself with her completely. I gave her everything. Everything I have, all my hopes and dreams. And everything I <u>am</u>, at the most fundamental level. There is nothing more to give.

And it just wasn't enough.

And if, after all this, it wasn't enough for her. How could it be enough for anyone?

How can I give my entire being and all I ever could be along with my complete and undying love to someone, and it not be enough?

How is this possible?

I know she cares for me. She may not love me, but I know she cares. Afterall, she is still here. And furthermore, she is going through a tough time too. Watching me in utter turmoil.

I hope she isn't just staying around because she feels responsible for my current state. I *will not* be pitied. The only thing I can see that she has done wrong is timing. She could've handled it better, so it didn't hit me all at once. I have no idea how of course; how do you break this kind of thing to someone who loves you completely and not cause untold damage? I am sure she does feel responsible. How can you rip the heart out of someone you have lived with for 15 years and then pull the pin on the oh so carefully hidden hand grenade in their head and not feel responsible in some way?

But I choose to believe there is more than just guilt. I choose to believe she has some level of care for me. It may not be love in the romantic sense, but there must be some feeling for me and my well-being. There just <u>has</u> to be.

I know she wants to fly. And I want to let her go. And I feel terrible for being such a complete basket case, clinging to the last of our love with my fingernails. I am a selfish bastard, but it is all I have left.

At some point. Eve will leave me.

In my heart, I know this to be true. I can't hold on to such a free and beautiful soul for ever. I should be thankful for the time we have had and cherish the little time we have left.

When she leaves me, it'll be the end.

I'll stop writing in this journal, I will just check out. Eve will be truly free, and I won't hurt anymore. I <u>will not</u> face a long and lonely life in abject misery. I will choose to go as I choose to live. <u>My choice</u>. If you have learned anything from these pages, it is that:

I need to choose who I am.

I have done it in the past, and although my current status was forced upon me, I am choosing to make the best of it.

It won't happen straight away, days, weeks or months will go by. I will procrastinate, I will find a myriad of tiny, inconsequential reasons to continue. But, when Eve is safe in her new life, I will have one of my "bad days" and it'll be too much for me.

At this point, I will take life in my own hands. I will, through my own determination make it, *finally*, atone for all the shit it has thrown my way over the years. I'll stand there with my destiny, and for once, just once, truly be its mistress.

And I will finally know peace.

And Eve will be free.

But no one will understand.

This book is categorically <u>NOT</u> a suicide note. But from where I am now, as much as I am fighting it, this remains a very real likelihood. I am desperately trying to find something, anything worth living for. But I have been shown how good life can be. The years spent with Eve were/are the very best years of my life. If I had seen this coming, I would have cherished each and every moment and made ALL of them count. So much time has been lost, lost to memory and now that I feel there isn't much left, I have such regrets that I have let so many of these precious moments slip through my clumsy fingers.

If I thought, for one moment, that I could have just the tiniest fragment of what we once had again, with Eve, or even with someone else, then it would be worth carrying on. I am clinging to life as Eve's sister, or maybe someday, as her brother again if I can. She is and will always be my best friend and there WILL be good times again with her in the future, indeed we are planning them now. And this is good. Because there really is no one else out there for me. Actually, there never was. If Eve couldn't deal with who I am and love me, then who could?

So, I will gladly take whatever I can from our remaining time together. I will make as many good memories as possible and I will hate myself for being a selfish git, not letting her fly away.

And when she does? Who knows?

I hope I will be in a better place, but it is hard to see from my current position. There really are only three options.

1. I go on. I am miserable, but I live for just the faintest glimmer that there is someone else out there for me. If I can, I will live as Adam and be, well at least as far as the world can see, someone "normal". So that when this mythical person comes along there is a chance for us. In the meantime, Eve and I stay friends and she shares the parts of her life that she wants to with me. I will gladly take these scraps, these slim pickings, these left-overs. I hope that I will always be welcome in her life, and I hope that she is happy.

2. I fully embrace Julia, likely travel, likely to the far east and mutilate my body to become as close to physically female as I can approximate. I will never be truly happy with my body, just as I am now, I will be a freak and will not be fully acceptable in society, so my life will have limits imposed on it. This does not end well. But at least I will be genuine, will this be enough? It is more and more feeling like it might...

3. I end it all.

Given the above, you can see that I really don't have any choice at all. All three are very real possibilities at this point in time and this is a truly frightening place to be. I can see that working on option 1 could fail at any time and I'll end up taking options 2 or 3, or both.

I don't want this.

My life was great, the very best. But it is gone, at the most fundamental level. And there is a very real risk of it going completely and permanently. So, I am fighting, fighting for my actual life.

This book helps. It helps me on days like today. When all I can see of my future are dark clouds and loneliness.

I love Eve. I think I always will. She is welcome in my life always and I will take as much joy from whatever time we have left as I can. But I am hurting now, today more than most. So, I write, and I write, and I write...

This book helps.

One survey to do this morning, then the long drive home. I will see my love tonight. So, I go on...

The survey was OK. I was acceptable to others, and I was diligent in my work. But once I was sat in my car, I fell apart. The entire length of the M4 is drenched in my tears.

I arrived home around 1pm, Eve was out at a costume fitting for one of her acting jobs, so I had the house to myself for an hour or so. I used this time to try to resolve an issue with Patreon. It turned out to be <u>very</u> frustrating and to be honest, I had zero patience for it. So, when Eve came home, she found me in an all-time foul mood. Tired and upset, now irritated too. In the end, I think I was successful, but I should have made more of an effort with Eve. I am such an idiot. I needed her badly today and her first impression of me was as "Miss Ranty". I apologised and the hug was both wonderful and very much needed. My shit day then, finally, slowly started to improve. Eve and I had a long chat, I didn't go into the depths of my earlier despair. It wasn't massively emotional; I think I was all cried out. And then we decided to go out for dinner. A pub meal, it was lovely, if a bit chilly, and we had a nice evening together.

I started a new book today, "Language Hacking", I am sick of not making any progress on Duolingo, time for a new approach. Eve had a nice bath and then, after I had got changed, we watched "Death in Paradise" for a bit – such a great show.

All in all, a good end to a really awful day. I hope tomorrow will be better.

Thursday, April 22nd

Day 2 - Fuck.

Woke up alone and lonely, I <u>hate</u> it and I don't think I will ever get used to this.

I literally have no future.

I have given Eve <u>everything</u>.

All I have, all I have built, all I am and all I will be.

I have let her in at the most fundamental level. She knows <u>me</u> intimately, in every way. And it isn't enough for her. She has ripped up my whole life, thrown it in my face and said she wants more.

How can I possibly let anyone else in again? To open myself up like this, be completely vulnerable and then be rejected and trampled?

So, <u>when</u> Eve leaves me, I will be utterly alone. For good. I can't put myself in such a vulnerable position again. I just can't.

And all I ever wanted was her love, to share her life and make her happy.

That's not too much to ask, is it?

Eve is the most astonishing and spectacular person I have ever met, I want her to be glorious, amazing and everything she possibly can be. So, I have spent my life giving her a stable base to fly from. All I wanted in return was to share this astonishing life and for her to come back to me, to our home.

And for that, I was willing to give it all. Absolutely <u>everything</u>. I still am, it's just "The Deal" and I committed to it completely. Even gambling my very identity on this one shot at happiness.

But I can't do this again, not now, not now I know how painful this is. How can I share myself this openly with anyone again?

I CAN'T

So, I am facing my twilight years alone and miserable.

I <u>refuse</u> to live like that.

> I only have two things left to give to Eve. Her freedom and the price of that freedom.

The irony is, she was always free...

Our life together is categorically <u>not</u> a gilded cage, if anything, it is the EXACT OPPOSITE.

Eve has my life in her hands. I am on my knees, begging her to be careful with it.

> The cost of her freedom from me
> **IS MY LIFE**

I will <u>not</u> live in misery.

Without her there is no joy in my life, only loneliness and misery. I hope you can live with this Eve, my true love, my life?

You have brought me to the very brink. You have taken away my ability to share your life, slowly and deliberately, you have shut me out.

But I <u>always</u> knew you loved me.

So, I always trusted you completely and I knew with absolute certainty you would come back to me. You would walk through our door, to your home and be bright, refreshed, and eager to share your adventures with me.

And although shutting me out was astonishingly painful, I could live with that. Because I knew in my heart that you loved me and would <u>want</u> to come back and share.

NOW I <u>DON'T</u>

Now, I am sitting on a ticking timebomb. Just waiting for the day you don't return to me.

BOOM!

GAMEOVER

Deposit more coins to play...

But why would I want to play again?

On the astonishingly rare possibility there is someone else out there who could love me. How can I open up to them? Knowing just how painful it is to have everything that you are, not be good enough. And to watch helplessly as they utterly destroy you?

I am truly alone now and will be completely alone for the rest of my life.

AND I <u>HATE</u> IT!

...this does not end well.

I am clearly not in a good way today, so I fled screaming back into the female side of my nature, but although she is my new reality, she is unlikely to ever be real out there in the world.

- I need to live in society as Adam, it's what "they" insist I am, "they" are completely wrong and what little is left of Adam is suicidal.
- He <u>must</u> get better if I am to live. But how does he come back from this? He can't.
- How is it possible to avoid the inevitability of the final outcome?

I thought Eve and I had it all. Life was good, the very best and it was worthwhile.

I didn't want much, just some companionship with someone so special and maybe grow old together in a cute little cottage by the sea. A couple of cats and a camper van to go on adventures in.

And it would have been so perfect, a life worth living. Filled with joy and happiness.

To sit there holding Eve's hand, watching the sun set over the sea on a perfect summer's evening.

I am so upset right now; I can't write anymore – I'll come back to this later. For now, I am crying again. But crying is temporary, So I will be back...

I cried with Eve this morning. She cried with me too. It was very touching; we are <u>both</u> going through this. In the end though she said she can only help so much and that i should speak with a counsellor. She is right. I have emotional support, but what I need is a map to show me the way out of this.

So, I have a session with a lady named Kay at 11am in 2 weeks' time (Tuesday 4th).

This feels like a positive step. We'll see if she can help, but from the little I know she seems nice and experienced in what I am going through.

I went to work, and little by little the day got better, as I knew it would. And by the time I got home I was more or less OK, much to Eve's surprise.

Suicidal at 9am, OK, by 5pm – my emotions are all over the place. Not good.

We had a lovely walk in the evening sunshine with Eve on the local footpath. Very nice and equally special. I made a memory – a good one.

Note to self: Ring dad tomorrow, he rang while we were walking so, we couldn't really chat. I said I would call when I could, I will do so tomorrow.

I have been dressed properly all night. I needed it tonight. Nice to (literally) let my hair down and truly relax after such a stressful day.

Going to sleep now. I hope tomorrow will be better...

Friday, April 23rd

I am alright this morning. Not good. Not bad, just alright.

I began to get upset again, but instead, somehow, I got angry instead. I am not sure this is an improvement to be honest, but it is a welcome relief from all the crying and sadness. A change is as good as a rest, as they say.

It began with a single thought: "This is NOT my fault; this was done to me".

That statement alone should be enough to make anyone angry. But as I have mentioned, you must focus anger to manifest it. And the truth is, it is not Eve's fault either. So I can't get truly angry. I can't focus it. It's a fizzing mess inside my head, like a swarm of bees bouncing off the walls of their hive with no exit. But I began to think about **"THE DEAL"**. You know, the unspoken deal that all couples have? Eve and I included. I give her my love; she gives her love to me. We share each other's lives, and we show our true selves to each other, let them in, behind the curtain that the whole world sees. And we support each other when times get hard. <u>We are a team.</u>

Eve has changed "The Deal"

She started by not letting me in.

I didn't notice this at first, we stopped talking intimately, you know, pillow talk about what is going on with each other and if we needed to make changes for them and for us.

She then began to take parts of her life away from me.

And this <u>REALLY</u> hurt. Firstly, because I was confused, we had a "Deal" right? This has continued, slowly, inexorably, and painfully. She has built a large part of her life, parts that she is passionate about, parts that are truly meaningful to her, that are entirely her own. Of course, she is allowed to have things that are for herself, but I am not welcome, she doesn't <u>want</u> to share them with me and indeed has structured them such that I can't share them. At this point our relationship flat lined.

And now she has taken away her love.

Love is the foundation it all sits on. Love is what gives faith and trust in each other. Faith that they will be there, regardless, if the other one needs them. Trust that when they walk out the door they will come back. Love is what binds us together and makes everything worthwhile.

I love Eve, but she doesn't love me.

I am upholding "The Deal", she is not.

We don't have an equal relationship anymore, I am giving her my love, my life, and my support, and she is not returning these fundamentals.

By taking away her love, my absolute faith in her is rattled. I can no longer trust her to be there for me if I need her.

I <u>NEED</u> THIS.

Without it, we are no longer a team. A couple is stronger together, stronger than the sum of their parts. And if we are no longer a team, why am I still giving her everything?

So, I began to get angry. Even though it was the genesis of this new emotion, I was not angry about this being done to me. I was angry about the years she slowly and methodically took it all from me but gave nothing back. But most of all I got angry at myself for not spotting it <u>at all</u>. Love truly is blind.

I am such an idiot.

So, at some point Eve and I need to have a frank conversation about what we want and how this is going to work (or not). To be honest, I am not sure I am mentally in the right place for this yet. I suspect there is still more to come out of the woodwork, it looks like she has an agenda, an end-goal that she has been working towards. Or maybe that is just me being paranoid? – I am still in a huge amount of pain and may well be seeing conspiracies where there are none – my mental state is fragile and vulnerable, so this could just be me jumping to conclusions. And me? She knows what I want. I want "The Deal". But I can't have it anymore. So, I need to think about it and decide what I want, but those things need to be achievable.

For example: I want to NOT feel desperately sad and lonely.

Eve can no longer give me this, at this point in time, this is not a realistic want. Sadly, as I have written before, I don't think I can let anyone else in, my pain now makes me very guarded. I can't just willingly hand someone the ability to hurt me this badly again. So, I think I am going to be lonely for the rest of my life.

The goal is <u>unachievable.</u>

So it can't be on the list, regardless of how much I want it. Besides being lonely is vastly preferable to being suicidal.

The list needs to have tangible, realistic things on it. I suspect Eve's list will have things like "travel extensively" on it, which of course she always could have done, and still can, I would even have funded it for her gladly. Because although I would have worried about her, missed her company dreadfully, and would have been very hurt that she wanted to do this without me, I had <u>absolute</u> faith that she would come back to me and tell me all about her adventures, and that would have been OK.

I don't have that faith anymore.

If Eve wants to travel, she will fund it herself, and by this, I mean completely.

I am very seriously thinking of turning off the "money tap". Part of me, the horribly hurt part, feels like she has been taking the piss out of me for years and this part of me resents it. Eve's finances can best be described as "erratic and unstable" and that is because she has rejected any kind of a traditional work model. She works when she can and when she can't, she works on setting up passive income streams. The truth of it is:

I support her financially.

And I see that this hurts her. She <u>wants</u> to contribute more. She <u>wants</u> to be financially independent and now, more than ever, it hurts her to have to come to me for anything. This is, perhaps, her last tie to me. And I see her doing everything she can to cut this tie without compromising her freedom to work as she pleases.

As much as I want her to stay, I genuinely want her to succeed in this. She has worked her arse off and this much effort deserves to reap rewards. But it scares me too. If she was financially sound, then she could literally up sticks and spend the rest of her life travelling and living wherever she wants.

I think this is her end-goal. I think this is the reason she is breaking up with me. She literally wants the whole world and doesn't want me tying her to her home.

I can't change my life to follow her on this amazing journey – I want to, who wouldn't? I want to be by her side and experience everything the world has to offer. But unlike Eve, I live in the real world, the one where people have a job to earn money so I (we) can have a home and a life. The compromise is my time – it's a Faustian pact with the Devil, my time at work in exchange for money. Money that enables me to live – but not in every moment – only those moments that I've not traded. Eve wants both, she wants the impossible. She wants the money to live AS WELL AS the time to grasp everything this world has to offer.

And I was prepared to give her this, indeed I have done so for most of the past 15 years. I traded my time, and I gave her the money I earned, so she didn't have to. Her love was there so I gladly did so. Because I <u>knew</u> if she went away, she would come back to me. *But now I don't.*

Our home, my work life, the unholy pact I made to trade my oh so precious time for money, gives her a platform to do all the things she wants to do.

But <u>only</u> if there is love.

<u>Only</u> if she comes back to me.

> So, I am angry. Angry with myself for being such a fool and angry with Eve for throwing it all away.

She had it all. The possibility for the whole world and all its' wonders at her fingertips unshackled by financial burdens – so few people get this opportunity, it is a gift; I would have given her anything.

But not anymore.

She wants to do this on her own? Fine.

Our lives were set up so she could fly and be everything she could be. My life was set up to enable this to happen, up to and beyond my death. She is my sole beneficiary, and I am 15 years her senior, so I have made provision for her.

But it was all for love.

She is throwing it all away...

Her life will be amazing, I am sure of this. But without me it will be on her own terms and sadly will <u>always</u> be compromised by her income. Maybe that will make it more worthwhile for her? But I think she will always be limited by what she can earn without compromising her lifestyle.

And this is the point.

I was happy to take that limitation away.

For Love.

A good deal.

The very best.

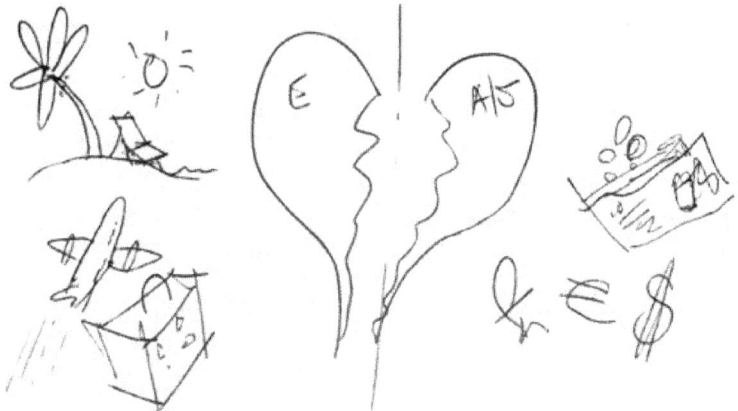

I went to work, and I was OK, my anger subsided – it had no focus. But this is a new emotion, and it is now with me. I have no idea where we are going to end up, I really don't. She is my very best friend and I love spending time with her, but this could end badly. I hope it won't, but she has changed "The Deal" and hurt me profoundly in the process. At the moment, my anger wants to reciprocate in kind, and I may well end up doing so. Anger flares up at the most inopportune moments, can be uncontrollable, and I am still very unstable emotionally. But more so than ever, everything I now do needs to come from a place of calm and a place of logic. It also needs to be absolutely fair. If I do anything now it will come from my pain, my anger and it will <u>all</u> be about me, so it won't be fair.

My anger is saying "She did this to me, sod being fair, how has she been fair to me?" And this is <u>exactly</u> why I can't do anything about it now. I am very much <u>not</u> in the right headspace, and I will react emotionally out of resentment and anger. This will kill any chance of a workable arrangement and we'll go straight to animosity, divvying up the house and going our separate ways.

Speaking of the house, this is likely to be the biggest hurdle in a full-on breakup. We have a joint mortgage; the house is in both of our names. She can't buy my half of the house, with no fixed income, she can't raise the money. I <u>could</u> conceivably buy her out. But then, I'll be left on my own, with very restricted finances, in the house we built together. It won't feel like home, it will be empty and a constant reminder of all I have lost. I don't think I can live here without her. This is <u>our</u> home.

And more importantly, her income has been erratic for years. I have paid 95% of the mortgage repayments. If I buy her out, I will effectively have paid her share twice. Rewarding her for shirking her responsibilities all these years so she could chase one pipedream after another. It's no wonder I am feeling angry...

The third option is to sell up and split the proceeds. 50 / 50. Half of the sale would give us both a sizable deposit, in the region of £80k to £100k each. I can use this to get a mortgage on another property. I'll have a large sum of money, a proven history of making mortgage payments and a steady income that, without Eve, is at least for the time-being, a tad generous. I

90

could potentially move up the housing ladder and get something larger with space for all my cars.

What could Eve get for £80K? And actually, that £80k is pretty much **all** down to me paying the mortgage on my own month in, month out. Sorry, anger again, not helpful. With no fixed income, she won't be able to get a mortgage. She couldn't pay it every month without compromising her principles and the lifestyle she loves so much. No financial institution will lend her the money – she is a bad bet. She could move in with her folks, but they are so far away from London now I don't see how she could continue working. The logistics of travelling to the epicentre of her work just don't stack up. Speaking of travel, her car is in my name! Wow, I just realised that. She couldn't get the finance (unsurprisingly), so it was bought in my name. She pays the bills, but technically I own it – it's like the house, but in reverse. We own it, but I pay for it. I own her daily driver, even though she pays the bills. Actually, I don't want her car. But if things get nasty, then technically it is mine, my name is on the agreements and the registration. How does she generate passive income from a channel about her car if she doesn't have it anymore? Anger again – shit. You see how counter-productive it is? I need to be *very* careful.

The most important thing is that I fund her lifestyle. And I ONLY do this for love. I am not going to fund her leaving me that's for sure. And if she won't give me her love, why should I keep paying for it?

She has changed "The Deal"...

I give her everything. The house she lives in? I pay for it. The food she eats? I pay for. The water she uses? I pay for. I even bought her a bed so she could choose NOT to sleep with me! I did it for love. She doesn't love me. I paid for her to make me miserable and to keep her comfortable!

Love is blind they say. They are fucking right it is! Why the hell did I do that? Why?

- We are not married; she has common law rights – that's it.
- We have no dependants, so I don't have to fund their upkeep.

If we split and it goes badly, I think her only option is to spend the £80k travelling, or setting up a new life, likely in mainland Europe. And she'll love it I am quite sure. Right up the point the money runs out and the real-world starts knocking on her door.

Love is reciprocal, for love, nothing is too expensive. She has taken her love away, I am now paying for a broken heart, she has changed "The Deal".

When the real world comes calling, she can't rely on me anymore to bail her out. We are no longer a team, so she can't rely on me to support her when times are rough. These are the terms of "The Deal", she can't take everything and give nothing in return.

The European rally later on this year? I am not going. I can't see how I can. I am not going to go there to be side-lined and ignored by the woman I love in front of my friends. Why would I, or anyone for that matter, do that? She has done EXACTLY this to me before, not once, but twice now. I won't let her do this to me again. It hurts too much to have the most special person in the world to me blank me totally. And then, to expect me to pay for the trip! That's just not on, it really isn't.

We go together, as a couple, and she gives me some God-damned respect - I've earned at least this much. She doesn't treat me like dog shit. She doesn't ruin my entire holiday and most of all, she doesn't humiliate me in font of our friends by ignoring me. If she can abide by these rules, then, and only then, can I go with her.

She's done this to me twice before, a repeat offender. It was unacceptable then and it still is, it's also just bloody rude and shows no consideration for me at all. I will not be treated like that. I won't.

Anger again, see? Anger.

Or we take 2 cars and go separately. In every way. She pays for herself, completely. And it is too soon, so it will be awful. Our friends will be drawn into what is going on between us and we are both equally unhappy, with our holidays ruined. Of course, that's **if** she can afford it - at the moment, I don't think she can. She is really good at living and travelling on a shoestring budget, but this is not some AirBnB for €20.00 a night. It's a series of good hotels, with good hotel priced meals and a rally that costs actual money. She could save for it and make it happen; indeed, I suspect this is exactly what she will do. But it will be hard for her. I don't think I could be so spiteful, I don't think I could air our dirty washing in front of our friends, so I won't go at all.

And that's where I am with it. I'm not going and Eve, if she can afford it, will go on her own and explain to everyone why I am not there.

And most likely, I will lose a circle of friends.

I really only have 2 options:
1. Try to live with Eve.
2. Try to live without Eve.

And, actually, without her love, she could force Option 2 at any time. I have the Sword of Damocles hanging over my head, just waiting to fall...

At the moment, I am so fragile, I think that Option 2 ends really badly. But it may not always be this way. At some point, I may be robust enough to deal with it. I hope so, because even if I don't force the situation, she could, if she chooses.

So, I am currently clinging to Option 1. But I don't know if I can do this. Or even if it is possible.

How can I live with someone I desperately love, but not get anything back from her?

- Neither of us can move on. We are bound together, and quite possibly, I will be in pain forever.

Or

- She will walk out. I will be devastated and alone for the rest of my days.

Hobson's choice – damned if we do, damned if we don't.

As much as I want Option 1, it is fragile and at best temporary, I think.

She really has fucked up everything.

And it seems it is only a matter of time now before it all falls apart.

She has changed "The Deal".

She is living in Cloud Cuckoo Land if she thinks she can have the life that she wants without compromising the time that she has. Her only hope is to find another sucker who loves her enough to make it happen.

I was that person.

I am not anymore.

I should be free, but I don't like it at all.

I love her, but she has hurt me, not just hurt me, she's damaged me. She has hurt me so badly I tried to kill myself. She has damaged me so badly the person I was is now gone and I am literally someone else, my female self, inside my head.

And she expects things to carry on as normal! She expects me to continue giving her everything but get nothing in return! Right up until the point that she leaves me...

This is NOT fair. Not fair at ALL.

She has changed "The Deal".

So, what do I do now? Massive change is coming, I know it. Mentally I am not in the right place to deal with it yet, but it is going to happen. From where I sit, either:

- Eve walks out on me at some point.

Or

- I live with someone I love and not get anything back.

I am in a holding pattern; my life is on pause until I am healed enough to deal with this.

Life will never be the same again.

And now I am angry.

This was done TO me; I did NOT do this.

I have every right to be angry.

But anger is <u>very</u> negative. Not as negative as depression, loneliness, or misery, but just as destructive. I <u>can't</u> do anything out of anger. It's a knee-jerk reaction to my situation and it is highly likely to make me do or say something stupid, something that I will regret and something I won't be able to take back. Something that will hurt Eve.

Revenge sounds <u>very</u> appealing to me at the moment. **I do not want to feel like this**. I am allowed to be angry. But revenge is unforgivable. Causing pain to make myself feel better is not acceptable and causing pain to the person I love and hold most dear? I can't live with that. I am not a spiteful person and if I react out of anger, then I am not sure I will be able to look back on my actions and be comfortable.

I keep talking about "The Deal", but what exactly is it?

"The Deal" has five parts, it is very simple, but also utterly profound.

1. I love you and you love me.
2. We share each other's lives.
3. We share our true selves, honestly.
4. We are there for each other, no matter what, when we need it.
5. We face the world as a team.

"My Dearest Eve,

For the first 10 years we both committed to "The Deal" and it was glorious. The absolute best of times. But then, bit-by-bit, instead of working through stuff with me, you just decided to give up on our relationship. Instead of being honest with me, sharing what you were going through, so we could work together as a team should, allowing me to be there for you (3, 4 and 5), you stopped living for us and began living for you (2) and as a consequence, you stopped loving me (1)."

You stopped honouring "The Deal"...

I think, back then, there may have been a chance for us. Back when things were great, and the storm clouds were still away on the horizon. Couples have rough patches and if most of "The Deal" is still there, then things can be fixed if both parties want to, and they put the work in. But now, Eve you are not upholding any of "The Deal". And as long as I still am, well it is very comfortable and convenient for you to carry on taking everything I can't help but want to give.

You know what? I think I am going to be alright. I can see a future for me at last. It isn't great, certainly not as great as the first 10 years when we both worked on "The Deal" together, but it will be OK. I will be better off financially, that's a given. But I will be lonely. I can't ever let anyone in again, I just can't risk this agony and being this close to the edge. But I will feel better someday. I know it. I will always have this sadness in me now, but it won't be all consuming. And although I will be lonely, I **will** be OK.

"I am worried for you Eve."

You are going to have a life of adventure. But you have lost the best, most stable platform to launch your adventures from, and return to. And you want to live your life completely without compromise. No one ever gets to have this; everything comes at a cost. Passive income is great, but it is only ever going to give the brass ring to a very few people. The game of life is rigged my love. You can get small wins, but the big one is a billion to one shot. I can see your dreams being constantly thwarted by money. Everyone's dreams are to some extent. In my case, like most folks, I have traded my time for money, and I spend that money on us. To give us both a life. And, because I love you and you loved me, to give you a life with as few compromises as possible. You lead an unconventional lifestyle my sweetheart, where you want it all – and I was prepared to give it to you. All of it. For love, for "The Deal". It is a good deal, the very best of deals and the only deal in this world that is completely fair. You haven't upheld your side of "The Deal" for years. You have taken, but not given. And you have traded "The Deal" for a fantasy. One that will be compromised by money, due to the unconventional lifestyle you so adore.

I truly wish you could have it all. I really do. I was prepared to do whatever it took to make it all happen, but you just couldn't see it. You have given me the best 10 years of my life and in all likelihood, the next 10 will be the worst, none more so than now. But in the end, I will be OK, not great, but OK.

And you? You will be poor. You will likely live day-to-day and won't be able to afford your dream. Or you will end up having to compromise your unconventional lifestyle in order to make your dreams happen. You will trade your time and opportunities for money, money to fund your dream. And you may well be happy. I truly want you to be. But this is a worse place to be than the one you were in with me my love. And I have seen what a 9 to 5 job does to you. I hope you can find something fulfilling to do for a living, I genuinely do. But I am worried for you my sweet. Assuming your damned pride doesn't get in the way, I can see you looking back on the good times we had together with regret, wishing you had tried a bit harder to keep "us" going. Knowing you had it all and the potential to be the spectacular person I know you are, but you threw it all away chasing a pipedream. Because the hard fact is, you need money in this world to survive. And you need LOTS of money to follow your dreams. And the <u>only</u> way to get this is to bargain away your time, or love someone who will bargain away their time for you.

I AM worried for you Eve. We are both much worse off at the end of this.

But I will be OK.

Your future is a gamble.

And I am worried for you."

Saturday, April 24th.

I am OK this morning. Epic entry yesterday, I feel like I have begun to sort things out a bit. And, importantly, I am not angry today. I am not miserable either, I am OK.

At the moment, I am in limbo. I am just grateful to live day-by-day and make the most of what we have, right up until it all comes crashing down. Make the best of the whatever time we have left together. And my misery will get in the way, so I am not going to let it. I need to be able to look back on this time and find some joy. So, I <u>will</u>.

And as I start to put myself back together, I will begin to prepare for the end. I will at some point be able to have the discussion with Eve about what she wants, and we will begin to go our separate ways. There's lots to sort out, lots to unpack and it will be painful to do. But I think it is going to happen anyway. So, I might as well do it right and if it comes to it, allow us both to walk away with the best possible outcome.

Looking at "The Deal" from my side of the fence, for the time-being at least, I am still giving her all of it. But there are things I need now more than ever, the most important of which is:

4. We are there for each other when we need it, no matter what.

Sheez, do I need it now. Furthermore, I think she does too. I hope that this is something we will never be able to change, and I don't think I want it to. We don't have to be in a relationship to be there for each other when we need it.

I will always be there for Eve.

She is my best friend, she is my sister, and I am there for her, always.

But the other parts of "The Deal"?

I think, I can stop them all, not entirely, but I can close the taps off on most of it.

5. We are a team.

This is the one that has the biggest tangible impact and therefore contains the most knots to unpick. But it is do-able, and she will hate it, although maybe not at first, and I will feel terrible. But it may have to be done. I am not going to continue giving her everything for nothing in return, she needs to come to the table, or lose it.

3. We share our true selves openly and honestly.

She hasn't done this for years. It is a betrayal at a fundamental level. If we had talked this through as it was happening, there is a good chance we could have made it work. Consciously or not, she **chose** to hide something so momentous from me that it has ruined our entire lives. I am sharing myself with her now, as always, openly, and honestly. She is, for the first time in years it seems, doing the same. Ironically. we are closer now than we have been in ages. But without love, it is irredeemable. But it *may* be enough?

2. We share each other's lives.

She already isn't. I am working on this. It will happen, it must, I think. I am going to have to find things to do and enjoy on my own. With friends, with family, for me and without her. This sounds really harsh and spiteful, but I need to move on it seems. She already has and I know how much it hurt me. It still does.

1. I love her and she loves me.

The <u>**MOST**</u> important one. The one that enables everything else to happen. My love for her is all consuming. But I need it not to be. This is the healing process and the one that will take the most time. It is also, by far, the hardest thing to achieve. I will always love her, I know this. She is the one, my soul mate and I can't just turn off my love for her. But I need it to be manageable, because without it being returned, there is only despair. And despair, as i have found out, leads to some very dark places. Despair ends it all.

So, this is my goal. To make my love for Eve less, or turn it into the love of a sister, just as she has. "IF" I can do this, then we can continue to share a house (not a home, there's a difference) and I can live with her being just out of my grasp. I can take joy in the things she wants to share, and I can also take joy in the things I do for myself. Most importantly of all, I can take joy in the things we do together. It is a big "if", but I have hope.

If I can't, then we <u>cannot</u> live together. Having her so close, but forever out of reach <u>will tear me apart</u>. Just as losing her, little-by-little, piece-by-piece over the past few years has done. Small, constant cuts that eventually add up to a whole. We'll have to go our separate ways, or it'll kill me. And this will be extremely painful for both of us, and we both lose out massively. The consequences of this cannot be underestimated, they are also unknowable at this point, so she is recklessly gambling with both of our futures.

It may happen anyway, indeed at this point I would say it is likely. But as I said, I can't do it now – no big decisions – not while I am so raw and need to heal. That way leads to disaster.

We do not, and never have, fitted into to societies' neat little pigeonhole. We have <u>never</u> had a conventional relationship. So, we should be able to deal with this equally unconventionally.

> I think we need a "New Deal".

At the moment, I don't know what this deal should be. But I do know it needs to be built on respect. In the absence of love, what else can it be built on?

So, the first part of the "New Deal" needs to be:

1. I respect her, she respects me.

I also think the next part needs to be:

2. We are there for each other, should they need it, no matter what.

I really want to stay a team with her too, but at this point I am not sure if this is possible. We a definitely are stronger together than as individuals, but Parts 1) and 2) are what best friends do for each other, this is definitely do-able, we do it already. But being a team, facing the world together as a unit, that is the definition of being a couple, something that Eve sadly doesn't want anymore. So as much as I want it, I don't think it can happen, or at least our team is now a *lot* less strong.

From here I am a bit fuzzy. The "New Deal" needs some work, but I think sharing ourselves honestly and openly is sadly not transferrable from the old deal to the new. It is too strong and too much of a commitment outside of a relationship. Even siblings have secrets from each other. But despite this, siblings have love, just not the same love. There is a bond that goes beyond friendship, indeed in some cases, exists independently of friendship. Siblings can love each other, but not be friends. It happens. In our case I think the opposite is true, we <u>can</u> be friends, we just need a different kind of love. A love that is not a foundation, our shared life experience is. I think this is the difference. Sibling love is based on time, common family ties and shared life experiences. Eve and I have this. We have over 15 years of this. So, I think this can work. And, actually for Eve, it already is.

So maybe something like:

3. Our shared life experience has given us a bond. This bond is important and makes us family.

Next, I think we need some kind of commitment. Something that says we recognise that respect, friendship, and family need to be maintained and that we will both put the work in. In fact, exactly that.

4. *Friendship, respect, and family are to be maintained.*

As I mentioned I still want us to be a team, sadly I don't think we are anymore. Being a team in this context means we take the world on together, supporting each other unconditionally and I think that can only come from love. Some of this comes from being family, but I was prepared to give Eve everything before, up to and including my actual life. I am not anymore. So, regrettably, our team is the second casualty of this, after her love.

Looking at the embryo that is the "New Deal", I think that between 1) and 4) she won't be able to hurt me like this again. 2) gives us a safety net and 3) allows us to still have something special and important, but with fewer of the burdens. So far, I think this "New Deal" is quite good.

I am not sure if there are more clauses to find, or if the four outlined above need some work. I suppose we *should* work this out together. But not just yet. I am too fragile to face the consequences if it doesn't work – no big decisions – not while I am healing.

As positive as the "New Deal" is, it only works if I can change my love for her into a sisterly one. It is possible, Eve has done it. I need to do the same or we both lose everything.

Work in progress…

I wonder if I am clutching at straws. I still think this is a huge longshot. But I don't want to be lonely and alone, so I am working on an alternative.

Sunday, April 25th

I am OK again today. I still have this calm over me, this lull in the storm where I am not quite 100% plugged into the world. Everything is just a tiny bit detached. It's an odd feeling, trepidatious, I feel something is coming, I don't know what, I hope it is me starting to heal. I hope this calm, this eerie stillness, is providing me the space to heal and the clarity to assess the situation in a non-emotive manner. It's what it feels like to me. But it could be the calm before the storm. I <u>really</u> hope not. I am exhausted and so is Eve. For now, I am appreciating a break from all the rampaging emotions. I feel like I am at last in a position to try to make some rational sense out of the situation.

Dad and my brother, bless them, can only see one outcome. The very worst outcome. And when I am angry, they cheer me on! What kind of support is that? They can't comprehend an alternative, they can <u>only</u> see a short, sharp shock and the loss of everything. They tell me to be strong and not roll over or accept any compromises. They truly do not have a clue, they think this is some kind of war, an epic battle. And like all wars, there are no winners, only which loser ends up with the most stuff. And I love them for standing by me and being there for me, but what kind of support *IS* that? Encouraging me to throw my whole life away and carve up the ruins? Eve was never my enemy; I hope she never is.

It is destructive, just like my anger and DOES <u>NOT</u> HELP.

...it is not what I need right now.

I hope the "New Deal" isn't just a pipedream cooked up in the tortured mind of a woman in despair, at the end of her tether. It gives me hope, a mad, desperate hope maybe, but hope never-the-less.

And the likelihood of failure is very high. I am under no illusions here. But it is worth the effort because it promises something other than misery. It promises something other than the complete destruction of our lives. And this gives me hope.

The mechanism to get there is now clear to me. Manifesting it will be astonishingly difficult, I think.

It involves a trick of timing and a true balancing act. And even IF I manage to pull off this astonishing feat, other factors threaten to ruin it at any time. Here's what I think needs to happen...

> **My love for Eve is unconditional,
> it allows me to forgive her anything.**

She has hurt me deeper and far more than anyone ever has, or possibly could. She has taken me to the very edge, made me consider suicide as a rational and viable option and in the process, shoved me across the gender divide in my psyche and shattered the way back. It is no exaggeration to say she has turned me into a woman. Or rather, she has forced me to face my true nature, by destroying the mask I've spent my life hiding behind. And, just as puberty determined my physical gender and set it in stone against my will, she has done the same to my soul. In both cases it was an assault and massively traumatic.

But my love for her allows me to forgive her. It allows me to face it and it allows me to try to make the best of my situation. I kinda like being a woman. I hate no longer having a choice, but being a woman is, so far at least, really nice – the only bright spot in the past weeks. And furthermore, I like the person I am becoming.

> As long as I love Eve, I can forgive her for hurting me.

But...

> I can't live with her and still love her like this. To have the person you love be so close, but be forever just out of reach is impossible, maddening and more powerful than <u>anyone</u> could bear.

<u>This</u> is why both dad and my brother can only see a huge breakup and nothing by destruction.

> So, this HAS to change.

To make this work, I have to stop loving Eve unconditionally. And I can do it by loving her as her sister. I <u>want</u> to be her sister. And she has shown me that it is possible.

> The trick is to do this **without** getting angry **at her** for all the pain.

I need to love her enough to forgive her, but turn my love into that of a sister, so that we can continue to live together.

It's a trick of timing and a process with no road map. Eve showed me it can be done, but she isn't dealing with the worst pain imaginable, or the anger feeling like a victim imposes.

I am a nice guy, well, girl now I suppose. It is <u>really</u> hard to get me angry. And I have more cause to be angry now than I ever have. She has hurt me more profoundly than I ever thought possible, and I <u>can't</u> get angry at her for this, because that will destroy us both and it will destroy any chance of a life with her still in it.

> **THE TRICK**
> **So, I need to stay loving her unconditionally so that I can forgive her but begin to love her as a sister so that we can stay together.**

Neat trick eh?

If I can pull this off, it'll be the best trick ever!

I want to be Eve's sister. So, I am motivated to do this. It's a balancing act that will take both time and precise timing but is also something that will happen organically I suspect. A natural process of change. And it will happen because this is where I want to be. It won't happen if I try to force it.

And it will be very painful.

And I am going to have bad days.

And external factors will try to ruin it all, they won't understand.

And Eve could up sticks and leave me before the trick is complete.

But I have hope. I have a goal to aim and even live for. And although very small, there is a chance here.

A chance for me to not be lonely forever.

A chance...

But it is a chance for me. Not for us. So, I am sad. We have lost so much. And the biggest unknown of all is:

WHAT DOES EVE WANT?

- We NEED to have this discussion.
- I am not ready yet.
- But it has to happen soon.

- I am unlikely to be ready when it does, but I am working on it.

I <u>think</u> Eve is now where I want to be. My sister and comfortable living with me.

I <u>think</u> she sees what I am going through as temporary and although painful, not as earth-shattering.

I <u>don't think</u> she realises that she has gambled literally everything and that the most likely outcome of what she has done is us splitting up, salvaging the wreckage of our lives, and going our separate ways.

I <u>truly think</u> she thought she could tell me she didn't love me anymore, I would be hurt, but brush it off and life would continue more or less as before. But with us in separate beds.

I <u>believe</u>, me going completely off the deep end has come as a total shock to her. How close I have come to killing myself scares the shit out of her. And me too.

I <u>don't think</u> she has a clue, just how deep and profound my love for her is. And what taking her love from me has done.

And I <u>don't think she could have possibly known</u> that doing this to me would destroy the man I was completely and literally, leave me with no alternative but to face up to the woman I am. To take refuge in the little I have left. I think she knew I would need more time as Julia to heal, but I don't think she could have foreseen a <u>permanent change</u>. I certainly didn't!

And lastly, I <u>don't think</u> she considered the damage and consequences of her not holding up her end of "The Deal". If she had realised that the likelihood of her doing this would be to literally throw both of our lives away, everything we had, everything we built and everything we could be together, just ripped up and thrown in my face. I think she would have worked harder at it. In fact, I am <u>sure</u> she would have. Afterall, "The

Deal" is the best deal in the world. There is none better. It is fair, it is profound, and it is worth everything. Literally everything.

We are left with just two stark choices as far as I can see.
- Ruination. Separation. Loss and pain. Rebuilding whatever we can, writing off the best years of both our lives and any chance of a bright future together. I will end up OK, not great, but OK. I can't really see Eve's future; it is too random.
- The "New Deal", whatever that turns out to be. It is not as good as "The Deal", nothing ever could be. But it just might give us something, it might just allow us to continue, and it is a billion times better than the alternative. <u>If</u> I can pull off The Trick.

Our whole lives are in the balance Eve.

You have done this to us, to me and to you.

You have played fast and loose, rolled the dice on everything we have, and lost.

There are consequences. Serious consequences my love. Consequences for us both.

And you did this without my consent. You just threw our lives up in the air without talking to me and without considering the impact on anyone other than you.

Reckless. Foolish.

You live your life without compromise. I love you for this. But there are compromises coming now my love. Big, unpleasant, serious and life altering consequences.

Reckless indeed.

The truth is we <u>were</u> stronger together. Stronger than either one of us, as a team.
- You have quit the team.

- You did this without talking to me.
- We are now much less strong.
- I am damaged as a consequence.
- We have both lost.

And carrying on is not a given. It is now a <u>very</u> difficult thing to do.

But I am willing to try. Despite everything I am willing to try. Because I see the faintest chance of something other than total ruination. I am willing.

The question is:

ARE YOU?

Monday, April 26th.

New week, I am reaching the final pages of this first book. Soon there will be a new journal – I am reaching the end of this first emotional tome and I have purchased a new one to continue in. So, this volume is drawing to a close. I look back at this journal and I can see progression. I can also see depression, obsession and despair – it's not an easy read. I can see multiple paths ahead of me, most of them are awful. But I can also see a glimmer of hope.

But most of all I can see me changing. Coming to terms with things and starting to deal with them. And if this continues then I think I am going to be OK you know?

Change is coming, Eve tells me change can be good, we shall see. From where I am it's a huge train and both Eve and I are tied to separate rails. I can see it now; Eve is choosing not to look but I have snuck a peek and am getting an idea of just how big it is.

And it is truly frightening to behold.

But, if I can see what is coming, then I might be able to adjust our positions so that the impact isn't so bad, a glancing blow maybe...

It IS going to run us both over.

And the way we are tied, it may well throw one of us to the left and one to the right. It has a huge cow catcher scoop on the front. This is the most likely eventuality. We are seriously injured and forced apart. But there is a very small chance, an infinitesimally tiny chance. That I can un-tie us just enough before the train hits. And <u>if</u> we can hold onto each other through the impact, then although we will both be seriously hurt, at least we will still be together.

I have already started on the knots. At the beginning of this journal the train was sure to kill me. I was about to take the full impact to protect Eve. Noble. Foolish. A final gesture to prove my love. <u>But not anymore</u>.

- I am going to fight to survive and
- I am going to take the impact and
- I am going to deal with the injuries.

And if I can, I will try to not do it alone.

There is a tiny chance. I have hope...

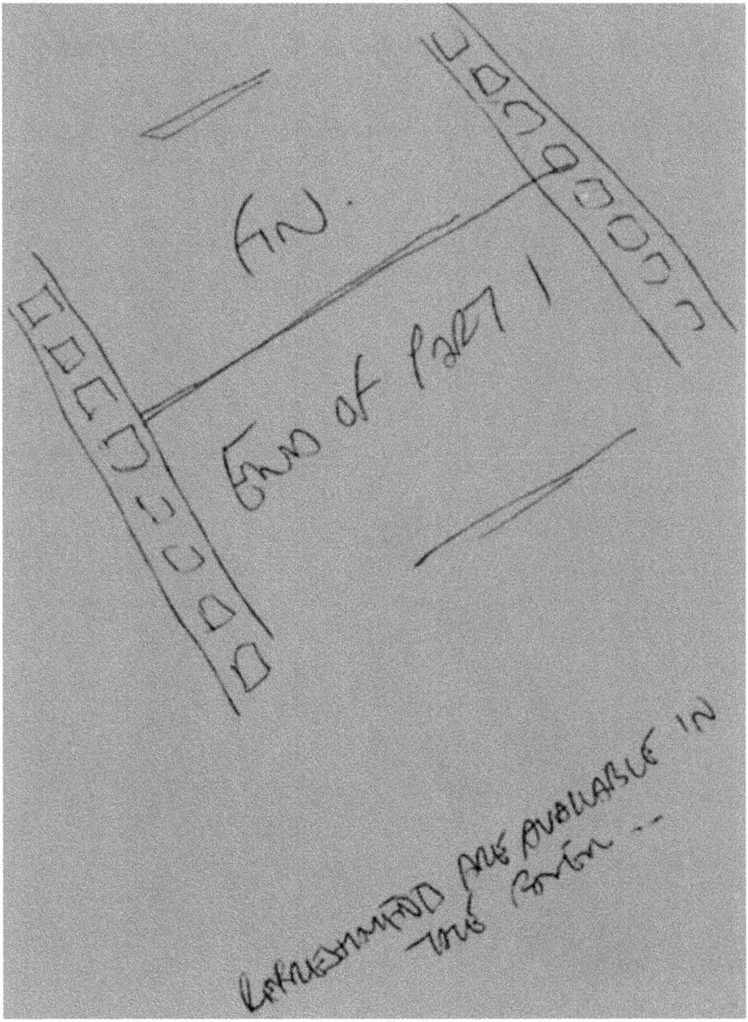

FIN.

End of Part 1

左手notations are available in the given.

The King is Dead, Long live the Queen

Volume 2

If the Shoe fits

By
Julia Phillips

Volume 2 – If the Shoe fits...

This journal belongs to: Miss Julia Phillips.

For Eve. Everything, always.

For me. These journals were necessary and saved me.

...and for Tanya, my new bestie, and the reason I finally sat down to type this up.

Without her support, encouragement, and motivation, you would not be reading this now.

Forward

I am writing this in April 2024 – welcome to the future!

    I won't spoil the finale, but I have just given a copy of Volume 1 to a very lovely person, and new special friend, Tanya. I don't mean special in a romantic way – stop trying to skip to the end! Although very intimate, these pages are not romance novel! I am not Barbara Cartland (I love pink, but there are limits!) Actually, looking back at these pages, they could very well be read this way – the end of a grand romance. I never looked at them in this way before, but love is definitely one of, if not **the** central theme. Anyway, I digress (again! I love a tangent; I just can't help myself! Back on topic. Where was I)? Ah yes, special. As in for the first time in my life I have someone I can be completely open with and, well, be myself. So special, very special. And she's a great person too, very good company – we just hit it off immediately, and although our friendship is fairly new, I feel like we've been friends for years. I guess, after all this time, I was at last ready to meet her and open up. This is not to say I was never 100% open with Eve, but I was a different, divided person back then, she knew me intimately, more so than anyone before or since, but she knew the old me. There is, as I am sure you can appreciate, a VERY big difference. I am just not that person anymore.

    As I write this, and as I have had some (great) feedback from Tanya, I realised there are a couple of blanks that I probably should fill in. Firstly, *there are four volumes*, this being the second – I hand wrote four diaries in the 8 months between the 4th April and November 5th 2021. Up to the point where I felt I didn't need to write anymore, so if you appreciated the first and I hope this one too, there is still plenty more to come. They are all different

lengths, have different tones to reflect my improving mental state, and the entries tend to become shorter in the last volume as I had less to write about and a rapidly diminishing need. This volume and the next are by far the biggest, I will apologise for any repetitions and a whole load of waffle now – but they are all completely honest and a true record of the time – I wrote what was on my mind and I agonised over topics, likely much more than I should, revisiting them time and again as my mood demanded. But these volumes were a huge part of me dealing with more than one earth shattering event and I didn't write them with a view to them being read by others, at least not until towards the end. Tanya liked Volume 1, so I am inspired to type up the other books (wow, there's a lot here, Volume 2 is much larger than Volume 1). I also should come up with an epilogue I guess as well. I feel a bit like her secretary – I kinda like this, of course I do! – you knew that right? Why am I drawn to all these female stereotypes? Probably because I feel I missed out on a hell of a lot growing up, I guess. Tanya is champing at the bit to read Volume 2, no pressure then, it's no wonder I feel like I'm her secretary!

Tanya asked me why I chose Julia?

This information isn't covered directly in the journals, simply because it pre-dates my crisis by a couple of decades or more. In my late teens through to my early to mid-20's I was in therapy, I have spoken about this in these pages, but my therapy was to come to terms with who I am (a process still very much ongoing today) and the ramifications of the ravages that puberty inflicted upon me. As part of this process, I accepted my female nature and decided I needed a name.

People are given names by their parents - ironically, if I had been born in the correct body, I would have been an Eve – this coincidence is not lost on me! Having the opportunity to give yourself a name is really quite an unusual, and very special thing.

And certainly, in my case, carries huge importance. I needed to get it right, after all, this is most likely a one-shot deal and I'll **be** this name for the rest of my life.

I tried a number of names 'on for size' – I really didn't want a name with an obvious male equivalent and an 'A' name, is just far too close to home to be comfortable, I am not and never have been comfortable with Adam. I was very nearly a Lisa, my Nan was Elizabeth (Bet), so it felt appropriate. I really like the name too, but it just didn't feel right for me. It didn't 'fit', you know? Mary is nice but has far too many religious connotations (I'm not religious at all). Marie is better, but still not quite right. If I had chosen a middle name, I think Marie would be a nice one & it scans well. I like Susanne, but I have an Aunt Sue (who is lovely, as are all my aunts), so it felt a bit strange and I'm not sure she would appreciate it, should she ever find out. I don't know, maybe she would have taken it as a compliment? All my aunts are far more open minded than my dad – it's a possibility. I like Melody too, but this felt a bit too feminine, I wanted something a bit less special, more real. Nice, but an everyday name for an everyday kinda girl. Eventually I came around to Julie. I like Julie and I know a couple of Julies who are really nice ladies. But I tried it on, and it wasn't quite a perfect fit – close, but not quite 'me'. Julia. Yes. I will be Julia. And so, I was born in a sense, but it took me a very long time to become a real person...

Anyway, I'm firing up the time machine to head back to 2021. Back to all the drama!

Julia, Monday, April 8th, 2024.

Tuesday, April 27th

New book! Can't believe I filled up the last one, and in only 23 days! Astonishing.

Still, I have had a lot on my mind...

Welcome, dear reader, to Volume 2. The continuing saga of Julia, an unintended woman. Caught in the maelstrom of who he was, the birth of who she is and the momentous events that forced the switch. The end of his relationship with Eve, the woman he loves more than anything, the woman he built a life around and for, and the woman he defined himself by. When she stopped loving him, he lost everything. And so, the person he was, took refuge in the only thing she had left. The femininity of her soul that she had denied and worked so hard to conceal. Julia.

Wow, I don't think I've ever read a paragraph with so many mixed-up pronouns. This would make a great film though! I feel *very* sorry for the scriptwriter.

> Great film or not...

> ...sadly, it is all too real...

Early start today. I am OK again. A little emotional as I whispered my goodbyes to a mostly closed door and to a sleeping Eve. Even Tara the cat didn't stir.

Out the door at 6am, heading for Southampton. Two surveys and then a hotel. One more survey tomorrow and then home.

I had a secret today though...

I've been in a bra the whole day!

It felt great, one of my discreet, well fitting, non-wired ones. But I don't think it could've been spotted through my T-shirt, fleece, and backpack.

Both surveys done around lunchtime – a nice easy day. At the hotel mid-afternoon, chillin', comfy, nice.

I spoke to Eve around 7pm. To be honest I wasn't sure she would want to chat, but we did, and it was also nice, as well as very much needed. I'm glad.

Gonna watch some TV and have an early night.

A good day.

Wednesday, April 28th

I seem to be OK again today, it is 6:51am and I have just showered. I am back in bed and have an hour or so to relax before the day begins.

In fact, the only fly in the ointment is work. I received an email from one of our clients yesterday evening in which, further down the email chain, he has slandered us to his boss about something we are not responsible for. What an idiot! It is one thing to spread lies to his boss and other 3rd parties behind our backs, but to copy me into a smoking gun! Well, it just beggar's belief...

I think I am going to have to call him today. I don't want to. With everything else that is going on, I am not in the best frame of mind to be honest. But I won't have him lie about us to his boss. Actually, I am thinking about demanding a written apology.

Anyway, I am supposed to be relaxing, gearing myself up for the day to come. Other than the above unpleasantness, it should be a good day. A small survey first thing and then a steady drive home.

Something interesting has happened though. I don't know if I should read anything into it. But I towelled myself dry and stepped into a pair of underpants, not knickers. I did it without thinking about it and I have only just realised I am wearing them. Now that I know I will slip back into my nightie, but maybe it is a sign that I am sub-consciously feeling a little more comfortable as Adam? Or not. Maybe it just means I was irritated and distracted thinking about idiot Clients and just didn't notice...

Anyway, I am putting this book down for now. Time to relax. I will check back in later to record how the day went.

It's quarter past ten, comfy from 6pm, so 15 and a half hours in a skirt today, expressing myself truly.

The site was further away from the hotel than I realised, about 40 miles east along the south coast. I arrived around 10am and the survey went well. On the drive home dad rang and he started cheering me on when I started to talk about the various paths ahead and how the most likely is the worst of all the options. He sees I am in turmoil and wants the pain to end. But he can't see anything that isn't black and white. So, he is encouraging me to "don't take any crap" and to "stick up for myself". I snapped at him. I feel terrible for it. I want and need his support, but this is NOT helpful. Encouraging the end, even if it is likely to happen anyway, is not only surrendering to the situation, throwing all I have away, but it is also a sure-fire way to make me miserable for the rest of my days. Because, if I pull the pin and throw a grenade into the little that we have left, I not only lose my love, but I also lose my sister, my extended family, a circle of friends and most of all, my very best friend. There is much more at stake here than just money and stuff. My whole life is in jeopardy, up to and including both my physical and mental gender.

> If the most likely scenario plays out and we split. It needs to be done sensibly, over time and without emotion. The most important factors are empathy for each other and sensitivity to how we are both feeling. If I rush at this while I am still raw, I will be at the mercy of all the negative emotions I am experiencing. I will react. I will say stuff I will regret and won't be able to take back. And I will lose Eve from my life. This is the worst possible outcome, the worst of all things.

If we split, and I get the irony here, I want to do so as a couple. Our lives diverge, but we remain family and we remain friends. We just won't be partners or a team anymore and we

will live separate lives. This is still awful. It is NOT what I want. I will hate it all. But I CAN live with this because we will have done right by each other. Furthermore, we will still be on good terms into the future. I want to be able to call her up and go out for a meal, or to the cinema, or just get together for a chat. Do stuff that friends and family do. And then go to our separate lives and homes.

> This is the best of a bad set of options.
>
> This, I think, is possible, but needs handling carefully.

And then, there is the 100-1 shot. The one that gives me some hope. The one that I want to try for but am under no illusions as to the chances of success. The one that dad cannot even see, let alone comprehend.

I become Eve's sister. I relate and love her as a sister and best friend <u>only</u>. And then we can continue to share our home together. I want this. It is <u>nowhere near</u> as good as the life together we have lost. But it is a million times better than going our separate ways. This relies on me stopping loving her unconditionally, without getting angry at her for doing this to us and to me. It is ultimately a question of timing. I need to be able to forgive her beyond my time loving her. Actually, I think me being Julia now is an advantage. The more time I spend with Eve, expressing myself fully as a female, the more I begin to relate to her as a sister, not a partner.

> Validation of who I am from Eve would help enormously with my mindset, but as I have said, I won't push her for this. She hasn't felt comfortable with this last step in the past, so as helpful as this would be, it needs to be something natural, not forced. I hope Eve will come around to this on her own, in time.

> Julia can do this, I think. I am pretty sure Adam cannot. The more fully I embrace being Julia, the more likely I can change my love for Eve into that of a sister. It would help massively if Eve would start treating me as her sister, but it is hard for her. I understand.

I have a regular site visit on Thursdays, I am hopeful I will be OK again when I wake. I don't want to be miserable again...

Thursday, April 29th

I am irritated this morning. Not about my situation (thankfully), about work.

I have caught a client red-handed lying about my company in writing – setting us up to take the blame for a project delay and now I have to respond formally.

I detest politics.

Still, that is a job for tomorrow. Today I have my regular weekly site meeting (meeting number eighty-six!) And I am quite looking forward to it.

I had a nice evening with Eve last night, pizza, TV, me dressed comfortably, Eve taking her evening bath and then another episode of Death in Paradise together. It's a good show, we both enjoy it, and I am cherishing these fleeting moments together.

My appetite seems to be a bit erratic lately. I am concerned because, from the little I know, it is a sign of clinical depression and I do think I am depressed – given what is going on with me right now how could I not be? Mood swings, bursting into tears, little things triggering a big emotional response, finding it hard to find any joy in life, all classic signs. I hope Kay can help me with this when I start seeing her next week. Fingers crossed.

I am trepidatious about seeing her though. The first step through her door is an acknowledgement that I can't handle this and as such is a really big deal. I never thought I would <u>ever</u> need therapy again. NEVER. But I definitely think I need some help. So, this is a positive step, regardless of whether she is right for me or not. I hope this works out.

- Eve is supporting me, but she can't show me a way through this.

- Dad is supporting me, but he can only see utter disaster.
- My brother is trying to support me, but work gets in the way.
- I think one of my colleagues may be able to help, he has been through a nasty breakup, and I could do with a friend, someone impartial and not directly involved…

But I need a map to find the way, I am hopeful Kay can give me one.

This is a big step to take, a good one I hope, but it is momentous, *one of life's pivotal moments.*

I have hope.

Time to get up and face the day **again**.

3:20pm…

I have taken the afternoon off, and I feel guilty about it. I shouldn't, but I do.

I watched the season two finale of Veronica Mars, it was excellent. I have heard season three isn't as good, but I am sure I will enjoy it anyway. And there is a movie too. Season four is not available yet as far as I can tell. At least not on DVD.

My new skirt and undies arrived; I really like it all. The skirt fits well, I've not tried the bras and knickers yet.

Eve is home, in her room, working, or studying, or both. I am looking forward to spending some time with her this evening.

I am no longer irritated, but I am feeling a little fragile, more so than I have been recently. I need to step up at work, it is the one thing in my life that is going OK at the moment. It is totally manic, flat out and high pressure – we are all feeling it, but me taking random time off is just putting more pressure onto the others. I am not pulling my weight – I know it. This is why not going back into the office this afternoon isn't sitting very well with me. I think I am going to need to work some long hours fairly soon, I am piling up a backlog of work and I need to climb on top of it.

> Work = money. Money greases the wheels of our lives.
>
> As bad as I feel, I can't screw up work too.

So, I need to stop feeling so self-absorbed and step up to my responsibilities, at least in work hours.

How else am I going to be able to afford more girl stuff?

Bras and knickers are a perfect fit. I think I have finally cracked my sizes.

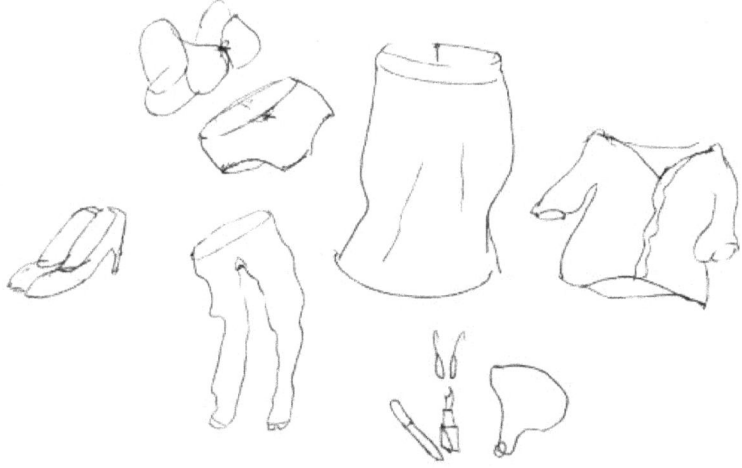

Bra = 50C (non-underwired)

Knickers = 24 (briefs)

Everything is sooo comfy!

I love it all – a <u>very</u> successful shop.

A nice, chilled evening with Eve, I am feeling OK again, nowhere near as fragile as earlier. It's amazing what 4 hours dressed in a pretty outfit can do to a girl's mood!

It's been nice. Too nice to bring to an end just yet. It is coming up to 10pm and I don't want to get ready for bed. Will stay like this for a little while longer…

…and Eve said I looked nice!

Validation: My heart soared!

Friday, April 30th

I am OK again today. I slept in my new white bra and knicker set, although I had to strip off my nightie in the wee-small hours as I was too hot, but the lingerie remained through the night. It's lovely waking up feeling the warm embrace of a bra hugging me, no underwires – much better.

I have a stressful day ahead. I need to write an unpleasant email to my duplicitous Client. Also, my new attitude will be implemented at work today – I need to step up my game.

And then there is mum...

Tomorrow is the one-year anniversary of her passing. I miss her so much, she is on my mind a lot, I mean, I think about her daily anyway, but more so at the moment. I wonder how upset Eve's and my situation would have made her? She was close to Eve, it would have been really hard for her, I am sure.

I would give _anything_ for a hug from mum right now.

I have to move one of my cars from a lockup to a storage facility tomorrow morning, then I am heading over to see dad. Alone.

My brother and his family will be there too – Eve can't face them, given they know what is going on with us. But I want her to come. I need her support on this, of all days.

...but she can't face it.

And this is the first, real, tangible split between Eve and I, beyond the sleeping apart business – mum would hate this, she would hate that Eve doesn't feel welcome.

> There is a wedge being driven by others between Eve and my family.
>
> I FUCKING HATE IT

I am trying so hard not to set myself up for a fall tomorrow. I have had such a good run of OK days. But if it is going to happen, it'll be tomorrow, I am sure.

And I think that, although we will muddle through as a family tomorrow. My niece and nephews will not understand why 'Auntie Eve' is not there with me on such an important day for us all.

I am actually more worried about Eve being on her own. I am sure she misses mum too. And I want to comfort her, but don't know if I can. Or more accurately if I am *allowed* to. I also think a lot of stuff is going to come out tomorrow.

And now that I think about it, I am not too sure about Majorca later in the year where we, <u>as a family</u>, say our final goodbye to mum in her favourite place.

Mum would want Eve to be there. I will need her to be there too.

But how can she come if there is a rift between her and the rest of my family? If she can't come tomorrow, how can she come with us to Majorca for a week?

> We need to talk this through tonight, ahead of tomorrow.
>
> There is a real danger of setting a precedent here.

Shit.

I think Eve and I need to face my family as a united front. To say we are BOTH going through this and that we have put aside our troubles for mum. And then the way is open for us to say our final goodbyes later in Majorca.

Or

The wedge gets driven deeper, and Eve and I have taken a **very** painful step further apart.

How can she be my sister and not be a part of my family?

This is a very **big deal**.

...and the timing of it REALLY SUCKS.

> Eve needs to know that she is welcome.
>
> I think I need to talk with dad and my brother before I can chat it through with Eve.

In the end I didn't do this in the order I intended. I ended up chatting to Eve first. I knocked on her door and asked if she was awake and if we could chat. She said yes, so I entered and sat on the floor next to her bed. And then we talked.

Eve doesn't want to come, I get it. She has a choice. I do not. But she *should* be there and she reluctantly agreed. But it is going to be really tough.

I then went to work and as my brother and I were the first in, I asked him for 5 minutes and we talked. Eve is <u>definitely welcome</u>. He agrees, what we are going through is absolutely a separate matter. This is what mum would've wanted.

It got to lunchtime and my nephew, and I headed to Tesco. When we got back, my brother called me upstairs to chat. Dad had rung him in tears. He wants to scatter some of mum's ashes tomorrow at the local church. I can't talk to him about making Eve welcome when he is in this state. My brother dropped everything and headed over to see and comfort him. Neither of us think this is a good idea to do this on the first anniversary of her passing. But we will go with what he wants – even if the 1st of May will now hold double the painful memories of mum from now on. I hope it is beautiful. I think it will be. But it will also be hard for all of us.

Later, I received a text from my brother. Dad was feeling better, and he had spoken to him about Eve. <u>She is welcome</u>. I am relieved.

Knocked off half an hour early, only my nephew and I in the office. Had a touching 10 minutes with him as we locked up. He knows Eve and I are having difficulties, and we had a moment or two – it was nice.

Eve was mid-tandem call when I walked in, full on foreign language – very impressive. It was also nice to hear her laughing again. I love it when she laughs. It's been so long…

I went for an early KFC for us both and so was dressed correctly from around 6pm. 14 much needed hours today. And all of my outfit is a 100% perfect fit. I feel so comfy, it's amazing. My new skirt is long enough to wear with a long slip, so it is even more comfortable, and I adore zipping it up behind my back. It feels so feminine.

Good for my soul.

Eve has been busy today; she has created a little pond in the garden using an old plastic barrel/tub that was a large flowerpot. It's great, I love it.

Eve and her sister have an early gym session tomorrow, then we are moving my sports car to its new home around 10am. We head over to dad's place after to scatter mum's ashes around mid-day.

Dad's lady friend is coming over for the late afternoon, so we will leave dad with her. Eve and I will then see to the horses on the way home.

I hope to be back in a skirt before 6pm. I think I am going to need it tomorrow.

Time for bed, but I don't want to get changed just yet – maybe in a little bit...

A Good Day.

...Oh, and I put my idiot client back in his place too.

We'll see if there is any fall out as a consequence...

Saturday, May 1st

Not much of a lie in today, Eve is going to the gym, she is meeting her sister there at 8am. I am done in the bathroom, but my face looks odd. I am so used to seeing makeup, it now looks unfinished without it. Eve is also done in the bathroom, it is 7:35am and she is running a little late. I am sitting on my bed in my nice undies and my nightie thinking about what is coming up today. It is likely to be so difficult. But I am OK at the moment.

I'm just trying to find a bit of calm and comfort before the impending maelstrom of emotions.

I want to do my makeup; I look weird without it. I don't look like me. Strange.

I have stuff to do myself anyway. I need to get prepared to move the car. It's happening at 10am, so we should probably leave the lockup around 9:50 – I'll be ready to go when Eve gets back from the gym. **But my face. It belongs to someone else. It looks a bit like Adam, and he's upset.**

While Eve was at the gym, I popped to the local ATM to get some cash. I also bought a couple of chocolate bars and some drinks for us later. The cash is for the storage of car #3 – I thought as we are going to Thaxted anyway we could drop the rent money off. Too many cars, it's just what happens when you grow fond of them, enough to not want to see them written off by the next owner – it's happened to me, twice now. It's not nice to know your pride and joy has been thoroughly abused by a total idiot with zero appreciation for something well looked after and, well, nice to have. I'm at the point where I feel no one deserves to have any of my cars, they mean too much to me to risk them being run into the ground by an uncaring fool. So, I have ended up with 3 pseudo-classics and my daily driver – excessive? Absolutely. Impractical? Totally. But there's just too many good memories to let them go.

Eve returned, so we headed off to the lock up. Car #1 started first time on the key (good car). We dropped the fob for the security gate into an envelope and then headed to the new storage facility a couple of miles away. Wow! What a place! Full of exotic cars, my old banger is in very rarefied company. Dehumidified, dedicated vehicle storage. It's awesome.

Once done, we headed home to swap cars and then off to dad's place via McD's.

I have been so stressed about this, for so long. But in the end, it was fine. Eve was welcomed and we all chatted away. My niece was a little upset, and dad too. But generally, it was good, if appropriately subdued. And then, we visited the church yard. Dad scattered mum's ashes and I cried a little. The sun was out, and the trees were in full blossom. It really was very beautiful.

We wandered to the windmill, chatting and generally being there for each other as a family. I think we did mum proud.

        A perfect moment.

                I love you mum. X

We said our goodbyes and then headed home. Later in the day we visited a couple of garden centres but didn't stay for long.

I am so tired now. I think it is due to releasing all that stress. My new bedding was on the doorstep when we returned. It's taken a while to get here, but it is lovely, and I need it tonight.

Going to sleep now. Today was amazing.

Going to sleep now. Today was exhausting.

Night mum. x

Sunday, May 2nd.

I didn't sleep well. I'm not sure why, maybe I was overtired? My new bedding is so nice, but also different. I've never had satin sheets before, and it is a very different experience. Still, I have a lie in this morning. The only thing on the agenda for today is to drive up to Eve's folk's place and stay over. It will be great to see them.

I cried again this morning. The first time in a while. I just felt overwhelmed by it all once more. I think mum was the trigger. She is on my mind a lot - how could she not be?

Eve is talking about telling her mum and dad what is going on with us. She feels that by not telling them, she is keeping it from them. My experience with telling my brother makes me worried. I think that if I could wind the clock back and avoided telling him, I would have. <u>It made it real,</u> and <u>it **has** changed things.</u> But this is not my decision, and it will be good for Eve to have someone to talk to. I suspect it will change things between them and me, so I am concerned. They are my family too. This is not something she can do on the phone, it's a face-to-face thing. But, with them now living so far away, it's difficult for her to get there on her own. We go up there together, so I think I will be there when she tells them. I can make myself scarce if she wants but actually, I would like to be included. However, if Eve wants to do this on her own, I will respect her wishes.

I'm crying again. Shit.

Eve heard me crying and came to see me. We had a hug, and it was lovely. I had built up all this tension about yesterday's anniversary and was expecting a very difficult time. It being the first time we had all been together since Eve's and my issues began. But it was perfect. All my tension had nowhere to go. I

think this is why I felt so weird yesterday, disconnected. It was the calm before the storm. The storm crashed over me today.

I had a bit of a lie in this morning, I do like my new bedding, it's just a bit too different, I'll get used to it, I'm sure.

I rose around 10am, then headed off to the horses with Eve. It's lovely there, peaceful. And it was nice to be outside. From here, we started driving up to Eve's parents' place. A very odd journey. The cross-country part took ages as we were starting from the horses' yard so there was no main road for quite some time. Finally, we approached the M11 at Duxford and took the opportunity for a spot of lunch at McD's. The Sat-Nav was playing games this time, it kept us on the main road all the way up to Peterborough, before hopping us across to the east and their place. Some of the roads were not much more than tracks – they were very bumpy.

Eve's sister and her girlfriend were there when we arrived. It's always great to see them. I sat in the summer house, Eve sat by the back utility room door in a garden chair. Eve's dad and her sister popped out to the local DIY store and her sister's girlfriend was elsewhere in the house, so, when her mum sat with Eve, I just knew she was going to tell her. Eve looked upset, and then they both went indoors.

- I fell to pieces -

I couldn't stop crying. It must've been a good 45 minutes. Not just because I knew what was going on, but thoughts of mum kept popping into my head too. I am glad Eve can now talk to her mum if she wants to, I would give anything to be able to do the same...

Eventually, Eve appeared at the kitchen window, and she saw I was in a state in the summer house. She came out to see me and her mum followed. We all had a hug, and it was lovely,

I felt welcome and part of the family still, but I was in floods of tears.

This weekend has been really awful. But also in places, beautiful and very touching too.

Eventually the others returned, and we had tea and cake in the summer house. My mood began to stabilise.

Everyone who needs to know, now knows. Furthermore, Eve now has her mum to talk to about it. I hope it won't change things between Eve's folks and me, it likely will, but they are my family too – after 15 years, how could they not be? Who knows what the future will bring...

A nice dinner, then Eve's folks, her sister and her girlfriend settled in to watch the finale of a TV show called 'Line of Duty' – apparently, they have all been watching it and it's a pretty big thing. With all the stuff that has been going on with Eve and me, we have missed it entirely, so we retired to bed, I changed into a much-needed nightie and wrote this piece in my journal.

A <u>very</u> emotional day.

Bank holiday Monday – May the third.

Mum's birthday.

I am OK this morning. Eve and I shared a bed for the first time in ages. It was very nice to wake up next to her again. It feels like a real privilege. I was a little teary, mum is on my mind again today, understandably so. Eve helped; she was there for me when I needed her. She finds this kind of thing particularly difficult, but she made an effort today and it was very much needed and appreciated.

Up and breakfasted with the others at a reasonable hour. It's cold and cloudy today, we couldn't spend the morning in their beautiful garden as we would've liked. So, with the horses to attend to, we said our goodbyes and hit the road around midday.

We are both shattered. It's been a <u>very</u> emotional weekend, and it has taken a toll. Eve drove and I snoozed for a bit in the car. I woke up as we reached the M11, and we had a chat about it all for a bit. I said I wished she had shared how she was feeling with me earlier, as she was reaching the realisation that she was falling out of love with me. But that we would likely have ended up where we are now anyway. She said it was gradual and then she couldn't talk to me because it would have hurt me so badly. But eventually, she had no choice but to tell me.

> She has carried this burden for <u>years</u>; I really don't know how she managed it.
>
> I feel so sorry for her, it sounds trite, but I would have gladly shared the load.

I had a couple of chats with Eve's mum before we left. Five minutes here and there. For the first time someone has told me that this doesn't have to be the end. Eve and I can still be best friends and <u>I am **always** welcome</u> at their place. This means so much to me, it has given me some much-needed hope.

Freezing at the horses, we fed and watered them in double quick time. Then home. It's good to be back here after such a roller-coaster of a weekend. Eve is snoozing on her bed; I am at last dressed correctly. We are planning a quiet night.

Day off tomorrow, I am seeing Kay for the first session. I hope it goes well.

Tuesday May 4th

One month on from J-Day...

I'm going to see Kay this morning, I am very nervous, but OK. Eve was up early today, she has a day's filming lined up in Hadleigh, something called 'Magpie Murders'. It's bloody cold out there today though, I hope she is alright and doesn't freeze.

I slept really well last night; I was emotionally exhausted I suppose. I am getting used to my new satin duvet set, it is lovely, but any rough skin on your body can snag the fabric and a satin sheet with a satin duvet over, combined with a long satin nightie sounds like heaven, but is in fact a perfect recipe for a duvet on the floor – you need to hang onto it and I am not sure how this would be possible with two people in the bed together – it's hard enough hanging onto a regular duvet without the other person getting a bit possessive of it in the night!

I have taken a much-needed day off today, and I intend to spend as much of it as I can in a skirt. I am seriously considering wearing bra and knickers under Adam's clothes to my session with Kay, a little confidence builder. It would be great to spend the entire day dressed in full, or in part as me.

Eve said good morning and we had a hug before she left, special you know? I think she still loves me, not in the same way, but I think there is love there. The love of a sister and a friend. She cares for me, and it hurts her to see me in such pain – or it may just be wishful thinking. I am sure having a day at work on her own will help her. She needs a break from me, but I am like a love-sick puppy. I can't help myself, every moment we spend apart is painful. This <u>must</u> get better – it HAS to, or we will both burn out. We are both exhausted.

I think I need to take a week, or a long weekend off. Or maybe a regular long weekend. Rent a cottage somewhere private maybe and live as a woman completely and continuously.

If I am dressed as Adam, I won't be able to leave Eve or stay away, so I think I can only do this as me.

My appetite is depressed, I am worried. Not because I am losing weight, but because I need to keep the fire fuelled to stay positive. I also need to get a bit fitter – I see this now – maybe I'll take the odd evening walk. It'll be hard to fit this in as it means more time in Adam's disguise and less time as me. But it'll be good for me I think, and it is something I can share with Eve, if she wants to join me. But I'll wait for some better weather though, brrrr.

It is coming up to 8am, I will send Kay a text shortly to confirm our session and then shower for the day ahead. I need to get her some cash out for our appointment, I hope there will be enough time for the first one, I am thinking there is a lot to tell her, and I might need a double session. It'll have to do; she likely has someone else booked in for mid-day.

I am really starting to like who I am becoming. I know I have written about this before, but I just can't wait to get changed each night and relax. I look in the mirror as I apply my makeup and I love seeing myself come forward, it's an honest expression of who I am, rather than a façade I need to maintain to fool the rest of the world.

Nine am, time to get up, I think...

10:50am – I am sat in the car outside Kay's house – I am very, *very* nervous. Watching the clock...

10:59am – NOW! I knocked on her door and our session began. Her home is very new age, bright, multi-coloured walls and pictures everywhere, it took me aback a little, I wasn't expecting this, actually I didn't know what to expect, but I like it – it's full of good feelings and memories. Kay was very professional and more importantly, very nice. We sat in a room upstairs and I told her <u>everything</u>.

I broke down in tears a lot, she just listened and let me unpack it all. I think I was understandable, in between sobbing. I started with who I am and that it has been 25 years since I was last in therapy. I did NOT expect to be doing this again.

She asked me if I was on any medication, or anti-depressants – I told her I wasn't. She then asked me if I was suicidal, or self-harming – I am not... Anymore. And that is when the flood gates opened, and I laid it all out.

I must have talked for a good 45 minutes. I then told her about me, my nature, Jane (my previous therapist), Julia and then Eve. From there, the good times, the recent times and how Eve has matured into someone else, someone different from when we first got together. I spoke about how she had gradually turned the taps off on her half of "The Deal" and how she gradually stepped away from us as a couple and began to build a life for herself without me. And how much that hurt. And how much I feel like I have failed her and us. How I failed at being "a man" and as a consequence, who I am now.

And it felt good. It felt positive.

She gave me some sound advice.

- Draw strength and support from others, but don't heed their advice, unless I want to. They cannot know what I am going through, only what they *think* I am going through.
- There are all kinds of relationships, **most** do not conform to the stereotype. We can find our own path.
- Find out what I want, and importantly, who I want to be – be true to myself.

It was very empowering. And although drained, I feel positive. Have booked another session for Friday 14th.

It's the weirdest afternoon, the weather is cold, wet and windy. The mogs wanted in and out all day, they kept coming in soaked and messing up the house. Larry left a bit of bird carcass in the kitchen too, so I decided enough was enough and cleaned it thoroughly. Second shower of the day!

I am feeling out of sorts again, likely because I have had an emotional morning and then alone in the house afterwards. I am just gonna have to get used to this I suppose. I can't help it though, I miss her. It's bloody stupid, it's only been one day. I'm so fragile and I hate it.

I will get changed shortly. I need it.

I went for comfort rather than my usual smart attire. Jumper, skirt and heels, tights, knickers and a non-underwired bra. Simple jewellery completed the outfit, no makeup today. I wasn't sure if I would be crying again later on, and Panda eyes aren't very becoming.

Eve arrived home around 8pm, then pizza shortly after. We had a good long chat about today's events and Eve actually said she is liking me as Julia – she used my name! It was amazing.

She was also freezing. It was so cold today and she was either in a graveyard, church, or an open sided marquee. Furthermore, she was dressed in a 1950's period costume. I wrapped her up in blankets, fed her pizza and then she had a hot shower. She is toasty warm now.

Such a lovely evening, we retired around 11pm. Eve will sleep well tonight, and I will too, I am sure.

A good day and another significant step taken on the road to recovery. Eve is proud of me, and the good night hug was very special.

Wednesday, May 5th

I have a potentially difficult site meeting today; I will be face-to-face with the idiot Client I had to write a harsh response to last week. I am not looking forward to it, so I am feeling a bit stressed this morning. Hopefully it will be OK – my first day back at work after quite possibly one of the most intense weekends of my life and I am plunged straight into this crap – sheesh...

So, how am I this morning? It's hard to describe, I am feeling disconnected again. Everything is just a little off-kilter, and it is a VERY odd sensation. But I am not miserable, so that is a bonus.

I do, however, feel fragile again. I feel like it wouldn't take much to push me into a hole again. I have no patience today.

The cat being sick at 3am didn't help matters, she woke Eve up, who then visited the loo, I suspect to clear up the mess, but this woke me up too and I found it hard to get back into a deep sleep, just fits and starts. So, I am a bit tired today.

Yesterday afternoon was strange. I have been thinking about it a lot. I didn't want to don my clothes initially. I kept putting it off. This meant I spent longer in Adam's clothes than I could've or than I expected to. I am wondering if this is contributing to my mood this morning. Likely I would say.

But I am feeling my way through this, there are no hard and fast rules, I am going with the flow. I am just expressing myself how I want, when I want. And it doesn't have to be 100% female all the time. I think that for the first time in ages, I was feeling OK in Adam's clothes. I hope this is a good sign. I am not so sure it is. It could be that I am beginning to get some of my gender balance back. Or it could be that I have spent too long as Julia and the little of my male my nature left is beginning to rebel. I suppose it is just a matter of perspective. I choose to

believe this is a good thing. The problem is that if I try to go with this, I run the risk of a bad morning after, so I need to take it slowly and just let things pan out naturally.

I headed to the office to pick up the project file and drawings for my meeting. I was delayed leaving, so I was stressed driving down to the site. A Police cordon and an unplanned diversion didn't help. But importantly, I had a phone conversation with my brother that ended badly. It started out OK, but then he told me why dad wants to see me this week. Dad wants to make sure that Eve doesn't benefit from his Estate. And while this is his choice, I get it, it also pressed all the wrong buttons and I reacted <u>VERY</u> badly. And then, he broke down and said that I wasn't the only one in pain, or the only one that was suicidal recently. I was floored. He hasn't slept properly in years and feels the burden of responsibility for everyone's salaries and their families terribly. It keeps him awake at night and he spends most weekends at the bottom of a bottle. I had **no** idea. I mean, I knew the stress of the business kept him awake sometimes, but not to this extreme and not for so long.

> I feel awful. He's my brother and I didn't for one moment consider his situation. I was so self-absorbed.

It took all the fight out of me and as a consequence my meeting went well. I rolled over and was professional, my Client was nice as pie (two-faced) and didn't bring up anything (coward). I was diligent and did my job. And then after, I came home and cried on Eve's shoulder.

I feel like telling my brother was opening Pandora's box. I would give **<u>anything</u>** to take this back. My whole life, even beyond my current situation, is a house of cards and the slightest breeze could blow it all away.

Later that evening I called my brother back to apologise. I think we are good, but I also think his support is now very flawed. He, like me, is not a reliable source of objectivity. Dad is also the same. It explains both of their attitudes towards this. Business-like, dispassionate and eager to do things to fix stuff that don't need it or protect me from an inevitable disaster.

But these things are making it worse between Eve and me. They are moving in the background to hasten a huge bust up between us.

> I choose **not** to follow their flawed advice. I categorically am **not** going to make any big or important decisions now, while I am raw, hurt and fragile.

But I am now hugely worried about Majorca.

I think it will be VERY difficult for Eve to come. And I don't know if I can put up with such a toxic atmosphere for this length of time on my own.

They are driving wedges between Eve and themselves and they are trying very hard to do the same between her and me.

Paranoia tells me that they have an agenda. This is patently ridiculous. They are blinkered and damaged and are not in the correct vantage point to see the whole picture. They are missing both vital and fundamental pieces about me and my relationship with Eve, so of course they are not able to see the damage they are doing. This makes them dangerous. So, as much as I love them and need their support, their advice is poison.

Pandora's box indeed.

Eve was there for me today. In a way my brother and dad were categorically not. She listened, comforted and was a genuine friend in need. She also validated me as Julia today, in a very small way, but it meant the world to me.

I told her about me wondering if Adam is ever going to come back and she agrees that there may be some green shoots, so I think now that this is a positive step, although I'm still not sure if any of it is real, I may well be seeing what I want to see and Eve may just be telling me what I want to hear – I'm trying so hard to be genuine, but I'm so broken emotionally I am struggling to sift through what is authentic or just wishful thinking.

Writing it all down helps, it means I can sort through my emotions, ponder different interpretations of what I'm feeling then re-read and review. This journal is a very powerful tool.

I did my drawing amends from home, and we had a nice evening together.

I am going out with a colleague tomorrow night. Just an evening out with a mate. I could do with a friend right now. Hopefully it will be good.

Lastly, I am seeing dad on Friday night. We will discuss his Will and how he wants to play it. Personally, I don't want any of his estate. I want him to enjoy it all, every penny, **with me** while we still can. I have no one to pass it on to anyway, I'm very happy for it to pass down to my Niece and Nephews. The only real question is whether I see any of it in between times and how we ensure it goes to my brothers' kids.

It's his Estate and it will go where he wants it to. If it means cutting me out, then so be it.

After the weekend from Hell, this week isn't shaping up to be much better...

Thursday, May 6th

I am in an odd mood today. I am beginning to think that this is, maybe, Adam starting to come back. The male side of my nature beginning to re-surface as it seems to be tied to a lessening in my desire to be as completely female as possible.

...or it could just be because I overheated in the night and had to take off my nightie. So, I've not spent the full amount of time in it, although the earrings, knickers and make-up remained. Plus, the satin duvet set is currently fitted, so I am enveloped in silky fabrics – it's not like I spent the night as Adam, far from it. I'm over analysing stuff again, I'm kinda hopeful he is starting to reappear, but equally I'm not sure why? I miss who I was hugely, but I really like who I am now. If he never comes back then I'm good with that – I like being Julia very much, a longing for the familiar maybe? As I said, an odd sort of mood...

My brother and dad set me off on a train of paranoid thoughts and it's continued this morning. I <u>know</u> it's all utter rubbish, but I'm not in my right mind and I am jumping at ghosts and shadows. Joining dots that aren't there and assigning malicious intent where there is none. Not good.

This is exactly why I can't make any big decisions at the moment.

And this is why them moving so quickly on this has caused such a strong, instant, and adverse reaction.

I'm in a holding pattern until I heal enough to deal with things rationally. In the meantime, I am desperately clinging onto the tattered shreds of my life, trying to keep it together until I know what to do. And them dictating to me what I should do is very unwelcome, them putting wheels in motion to serve their own blinkered agendas is even more so.

My blow up with my brother is exactly what I am desperately trying to avoid with Eve.

I am categorically NOT ready yet, this proves it.

But Pandora's box is now well and truly open. Other people are now involved. Things are moving without me, whether I am ready for them or not.

I am NOT ready...

Eve popped into my room (I still can't get over this, it'll always be *our* room), to see how I am this morning, and it was (as always) lovely.

I recounted the above to her. She agrees that dad and my brother are not reliable sources of advice, but of course, neither is Eve, they all have their own baggage and neither dad nor my brother can see any other options beyond the absolute worst. They also don't think I am capable at the moment, mentally – they may well be right. I certainly don't feel like I am.

What they don't see is the improvement in my relationship with Eve, it gives me hope – not hope that we will get back together, that horse has long since bolted, both she and now I, are very different people and she has her own agenda to follow. But our relationship hasn't been this communicative and open for literally years. I see hope for us all the time now. A different life, apart, but hopefully still friends. A life where we are both truly free. Free from the expectations of society and free to be who we really are. We were never a traditional couple, we never fit into that particular pigeonhole, maybe we can be something new?

I am thinking about "The Deal" again.

I am wondering if some of the other parts could be salvaged?

I would very much like it if we could be a team again, I am not sure if it is possible, Eve seems particularly intent on destroying this part, but would like it VERY much. We were stronger as a team than we are as individuals, and I really liked being there for someone important to me.

I am also wondering if we can share our true selves again. I very much still am, and she has come to the table a couple of times recently. As I said, we've not been this close in years...

1. I love her, and she loves me.

    The second part has gone. I am working hard on dismantling the first part, slow and painful.

2. I share myself openly and honestly with her and she does the same.

    The first part is in place, the second part I'm not sure about, sometimes and to a lesser extent maybe. It might be possible to work on this, but only if she wants.

3. We share our lives with each other.

    This is the one that hurts me the most. This is where I think the big changes are going to happen and this is why I need to change my love for her. She doesn't want to share her life with me anymore, indeed she is planning on taking her life places I just can't follow. I can't help it; this cuts me to the core and is the source of most of my pain.

4. We are there for each other, no matter what.

    This is <u>still</u> very much in place. I will always be there if she needs me, I just think she won't need me anymore and as much as this is empowering for her and I am genuinely pleased she is strong enough to spread her wings, I love being her safety net, it's what made me a man and I am not one anymore because she doesn't want a safety net where she is going.

5. We are a Team.

> I want this so badly. It means we are stronger together and enables us to do great things. It gives, certainly in my case, life purpose and it ties us together in a myriad of ways. These are really difficult and painful knots to undo. I think it's inevitable at this point that some of these will have to be untied, without love, there needs to be respect and this means equality and fairness. But I am thinking now that this can take as much time as it needs and we don't have to undo it all, or even most of it. Just the ones that are unfair to one or the other.

This ***could*** work…

Wow, I never really believed this until now. It was always a pipe dream, a one in a million shot, just to give me some necessary hope. A fool's hope but hope never-the-less.

And I think we would <u>both</u> be better off as a consequence.

> I think I would like this very much, I'm not hopeful that this is a realistic possibility, it's still a one in a million shot, but it would be good, very good.
>
> **But what does Eve want?**

If this happens, then neither of us can move on. I don't think I will find anyone else, but she conceivably could. And if she does, then she will form a team with them and break up whatever we have left. Maybe it is for the best we dissolve our team now? At least we are both free to embrace whatever life throws our way in the future?

I'll be getting up soon, regular Thursday site meeting again today and then a colleague and I are going out for a mate's night out. I need a friend, someone without an agenda and this is the very first step in doing something <u>*for me.*</u> The first step away from our team.

I feel like I've sorted some stuff out this morning, although I am not sure how real any of it is to be honest, but I feel better for working through it. I'm actually smiling as I write this!

The site was OK, a last-minute glitch with the fume extraction to the lamination bench, but it was solvable. I took a leisurely drive back to the office. I stopped in the motorway services for an hour and a half, just dozing in the sun, some much needed quiet time, then the short hop to work for the afternoon. I finished the NHS mental health facility drawings and sent them out officially. Also, I updated a client's HQ master plans. I have a long meeting tomorrow with another client.

I headed home to change (not in *that* way), then out to Chelmsford for the first thing I've done for myself and not for "us" in 15 years. It felt **really** odd walking out the front door. But the Orange Tree pub is lovely, good food at great prices. He's good company too, we had a laugh, and I shared my troubles, well as far as I could anyway. He's a bit like my brother and dad in so far as he thinks a split is inevitable, but he doesn't see it having to happen any time soon. It can happen when the timing is right.

Overall, it was a good day I think.

A road closure in Chelmsford meant an excessively long diversion to get home, I filled in tonight's events for Eve after I got changed, then off to bed. Nice.

I think I've made another positive step today. And I had fun too.

But I haven't spent much time as myself today. Consequently, tomorrow's mood is uncertain. Hopefully I'll be OK...

Friday, May 7th

I am OK. Perhaps a little sadder than I would like, but I am not in a dark hole again. Thank God.

Work should be pretty intense this morning. We have a client coming in to go through the two new designs for their roll out. This information has been much slower in coming through than needed so we are coming under increasing pressure to complete our work segments. But we can't start without the information and there now isn't time to re-do anything should it go awry. Tweaking things or adding in extra items will sink the ship.

I am going to see dad later to discuss his Will. I am **NOT** looking forward to it. This is the first, real, tangible step towards Eve and I breaking up. One of the knots that tie us together, all be it a small one, is about to be untied.

Also, I **really** need a night at home relaxing as a female. This week has been just too much.

Eve left early this morning; she has a Covid test in West London today and another one on Sunday for a job. The house is empty. I am alone.

I miss her.

Both cats fed and out for the day, I then headed for work. It was a full-on day, the Client arrived around 9:30am and didn't leave until gone three. I was tired, so my colleague and I left around an hour later. Before I left though, I gave my brother a hug – it was lovely. We are there for each other.

Off to see dad afterwards, it was a very emotional chat, but it was good. Mum and he had/have mirror Wills and both of them leave a sum of money to both my sister-in-law and Eve, our respective partners. It was done with the right intent but given how badly Eve has hurt me and the change in our status, he doesn't want any sums to go to her now. With mum now

gone, he doesn't know if he can alter her Will, or if he even needs to as I suppose, mum's Estate is now his to do with as he sees fit. He is going to seek advice next week.

Additionally, in the event of <u>my</u> passing, he doesn't want any of his estate ending up with Eve. This is his choice and I respect it.

So, I need to make a change to my Will. I am thinking I need to ring fence a sum of money equal to his eventual estate and specify that it doesn't go to Eve. I have no one else to leave it to, so I think it best if this sum of money is split 3 ways between my niece and nephews. It seems appropriate. Anything over and above this sum still goes to Eve. Unless things change for the worse – I hope they don't.

All very morbid, but it's a case of planning for the worst and hoping for the best.

We had a nice takeaway from a local pub and then hugged our goodbyes. I arrived home around 7:30pm and was in a skirt by 8:00.

Phew!

What a nightmare week.

It was so nice to relax with Eve tonight. Her Covid test went OK, it was in Hayes, near Heathrow, so a bit of a trial to get there on the M25 though the rush hour. She's not looking forward to doing it again on Sunday morning, although I suspect the traffic will be less, even if the driving standards of her fellow road users will be worse (Sunday drivers are a real thing).

Speaking of which...

Eve's sister has slipped over at the yard, her ankle has ballooned up, so no Gym tomorrow for her and Eve has to tend the horses. She's not happy, it's forecast rain tomorrow. I have volunteered to help, but she is non-committal. I suspect she will go on her own.

Because of her next Covid test on Sunday morning we can't stay the night at her folk's place and because she now has to do an extra turn at the horses tomorrow, 2 hours driving each way means not a lot of time there, so I don't think we are going this weekend.

Shame, I was looking forward to it.

I told Eve about dad and his wishes, she doesn't seem bothered at all. I also said that she is still very welcome at the hotel in Majorca, it may be awkward, but he's promised not to make it so, so she is welcome. Mum would've wanted her there and I certainly do.

The bigger issue is our planned European trip, I'm still undecided. I am, I think, going to play this by ear. If I do go, I think there will need to be some ground rules. I will not be abandoned or humiliated in front of our friends again and I certainly am not going to pay for the privilege. If we can establish a mutual respect, then I think it can still happen. This will stop her treating me so badly. She needs to remember it's my holiday too.

Worst case scenario: We go on holiday; she abandons me again. I fly home and leave her to it. She can explain it to our friends. I may even buy the plane ticket in advance. Just as an insurance – I **will not** be treated like this again. We go together, or I don't go.

Couple or not, **friends** do not do that to each other. I need my own safety net in place, but if it happens again, she does not respect me. Twice is two times too many, a third time **will not happen**. I will make sure of it one way or another.

This week has been one of the worst of my life. But in the midst of it all, some truly amazing moments:

- Mum's ashes, a perfect moment.
- Seeing Kay, a real positive step forward.

- Night out with my colleague, another step forward.
- Some cherished heart-to-hearts with Eve.

I hope the weekend works out well. It's a bit up in the air at the moment, so it could go a number of ways.

Providing I am feeling OK it should be alright.

Saturday, May 8th

I am OK this morning, as predicted, the weather is a bit grim, so Eve is going to get soaked at the horses. My offer of help still stands, but if she doesn't want me to? Well, this is OK.

I have no idea what I am going to do this weekend. Normally we have a plan, but it has fallen through spectacularly so it will be a play it by ear thing I think, and this will be largely weather dependent. If it stays poor, I *could* I suppose, spend the entire day as a woman. That's one (very nice) option. But this will mean I <u>can't</u> go out, so it will limit my movements should the weather improve. I am a bit torn to be honest, it is very rare I get an opportunity like this, and I want to make the best of it. I can't remember the last time I spent a full 24 hours in a skirt, likely my 25th birthday. Wow, literally half a lifetime ago. But equally I don't want to be tied to the house all day.

So, 11:30am I showered and chose to wear an acceptable face to the world. It's now 6:45pm and I'm about to lose my disguise and be comfortable. In the end we went to Colchester, and I bought another duvet set (not satin!) and a frying pan – my life. So exciting! Seriously, it was nice to go out with Eve and mooch around Colchester for a bit. Back home now, it's time to relax for the evening.

A nice, chilled evening. I watched a film (Elysium) while Eve relaxed in her room. Then we watched Death in Paradise together before retiring for the night.

A good day in the end.

Sunday, May 9th

I have uploaded my last holiday photo to Facebook. I have been doing the "10 days, 10 travel photos" challenge and even though it is spam, I've quite enjoyed it.

I overheated in the night again. My nightie is hanging up to dry and I spent the second half of the night in my bra and knickers only.

I am feeling OK at the moment, but I think it wouldn't take much to set me off crying again, my emotions feel very close to the surface today.

I had a (brief) episode yesterday. I dozed off for 10 minutes on the sofa. Eve was in the armchair opposite, and she had some music playing softly. I woke up to hear "If I could turn back time" by Cher playing, which is a great song, but the lyrics are too close to my situation at the moment. I started crying. Eve skipped the track when she realised it had upset me.

This is not the first-time music has triggered an emotional outburst in me. I can't listen to "It Must Be Love" by Madness any more as this is **our** song. Consequently, I am listening to Classic FM in the car now. There are loads of contemporary songs that will set me off at the moment, some more than others. Also, I have next to no patience currently. The DJs and the adverts wind me up terribly.

Eve will be up soon, it's 7:15am as I write, and she has to drive back to Hayes for a second Covid test ahead of her working tomorrow. I will be alone for a couple of hours or so. I suspect this will set me off crying again as I'm feeling a bit fragile this morning. I will try to distract myself...

It's been an odd day. I was up around 10am, so a bit of a lie in. I would've loved to stay female, indeed I delayed my shower for as long as I felt I could – I didn't want to take my make-up off. But I had bedding to get in off the line, more bedding to wash

and hang out too. So, I had to hide behind Adam's façade earlier than I wanted. Consequently, I have been a bit out of sorts all day and I also missed Eve greatly the entire morning.

Julia **definitely** misses Eve less than Adam. That's a weird thing to say, it's **really** strange – I am only one person after all, but when I am disguised as Adam, my emotions are cranked up to the maximum. When I am me, Julia, I can be civil, less emotional, logical, and even happy to some degree for short spells. I think I am much better company and I feel generally a great deal more comfortable.

When I look like Adam, I feel everything much more acutely. I am like an open wound and crave Eve's company. It's maddening – I feel pathetic, following her around like a shadow. And a shadow of my former self too. Adam tries to be pleasant, he succeeds occasionally, but there is an inescapable sadness about him. Julia has some of this too, but it's nowhere near as intense. Adam feels awkward, he is not comfortable in his skin. And it shows. I have always felt dysphoria, it comes in waves, sometimes it's overwhelming and sometimes it's a maddening background hum. I live with it. My dysphoria has changed – Adam feels it constantly now but it has been joined by an intense emotional pain – this is pretty much all he feels, this and a longing for Eve. He's not a real person anymore, just a receptacle for all the hurt done to him, a thin façade to hide behind. I need him to be real again, hiding myself behind another's face is exhausting. It was never an issue before, I **was** Adam, he had to live within a stiflingly cramped and confined box labelled "male" and he just didn't fit.

I expressed the important, but unacceptable parts of myself whenever I could, I named her Julia and she, although every bit as real too, was not able to be my everyday face. The reality is puberty made this impossible for me, I have a 6ft-2inch frame that is broad and I hate it – it just doesn't look like me and

despite being as big as it is, I simply don't fit into it very well at all. I never have.

This is the conundrum I am working on trying to resolve. I **have** to be more comfortable as Adam again. He can leave the house and do stuff. He can have a life. A good one even, *if* he can make the best of things as he has done in the past.

Julia cannot match this.

But Adam doesn't exist anymore, only Julia remains, and Adam's façade is paper-thin. It has never felt so false, or so raw.

This is the paradox of my life at the moment.

Most of me cannot exist outside of these 4 walls. And it is such a shame, as now that I am exploring being her fully for the first time in my life, I really like who she is. I like who I am. She has so much to offer and to give. I adore being her and she is so full of wonder.

It's a tragic thing, to be gifted with this rare insight and ability to actually be another gender and love it. But not be another gender and **live** it.

...and it **is** a gift. No question.

I know this now. I have spent my whole life denying who I am, running from it, being scared of it, the ramifications of such a profound truth. Trying to force myself into something I am not. Then, finally as the dysphoria and inner turmoil reaches a crescendo, expression, in a limited, but just barely satisfactory way. A pressure release valve and a way to manage the important, but unacceptable parts of who society expects someone with my physique to be.

I came close to acceptance in my '30's. I had given up on finding someone and was struggling to "manage" my female nature, so I began to explore who I am a bit more and take things a bit further. I began to visit a salon in Cambridge and started a regular waxing and pedicure routine. I truly hate and detest my

body hair; it turns my stomach and is quite disgusting. There is so much of it, and it really doesn't like being shaved or removed. My skin pays the price when it regrows with extreme sensitivity, like electricity at the slightest touch and acne, oh so much acne. Ultimately, I took female hormones for about 6 months. I began to develop my breasts – I truly love them, even if they can be awkward to hide when disguised as Adam sometimes. And I truly love wearing a bra, or more accurately, I love being able to fill one – having a bra that pretty much fits me is mind blowing. It was unsupervised, which is unwise, but no doctor is going to prescribe HRT for me, I am never going to be able to pass the living for 2 years in my true gender test. I suffered with gynecomastia during my teens – I use the word 'suffered', but this is not true at all, I loved it. So, my breasts had a head start and by 6 months on HRT, I was between a B and a C cup. I was not on anti-androgens, better known as blockers, then. To be honest all I could get was oestrogen and progesterone online by ordering from abroad, but testosterone blockers were nowhere near as readily available, and I didn't have a clue about dosages. My breasts **need** support, they require it. I miss my bra when I can't wear one.

And then, just as I was beginning to take my acceptance of who I am to the next level. A dangerous level where things would become harder to hide. Eve came into my life, and it took the most astonishing, joyous, and unexpected left turn.

I was at a turning point; I chose to become Adam and not continue exploring who I am as Julia. I did it so I could build a life with Eve. A good life, one that I had given up any hope of having. One that ticked all of societies' expectations of me, a 'relatively' normal life. And it was good, so very good, for so long.

I invented a man, his name coincidentally matched that given to me at birth, Adam. He was a good man, a genuinely nice guy. People like him and he's worth knowing. He is good

fun and can light up a room if the mood takes him. He is good at his job and is great at providing a home. First and foremost, he is Eve's best friend, he is loyal and dependable. He's not perfect, but he knows this and tries to overcome his flaws. He is kind, honest and has a good moral compass.

Even though he is an invention, he has defined himself as Eve's boyfriend. This is the central keystone of who he is and why he exists. And this key attribute has only grown stronger and more important as his love for Eve deepened. I am wondering, as I write this, if this depth of feeling may have smothered her?

Eve is and always has been an incredibly independent person. It's one of her defining characteristics and a big reason of why I love her so much. She was **never** comfortable being part of a couple. I see this now. What has been going on over the past few years is Eve separating herself from me and reasserting herself as every bit her own person. To be fair, it wasn't a big leap for her. She is amazing and this is something to be celebrated, I am in awe of her ability to do this, it was an act of sheer will and was spectacular to witness, if heart-breaking. I should feel privileged to have had such a ringside seat.

But.

This process hurt Adam. It undermined his very reason for being.

Every glorious step Eve has taken to discover herself and step out of the shadow of being in a 'couple' has been astonishingly painful to Adam as it has come at his expense. Culminating in the ultimate blow, Eve not loving him anymore. This was devastating to him at a fundamental level. Much more so than Eve could have ever realised or comprehended.

Breaking Adam's heart was bad, but destroying his core, who he actually was, was much, much worse.

And she didn't just destroy the construct, she laid it bare, ripped it to shreds along with his heart and took the rest of Adam with her. There is nothing male left in me – it's gone and I'm certain that I would be gone too if that were all that I am.

Julia was revealed as the real person. I am Julia and I see now; I always have been. She is all that remains of the strange mix of genders I used to be. She cannot exist, and yet she is all that I am, so has to be. A paradox. I have to make this work, so I am exploring who this lovely new lady is. She has been neglected for so long, but I really like her, I like being her very much indeed. She's great. I am healing, I hope that Adam is healing too, but that is all it is at the moment, hope and seeing green shoots where there may not be any. I sometimes think he makes me hesitate when I dress comfortably as a female. I think he is also stopping me dressing in a more feminine manner. He took the joy out of my satin duvet set too I imagine; he just didn't feel comfortable. Or it could all be in my head, and I just don't want to face the truth. I really hope he comes back; I need to feel good as him once more. Life will be simpler if I can embody him again, but this is not a given. Just a hope.

I like to think that Julia is getting me through this, giving Adam time to heal as well as some perspective on the situation. She is **much** stronger now, I can feel myself growing, trying to live authentically as who I now am. I am permanently changed by these fundamental and unprecedented moments in my life. Julia is providing the missing strength and I know for a fact that I will emerge from this as a **much** fuller and better person.

But at the moment, there is at best a long and protracted "shift-change" going on. This is why I think I have been feeling so odd lately, I am sure.

I hope that Adam is trying to come back – my life was much easier when I could inhabit this body without dysphoria constantly screaming at me as loud as it can – it's deafening

and I never get a break from it anymore – I look in the mirror at Adam's face and my mind rejects utterly what it sees – THAT, is not me, it CAN'T be – I put on my make-up and the dysphoria quietens a little. I do my hair and it quietens a little more. I dress to align with who I am, and the dysphoria now shouts in my ear rather than deafens me.

I used to think I was Adam and "managed" Julia. But now I know it's always been the other way around. I have always been Julia, but I denied her and hid behind Adam. The only difference is that Adam used to be real, I was able to BE him for a short while. Now he's just a mask, the skin I walk around in. I want him to come back, to be real again - it was so much easier when he was around – he could be the acceptable face for the world. I'm bloody good at hiding who I am, after 50 years practice, anyone would be, but it's really hard work these days. Such hard work, I am shattered in a myriad of ways, including being both physically and emotionally exhausted.

I hope Adam is trying to come back, it'll help me more than you can imagine, he's always been my rock, but he's not there anymore, just a face I have to look through and a face that the world expects me to be. That's not who I am. It used to be, partially, but not anymore.

It's more than possible I'm seeing green shoots just because I want to see them...

Monday, May 10th

I am in a better place today. At least I think so. Tara cat came to see me in bed this morning. Cute mog, it's been sometime since she did that. Cats are empathetic, but on their own terms, maybe she came to see me because she could sense I was in a better place? Or maybe she just wanted cuddles.

I've been thinking about Eve and my financials. Who pays for what etc. Partially because dad and my colleague (but dad in particular), think she is taking advantage of my good nature. She has stepped up a bit over the past month, I have noticed her paying for more food for instance. It has hurt me a bit to see it happening to be honest. I **like** to do things for her, it gives me purpose, I **want** to, and it makes me feel good. But she has **always** strived to be financially independent, though she has never had the fortune to do so. She still doesn't (although she is working **very** hard to change this), but she has made a noticeable effort despite very meagre incomings.

The problem I have is despite her best efforts, she is a very long way from pulling her weight. When she loved me and we were a team, it simply didn't matter.

But now, through her own choices, it does. A lot.

Now, my best friend (I suppose 'sister' is more accurate at the moment?) is living rent free in a house that I am 100% paying for. A house that is an appreciating asset, that she legally owns half of. She is also 15 years my junior and is almost certain to outlive me by a long way. I am buying her a house. And I am getting nothing back from her. Indeed, I am only going to get less from her from now on.

I don't want her money, but I do need the financial situation to improve – not because I can't afford it, but because **it just isn't fair**. She has a legal commitment to pay half the mortgage and a moral duty to pay half the bills.

- She physically can't.
- This is not fair.
- She has to step up.

It all comes back to us being a team, the fifth pillar of "The Deal".

We are stronger together. As a team. She gets strength from me, and I get strength from her – it's mutually beneficial and actually, quite beautiful.

I am asking myself if the situation were reversed, would Eve support me in the same way?

Before, she would have said yes, with no hesitation. Now? I really don't think she would. I think that without my love, she would resent paying for the roof over our heads, especially if I was actively **not** trying to get a job. Instead, I was putting all my efforts into (yet another) passive income scheme/project.

I am desperate for just one of her projects to pay off. She works so hard to make them come to fruition, she deserves success, and she is so passionate, she truly loves what she is doing.

But it's a slow burn and hard work and diligence is no guarantee of success.

And in the meantime?

I continue to support her.

What choice do I have? I need a place to live, and I can't leave Eve, plus as I mentioned, I *like* to support her, supporting her has been my entire life for the past 15 years. Even if she was paying her way fully, I'm not sure what I'd do with the money – I don't want to take it, it feels wrong. But what she has done to me and is continuing to do to me is not fair and at some point, it has to stop.

...or she has no respect for me.

And respect for each other is the only way I can see us remaining friends.

- I want to remain friends so badly. She has to step up somehow.
- And I **really don't want to have this conversation with her.**

Financially at least, she needs us to still be a team, in the short term anyway, but she has made this **much** more difficult now.

There are consequences to her actions, real, actual consequences. She can't shirk her responsibilities. Without her love, there are now limits to what I can give her. And I detest this.

This is the sad truth of the situation she has put us both in.

I never wanted any of this.

...and now I am upset again.

But this doesn't have to happen now, or indeed any time soon. But it does need to happen.

When her website starts to make money, she needs to contribute more. It **has** to be her priority, and this is going to be very hard for her to hear.

Of course, she contributes in other ways, lots of them, likely some I don't know about too. These are not insignificant, far from it. They are also very, very much appreciated.

But I could pay for a cleaner, or have our laundry done if she paid for her half of the mortgage and bills. Similarly, a regular grocery order would be easy and affordable too. A lot of the maintenance items outstanding on the house would also get done. And she would have more available time to put into her website. Simply put, there would be a lot more disposable income to deal with the chores.

I don't want to sound ungrateful for Eve's contributions. I am truly grateful for everything she does. But there is a _fairer_ way.

...and the way forward **has** to be fair.

I hate this. I really don't want to do it. I feel like I'm kicking both her fledgling business and her dreams in the teeth and more importantly, it feels wrong, actually, much worse than that, **_it feels mean_**. And that just isn't me. It has the potential to ruin everything. But I didn't set this train in motion, she did. I am just trying to manage the damage it's doing and will continue to do.

It's strange that financials should suddenly become a problem. I never thought about how one-sided they were before. We were a team and so we supported each other, filling in where the other needed help to create a balanced whole. Regardless of our individual financial situations, where she struggled, I happily stepped up – it was my duty and my pleasure to help. Can we be a team again?

I think it ultimately comes down to:

- Eve literally **can't** pay her share of the mortgage and only contributes to the bills when a referral comes in.
- I **have** to pay the rest, or we default on the mortgage and we both lose the house.

> This is not fair, but it is the only solution that works given the circumstances.

- If the circumstances change, then the solution needs to change too.

What does Eve want to do?

Does she want to live here?

Does she want to own this house ultimately?

- If she wants to live here and/or own the house, when she is able, she **must** contribute. If not, if she wants to up sticks and go live somewhere else, then she can. But I will need to buy her out and leave the house to my niece and nephews, or sell it, pay her 50% of the equity and move.

> I won't buy the house for her if she is not going to live here with me.

Fairness… I hate it. But how can I hate fairness?

Eve arrived home close to midnight. I was in bed and said 'hello' and pretty much 'goodnight' at the same time.

I missed her today.

But I am OK.

Tuesday, May 11th

I seem to be OK again today. Epic rant in here yesterday, no idea how much, if anything I am going to move forward on. But I think I have a loose plan for the future.

I spent the evening in my casual clothes, comfy bra and knickers, minimal make-up, hoop earrings, heels, skirt and blouse. I am finding it hard to do 'casual', I think I'm quite good at 'formal' and I really like making an effort with my appearance (odd because this is the exact opposite of Adam, he's a scruffy beggar because he is a prison, likely the most escape proof and effective physical prison there is, and I don't have any intentions on living in a gilded cage) – but I just don't look female enough when dressed casually and scaling back my formal look is proving difficult. This is a work in progress. I feel comfortable but am dissatisfied with the way I look.

My legs are another issue, in fact, all of my body hair is. I would love to shave it all off. Waxing, I've tried, but it makes my skin react badly. An hour or two of pain, for at most 2 days of nice, acceptable skin and then 2 weeks of acne, itchiness, irritation, and hyper-sensitivity. It's just not worth it. But Summer is on its way and soon, I will need to buy some Adam shorts and T-Shirts. Shaved legs will be noticeable in shorts, just as unshaved legs are noticeable in a skirt. I have been dealing with this with stockings or tights. But it is getting warmer...

I have a day in the office today. I will lose myself in drawing work and it should pass quickly enough.

Eve is having a well-deserved lie-in. I am looking forward to seeing her tonight.

I need to chat with my brother, he has invited me to dinner tomorrow night. Was it for me alone, or did it include Eve? I hope it included her. She and they are my family. At least until I am in a better place, I need them to get along.

I spoke with my brother; the dinner invite is for me only. He says it is to get me out of the house, but really, what it means is more time feeling utterly awful in trousers and less time feeling better in a skirt. He means well and has no idea what I am going through beyond the surface, how could he? How could anyone for that matter? He is trying to get me out of what he sees as a toxic environment, but in actuality, every remaining moment I have with Eve is precious there is a ticking countdown to the day she leaves, furthermore I need to express who I am as Julia as much as I can, to deal with Adam's pain and not go completely crazy with dysphoria.

I'm sure it'll be nice. A bit awkward being there without Eve. But despite the above, I'm looking forward to it – I just wish I could go as myself instead of putting on another stressful acting job as Adam.

I have been thinking about the possibility of transitioning. I suspect that, if I ever transition, immediate family will be the biggest hurdle to deal with. I think I can transition physically, it'll be hard, painful, and challenging, plus I won't ever be completely convincing, I am just too big.

If I can train my voice, I think I can transition socially, this will also be difficult, there will be a number of friends I will lose – I'm GenX, as are most of my friends, so although we have much broader attitudes than the Boomers before us, there are still a lot of bigoted folk when it comes to people like me – to be honest, if I can't convince them, then I am happy to lose them from my life – no one needs this negativity.

Transitioning in public is less certain, I think I will be read <u>a lot</u>, but is this really an issue? It is for me at the moment, hopefully this will change. **If they see a man in the woman, then they are missing the woman in the man. This is not my problem, it's theirs.**

Transitioning with my neighbours, well, I'd like to avoid this if I can – I am very lucky, I get on well with all of them – I don't want to upset them, but it's doable, if tricky, & I'd love to come and go as I please. It may be better to just up sticks and move somewhere new, somewhere more rural, or somewhere where my new neighbours only know Julia.

Transitioning professionally is a big showstopper. Not because of colleagues, or even clients – yes, it'll be awkward, but I'm not really worried about this. I am worried about my brother – he will 100% see this as a threat to the business, he may well support me personally, but he will want to dissolve our business relationship, I am sure. So, it can never happen sadly.

And this leads me onto transitioning with my immediate family. Dad, bless him, has categorically denied my existence my entire life – he will never understand, or condone and he will sadly, never actually meet his daughter. It's such a shame, I love him, but it's his own blinkered attitude and unwillingness to open his eyes that has put us both in this situation. My brother, well, this is as I mentioned, inextricably linked to our professional situation. I think that me transitioning would also put him at odds with his wife – it happened with my mum, she became piggy in the middle between her child and her husband – she was in an untenable situation (she sided with my dad, this hurt her and me) and I think my sister-in-law wouldn't have any issues with me transitioning, neither would my niece and nephews – but I wouldn't want to put them in this situation – it is just not fair on them or my brother.

Transitioning with my wider family would be a very mixed bag, likely split along generational lines. Younger people have a much better understanding and are hugely more accepting of folk like me, whereas people of my generation and above have ever increasing ignorant and immovable attitudes, based upon narrow minded views, influenced by the society they grew up

in and were formed by. It affected me too – I have such hang-ups about going out as me in public – it's just how most of my generation were moulded by the world back then. The world has moved on, but there are still lots of old dinosaurs like me roaming the earth... We can't help who we are, or the world in which we were raised.

All that said, I'd much rather the world see a man in a dress, than BE a woman in a cage.

I set up an appointment with a local financial firm to deal with he changes to my Will, following dad's wishes. It's a week on Friday. I feel like (at last), I've made some progress with the first of the batch of drawings. I will try to do the same tomorrow.

Home around 5:30pm, fully female by 7:00pm, so, 13 hours clocked up today. I've also made a bit more of an effort this evening. I feel extra feminine. Sexy black satin and lace lingerie, including stockings, suspenders and an underwired bra for extra support and lift. Long, black pencil skirt, black satin blouse and high heels. Simple make-up, jewellery, hair and perfume. I look nice and feel really good about myself. I'm smiling for once.

Eve told me about her day yesterday, it was pretty epic apparently. 2 locations in North London and a crowd scene at Wembley tube station. She had a bath and we settled in to watch a couple more episodes of Death in Paradise before retiring.

A good day.

Wednesday, May 12th

I didn't sleep very well last night. I fell asleep fully clothed and woke up around 2am with an underwire digging into my right boob – ouch. The downside to wearing a bra, I guess... It's not all roses. Or it is, but I've found a thorn! I was so happy with my appearance; I delayed getting changed for bed until I inevitably fell asleep. I also added to my make-up before I retired, I was feeling so nice, I felt I wanted to go the whole way. Eyebrows pencilled in, eye-liner (still very much developing skills here), eye shadow, blusher and lip gloss to complete my face. I adore seeing my face like this, it just looks 'right'.

From 2am, I undressed and slipped into a very welcome nightie. But my brain wouldn't switch off, so I didn't drift back to sleep for another hour or so. Some of it I am sure was related to looking less female in my attire. Some of it was related to my thoughts on transitioning too. But I'm having paranoid thoughts about Eve and Steve again. It's all rubbish. I am absolutely sure neither of them would do this to me. But this is the last red line. The <u>most</u> destructive one, so I fear it, and this fear gives it the power to disturb me and my thoughts at a fundamental level.

I am thinking that I might be ready to sit down and have the financial talk with Eve soon. But it'll be between Eve and Julia. I am <u>not</u> ready to do this as Adam yet. It's an additional level of emotion and stress that I'm just not up to at the moment. I am <u>much</u> calmer and rational as myself. I think I can handle the conversation if I am properly attired. And actually, the more female, the better. I may need to set some ground rules though. I may need her to call me Julia throughout to stop Adam responding out of pain. And if she *has* crossed the last red line, then this topic is not up for discussion yet. She may have ended her side of our relationship, but my side is still very much intact and until I can resolve this, betrayal is not an option. That'd put me back to worse than square one, I suspect it would literally

kill me – I'd be more upset than I was on "J-Day", when I went out to do something incredibly stupid. Make no mistake, from my side of the fence, this is the biggest possible betrayal – if this red line has been crossed, she is unquestionably *"the bad guy"* and I kick her out. We lose everything we have in the most painful way possible.

So, it cannot be a discussion point, unless I suppose, it is a future aspiration for her. To find a new partner when our relationship has dissolved **from both sides.**

At this point I can be happy for her.

But **not** before.

I will be getting up soon. A new day awaits and despite being very tired and all of the above paranoia, I am greeting it with hope.

Initial thoughts on "The Talk". Sheesh, I suppose I've got yet another a new phrase in quotes now, along with "Red Line", "The Deal" and "Five Pillars"...

- What does Eve want / not want?
- What do I want / not want?
- Possible timelines (maybe including a discussion on the "Red Line")
- Changes in our relationship and how this affects us in public.
- Respect and finances.
- What is and what isn't possible.

What do **I** want?

> I want things to go back to the way they were. This is what I was trying to achieve over Christmas when she blew our whole lives apart with those 5 utterly devastating little words. I now know this isn't possible, so...

I want some of the pillars of "The Deal" to remain. Being there for each other no matter what and as much of being a team as possible. I also want us to share our lives, albeit not together anymore. I strongly suspect however that this will be a case of diminishing returns. Her shutting me out is still hugely painful to me.

I want some respect. And with this comes **never** hurting me like this again. Something this fundamental **has** to be discussed beforehand, ahead of a crisis point. To spread out the impact and allow me to be involved in any decisions that affect my life on such an enormous scale.

I *want* us to continue living together, but strongly suspect we are on a clock ticking down to her moving out. It feels like it is only a matter of time, and the timeline is most likely tied to Eve's finances.

I don't want to continue to pay for 98% of everything and get nothing back from her. When we were a couple, our love meant it didn't matter. Her love for me is all I wanted. Without this, it now matters a lot. This comes back to respect. I see her financial situation and know she contributes as much as she can. But I didn't do this, she did. Her contributions are not equal, so are not fair. It is not enough. **When** her finances improve, she has a moral duty to me and a legal one to the mortgage. I always had faith in her, she is immensely talented and always puts 110% into everything, so at some point, she **will** be successful. At that point, I will need her to reimburse me and/or shoulder her responsibilities. Until then, I will continue to support us both and her other, less tangible contributions need to continue also.

I need to continue to live as Julia. She brought this change upon me, she forced me to face and then inhabit who I fundamentally am. It was **not** my choice. Adam may well be coming back; I hope he is. I believe I feel him being uncomfortable occasionally with so much time as a woman. But IF he does re-emerge, he is highly unlikely to return as he was, he is far too damaged and will always play second fiddle to who I actually am, Julia has **had** to come forward and I really like being her. Furthermore, I think I will ultimately be a much more balanced person as a result – with less extreme swings in my nature. This is a good thing, possibly the **ONLY** good thing to come out of all this.

Importantly, I think being Julia also gives me the ability to manage my love for Eve. Adam loves her completely; with everything he has and is. He was, and what little is left of him remains totally committed to her as her boyfriend. This is why he was so completely damaged. Julia is not, she wants to be Eve's sister if possible and as such, loves her also, but it is not the same. It is not as fierce, so she is not as hurt. I can deal with what is going on as Julia. Even if I could inhabit Adam again, I can't deal with *anything* as him. I hope to be able to be Adam again, instead of looking through his eyes at a face in the mirror that isn't me anymore. I'd like to be him again; he had a great life and I'd like to like myself in his guise once more. But I still very much feel like Julia in disguise, playing a part and too much time in his shoes is hugely damaging to me at the moment, it's maddeningly uncomfortable, my dysphoria is turned up to 11 and it's all consuming. I just can't settle and am emotionally unstable. I hope this will change with time; it has to as my current situation is unsustainable. Living a lie never is. But Julia is there to give Adam space to heal. This process has to continue.

I don't want to be alone. When Eve and I are apart I experience a loss akin to physical pain. I need this to change and I am working on it. This too will take time. My worst nightmare is being lonely, but I suspect that that is exactly what my future now holds. I have always lived with someone, be it my family, or with Eve. Regardless of what happens in the future, Eve is my best friend and Adam's soul mate. I need her in my life, hopefully to a greater degree, but think it will be much sparser and more sporadic. Ultimately it will be whatever she feels comfortable with I suppose.

Whether we are living together, or apart, she will **always** be welcome and will always have a home with me should she want it.

If we go out together, we do so **together.** I will not feel abandoned by her again, I will not put myself in this position anymore. If we are together, we are **not** free agents. If we are not together, then we are – it's that simple. I think this needs to be a rule, I will not have her ruin another holiday, or any activity again. It was heart-breaking, humiliating and extremely painful – I am NEVER going to be in that situation again. So, she needs to include me. This comes back to respect. Together, does not mean 'a couple', it means a team and our first priority is always to the team. The team is about being fair to each other, this includes finances, but is not limited to them. Treating the other person is fine, but we should both pay an equal share. More importantly, we strive to not hurt each other – I can't stress this enough.

The Red Line

The above only works if she does not betray me. At some point she may well find someone else. I **have** to be in a position to be happy for her. Happy that she is happy. I am **not** there yet. This will take time and I don't think I can rush it.

> Betrayal is the last and only unforgivable thing. It cannot happen, or everything we have, our lives, our love, our friendship stops immediately.

We can move on, but only when we are both ready. I am not yet. She may no longer consider herself in a relationship with me, but the reverse is very much not true. I am working on it, but it is not like I can just turn a tap off on my feelings. It will take time. She has had years; I have had just over a month. She does **NOT** have permission to see other people. Not yet. But there will be a time when she does. I don't know when. But I am genuinely happy for dad and his lady friend, so it will happen, I think. I only ever wanted to make Eve happy. This has not changed. When I have let her go emotionally, then I will be happy that she is happy, with whoever she finds to be with.

I want to be happy again – sounds simple, it should be, but it is not.

I don't want to live in 'our house' alone. If it comes to this, I will likely sell the place.

I don't want to be lonely, and I adore being in her company. So, I desperately want us to remain friends and see each other regularly.

I want to achieve a gender balance again. An equilibrium to my nature.

Boring day at work. Went around my brother's tonight for dinner (chicken stir-fry, really lovely). Eve stayed home and I found this very painful. Walking out the door without her was very emotional and difficult. Once I arrived though, it was nice hanging out with my family. Really nice. But I missed out on time in a skirt. Will make up for this, err... in both senses of the word, likely on Friday.

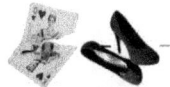

Thursday, May 13th

Site meeting again today, I have tomorrow booked off work, I'm taking a much-needed break and some time for my well-being. I am seeing Kay for my second session too. I hope it goes well.

It is 6:50am as I write, I am done in the bathroom (as usual), but Eve is in there now. She has another Covid test this morning ahead of a day's work tomorrow. This time it is just south of the Olympic Park, so not too bad for her to get to.

Everything about my life has changed...

...and yet...

...nothing about my life has changed.

The day-to-day stuff, like using the bathroom early so as not to disturb Eve, Tara cat coming to see me in the morning in bed, NHS site meeting every Thursday (meeting #87 today!) Sleeping on the left-hand side of the bed, Eve going to work at random times, Eve going gooey over the cat. All the little moments and routines that make up the day are the same.

And yet, I feel it is all about to end. She has gambled both of our lives and lost heavily. Whatever happens from here, we have lost a fundamental part of what we had.

The site meeting was OK. I spent more time there than usual as I updated the snag list. I didn't go back to the office after, so I was therefore an hour early home and after dinner, dressed properly from around 6pm, so 13½ hours as a woman today.

Eve had her usual bath; she has a groin strain at the moment from her weightlifting. It's causing her some discomfort and I feel useless. I want to help her, but do not feel like I am wanted. She retired early to watch some foreign TV on her laptop in bed

– effectively shutting me out again. If I was Adam, this would have upset me. It has in the past. But I am **not** Adam. I am Julia and not only am I Julia, but I am also expressing myself openly and genuinely as Julia. So, although I am missing Eve's company, she is doing something for herself, and I am doing the same. Fair enough.

It occurred to me that we do not fit traditional gender roles at all. I mean we never really did very much, but she is now even more assertive and capable, taking charge of the situation and her emotions, and making things happen. She has a goal and is working towards it in a methodical and definite way. She goes to the gym to lift weights and dresses practically; she literally wears the trousers – actually, she truly hates to be in a dress or a skirt, it makes her self-conscious, very uncomfortable and always has. Some of her family photos of her as a child in a dress, at weddings, formal events etc (there are precious few of them), she has a face like thunder. She also hates me giggling at them! As an actor, she is often required to wear a costume and she does wear some beautiful clothes (and looks equally beautiful). But she only puts up with it because she is being paid to do so.

I am literally wearing the skirt in this relationship (and I love it! I genuinely can't get enough time in a skirt or a dress). I am emotionally overwhelmed and unable to make any decisions without hours of deep thought and contemplation of my feelings. I am following her lead and supporting her, even though I don't like where her decisions are taking us. I make myself pretty for my self-esteem, well-being and in some small way, for her – although I don't think she appreciates, or even notices it anywhere near as much as I do, even when I go the extra mile. Living like this feels right, it's who I am and who I am meant to be and while I am showing my true face, I am content and most importantly, comfortable. There are no family photos

of me in a skirt, God how I wish there were. I would give anything to have been a bridesmaid at the many family weddings that have happened over the years. I sometimes feel that most of my childhood was robbed from me – so many experiences I should have had, that just never happened. Mum teaching me make-up, learning her skills, tips, and tricks. Being encouraged to play dress up, mum helping me buy my first bra and being fitted, instead of the furtive, stressful rabbit in the headlights, solo experiences I had buying, and then throwing lots of them away until I found my size and a style that I like by trial and error. Going to school in the correct uniform (God how I hated my school uniform, I would've given anything to have been like the other girls), having a circle of close female friends, learning to swim in a swimsuit, having my ears pierced with my mum, her passing down to me recipes and domestic skills. There's just so many, both huge and tiny, rites of passage a young girl goes through that I will never know. Some things I can experience, but some of the more profound events are forever denied to me. I can take hormones and develop my breasts; indeed, I have taken a few steps in this direction in the past, enhanced what I already had and will likely do so again in the future. I have had my ears pierced, and although I had to do it on my own – it was still a pivotal event in my life, and I adore wearing earrings. But I will never have a period. To be honest, it's not something I desire, I suspect no woman does. From what my limited outsider's perspective affords me, it's painful, uncomfortable, inconvenient, a chore (a potentially expensive one too) and kinda gross. It's also a magical, affirming and profoundly female experience that comes with a huge mother/daughter bonding moment in most cases. Something really very special. Dad teaching me how to shave my chin is not nearly the same – it's a necessary life skill and nothing more. I'm sure dad got a kick out of it, for me it was yet another confirmation I am not who I

should be – actually, shaving every day is my number one hate – it's a literal punch in the face first thing every morning and comes close to ruining every single day before it has even begun. The only thing I like about it is how I look afterwards, when that horrible hair is gone, but it's an insidious and pernicious thing, slowly growing on my face, making me look less and less like I feel every moment of every day. I hate it so much and am definitely going to have it permanently removed, along with any other body hair, I hate it all.

Anyway, I digress... Hey, it's my journal, I'm allowed to go off on a tangent! Suffice it to say:

Eve, more than ever before, is the husband and I am absolutely the <u>wife.</u>

I like it a lot, sheez I am odd...

Eve has a job tomorrow in Stansted Airport. She is very excited! Fairly local, a good payday and it is in her favourite airport. It is a 6:30am call time too, so not too early. Plus, she had a call from Rachel (one of her booking agents), they are putting her forward for a regular slot in Sevenoaks, Kent (her original home county), in a show called "The Larkins". We think it's a remake of the Darling Buds of May, one of Eve's very favourite shows. She is very happy, and I am equally happy for her.

I have tomorrow off work, I am thinking of spending much of it in female attire. I also have an 11am session with Kay – I may well do so in the correct underwear – I think the knowledge and feeling of wearing lingerie may help my mood. If not this, then the constant reminder of my bra will definitely help keep me centred and give me confidence. I am curious as to how tomorrow will go. There is a lot for her to deal with here, will she look at our relationship first? This is, of course, the most pressing issue. Or my gender? Or the healing process?

I would very much like her to call me Julia, but I am not sure if this is a good idea. Or if she will read more into it than intended. I just want some validation of who I am, that's not too much to ask is it? If I get the opportunity, if it arises, I will ask her to do so. Maybe she will ask me how I want to be addressed? I want to shout as loudly as I can SHE/HER, MY NAME IS JULIA! But no one **ever** asks me this and more importantly, if they did, I would be too shy to follow through with it. But Kay knows about me, this is not an out of context conversation, she may well extend this courtesy. I hope so. I hope she is good tomorrow. I am actually in a much better head space than I was last time, so I think I am making some progress. But her help is very much needed still. She needs to show me the way. I think she will want me to have "The Talk" with Eve fairly soon, maybe this weekend. I am not sure how we, and more importantly, I, can progress without knowing what Eve wants and therefore what we are both facing.

I am beginning to think I will never be ready for "The Talk", but I also think I have a good chance of getting through it if I am fully female at the time. I am not sure if this will work for Eve, I hope so. Fingers crossed it will work for her too – it *should* take a lot of the emotion out of the conversation on both sides, I think.

Anyway, not a bad day all in.

I am very comfortable right now and have been for hours. I really like myself like this and I like who I am becoming. Julia is a nice person and I like being her very much. I also love being Eve's wife, even if just in spirit. Such a shame it's unlikely to continue...

Friday, May 14th

9:30am, nice lie-in. Time to get up, time to don Adam's face again and once more play the charade for the day. I'm seeing Kay at 11am, it will be good, I am sure. Eve left around 6am, I hope her day is going well.

In the end I decided to be Adam for Kay. Julia doesn't need her I think, Adam, or what's left of him, definitely does. I worry that when I write things like this, I sound like I am schizophrenic, this is not the case at all, but my situation is just so difficult to put into words – I need to differentiate between who I am and who I used to be, and this is the only way I know how.

I am early for my session, parked by her house. I will knock on her door in time and am writing in this journal in the car, with an eye on the clock.

I've mentioned that Kay's home is very unusually decorated, it is obvious which one is hers. The estate is very 'toy town' but has a uniformity about it. Kay's front door is painted sky blue and has a wolf's head door knocker – it stands out a mile surrounded by all this conformity – It's a bold and authentic statement about her and I love it.

Dad texted me about my week, we had a short chat – actually my week hasn't been too bad. Sunday was the last time I was feeling really low, but even then, it was better than it has been. I hope that this is a trend, a sign that things are calming down a bit. Never say never...

We are planning on visiting Eve's folks this weekend. I expect her mum has told her dad by now. Hopefully I am still welcome. Not that I have done anything wrong you understand, but I could never compete with Eve (and wouldn't want to) for their support. They understandably will always put her first, just as my immediate family do with me. Her folks and her sister though are my family too, how could they not be after 15 years?

I don't want to lose them; they are genuinely good people. I would miss them terribly.

10:55am, nervous again. I am about to knock on Kay's door...

It was a good session. Phew! The dialogue has begun, and I have a piece of paper illustrating something called "The Whirlpool of Grief". It sums up my relationship position perfectly. I am going around in circles; this journal is testament to that. I need to accept the loss of our relationship, the loss of Eve's love and then I can get out of the whirlpool and swim to the side to move on.

Fuck, this is hard. I am mourning the loss.

It's the only way forward.

This is my path.

I really don't like it...

The Whirlpool of Grief

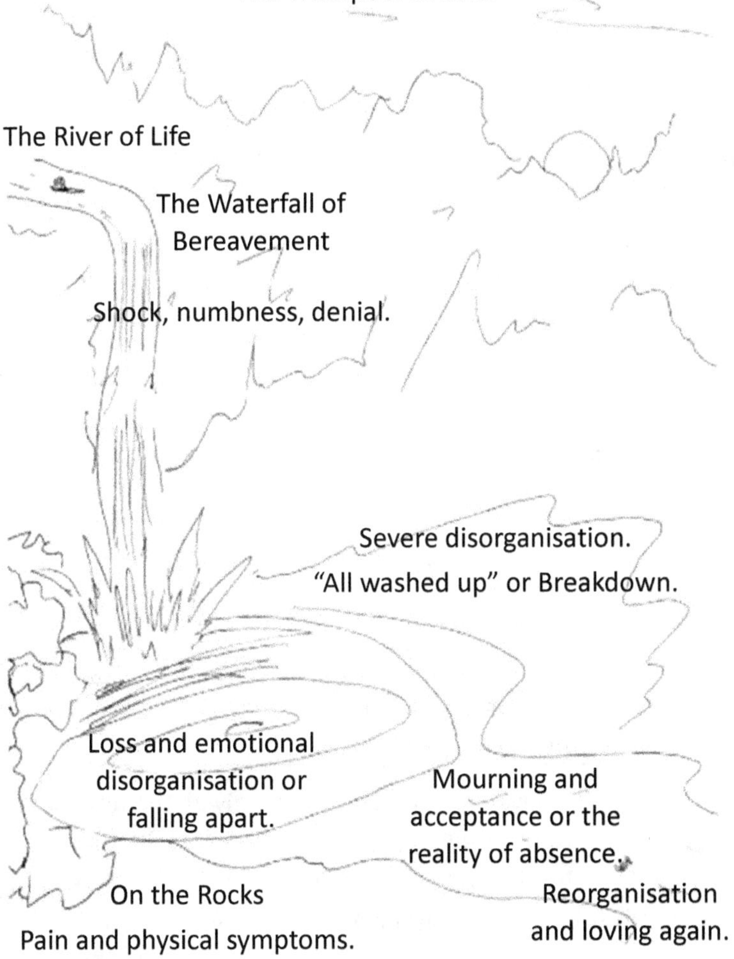

The River of Life

The Waterfall of Bereavement

Shock, numbness, denial.

Severe disorganisation.
"All washed up" or Breakdown.

Loss and emotional disorganisation or falling apart.

Mourning and acceptance or the reality of absence.

On the Rocks
Pain and physical symptoms.

Reorganisation and loving again.

Bereavement is what happens to you / grief is what you feel / mourning is what you do.

Loneliness – Part 1

Kay asked me what I want. We had a chat about who I want to be as well. I think the two are intertwined so one will help resolve the other.

I have begun to think along these lines anyway. Wednesday's journal entry speaks to this and goes into some detail on the subject. But it needs some clarifications, and I am sure there will be new goals and aspirations to work towards.

> Kay asked me what I **don't** want too. I don't want to be alone, more specifically, I don't want to be lonely.

I am lonely.

I still live with Eve, but I am more alone now than I have ever been. Every step she takes away from me makes it worse. And I desperately fear the day she moves out, for I shall truly be alone.

I think this is now an inevitability. I think Eve will become more and more independent, until she moves out.

> I need to structure my life such that **when** it happens, I am not lonely. Friends, family, activities, doing things for myself will help.

I think I can live alone and not be lonely all the time. Some of the time I think is inescapable at this point. But I can take responsibility for my own happiness and make it happen.

I also think that, whether Adam returns or not, I will be a much more complete person after, at some point in the future when this turmoil is behind me. I hope to be a person with a better balance between my opposite gendered body and mind. I hope that being a more balanced and complete person and by putting myself out there, well, there just may be a chance of someone else for me. Who knows? It happened once before

when I was least expecting it, can lightning really strike twice? But I won't find them by shutting myself away that's for certain. And I may well have some fun along the way.

I think I am going to be alright.

I think I am going to be lonely too. But not all of the time.

I just need to swim out of this damned whirlpool...

Sunday, May 15th

Morning World. Mourning World.

I am feeling like "The Talk" may happen this weekend. Scared? Absolutely, I'm terrified.

Adam lived to be Eve's boyfriend – this was his purpose in life. To have any chance of returning, he needs a new purpose, or series of purposes. Something to live *for*. That something should be himself. If he lives for himself, no one can ever hurt him like this again.

- I need to take control of the Joint Account

I control the money going into it and can turn off the taps if I want. But I don't have access to the joint account, therefore I don't control the money leaving it. I need to know just what I am paying for. If Eve leaves me, I need to be able to continue to pay the bills, ideally from my own account, not a joint one. This will take some time to alter, but I can't do it without access. And Eve controls the access.

Plan for the worst, hope for the best, as they say. Sorting out the joint account also gives Eve the option to leave if/when she wants. Our day-to-day finances will be separated. But it also stops her contributing directly to the household bills. She could set up a standing order to me I suppose... That would be fair.

Time. This is all going to take time. And it's going to be very unpleasant, I can feel it. Eve has lost her safety net and is now expected to contribute more. This is going to hurt us both.

But it is potentially a project for Adam? Something he can do for himself. A reason to live, a purpose. Taking back his life. Assuming he is still there to do so...

How long am I prepared to keep supporting Eve?

I really don't know.

I suppose it will carry on until I stop loving her. The truth is that this is an indeterminate period of time.

To some extent, Eve controls this. If she continues shutting me out, which I am sure she will, causing me pain, then this process will accelerate. But equally, she runs the risk of losing our friendship if she moves too fast.

I don't want to lose her completely.

She is my very best friend and I suppose, my sister. I don't want to lose this too. But she can't take the piss out of me. Without her love, she needs to contribute in other, more tangible ways.

> Nobody rides for free.

Fuck. I hate this.

I want to continue to pay for her. I like it. It makes me feel good to treat her. Love again. Shit.

It is in my benefit to carry on supporting her until she is capable of supporting herself. I think this will be a gradual process, she is not in this position yet. But she has commitments and responsibilities, both legally and morally.

> I will continue to help, but she needs to step up.

Example: We are going to see her folks today. Eve's car can get there, but without a charging point at her parent's house, cannot get back. So, we are going in my car. I will pay for the fuel. I am benefitting too, but I am supporting her. QED.

She needs to organise a charging point at her folk's place. This is fair.

It is also in her interest to do so. It means she can visit her parents any time she wants, without relying on me.

- Why should I pay her bills if we are no longer a couple?
- I pay them because they **have** to be paid.

    This is not fair.

    Without her love for me, this **has** to change.

NOBODY RIDES FOR FREE

    Fuck. This is going to hurt.

Eve went to the horses; I got up and got ready for her return and our drive up to her folk's place. When she arrived home, we set off on the 2-hour drive. I confess I am feeling a bit raw today, but I managed to contain myself. I tried really hard not to snap at her and pretty much succeeded, only rising to the bait when she brought up my backseat driving again. It was uncalled for, especially as I was actually doing the driving today and more importantly, I haven't done this since she broke my heart. I said, "I don't do that anymore". She was surprised (she hadn't noticed) and asked why? And I blurted out, "Because I just don't give a fuck". Sadly, it's true. I don't. If she crashes the car now, I don't care if I am injured or worse. And I am finding it increasingly hard to care about her to the same extent I used to. My trying to help from the passenger seat was never a critique of her driving, she is an excellent driver and I feel perfectly safe with her behind the wheel. It was always about being part of the team, looking out for each other and 2 pairs of eyes with double the driving experience is a genuinely worthwhile thing to have. I couldn't help myself; I was never over the top with it, not like the stereotype "backseat driver" pointing out anything and everything, but I was engaged in the journey and cared about her and her wellbeing – if I had spotted a hazard that she hadn't and we ended up in an accident because I didn't say anything, well, I would never have forgiven myself. Some of this

is to do with our different driving styles. I used to drive like she does, confident and reliant on her reactions. I am older and (a little) slower than I was, I am also wise enough to realise my reactions are no longer to be relied upon. So, I try very hard not to put myself in hazardous situations if I can help it. I signal and manoeuvre way in advance, I am always trying to keep out of blind spots, and I look for openings ahead of when I need them before making use of them as they arrive. Eve drives like my brother, and actually, like my 70-year-old dad too (he scares the shit out of me when he drives) – they all signal first, then make a space. They drive close to the car in front and rely on their reactions to get them out of trouble and they take no prisoners. This is fine when you are young. I've had too many near misses and actual accidents to drive this way anymore. So, I try to help, and it is very much *not* appreciated. She takes it as a personal affront to her driving ability – which is bizarre, considering I was perfectly happy to sit in the passenger seat of her car whilst she drove the Alpine passes, the Stelvio, Autobahns and even the Nurburgring. She knows for a fact I have confidence in her skills behind the wheel, I'm just trying to help because I care. <u>*I don't care to this extent anymore*</u>. Fact is, she has hurt me, the one person in the world she is *not* supposed to hurt. The person that loves her, is her teammate and who completely trusts her never to hurt them. She hurt me. This was actually the very first change in our relationship from my side, it happened almost immediately after she broke me. And she didn't even notice. This stung – I spoke from my pain instead of from my rational side.

And I immediately regretted it.

There was a silence, I composed myself. I think Eve was shocked to be honest – outside of this journal, I don't swear. I think it crass, and actually, not very ladylike. I'm so strange, just writing this down makes me think this is weird. But it's true, I'm

never offended by others who swear; indeed, it can be funny, just a natural part of some folk's speech patterns, or most often, just to make a point. I've always been a "nice guy" – I've said it before in these pages. Swearing is unnecessary for me and actually distasteful. But if you kick a dog, it'll bite you. I calmed down, but the floodgates were now wide open. Time for "The Talk" ...

We began to talk about financials. I think Eve is beginning to realise just how much she has lost. She needs to have the rust sorted on her sportscar but can't afford it. She hasn't been able to afford it for a couple of years now. Before, I would have gladly paid. Especially as it will only get worse, even more expensive to fix and will eventually kill the car if it is not attended to before it goes much further. I actually offered to pay over a year ago. She didn't accept and now it is becoming a priority. She is stuck.

I said that no one will lend her the money. She has no fixed income and no employment record. She agreed and I could see her face fall as the realisation began to hit home. I then said that before, I would have gladly paid, but the situation has changed. I am still happy to help, but I would need it paid back. Eve said she would try her mum and dad, apparently, they have loaned money to her sister over the past couple of years until she got a job. I said that sadly, I am now the last resort. But if other options don't pan out, I can help. I know she will be good for it in the long run. But I can see her damned pride getting in the way. I don't think she wants anything from me anymore. I truly don't. This makes me very sad. But I think it's for the best. This is her bed to lie in. And I will help if she needs it. The door is still open, she only has to ask...

We then spoke about money in general. She is very, very skint at the moment. It hurts me to see her struggling and coming face-to-face with the reality of her erratic finances. Again, her bed.

Pride is such a bag of shit. I swallowed mine to go and see Kay. It was bloody hard, but I don't think she has the fortitude to swallow hers. I admire her resolve, but she is just not ready to take on her full responsibilities. She just isn't. So, I took the pressure off (I used to be a nice guy remember, now I'm a nice girl). I probably shouldn't have done so; I probably should have pressed my advantage. But I just can't hurt her, intentionally or otherwise. Instead, I said that I needed her to step up and begin to pay at least some of her way. But it doesn't have to happen now, or even in the short term. But it does need to happen. I also said that I had noticed her already trying to pay more and it was very much appreciated. Lastly, I said we should begin to untangle our finances. She seems to think this is going to be simple. She said it is mainly the joint account. She hasn't considered the house, or the mortgage. I think there is a lot more to it...

But it is good that we have begun to talk about these things, a dialogue has opened up and despite not being dressed comfortably, with the exception of my initial outburst, it was rational and fair.

I just wish it didn't have to happen at all.

I want so much for her finances to improve. I want her to pay her way – it'll be good for us both and actually, should have been happening for most of our time together anyway. But I can't see it happening anytime soon – she will never sell her soul to a 9-5 job I am sure of it, so I will continue to shoulder the load until she can begin to help out.

Look at what I have written. Shit. I still love her – it's bleedin' obvious. Any normal person would have made her go out and get a regular job to pay her way. Not me, what a flipping idiot I am. I've given her an open-ended window of time to continue shirking her responsibilities at my expense and even offered to lend her the money to get the rust sorted out on her car.

I'm fucking stupid.

- I still love her -

I think the next time she hurts me it's likely to be financial. The potential is there, and I am vulnerable, I think. I am too nice. This is one of my very best qualities, but I think she may well exploit this. Intentionally or otherwise. I am likely to lose out here if I am not careful. I still **want** to support her. It **hurts** me to see her struggling. I **want** us to stay as a team. This is very hard.

We arrived at her parent's home early afternoon and had a very pleasant day with them. Our situation was not brought up. But I am already beginning to feel like a 5th wheel. It's nothing they have done; this is all on me. I am feeling less at home here and I really don't like it at all. I love them, they are my family. And I see the way Eve lights up when she is with them, I also see that she doesn't when she is with me anymore. I really miss it.

So, although today has been a good day. I am feeling sad now. Alone in my room with Eve only next door, writing in my journal before bed.

She is genuinely happy here. She is not happy with me. I have failed her utterly. She is not happy at home.

We used to be.

I miss it so much.

Sunday, May 16th

Awake from 5:30am, I didn't sleep well. I couldn't find my usual ambient raindrops playlist on Spotify, so ended up with one that was more dramatic, and the thunderclaps were a bit jarring.

Loneliness – Part 2

- I feel vulnerable when I am alone. It's a primal thing, I think. I could have a fall / accident / illness, and no one would know – I could die in a stupid way and not have any help.

This is unlikely, at least not until I am much older anyway. But it scares me, and I don't think it's too irrational a fear.

- Social interaction. I miss chatting with Eve about the mundane stuff, the important stuff too, but the everyday hellos and goodbyes, making her a cup of tea, just generally taking care of each other, and sharing time together. Not just being in the same room at the same time. I **hate** being shut out. It's painful. All these little moments are important and meaningful – I really miss them and they are not replicable by friends.

- Human contact. Physical and mental. I loved sharing a bed. Yes, there are disadvantages but physical closeness / proximity, being with each other when we are both sleeping / vulnerable (a primal thing again), sharing warmth when we are cold, listening and sharing our hopes, fears and aspirations, pillow talk. It's so special and I miss it all.

- Companionship. Someone to talk to, someone to share my life with and to share in her life. Someone I can rely on no matter what.

Someone special and dear to me.

I don't want to be alone.

                I am alone already.

                              It makes me sad.

An interesting day...

I woke up early and disoriented. Although the room is laid out the same as my one at home, window on the right-hand side of the bed, there are mirrored doors on the wardrobe opposite and I woke up looking at the reflection of the window in the mirror. It threw me for a moment, and I struggled to go back to sleep, so I got up and sat downstairs for a bit.

Eve joined me a bit later on, and then her dad.

Once her mum got up, Eve and I made a cooked breakfast for us all – it came out rather well and we all enjoyed it. The sun was out, so we headed into the garden, and that's when all hell broke loose!

Moon, their cat, caught a small rat, ran into the house, and then let it loose in the Living Room. It was a feisty little blighter! We ended up trashing the entire room trying to catch it. It took over an hour, but eventually Eve and her mum caught it under a blanket, and we released it at the end of the garden. Before putting the room back together.

We left around 12:30 for the drive back and Eve and I chatted.

It was good, we sorted out some more financial stuff and started talking about the future. I brought up the final "Red Line" and although I was a bit teary, I didn't go to pieces.

Eve does indeed want to travel. She wants to fund it herself though, it's a pride and self-accomplishment thing. I said that she shouldn't let pride get in the way. I am fully supportive of her endeavours to gain money as always and understand her

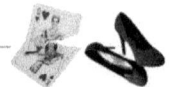

wanting to do this on her own. But, if she needs me, if she runs out of money or has an emergency, she still has her safety net. I don't think she will use it, but pride should never be more important than need. This is the same as me admitting I needed help and going to see Kay. If I can do it, she can. I think she was reassured. I think we can begin to feel out some boundaries now. There are no hard and fast rules, but I think we can begin to see how this might work. I feel like real progress has been made.

Importantly, she has no plans to leave home. She may just be saying this, but she just wants to travel. I said she always could have done this, and indeed her frequent solo trips to Europe are testament to this fact. I even would have paid. She said that is exactly the point. She has to do this for herself. I get it. I also don't get it! Eve said that if the situation was reversed, I still wouldn't understand. She said I would like to be a housewife! And she is right. I would. I would like this very much indeed. We are such an unusual pair. Circumstance has put us in these positions, but I think that if our genders were reversed, we would in all likelihood be the perfect couple. I would dearly love to be her wife. And I think that Eve would love and thrive with the physical strength, financial empowerment and even the responsibility of being the provider. She would flourish in this role I am sure of it. And so would I. I would have happily become a stay-at-home mother to our kids. I think, if our genders were switched, she might've liked being a dad, so long as I had all the female stuff to deal with.

Life has played a twisted trick on us both I think. And neither of us are likely to reach our full potential as a result. But we try. What else can we do?

Eve of course, is categorically **not** trans, she is happy and comfortable being female. But she is not a traditionalist in any shape or form. She battles against all of the restrictions society

imposes on women. Instead of seeing the advantages, as I do. Not least of which is the burden and physical damage that comes with motherhood. A traditional wife's role is poisonous to her, in every way it seems, even the 'girlfriend' part. But this doesn't make her unhappy as a female, far from it, she sees injustice and rails against it where I see love and comfort, and I long to fill this role.

I am really weird. I would genuinely love to be a girlfriend, wife, mother and especially a bride. I strongly suspect these are things that are forever denied to me, maybe, when this is all over, I will buy myself a wedding dress? It's the closest I'll get I think, to achieving any of the above.

Everything that Eve despises!

I once said to Eve that she didn't need to worry. I would happily wear the skirts in this relationship, so she doesn't. And you know? She hates wearing a skirt. She only does it if she has no choice or is getting paid to do so as a costume. She feels uncomfortable in one. I am the **exact** opposite!

We got home safely; I measured up the deck at the back of the garden so I can begin to start renewing it. We had an early dinner and then settled in to watch a film (Bill and Ted's Excellent Adventure again) and a little YouTube before bedtime.

It's been a very good day. The best in a very long time. We were both happy today.

Progress has been made.

And I was female from around 4pm.

Monday, May 17th

I am OK today. I had a nice sleep <u>fully</u> clothed – it just felt right and my underwires didn't dig into me in the night, so no sore boobs this morning. I showered yesterday evening, so I am still in my bra, skirt, and now heels (the 'trinity') – I am very comfortable. Given the way our conversation has been going, I am wondering if Kay will ask to see me appropriately dressed. It is a possibility I suppose. Logistically it will be difficult to achieve. It's been decades since I have gone outside fully dressed in broad daylight – I have had a couple of excursions, not hugely successful, but in the company of friends in the know, way back in my early '20's when I was coming to terms with my need to be female. Going out in broad daylight will be a very big deal. I am hairy, huge and the wrong shape. I shouldn't, but I care about not fitting in.

I have also begun to think about my gender journey, specifically where I have been on the gender scale. And I truly believe it is a scale, we are all on it somewhere, it's just that some of us are in the middle, body and mind, some of us are at one end, or the other completely and some of us are at opposite ends – the further our bodies and minds diverge, the more trans we are. Hey, it's just a theory, OK? I'm not a professional, just extrapolating from my own situation after 50 years' experience. Take it all with a pinch of salt...

I was born, with both my body and mind close to the middle, maybe with just my mind some ways into the female side. At least I knew I wasn't a "boy" from around the age of 4 or 5. Pretty much for as long as I can remember. But I don't think I was too far away from centre – I was stable if you know what I mean?

Puberty came along, and I was in complete turmoil – every day my body moved further away from my mind and the

changes were permanent, irreversible, and hugely damaging to me. I cannot express how distressing this was for me, I am not ashamed to admit that I was in a complete panic for most of it, and when I eventually, in my early 20's faced up to the reality of my situation, not only had the damage been done, but I couldn't handle the image staring back from the mirror and went out to take my own life. I was faced with a transwoman's ultimate nightmare – a body so male there was little to no hope of a successful transition, a completely non-supportive family, and the prospect of spending my entire life trapped in the hulking great body of a man. I accepted my fate in the end. I decided to make the best life I could with the horrid cards I had been dealt. I would try to be true to myself, but I would accept the role society had laid before me. It would be hard work, but I would show the world Adam's face because that is all that the world will accept from me.

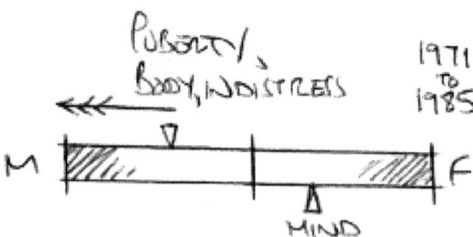

For a while, this worked, my dysphoria was still ever present though and by the time I was in my early 30's my female nature was exerting herself more and more. I think that I was ready to start my transition then, baby steps, but important steps in the right direction.

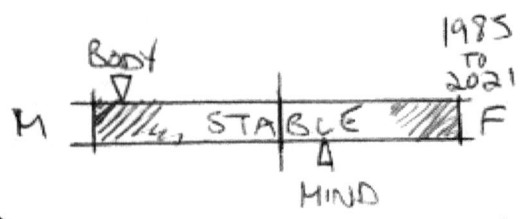

This changed when I met Eve — My decision to present as a man was a conscious one and I truly became that man for the sake of our relationship — I became the man Eve needed me to be, I embodied the face I had shown the world and the face Eve had fallen in love with. Instead of embracing my female side, I managed it, I fitted it into our lives together to allow me to function. It wasn't perfect, but it worked. Well, I was more or less stable for 15 years anyway. And most importantly, we were both happy. It was a poor bargain, but it was worth it. Love and happiness always are, in my limited experience.

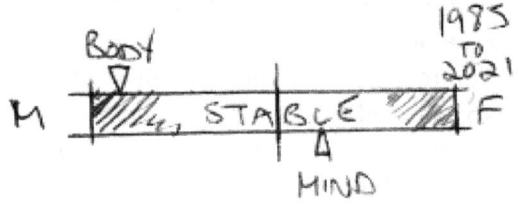

And then Eve broke my heart, the loss of her love literally destroyed the male construct I had built, my mind escaped into the only safe place it had left, the feminine side of my nature. I was always this side of the divide, but I was forced to inhabit this part of me fully for the first time in my life. It was a traumatic experience, one that I **never** want to go through again. And there was no way back, everything behind me was murdered, the broken mess of a fake life...

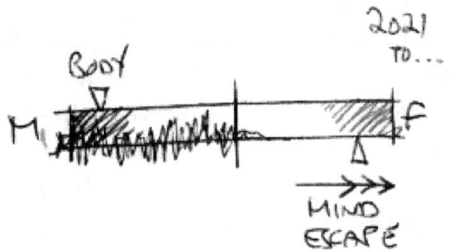

The further the two poles move away from each other, the harder my gender issues are to deal with, and any movement of the poles causes me unimaginable distress. It's no wonder this seismic event brought me to the very brink again. It was a violation, a very real destruction of a significant part of who I am. And it left me with the twin poles of my body and mind diametrically opposed at either end of the scale. My dysphoria went through the roof, I have never felt this awkward in my skin, I've never felt this 'wrong' on so many fundamental levels and I've never felt my body so far away from the person I truly am.

I am trying to find a way to rebuild the male side of my nature, but moving the poles requires a traumatic event I think, something that is literally life threatening, something that brings me to the brink of throwing in the towel on life. Puberty did it once, a dramatic, irreparable, and physical event that was tantamount to a rape of my mind. I was powerless and helpless, screaming as my body was hormonally assaulted leaving irreversible physical damage & mental scars.

Heartbreak and the removal of my entire purpose in life did it again. I have never felt this much pain, the term emasculation doesn't even come close to describing what I went through. I wasn't just emasculated, I kinda like being emasculated, my male side was eviscerated out of existence. How can I move the poles together if this is what it takes to do it? It is not a tangible thing either, there is nothing I can do to undo the damage caused. My body is stuck looking like a huge man and my mind is not only completely female but craves to be even more so. My healing process is about not feeling in so much pain primarily and I achieve this by expressing myself as who I actually am – it's the only way I can be comfortable, to physically be closer to where my mind is. And my mind's gender position is growing stronger over here as I continue to embrace who I truly am. Dysphoria is my ever present and hugely unwelcome companion though – whatever I do is never enough for that spiteful bitch...

I am exploring who I am now, as a female fully in mind. This is new to me, an unprecedented shift and equally, an unprecedented opportunity. It is fascinating to me, rewarding and it gives me some self-worth back. I like it, I like who I am, and I am driven to want more.

I am thinking of doing something, anything with my body to try to move the poles closer together. Electrolysis on my beard would be amazing, I loathe my body hair, all of it, but my beard in particular. I have bought a batch of female hormones too, oestrogen this time, no progesterone. It came through an official channel by me lying on a form, I declared I am female, which is true, although not officially, and I said I was going through the menopause, which is also kinda true, at least I'm suffering from a lack of female hormones and the hormonal imbalance has done a lot of damage to my body, seriously affecting my quality of life – I feel terrible about this, but I really don't want to delve into the dark web – what I end up with could be anything at all. Equally I can't do this supervised under a GP, no GP will sign off on HRT for someone who physically will never be able to live fully in the world as the woman she actually is. I can't see me ever being able to pass the "live for 2 years in your true gender" test, I know this, it is the tragedy of my life, and it is blatantly obvious to anyone who looks at me. I can jump through the psychiatric hurdles no problem at all, I AM a woman, so it shouldn't be an issue. Furthermore, I have ALWAYS been a woman, from the earliest point I can remember, I am supremely happy to live as a woman and I like who am a great deal. But it has brought me to the point of suicide twice in my life. That is more than enough to justify a full transition. But physically I am just not suitable. So, no GP will sign off on irreversible hormone treatments I am sure, I need to do this on my own, I want them so badly, I have to deal with at least some of the damage puberty did to my body, even if I end up

looking a bit odd. It will be worth it. But at the moment, I can't exaggerate my mood swings, I am emotional enough already and enhancing my moods will be counterproductive. So, when they arrive, I, in all likelihood, will not take them for a while. Furthermore, a repeat prescription is unlikely to happen as the source wants me to back up my 'existence' officially with medical records etc, something I just can't do. Maybe I'll treat myself to a beauty parlour session too? I would love a full make-over, a day of pampering as a woman. That would be amazing. Again, later in the year, I think.

It's fun to think along these lines, more fun than dealing with my current circumstance anyway – a very welcome distraction.

Off to work as normal. I am progressing through my heap of drawings to do and am up to date as far as I can be at this stage. I picked up a couple of my colleagues' surveys to draw too. I will finish them off tomorrow.

Home around 6pm, a nice early evening with Eve watching YouTube. Then dinner and me getting changed around 7:30pm. 12½ hours in a skirt today. If this is to be my life, I like it a lot. I am wearing my red and white summer dress, white bra and matching knickers, tights, and white heels. Apart from body hair, I look OK, I guess. This is one of only 2 dresses I own that zip up the back – I adore a back zip, it is so alien to a male sensibility, so exclusively feminine. Yesterday I wore suspenders, bra, skirt, and blouse as part of my outfit. **All** of these garments fastened behind my back – I love it! I love the uncluttered lines on my front, I like that they require dexterity and learned skills/techniques to fasten these items proficiently. A man would really struggle to put them on or take them off. I don't, therefore

I <u>must</u> be a woman, right? Well, the ludicrous logic works for me at least, if maybe not in the real world. Any kind of validation, even one built on such a shaky premise, makes me feel good about myself.

The same logic applies to make-up and all sorts of the uniquely feminine skills needed to build a successful female outfit. It's an artform, one that is completely lost on 50% of the population and even though I am entirely self-taught, I feel like I have a small insight, an appreciation, a peek behind the curtain, of what it means to live as a woman and the time, effort and skills needed to just exist in this world as such. Let alone be proficient, or even good at it. I look at some of the beautiful women around me and see the work they put in. No man has this kind of appreciation, furthermore, I do not judge them by their appearance, I just marvel awestruck – I am not competition for them, unlike other women, so there is no judgement here, I don't do the stereotypical 'look them up and down' thing, but I do see the artistry and have a real appreciation for what it takes to look this good as I fail to get even close, pretty much all of the time. Beautiful people, I aspire to look even half as nice.

All in all, a good day, I think. I am looking forward to tomorrow. It's been a very long time since I have thought this. Tomorrow is nothing special, just a typical workday, but I am hopeful it will be another <u>good</u> day.

I feel like I have turned a corner and hope that things are improving.

I think I am feeling good about myself at last. I am Julia, but Julia is a nice person to be.

And I hope that Adam is coming back, little-by-little. I have faith that someday, balance will be achieved. And if I am still Julia, but have a semblance of balance, so-be-it, this will be a good way to live. Not perfect, but good enough.

Tuesday, May 18th

So far, so good – I am OK again today.

It is in no way a substitute for waking up next to Eve, I do miss her dreadfully in the mornings, but waking up as a woman every day is nice. I feel privileged to be able to do so. Sure, I have slept in a nightie since I was 18, wow, 32 years... So, waking up in a satin dress is nothing new, I am very used to it, it is the norm for me. But this is different. It's not just the nightie (sometimes it is a LOT more), typically I am wearing earrings, make-up (you should see my pillows some mornings, sheesh, the endless washing...) perfume and underwear too. But again, although lovely, this is not the whole experience.

In the past, if I had fallen asleep fully clothed, I would wake up with a start and there would be a moment of confusion, almost shock at the realisation I am fully dressed as a woman. This would then be replaced by a memory of the previous night, comfort, and grateful acceptance of the situation. It was an interesting way to wake up, but a bit jarring.

Now, these clothes are normal, everyday clothes to me. They've always felt 'right' and more importantly, I feel 'right' wearing them, but never more so than now. I actually **choose** to sleep fully clothed on occasions. To the extent I'll remove my shoes and switch my pendant earrings for hoops. I prepare for sleep in the outfit I am wearing, the clothes never leave the house so are always clean. And when I wake, it is not jarring in any way anymore. It just feels nice and comfortable. Because I am not waking up as Adam, dressed as a woman. I am waking up as Julia, dressed correctly, all-be-it inappropriately for bed. So, it feels nice, not shocking, just 'right'.

So, when I say "waking up as a woman every day is nice" I literally mean I am a woman when I wake up, regardless of how I am dressed. If I slept in men's PJs (not that I own any), it would

be just as jarring for me to wake up in them I am certain. I would have the exact same moment of confusion, then memory, but absolutely no feeling of comfort or acceptance – just as any man waking up in a nightie would instinctively react by taking it off, I would be the same with the PJs, I am sure.

This is new.

I have always been divided, a woman inside a man's body, but my female side was reasonably close to the middle, as most folks are, we all have a male and female side to our natures, and I learned to cope with it. But now my female side and my male side are poles apart – opposing ends, "I" am actually a woman in mind, completely, and I've never felt so trapped inside this horrid man's body.

I *chose* to live my life as a man and express my female nature in a limited manner. This worked well enough when I was close to the middle. I loved who I was and the life I had built.

Eve took this option away from me.

I was living this way before Eve, and I was, in little ways, beginning to explore my female side more at the point Eve came into my life.

I *chose* to embody the man I look like and box my female nature in, for Eve and to be able to build as close to a so-called 'normal' life for us both. It was a conscious decision, to be the man she wanted and needed in exchange for her love.

It wasn't a great deal, but it was completely worth it. I would do it again in a heartbeat if I could.

But I can't.

Not anymore.

Eve no longer loves me.

The man I chose to become, no longer has a purpose, or a reason to be. He's heart was broken, and he went through

more pain than I ever thought was humanly possible. He was only a construct after all, and he didn't survive the turmoil. The whirlpool of grief? Adam drowned at the bottom of it.

In my mind, subconsciously, I only had one place to go. A place of safety, of refuge. A place where Eve is not the very foundation of who I am. An unexplored place, full of wonder, beauty, and mystery.

Julia

I have said it before, but Julia saved my life. Quite literally. Without this cosy bolt hole, this safe haven where I am a step away from the pain and loss. A wonderful distraction from my horrible situation. I would have been forced to face it all head on, all the time and it was overwhelming. I would have drowned in my own tears.

…and I came close. So very, very close…

I crossed a fuzzy line in my head, I fled from the agony into a new, welcoming, and unexplored headspace and I felt calm, rational, and most importantly, relief. But I found I couldn't go back. There wasn't anything left other than pain to go back to.

My male side is horribly damaged, and although I hope healing, this experience has had a permanent and catastrophic effect. I am no longer able to choose to embody the male form I am forced to live in. I can re-cross the fuzzy line in my head to play the part, it is very hard work as it's hugely painful and is no longer me – the effort shows sometimes. But I can't stay over there - it's simply not who I am.

I am a female in a male body. I express myself as a male to try to achieve balance and to facilitate my life in the most effective manner. But I **have** to express myself truly and as authentically as I can as a female much more than I used to – this is who I now am.

My time spent in each guise is very much 50:50 these days, indeed I strive to maximise my time in a skirt. My female expression is as full and as total as my life allows at this time. It is not just 8 hours sleeping in a nightie as it used to be, yes, time spent, but not any kind of real quality – I was asleep. It is the whole evening, fully clothed and ***living*** as a woman. An important distinction, as authentic to who I am as I can be.

And I like it. I like it a **lot.**

For the first time in my life, I feel like I am truly living as me. I am a bit too female sometimes, every now and again I get a fleeting moment where I am not quite comfortable and I wonder if this is Adam trying to come back, this is typically immediately after I have spent too much time looking through his eyes. There is occasionally a split second of resistance to me emerging. I need this to improve as there are times when I need to spend extended periods in his skin. On holiday for instance, or if I have to go on a trip for work. Or if I have to do something in the evening that requires me to leave the house. I need to be able to do these things without becoming more and more agitated or uncomfortable, but ultimately, the longer I have to pretend to be him, the harder it is to maintain. When I can do so again without too much stress, I think I will be happy with myself once more – balance will have been achieved. It is a <u>really</u> hard thing to do, even though after 50 years, I am extremely proficient at hiding behind his face, it is exhausting. But I am working on it.

In the meantime, I really like being Julia. I like everything about her. I want more, but there are limits to how far I can go. I am under no illusions as to my ability to pass as a woman in public. This will never happen fully, as much as I would like it to. I would love to be able to just walk out my front door as Julia and actually exist in in the world for real. This is not too much to ask surely? Half the world's population do this all the time without

even giving it a thought. Puberty did a right number on me; you can see why it was such a traumatic experience. I am big. Not just big for a woman, but big for a man. In practically EVERY room, I am typically the biggest person there. Out of context I look OK, not perfect, but OK. In a space with other people, I am middle to the top end the scale for a man, but off the chart for a woman – if I were to dress as myself, immediately my size would call into question my gender and that's before people look at me in more detail. The detail I can work on, but I will always be this size – I have a physique that most men would love, 6'-2" tall and very broad shoulders – to give you some idea, my bra chest band measurement is between a 48 and 50. I'm amazed I can even get a bra this big (but am so glad they exist, they are really hard to find though and I want them to be pretty, they rarely are). This is my curse, as Julia. But it is an advantage as Adam. So, my life has always, necessarily been about making the best of my assets. For Adam, being big is indeed an asset. I <u>must</u> function in the world as Adam, regardless of how female I actually am inside.

I am certain I can do this. I am not yet there, Adam's skin still feels incredibly uncomfortable, unbearably so at times - dysphoria is a constant and hugely unwelcome companion – I suppose, given what I have been through, his skin will never fit me, and I will always be dysphoric in his shoes from now on. But although I feel my dysphoria much more than I ever used to, it is less upsetting than it has been. I am happier in his shoes than I was even a fortnight ago. So some progress has been made. Furthermore, I am enjoying my time as Julia more and more.

Wednesday, May 19th

I am OK again today. My brother's birthday, so I sent him a text. Must get him a card and a bottle today. Eve was out the door at 6:40am, she has a day shooting 'Call the Midwife' today and the set is directly opposite us on the other side of the M25.

Me? Well, my colleague is picking me up at 7:30am (so I only have half an hour to write this) and we have three check surveys to do and a meeting in Milton Keynes. I am prepared though, I also have the transit file in my bag for tomorrow's site meeting, so all is good.

After writing so much about it yesterday, I decided to sleep fully clothed last night. Bra, knickers, stockings, suspenders, slip, skirt, blouse, earrings, make-up – the lot. Glasses and heels were the only things to be removed. Everything else stayed. All night. It was cosy, everything fits so well, and it was lovely to wake up feeling all was right in the world. Even if just for a moment.

I worry about the amount of baths Eve is taking. It's relaxing for her, I get it. But she has all day on her own and we have a limited amount of time together in the evenings. An hour of which, she chooses to spend away from me in the tub. Typically, it coincides with me getting changed, so paranoia (again) suggests that despite her protestations to the contrary, she is not comfortable with me as Julia. I am sure it is nothing. Just routine and a nice way for her to relax. In much the same way getting changed does for me. But paranoia is something I am contending with, likely because I didn't see my current situation happening, even though Eve's falling out of love with me must have been going on for years. So, I am jumping at shadows, over-thinking everything and trying to find hidden meanings and possible agendas everywhere. It's exhausting.

A very long day, 3 surveys and an extra-long meeting, plus 2 hours driving each way. Eve's day was longer still. I have spent

11½ hours today in a skirt, it was the best I could do, and it was very welcome.

10pm, time for bed, yawn...

Thursday, May 20th

I am alright, again. I like not being miserable, it really isn't me, and it wasn't Adam either. Long may my better mood continue.

Regular Thursday site meeting again today, it should be alright I think. I will try to cross off some more snags too. Hopefully I will be home early-ish too – just as well, I am tired today, not sure why, I slept really well, but it was a long day yesterday, maybe it is catching up to me today? Regardless, I still woke up tired and could've done with a little more time asleep.

I have tomorrow booked off work. No Kay though, she is on holiday. I do have a massage booked for first thing in the morning (I'm really looking forward to it, doing something for myself, you know?) Then at 3pm I have an appointment with a local financial advisor to discuss my Will. This is going to be difficult I think and maybe expensive too. Then in the evening I am going to see dad, we are going for a meal locally – a lovely way to both end the day and start the weekend.

I was finished on site around 1:30pm, I diverted and stopped for lunch for an hour at the Gridserve Electric Forecourt, it's a nice place, even if, like me, you don't have an electric car, and was home just after 3pm. Around 6pm I headed over to give my brother his birthday presents and after dinner, dressed comfortably for the evening. Close to 14 hours in a skirt today. A long, pink one, twinned with a blue blouse, tights, white heels, minimal make-up and a matching powder blue satin and lace bralette and knicker set. Very comfortable indeed.

Going to have an early night tonight and will sleep in a nightie rather than a full outfit of day clothes – let's face it I am weird enough without sleeping in a day outfit – still, the amount of folks I see in the supermarket in their PJs... I am tired, and have been all day, so an early night is called for, I think.

Eve is relaxing in the bath, she has a night shoot tomorrow, so I am not sure how she is going to prepare her body-clock for working so late. Lots of tea I imagine! She also booked her first Covid vaccine tonight. I am pleased and proud of her, she is phobic of needles, so this is a big thing for her.

Off to bed now, I need sleep and an interesting day awaits me tomorrow…

Friday, May 21st

Awake at my usual time, I am OK again today, but I slept fully clothed after all. I tried to drop off in just my nightie, but I ended up getting changed around midnight and fell asleep straight away – I am sooo weird.

I am about to head out for my massage and am really looking forward to it. I am not sure what I am going to say to her if she asks about Eve, we have both been to see her in the past and she knows we are, or should I say, were, an item. I suspect she is likely to, but although having a massage is a bit intimate (not in *that* way, she's a professional and I just wouldn't, ever). I don't think it would be good to tell her. Not least of which because I am there to relax, not get stressed out and of course, I will look like Adam, so my emotions will be less manageable. So, I think I am going to chat, make small talk and be polite, but not go into it. I am showered, ready and just relaxing a little, writing in this journal before getting up and heading over to her.

The massage was absolutely lovely, just what the doctor ordered and so very relaxing. Nice to see her again, we chatted for a bit, as expected, small talk, nothing too personal or raw. Then 45 minutes of pummelling – my back feels great. But I'm sleepy now and It's blowing a gale outside too, I'm feeling cold. I have a little time before an appointment later, might snooze for a bit...

My meeting with the financial chap was a little disappointing. I went there with one thing I needed to resolve, my Will. But the chap said he needed to take advice, so this wasn't done straight away and instead I got a sales pitch on their other services. It wasn't unpleasant, over the top, or very high pressure, but I came away thinking I may well have wasted my time.

I came home to an empty house. Eve had left for her night shoot. I watched a (poor) zombie film on Netflix and then headed over to see dad.

Dinner was lovely, but huge! I didn't finish my ice cream (this is a first). After dinner we headed back to his place and chatted. He got a bit teary, and we "bonded" some more.

Home after, then an early-ish night (10pm), in my nightie and snuggled in bed. Not enough time in a skirt today, I can feel it. I may need some extra time tomorrow if I can.

Eve come home around 4:30am, I am unlikely to see her until circa mid-day, I think. She will be wiped out.

Saturday, May 22nd

OK again – I like this.

Lay in 'till 10am, Eve was sound asleep next door. I woke her with a cup of tea and then we headed off to a car meet, in her daily driver this time, not her sports car. It was held at the Gridserve Electric Forecourt around mid-day. A fun hour or so catching up with folks and chatting amongst the cool cars. It felt very much like a sports car natter.

Eve called it a day and we headed home. She then retired for a snooze, so I took myself off for a bit of a drive. I confess to being a bit emotional. I didn't tell Eve where I was going, in truth I didn't know myself. I just walked out the door for a bit. I truly have no idea where our lives are going to next. I felt bad for leaving her, even though the alternative was to potter around the house on my own while she slept. I thought, if I am going to be on my own, then I may as well go and do something at the same time. I got in the car and drove, just for something to do.

Home around 6:30pm, KFC and then I got changed for the evening. 14 hours in a skirt today. Amazing. I feel better.

I'm not sure what tomorrow holds for us? Let's find out, shall we?

Sunday, May 23rd

8:04am, I am OK today, so far at least.

I am not sure how, but I checked my bank balance yesterday and I think I had £1,200.00 in my account when I got paid, suggesting I had a significant excess that could be saved. I transferred £750.00 into one of my savings accounts – I will see how June goes, hopefully I won't need to dip into it.

I am not sure what to do about Eve.

A sweeping statement, but I shall elaborate. Yesterday I went out on my own, for myself, without telling her. I felt bad about doing it, but not as bad as I had expected – the fact is she does this to me *all the time*. I felt like I was being mean to her. But I also felt like it needed to happen.

I don't want to be mean to anyone, it is not in my nature to be so, least of all to Eve. Love or not, she is the most important person in my life. But *I* now need to be the most important person in my life. And that means doing things for me. Not for *us*. So, I think this will continue. And I don't like feeling like I am being mean or selfish, but I think I am going to have to be. It's a horrible feeling. After 15 years plus of being as nice as I could be to her, this is the first time I have intentionally done something contrary to that – it is ingrained in me and I am a nice person anyway, even before I had someone special to be nice too. Doing things for me, being selfish, even if it is necessary now, does not come naturally to me. And I think I am always going to struggle with this somewhat.

I took the car to be cleaned while Eve was at the horses, but when I returned, her sportscar had the hood down. As I reached to put the key in the door, she opened it and was surprised to see me. She said she was going to Colchester and half-heartedly asked me if I wanted to come. I think she thought I had gone out for the day and had made other plans. I said I didn't mind, and

she could go on her own if she wanted. But she insisted I come, and we headed to Colchester. I wish I had stayed at home. I could tell I wasn't welcome, and this hurt. I was quiet, too quiet really, not good company. I felt I was an inconvenience, and she would rather have been on her own, or with anyone other than me actually. Conversation was stilted, she had upset me. If only I had arrived home 5 minutes later... I put on a stoic exterior, but she had effectively ruined my Sunday, just through an accident of timing. She had three phone calls too, each one she isolated herself from me to take. her sister twice, and her mum once, they are my family too? There was no need to do this to me.

None whatsoever.

All it did was drive home, just how unwanted I am.

I feel worthless and although I've had an amazing run of good days, I am upset now. Not crying, but close.

And now, I am alone – she has gone to see her sister for the evening.

And I don't begrudge her the time with her sister. I am happy for her. But I wasn't invited. She made it very clear she was going alone.

I don't recognise her anymore. Who am I living with? Where has my best friend gone?

The Eve I love, would **never** do this to **anyone**, not just me, anyone. And I have done **nothing** to deserve her distain, her condescension, or her cold shoulder.

If anything, the opposite is true.

I have been supportive, understanding and I have tried to be rational and calm. I have not always succeeded, but the effort has been there always, and I am much better than I was.

But at the moment, I am hurt and abandoned – **AGAIN**.

She doesn't want anything from me, least of all my company.

Not even my presence in her life.

I am trying so hard to hold onto something, anything of our life together. The house, our cats, our families, our friends. Anything.

But actively shutting me out of her life is fucking painful.

I have tried so hard to be patient, to roll with the punches and not react out of pain, hurt, anger or frustration. But there are times when it is really hard. This is one of those times.

At the moment, I feel like throwing her stuff out the front door and changing the locks.

There was no respect there today, none at all.

I was unwelcome, and she made me feel it. She made plans without me, it didn't even occur to her to call and let me know. And when I arrived home inconveniently, she felt obliged to ask if I wanted to come. Not because she wanted me there. She genuinely didn't want my company. She felt guilty, it felt like I had caught her out.

It was just so awful.

And now I have (yet another) evening on my own to look forward too.

This **<u>cannot</u>** continue.

If she wants to live in the house that I pay for she needs to appreciate what I do for her and accord me some recognition and respect. And that means:

Not fucking hurting me anymore.

I've put up with so much from her over the past couple of years. Stuff that no one should put up with. And it has ramped up to unbearable levels recently.

I really don't know how much more of this torture I can put up with.

I understand that she is not the person she was. I see that all the time now, and indeed I too am no longer the person I was, ***it's just that this was done to me, <u>by her</u>***. She lets me know she's different in a million different ways and although it is hard for me to witness, it does help me come to terms with my situation.

I understand that she doesn't love me anymore. It is utterly horrible to be in this position. But I also understand that I am not an average human being and recognise that, even though my nature is part of the cause, it is hard for a hetero female to deal with.

But there is no need to keep on hurting me!

None whatsoever!

Why?

Why?

Why?

I haven't done **<u>anything at all</u>** to deserve this treatment from her.

Absolutely Nothing.

I go to work, I come home to see, and be with, my love. She loathes me and can't stand to be in my company.

She is only here because, financially, she can't go anywhere else.

I could live with not having her love. I don't want to, but we could've stayed together as friends, or even sisters.

But if she doesn't want to be in my company, how can we stay together?

We can't.

It's fine for Eve to say that we need to do things for ourselves. She has been doing this for months, at my expense. _Everything I do and have done has been for "us" and for her_.

However, the amount of time we have left together is running out, I hope not, but more and more I am beginning to think it's true. It is **not** fine for her to spend the limited and now very precious time we have left together for herself. _Everything she does and has done has been for herself_.

It's bloody selfish and shows her distain for me.

More importantly, it hurts me.   This is not right.

> My misery is saying: Be Julia, it'll be alright.
> Transition fully and be female, you know you want to, and you are already there completely in your mind.

> My anger is saying: She has hurt you, and hurt you, and will hurt you again and again. Kick her out and sell the house.

Neither of these options are particularly viable.

We are stuck together for the time being at least. I need to make a life for myself, I have taken the very first few, tiny baby steps and I really don't like it, or the way it makes me feel. Eve has already made a life for herself. When I too have a life, we can split. Until then, she **has** to stop hurting me.

Monday, May 24th

Up early, off to Cardiff to do a couple of surveys. Out the door at 6:15am, the plan is to do both surveys, then head into Bristol for an overnight stop. Drive back tomorrow morning and then, depending on time, work the afternoon.

The first site was easy, the second one was huge. But both were done around mid-day (the early start helped), so I decided to drive home and not make use of the hotel. 430 miles today – I am tired.

Nando's delivery for dinner, Eve watched one of her foreign language programmes on her laptop, I re-watched the pilot episode of the X-Files.

Justice League, Snyder Cut 4K arrived today. The Blu-Ray player downstairs didn't like it. Hopefully the one in my bedroom will be OK.

I was back in a skirt around 7pm, not quite 50% today, but now I am correctly dressed, I am OK.

A very long day, I am going to turn in now if that's alright...

ZZZZzzzzzzzzzz...

Tuesday, May 25th

A short entry yesterday, pretty matter of fact and to the point. What I didn't mention is that I have paid for an app on my phone that is supposed to guide me into training my voice to be more feminine. I would **love** to have a feminine voice. My size is (pun intended) a huge issue, as is my shape. I can lose weight and take oestrogen, this will improve things, but there are limits. But ultimately, I will always be this tall and broad in the shoulders. Not much I can do about my skeleton. I am working on my shape; diet, exercise, shapewear, even hormones and blockers are not out of the question. But I'll never be 100%, or rather I will always be physically more masculine than the vast majority of other females. Additionally, I don't think I will ever be completely satisfied because of my size. But there are things I can do. However, my voice is a dead giveaway. It's not really deep, I have quite a wide range, but naturally a deeper register than your average female. It's not over-the-top male, but it **is** a male voice. I would **love** to develop a female voice, something that is mine and fits who I am. My biggest issue is that I have no feedback, the voice you hear inside your head when you speak sounds different to the voice that others hear – it's why if you record your own voice, it never sounds like you, but it does to others. So, all the YouTube tutorials I've watched (loads of them) have explained the principles, the science behind it and the techniques, but without feedback, I just don't know if I am getting anything right or making any progress. So, I am trying something different, an app. I hope it helps; I would adore sounding like I feel.

Going back to my shape, there's lots and lots I can do. Ranging from tiny things to make me feel good, to life-changing extremes that there is no coming back from. There are times when I absolutely want it **all**. And recently, these times are profound, extended and often. But most of them are

not practical. I have to live and operate in the *real world*, so there are, sadly, limits. But that doesn't stop me wanting a full transition, I never wanted a vagina before – I've always despised what is between my legs, for most of my early life, and once I hit puberty, it revolted me, and I couldn't even bring myself to touch it. I use the loo in much the same way as a female (unless I am desperate, this is the *only* (very small) advantage I can see - effectively having a hose pipe that can be directed). But I'd never really considered the alternative seriously. I love how neat everything is on a woman, it looks simple, nice and practical. Nothing to get caught in a zip, nothing to get cheese wired by underwear and nothing to get squashed or worse, sat on. The reality is of course that a woman's vagina is anything but simple though. For me, my appendages are in the way, horrible looking and apart from just not being very pleasant, they're the source of *all* of my gender issues – it's all just wrong in every conceivable way. Fine on someone else, but not me. Still, I never really thought about having a vagina instead – kinda bizarre really given my situation. I was just making the best of the cards I was dealt with I suppose and as I never really considered a full gender reassignment as a practical or achievable outcome for me, there was little point in dwelling on the subject. I've considered cutting it all off, in my darker moments when I was much younger, but thankfully I am squeamish and a bit of a coward when it comes to physical injury. Mangling myself down there is equally as stupid as trying to end it all. And then Eve came along, she appreciated what I have to offer, at least in the early years anyway. We found a way to make the mechanics of it work, although I do have to be in a particular frame of mind (Julia's) to achieve orgasm. It helps that, after taking hormones when I was younger, the breast tissue I have is 100% real, as is the extra sensitivity in them. We found that if I stimulated my breasts and nipples, or better still, Eve did, downstairs would

wake up and we could then be intimate as a relatively normal couple would.

I adore having breasts, any guys reading this, you are really missing out. Especially as without a menstrual cycle, they are nice to have, all the time, no aching or painful breasts at certain times of the month. There really isn't much about being trans I can recommend to anyone, but this is indeed one of the few genuine advantages. Well, this and being able to sing all the parts of a Boney-M song, highs and lows. Anyway, back on topic, despite limits, there are some smaller things I can have fun with:

Toe nails	-	Painted, I love having pretty toes.
Fingernails	-	Will be noticed, special occasions only. I really want a full professional manicure though; I will make it happen one day.
Shaved legs	-	Generally, wintertime only. Although I hate hairy legs in the Summer, so as far as I am concerned, it's a good trade off to shave them and not swim or wear shorts.
Shaved underarms	-	Done, although I hate the 'gravelly' feeling of the stubble under there when it starts to grow back – a good incentive to keep them shaved.
Eyebrows	-	Working on it. May have them waxed to define the shape and then maintain.
Other body hair	-	Too much of it. I hate it all. Waxing makes my skin react, as does shaving too close. Also, need Eve to help with my back. She is unlikely to

	ever help again. Hate stubble too. Would like a **permanent** solution.
Chin / beard	- Absolutely HATE, HATE, HATE. ***Have to have a permanent solution.***
Ears	- Pierced. Love wearing earrings. I may have them pierced again…
Hair	- Long and nice when down. Detest my thinning and receding hair line though. I may have to research this. Really want to visit a hairdresser and have an actual woman's haircut and style. Likely a step too far sadly and hard to achieve with the male pattern baldness insidiously creeping up on me.
Face	- I love make-up, I am wearing it every day, although at non-traditional hours. I love putting it on, developing my skills and adore the way it subtly makes my face look nicer, much more like how I feel and completes my outfit. I will buy a dressing table (I've never had one and would *really* like to). I want to spend time developing different looks, just playing, and having fun. I would love a professional make-over some day. It would be truly amazing.

A spa day sounds like an excellent idea. A full day of feminine treatments is my idea of heaven. I might make this happen. A full make-over, body, face and hair. Amazing.

Beyond this, we start making long-term and permanent changes. I would like it all and in a perfect world I would have already done so. But puberty has mandated that my best shot at a successful life (and this is a very broad term, open to all kinds of interpretations), is to face the world looking like a man. Before, this wasn't an issue – I had made my peace with the damage dealt to me by my hormonal teens, it took me close to 10 years to do so, but I was resigned to this fate. Physically, I **was** a man, so I chose to be so. I inhabited this ill-fitting shell as best as I could, it was more than a task, or a performance, it became who I was, and I was able to cope with it because it wasn't an act and because I was able to express my female side when I was 'off the clock'. But things have changed. My name is Julia. And I am a woman. I think I always was to be brutally honest, managing my female side was a release from the stress of living a dual existence. But this time, there is no choice open to me. I can't inhabit this façade fully anymore. This time, it was **not** my choice, I was left with nowhere else to go but confront who I truly am. And I can't go back. I've tried, oh how I've tried. But my male nature is hollow and meaningless. The only thing that remains is his agony. A hollow psychological shell to match the physical one I exist within. The pain is less, but still there and he *so* is damaged. Beyond a full repair I am realising. Bit-by-bit I think he is healing, or at least in less pain, but if I am honest with myself, I know he will never be the same as he was, and I am revealed as a woman permanently as a consequence. Given this fact, why shouldn't I make some long-term and permanent changes?

I am faced with the ultimate trans-woman's conundrum:

a. Live a lie. Be Julia; but disguise myself as Adam to face the world as it demands I do. Then hope that things improve to the point Adam's face feels comfortable again. Basically, try to maintain the status quo.

    b.   Transition. Permanently alter my body to become as physically female as I can. Live openly and genuinely as Julia and show the world who I really am for the rest of my life.

I so desperately want option b). There are times when I want it so badly, normally when I'm in the depths of yet another of the endless, mountainous waves of dysphoria. I genuinely **never** used to. I have thought about it (often) and even fantasised about it. Waking up fully clothed with a start, as I used to in the past, feeds into this fantasy. I have always thought that it would be nice, different, a real mixed bag as anyone's life is, but a much better fit for me you know? Unlike most males, being a woman has never threatened me. I could quite happily spend the rest of my life as a girl – no loss at all, all good, indeed that is what I'm pretty much facing up to now. But to do so honestly and openly would be a perfect solution for me. But it was never something I actively wanted, only an intriguing idea that would've been nice. Now? Well, now I want it, I want it all and I want it badly. And this scares the shit out of me sometimes. Because, as I said, this is the trans-woman's absolute nightmare scenario. Being female but being stuck in a huge male body with no way to transition successfully/satisfactorily. So, I think that I still have **no choice** but to continue with Option a) and live a lie.

This is awful, and it's fucking hard work. Furthermore, I think it will end badly...

It affects me mentally and after a time it manifests itself physically through my behaviour. If I spend too long locked up in hateful trousers, looking out at the world through Adam's eyes. I become agitated, I can't settle, and it becomes more and more obvious I am supremely uncomfortable in my own skin. Even my mannerisms change after enough time, my body closes down when I sit, like women in general, I take up less space. I catch myself swinging my hips as I walk too sometimes,

I am well practiced at walking with a feminine sway, at least in doors anyway – after so much time walking in heels it comes as second nature to me – but it can manifest itself inconveniently, regardless of my footwear if I am overdue some relaxation time in a skirt. Spending extended periods of time as *him* is awful and at this point, I **have** to be female in every way for an equally extended period of time rather than just overnight, sleeping in a nightie as I normally do.

I can fit this into my life at the moment, but only because my life is on pause currently. But sooner or later I am going to have to spend more time in Adam's skin. To go on holiday, or out in the evenings or at weekends.

I need to find a way to do this without going crazy. That is what it feels like when I am presenting as Adam for too long, when I am agitated. Like I have been forced to become a man against my will. Trousers are a prison; I utterly detest them and hate having to wear them even more. Julia does not own any trousers, she likely never will – I have spent far too much time trapped in them for one lifetime thank you very much. A skirt is freedom, freedom of movement, freedom of expression, freedom of emotion and most of all, freedom to be who I truly am.

I have to be free.

I have to wear a skirt.

I am Julia.

I am a woman.

But I live a lie...

...and it's now increasingly difficult.

8:00am, I'll put on Adam's face shortly and go to work, be sociable and exist in the world, as the world mandates I do. It'll

be OK. I will channel who I was and be proficient at looking like him.

My skirt awaits, trousers are only a temporary confinement. I will be free tonight once more and all will be good.

My life is so weird. I like being Julia, but it is much harder than it was. Playing at being Adam is *much* harder than actually being him. But it is a skill, and I am good at it, after 50 years I should be. My day awaits me, but first I have to step into my prison. One leg at a time...

I will feel better later on.

I can do this.

I must.

10:26pm, I am in my room after a productive day and a nice, relaxing evening.

Work was OK, I managed to resolve a few things and have put the pile of drawing work back on track after the latest curve ball. Later in the day, I sent an email to "The Beauty Editor", a specialist beauty place in Stansted Mountfitchet that does <u>permanent</u> hair removal. I have booked an initial consultation about permanently removing my beard. I feel great, the consultation is at 12:45pm this Friday.

Dinner with Eve at a local pub – it's fantastic to be able to sit inside a pub and have a nice meal again. I hope I will never again take such a lovely thing to do for granted as I used to.

Home and in a skirt around 8pm, so 12 hours again today. More than half the day, every day more or less - I am truly living as a woman now, at least chronologically anyway. I love it, it just feels the right way to live.

Wednesday May 26th

I am OK today. Yay!

I spent the entire night fully dressed though; Eve upset me a bit yesterday evening. She asked me to hide my relationship status on Facebook, so I did. Our status remains the same, but now no one else can see it. Yet another step along this awful road. I hate this so much, but it seemed to matter to Eve, so I did it. If she wants to change her status though, that will do me in at the moment. I am not robust enough to deal with that yet. It's a huge leap in the wrong direction for me, she may already be there, but I am a **long** way off declaring to all and sundry our relationship is over at the moment, regardless of if it being true. It really shouldn't matter, but it **does.**

I am beginning to think there is a direct link our relationship status and my mental position as a female. It seems that the further Eve and I separate, the more cemented my female gender becomes. There's a strange kinda logic to this notion, each step stabs Adam in the heart again and makes him even more unreachable. This is a very bad position to be in. It means that I am on a **direct course to full gender reassignment**. It feels more and more like an inevitability, when Eve and I go our eventual separate ways, I will be so completely female in mind I will really struggle to live in Adam's world anymore. His face will be so alien to me, maintaining the charade will be next to impossible.

Eve was my one shot at a so called "normal" life. I knew it at the time and consequently I threw everything I had and everything I am at it. She is my one true love, even now and I think she will always be. I committed to her completely and not only built my life around the concept of "us", but I also redefined who I am at the most fundamental level, my gender, for her love.

I am trying to heal what little is left of my male side to restore some of the former balance I had to my nature.

But every step Eve takes away from me undoes some of the healing. And there really isn't much left to heal any more.

Every step upsets the uneven balance and makes me more female. Every step deals another painful blow to Adam's remains. I truly am stuck now, the woman I am is here to stay, I think for good and it's only going to get more so as Eve continues her painful campaign to destroy who I used to be. She has traded his soul for her independence, and I wasn't even consulted...

There are some huge steps in the future, Eve is likely already considering some of them as rational and logical, but to me, still in the midst of an emotional maelstrom, they are anything but. At some point, Adam's corpse will certainly disappear, there is precious little left of him as it is, not enough to restore anymore, or even save – my male side will cease to exist. And at that point, wearing his face daily for the world's benefit will be unsustainable.

I will have no choice but to transition.

It will **not** be successful, for all the reasons previously covered.

I can live a lie as long as there is some part of Adam, damaged terribly or not, still alive. He may already be dead, this is debateable. If my nature continues to be divided, I can be Julia and disguise myself as Adam daily. It'll be enormously hard to do, let alone maintain, but it is possible. But if my male side becomes unreachable, my nature becomes singular and totally female, then I am living a lie completely and this is not something anyone could do. I will have to match my body to my gender, there will be no choice, it will be inevitable.

The consequences of this on my life will be earth shattering. This **cannot** be understated.

Going back to the whirlpool of grief, I am in mourning still. But I am mourning someone else too.

- Mum.
- Eve.
- Our relationship

...and

Adam

Don't misunderstand me, being Julia all the time is nice, really nice. I like being her and in a lot of ways, vastly prefer it. Furthermore, if I thought it was possible to do so convincingly, I would happily have full gender reassignment surgery and live the rest of my days as far as possible as a complete woman in both body and mind. In a fantasy world, this is the perfect solution. **But it is a fantasy**. My body is too male to transition successfully. I will still need to disguise myself as Adam to face the world, only it will be much harder to do with a female body. I will end up being the tallest lady with the broadest shoulders. As much as I want to be Julia physically, trying to make a 'successful' life as me will be exponentially harder. Does this make me a coward? Or is it, as unpalatable as it is to hear, just a logical conclusion?

> I will look odd, too big, and too broad. I will not fit into societal norms, so my life will be more challenging.

I think it's both. A logical conclusion *and* cowardice.

Also, and this is a big admission, I doubt I will every truly be satisfied. There will always be something about my body that I won't like. Most people have this, but the difference is that after such a transformative event as full gender reassignment, the odd nip and tuck here and there is very small beer. There

will always be something that isn't quite right, something that doesn't fit with who I am – dysphoria is the queen of all bitches – and a full transition will not shut her up, she's far too good at ruining my life to ever quit making me feel awful. I know it. But maybe I can quieten her down a bit?

As horrible as it is, my best bet for a reasonable life is to remain physically male. Regardless of how female I actually am inside, and how much I loathe the skin I am in, how wrong and uncomfortable it is and how much I crave to synchronise body and mind. Disharmony is a good way to describe it, everything, literally everything is out of step – the only variable is by how much and the volume it is being played at. These days, the disharmony is so loud, constant and pronounced, it is unbearable.

Dysphoria, I name thee, I call you out as the vile monster you are.

This is the hard, unpalatable truth of my existence.

I need Eve to be careful. I need her to understand that what she does now affects who I am at the most fundamental level and the course my life will take. *My life is in the balance*, this is quite possibly the truest statement there is about me.

My life is in the balance…
…it could go either way.
Or
My life is **in** the balance…
…I have to achieve some semblance of balance between genders.

Eve's actions affect the balance, it takes one of the few remaining weights from the male side of the scales and welds it permanently to the female side. At some point, **ALL** the weights

will be irreversibly female, most already are, and I will *have* to transition.

Please be careful Eve, you hold my entire future in your careless hands.

I have been trying to move some of the weights back to the male side of the scales. It's hard, there used to be a bowl on both sides to hold the weights, but she has smashed the one on the male side so the few remaining weights left are precariously balanced, and without a stable base they are ready to fall.

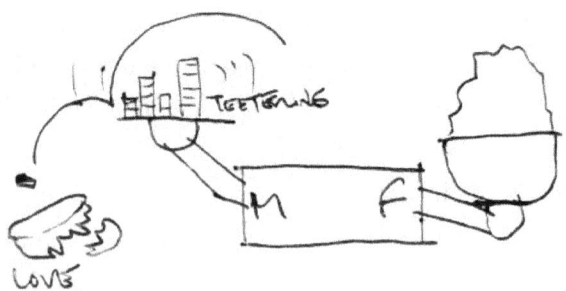

Every step she takes away from me moves a weight over to my female side. The shattered bowl on my male side, the bowl that allowed Adam to be full, was made from her love. A receptacle carefully crafted to contain the construct that was a man, Adam. It was a beautiful thing, practically perfect with only one flaw. The lynch pin that held it together was the purpose for which it was made – the love of my love.

When all the weights are female, this is the likely scenario as I see it...

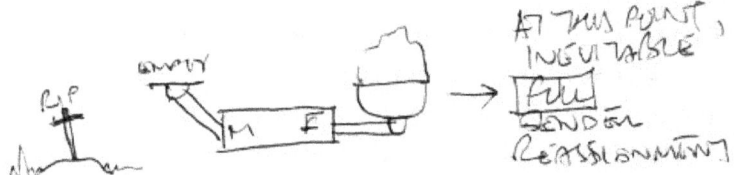

Adam remains the best way forward.

Eve stepping further and further away is erasing him and strengthening me (Julia).

I need to heal <u>before</u> she goes too far, too fast.

But I am not in control of the healing process, it'll take as long as it has to.

Eve needs to tread carefully, but she is emboldened and is accelerating towards her new independence. She cares not for the price I am paying.

> My life is in the balance.

And in the meantime, our lives are on pause...

Thursday, May 27th

I am OK again today, Eve left for work around 4:30am, she was quiet, and I didn't wake thankfully. But she was gone when I got up – an empty house. It's too quiet, not nice – but I am OK.

Eve's Covid jab went well yesterday, she had the Pfizer one in the top of her left arm. Her arm was a bit dead afterwards, but other than being a little tired and hungry, thankfully she doesn't appear to have had much of a reaction. I am relieved, I am sure she is too. I hope my second jab goes as well in a fortnight's time...

It's Thursday, so the regular site meeting again today, I think it will be tricky. Most folks have moved in over the past couple of days and things are starting to pop up as they settle into the new spaces. I think there will be the "want list", but with no money left in the budget, they will be very hard to accommodate.

Eve has 2 days shooting in High Wycombe, something involving bowling (hence the Covid jab in the *left* arm). She booked a cheap hotel last night and will stay away to save the time and expense of travelling. I miss her company already...

Despite this, I am, however, looking forward to tomorrow. Kay at 11am and then a consultation with Katie at the Beauty Editor in Stansted about permanently removing my beard. Hopefully it goes well, and I am suitable for treatment – I want it all gone, for good. Shaving is a massive waste of time – I am NEVER going to grow a beard, so keeping the option open is pointless in the extreme. It's also a constant reminder of my situation. And actually, it grows so fast it screws up my make-up in what feels like no time at all. I am doing something significant for me.

The site meeting was interesting, usual snags and staff making mountains out of molehills. Sian, our client, is stressed,

but grateful for all the work done. Today was meeting #89 and #90, the second one likely being the final Steering Group Committee meeting as the project is in the midst of a phased handover. End of an era.

Home around 5pm, I withdrew some cash ready for Kay on the way back. I then ordered a Chinese takeaway, but only ate half of it. The mogs are done, house is tidied so I watched some TV. Basically, dinner for one, chores and something to take my mind off the fact I'm alone. Actually, it's not so bad, and only for one night. I miss her though. Eve is on my mind again. Trying to distract myself with the TV, it's not working as well as I would've liked. Time to try the 'other T.V.' – it's odd that Transvestite is shortened to TV and Cross Dresser is shortened to CD – anyone would think the entertainment industry is a haven for folk like me... ...I'm getting changed now... ...I hope it's not weird with an unshaved chin (I need to be unshaved for the consultation with Katie tomorrow afternoon – have I mentioned how much I loathe my beard?)

Friday, May 28th

I'm OK, a bit lonely but OK. It's not nice living on my own. I just don't like it. Also, I have 2 days growth on my chin – it's horrible, scratchy, it looks awful, and I feel dirty / unwashed. My hair keeps getting caught in it, meaning I can't wear it down / loose, and I detest the dysphoria it is inducing in me.

I have <u>never</u> had this much hair on my chin, I am also concerned that approximately 2/3rds of it looks to be white. This is not good for Intense Pulse Laser (IPL) hair removal. I think I may need some electrolysis as well – ouch! I sincerely hope Katie can help with this, I have always truly hated my beard, but never more so than today.

But before all this, I have a session with Kay – I will bring my journals, she asked me to think about loneliness and I have made some notes… You may remember reading them? Teehee!

As I have such a horrible face today, I have compensated somewhat with my underwear. **Definitely** a bra and knickers combo kind of day.

The bra is a fascinating garment to me. I adore wearing one, even if it is ill-fitting and uncomfortable! I find them immensely comfort***ing***, it is like being hugged and I like and appreciate the support, as well as the reduction in the jiggling. I like the back closure too, it is so alien to males to fasten any clothing behind your back, a uniquely feminine experience and skill set. And then, of course, the bra has *no male equivalent at all*. Of the ultimate female clothing trilogy, high heels, skirt and a bra, only the bra is *exclusively* female. This is the reason for the trope about feminists burning them. It is so symbolic in so many ways. Me having breasts also just adds to the experience. I love having breasts and I find it mind blowing that a C-cup bra actually fits me. The bra I am wearing right now has an actual purpose. Lastly, I love the way a matching lingerie set looks

on me. Wearing a matching set – another uniquely feminine experience. So pretty! I love everything about bras, and I love wearing one every day. I am SO weird... This is a strange opinion, even for a woman!

10:44am, I am outside Kay's house, sitting in the car waiting for 11am when I shall knock on her door. I have had a sandwich and some OJ as well as some chocolate crispy bites (yum), just because. It is sunny and warm; I am beginning to regret my fleece somewhat.

The swarthy look is definitely <u>not</u> for me. I'll be shaving the very moment I walk through the front door after seeing Katie. I may take a photo for Eve – she is unlikely to ever see me like this again.

The session with Kay was good, as ever, I find her challenging – she is extremely good at playing the Devil's advocate – I think I have thought things through fully and she blindsides me with something profound I've not considered. We discussed Eve's financial and work situation and how it relates to our current living arrangements – how she needs to step up to her financial commitments to the house somehow, but that I am supporting her until she is able to do so. This is only fair, if we are no longer a couple, then we ultimately need to split the bills 50:50. I went through my fears and concerns about loneliness, Kay put me straight on a few things, but wasn't able to allay all of them. More like she made me realise that I was already alone. She opened my eyes to my situation and related how I am now, how I was a week, a month, 2 months ago to how I will be in time. She showed me a progression and then extrapolated it into the future. I still fear being alone. But I think I am better equipped to deal with it now and it will be easier as time passes.

The big thing today was living for me, not 'us' anymore.

And this comes back to where I see myself in the future. What do I want and who do I want to be? I said that I didn't know, and she tasked me with thinking about this for our next session. I also said I had begun to do things, just for me. I explained about beard removal, and she seemed OK that I was doing something entirely for my benefit. This led to a discussion on my appearance, formal vs casual, and whether I have any hang-ups about being seen as a woman or am I dressing for myself. In which case, how others see me doesn't really matter. I surprised her, I think. I said that I always dress for myself, it's just that dressed casually I am less successful at creating a female appearance. And to illustrate the point, I reached inside my T-shirt and 'pinged' my bra strap. Such a lovely, feminine thing to do (I've said it before, I sure am weird). A wry smile appeared on Kay's face. I'm sure she was genuinely surprised! I really don't think she suspected there might be more to my appearance than meets the eye and that I truly was dressing for me and not for anyone else' benefit. Afterall, if I hadn't have made it obvious, she likely wouldn't have known I was wearing a bra. I like to think she sees this as some progress – I know I do. I can wear female underwear under Adam's clothes now. I never used to be able to. It always felt like I was mixing my genders, one cancels out the other leaving me adrift, but now, I am female, and Adam's countenance is a façade. So, the bra and knickers feel right, furthermore there were fewer male clothes to worry about and that is always a bonus.

I think if I am male, female, or something in between in the future, I will be able to live. The only real variables relate to difficulty and success in terms of how the world relates to me. But the yardstick by which these are measured is not defined. Success and failure come in many forms… But providing I am comfortable with who I am and how I live, that is all that matters.

After a sandwich I headed over to see Katie. It was interesting and, I think, positive. I have booked in the next 3 sessions as a consequence. Fingers crossed it'll be successful and at last, I begin to lose my beard. Katie was nice, very chatty, I was concerned about the amount of white in my beard, but she was actually really pleased by the amount of colour still there. She was confident that treatment would have an effect and proceeded with the trial patches. I lay down on the table and she marked up 4 areas with a pencil, one on my left cheek bone, top lip also on the left, upper chin and neck. She handed me a cold air pipe and asked me to direct the cooling air stream at the areas. Then she applied a cooling gel and talked to me about pain. She said she would be asking me a lot about how painful each light pulse was and that I should reply with a number, zero to ten, with ten being broken leg or similar. Top lip, cheek and neck were a one on the scale, chin was a one and a half. But I think some of this is because it made me jump. In comparison, I would put hair waxing at a three on legs and back, chest and underarms are a solid 4. So, this is really nothing at all. To be fair though, my pain gauge has been massively weighted by the emotional pain I have been through and am still dealing with – my frame of reference is way off. In fact, the only unpleasant thing was the whiff of burned hair I got, likely from my top lip due to proximity to my nose.

> All in all, really good. I am looking forward to my next session immensely, it's booked for next Friday morning.

And the best thing of all, this is permanent! Not temporary. Awesome!! I'm so excited!

No more shaving every morning, no more irritated skin, or ingrown hairs! So brilliant!

Eve was home early; I wasn't expecting her until after 5pm but she was an hour early. Just in time for Tipping Point

on the telly. Great to see her, I really missed her company – being on my own wasn't too bad this time, but it is so much better having someone to talk to. Especially when she has a lot to say. Thursday was pretty epic for her it seems. A long day working, plus the journey time, shenanigans with parking at the hotel and all whilst being under the weather due to the Covid jab. She's such a trooper and the hotel was definitely the right decision. Having to drive back home and return after a day like that would've been crazy.

Today was, thankfully, less taxing for her, she felt much better, and they finished early.

A well-earned pizza for dinner as we swapped stories into the evening.

A good day.

I am worried about tomorrow though. It's our 15th anniversary...

...I hope I am not upset. It is likely our last one together and I don't want to spoil it.

Saturday, May 29th

Happy 15th anniversary, Eve and Adam...

15 years. The anniversary of the beginning of our life together is today. It should be a joyous day, and it always has been in the past. But I am sad. I am sad that we didn't make it to this milestone. And I am feeling the loss of our relationship a lot today. But I am OK. I am not in tears – I think I should be, today of all days should set me off, but I am not. So, I suppose this is a good thing – progress – to be honest, I'm just glad she is still in my life in whatever capacity.

15 years ago today, Eve and I sat around the kitchen table in my folk's place, and I took a risk that altered the direction of both of our lives. I put our friendship in jeopardy, by not only asking her if she wanted to take our relationship to the next level, but I also showed her who I truly am. I let her see behind the mask by removing a sock and showing her my (professionally painted) pretty toes. And then I said to take her time before giving me an answer – I gave her time to think about the ramifications and decide if she wanted to give "us", in whatever form that may take, a shot.

I am so grateful that she said yes. 10 of the last 15 years have been by far the best of my entire life, and this is entirely down to sharing them with Eve. The woman I love and my true soul mate, for I have *literally bared my soul to her*.

Given my gender circumstances now, I can't see how this could <u>ever</u> happen again.

> Eve truly was my one-shot at close to a "normal" life.

- I am not a man anymore. This makes finding someone else astonishingly difficult.
- Furthermore, I **NEVER** want to be this hurt again. I can't see me opening up to anyone else to the same

extent. Why would I make myself this vulnerable – now knowing just how painful a break-up can be?

I have so much love to give, but I can't anymore, and I have no one to give it to.

...In all likelihood, I never will again.

Now I'm upset.

I have pushed myself too far.

I just want our life together back. I don't want to have to live like this.

As much as I like being Julia now, it is not as good as loving Eve and being loved in return. No where near.

I have been forced to trade the best thing that ever happened to me for being truer to myself. And as good as being true to myself is, it was a **REALLY** bad trade. A deal I never wanted and a deal I would happily undo if I could in a (broken) heartbeat.

> I am _not_ crying. Progress has been made. I want to cry, but I am not.

And it's also the Mogs birthday!

Some small thing to smile about at last.

Meow!

I need to smile again.

Today, more than ever.

So, I will smile, and I won't cry.

It's been a difficult day. Eve went to the horses first thing; the Shetland had the farrier. Eve has a packed week at work ahead so will be looking after the horses all weekend. This means we can't visit her folks sadly.

Whilst she was out, I sorted out the sofa cushions and then hoovered under it. I also discovered 2 pairs of Eve's socks under there, likely from when she was sleeping on it in December / January.

I then settled in to watch Disc 2 of the Snyder Cut of Justice League. An astonishing film – so much better than the completely botched theatrical release.

Eve came home around 11:30am, we headed off to Colchester for some tea and cake. It was lovely and we had a great chat about us and how we can make our situation work. We also put the world to rights a bit. We disagreed on the meaning of the word 'blog' though – I am sure she is right, but there is a generation of folks out there who see the word 'blog' and think 'web log'. Literally a diary with loads of guff and not much relevant information... Writing this now, the irony is not lost on me... Eve however thinks the exact opposite is true, for her a 'blog' is a trusted and valid information resource, like an encyclopaedia. A healthy discussion and kinda fun.

It went a bit wrong on the journey home though. Eve played some Gotthard which was great, but the song "I Wonder" came on and she turned it up. The music really upset me, 'triggered' is the modern parlance I believe. The whole song is about a chap who has lost the love of his life. It couldn't have been a more accurate description of my situation.

And she said it was her favourite.

And she turned up the volume to sing along.

And I came very, very close to crying...

> Now I can't believe you are gone tonight.
> When I should be holding you so tight.
> I can't believe and I wonder.
> I wonder.
> Where we are going.
> Love don't live here anymore.

When Eve realised, she switched it off, but my good mood was damaged, and our nice trip out had been soured by a moment's thoughtlessness and a song that was eerily appropriate with lots of 'triggers' for me.

We drove home in silence.

Eve washed her sportscar, then took it for a spin. She then worked on her website for a bit. I fed the mogs and then ordered dinner. After which I got changed and immediately felt better. I helped her dye her hair (it was nice to feel useful) and we watched Robocop again. Such a great movie. And a good way to wrap up Saturday.

Sleep time now.

Night.

Sunday, May 30th

9:17am, I am having a lie in. I am OK today and it is sunny outside. I look forward to whatever the day brings and will get up shortly. But 9 hours in a dress already is a very good start.

Need to pop to B&Q today to buy a replacement bathroom light switch. The ceiling fitting is playing up I think, pulling the cord doesn't always activate the light.

I also need to clean car #2 and take some more photos – I am writing an article for a Club magazine. I am trepidatious about starting it up to be honest. I have lost confidence in it and don't want to cause any more damage. But it needs a run, and I won't go very far.

Eve was talking about spending some time with her sister today, but first she has the horses to do. She is up already and sitting downstairs in her dressing gown but will get dressed and head over to them shortly, I guess. I will be upset when she goes to see her without me. But it is good for Eve, and this is something I need to get used to. I can't help but feel un-wanted and rejected – it is painful. But I will find something nice for me to do, for me, while she is out, doing the same. I've no idea what though, I will play it by ear.

I am thinking about getting rid, or at least, not wearing male underwear anymore. From a purely practical standpoint, this will reduce the laundry. But I have discovered that I can now wear female undies below Adam's disguise, and it feels right, I no longer feel odd.

I have tried hard not to mix things up – when I am male, I am very male. And when I am female, I strive hard to be as close to 100% female as I can be. On the rare occasions I have worn knickers under Adam's trousers I have felt out of sorts. Like one cancels out the other, meaning I wasn't expressing either side of my gender.

This has changed.

I think because I am female now, or at least there is no longer any male conflict, female underwear feels right, all the time. Not just when I am dressed properly. I am Julia constantly now, regardless of my clothes. I really have lost my balance.

So, I can mix and match it seems. And I think this also opens the door to me dressing as a woman in a more casual manner. I don't have to be overtly feminine all the time, even though it is great fun and I like it a lot – looks like I'm a 'girly girl' – was it that obvious? Maybe I can enjoy women's trousers? Nah, I know I would miss wearing a skirt, it's always going to be my preference.

So, I think I can wear knickers under my day clothes 24/7 if I want to. I have done it a few times now, spent the entire day in lingerie hidden under Adam's façade. It was nice, a nice feeling to know I had pretty undies on and had support for my boobs. A bra, daily, is probably not a good idea. Why not? Other women do this all the time. Because bras can be seen through clothes – I see women's bra outlines all the time – I am not looking for them, they are just apparent and noticeable. So, as much as I would like to wear one daily, I don't think I can very often. At least I can't leave the house in one all the time. But I **can** wear knickers – I can stop wearing underpants. I might do it for a while. Just for fun and just for me.

The day started well. I had a very lovely lie-in. Eve left for the horses as planned and was due back for lunch before heading over to see her sister this afternoon. I got up around 11am and then headed to B&Q to get the new bathroom light switch. Whilst in there I also bought a fan for Eve's bedroom. Once the weather heats up for the Summer, there won't be any left on the shelves to buy.

Things went a bit pear shaped when I arrived back home. Eve's car was back, but her sportscar was gone. I had assumed that Eve had just taken it for a spin, so cracked on with fitting the new light switch and put off lunch, waiting for her return. By 2pm I was very hungry and actually upset – hangry. I had sent her a series of texts, eventually she replied saying she was with her sister already! Feelings of hurt and rejection flooded me again – it was such a little oversight on Eve's part, but I had an emotional reaction out of all proportion once more. I hate this. I actually told myself out loud that I didn't want to feel this way. I fell down the familiar rabbit hole once more of thinking I meant so little to Eve I wasn't even worth a simple 'goodbye' or a message saying she had already left, and I should sort myself out for lunch. Logic says this is not true, but logic has no part in the way I feel.

I had a sandwich for lunch and then spent some time on car #2, I fitted the extra grab handle above the driver's seat and switched the sun-visors over for a pair with illuminated vanity mirrors. I decided I would wash the car tomorrow and then sat in the garden under the parasol for a bit. I then went for a bit of a drive before watching some X-Files episodes on the TV.

Eve came home around 6:30pm. She had had a wonderful day with her sister, and I immediately forgave her in my mind, but I did ask her to let me know in the future so I can sort out my meals and not wait for her. Just a common courtesy is all.

We had a nice evening, I picked up a KFC and we watched a bit of telly. I painted her toenails again before bed, I like doing this for her, it makes me feel good and it's all great practice for when I do my own. I was dressed correctly from 8pm, so 15 hours in a skirt, well, dresses actually, today.

Day off tomorrow too.

Monday, May 31st

Bank Holiday Monday

Up around 9am, Eve was at the horses from 8. When she came home, we headed off to Stoke Poges, near Beaconsfield to a TV location set. Eve had a Covid test ahead of filming there tomorrow and I came along for the ride. If she had Covid, then in theory she could have infected the set, it seemed a bit odd to test her and others there to me. A pleasant journey in good company, despite the Bank Holiday moron drivers on the M25. The sun was shining, and the location was fascinating. It reminded me very much of the pits, during a race meeting at Silverstone or similar. A 'camping' vibe, but not in an amateurish way. They were filming while we were there too, Eve's electric car being so quiet was perfect, I could hear the on set instructions, but sadly couldn't see any of the cameras etc. Eve is so cool. She's an old hand at this and completely blasé about it all. She knew exactly where to go and what to do. I sat in the car trying not to look like a fangirl and trying extremely hard not to fall in love with Eve all over again.

We had to stop for 10 minutes on the way home after to top up the charge to the car's traction battery. No big deal once we found a rapid charger and waiting for a couple of minutes as a Kia E-Niro finished with it. We were both tired when we got home, Eve said she fancied a snooze. I don't blame her; I fancy doing the same.

After, I put her new fan together. She went for a walk and chat with one of her language friends. Then we went out to Nando's for dinner, which was lovely.

I watched a little YouTube and then some Netflix before bed at around 10:40pm. A really nice and interesting day all in.

More of the same please.

Tuesday, June 1st

White rabbits...

I'm feeling a bit weird today, not sure why, maybe it is because I didn't spend much time in a skirt yesterday evening? I slipped into my nightwear around 9pm, so pretty much 12 hours, but all nightwear and no day wear.

Anyway, I am a bit out of sorts this morning – I feel fragile – I am not upset, but I feel close to it.

I have a busy day at work today, so I need to shake this off if I can. Also, there's local sports car meet this evening, likely without Eve or her car. It'll be great to see friends again, but also strange given how much has changed in my life since I saw them all last.

I feel detached from the world somehow – I think that I have spent so long with Eve as my link to life that now this link is tenuous at best, I am at a loose end. I need to forge some new links – reconnect with the world somehow, find something I am passionate about that I can share with the world and throw myself into. Or multiple things maybe. But it's hard when I'm feeling weird like this.

<u>Kay's 'homework'</u>

- Kay asked me to think about what I want. This is a huge question and to be honest, I don't have answers really.

  What I truly want is to not feel like this anymore.

- My life has been on pause for the past couple of months. I need to press play (or is it record?) and start living again. I know this, but it's really hard to do. My life has been all about being Eve's boyfriend – how do I move on from here?

- I want to wind the clock back and fix all the myriad of things that brought me to this point in my life. I want to shake myself by the shoulders and scream "What are you doing, open your eyes to what is happening, you are losing her!" I want to undo all the tiny inconsequential and unnoticed steps along this road that with hindsight, were not inconsequential at all. Far from it, they all added up to a life altering situation. A situation that is the last thing that I ever wanted. And a situation that I would have strived hard to avoid if only I had recognised them as they happened.
- This is why I feel like a failure.
- I see them all now, clear as day. All the things I missed or did wrong. All the times I could've gone a different way and just maybe, maybe, avoided the terminus I now find myself in.
- Regrets, they are pointless and do not help. This train of thought stops me moving on. It stops me reconnecting with the world.
- What I want, what I truly want, is no longer possible. And I am really struggling to accept this inalienable fact. So, my life is on pause.
- Maybe the question should be what can I salvage from what I had before? And from here, what can I add to reconnect with the world?

- My friendship with Eve　　　　May be possible.
- My love for her as a sister　　　May be possible, but very difficult.
- My relationship with her family　Possible.

- All of the above I am working on, But I recognise that they are all changing, time and circumstance as well as outside influences are taking a toll, and they are going

to continue to change. I don't like it, they are moving targets, but it is happening, and I need to accept and deal with it. But I hope they can be salvaged, even if only in part or in a different format.

- Less certain, but things I still want to salvage are:
    - Living with Eve as a housemate.
    - Living in our home together.
    - Staying in this house.
    - Going on holidays together.
- These are all in the balance. Both Eve and I want them to remain, but they are really hard to achieve. The first one has all kinds of financial hurdles to jump. Mainly from Eve's side, but she is not in a position to do so yet. The second and third are related to the first, and the last, I think, is highly unlikely now. The problem is the word 'together'. I want to be together, she does not. So, she will <u>always</u> hurt me from now on unless I can change this somehow.
- I need to **<u>not</u>** want us to be together.
- It's the only way her actions will stop hurting me.
- How the hell am I going to do this?
- I must find a way. When she does stuff for herself, **I must not feel rejected.**
- The fact is, she already has rejected me, it is done and in the past. Every new thing she does is not a new rejection, it's not personal or aimed at me at all, or a deliberate attempt to upset me and cause me pain. It's just Eve connecting with the world, and I need to do the same.
- Somehow.

- So, I need to find things that I want.
- Things to do, things to work on, things for me and things that will plug me back into life and un-pause it.
- There's a whole world out there, I just need to decide what I want from it and then make it happen.

A weird day, I spent most of it working on a quantities analysis spreadsheet for one Client instead of the much more important pile of drawing work for another.

A full day of staring at spreadsheets is not my idea of fun. I'm glad I'm not an accountant.

Home around 6pm, Eve arrived 10 minutes after me, then she received a call from Rachael's People (the agency who has set up work for tomorrow and Thursday on The Larkins) asking her if she can ride a horse! Manna from heaven! She said yes of course, but then we had a search of the loft (riding boots found), so she can ride tomorrow safely, if the costume department will allow that is. This means we were late leaving for the sportscar natter. The first one in months.

We headed down to the meet in Eve's sportscar after all, with the hood down. It was a lovely drive, despite the awkward conversation. Eve asked me not to use the pronoun "we", instead use "I". This stung a bit, and I said how I feel. Firstly, what is going on between Eve and I is no one's business but our own. And, quite frankly, I am not ready for this. I understand that she has moved on, but I am not there yet. But I said I would try. Thankfully the opportunity didn't come up after we arrived, but while we were having this discussion in the car enroute, what I really wanted to say is "Fine, I'll recognise in public what you have done to our relationship, but in return, I need you to do the same, by recognising what you have done to me too – my pronouns are she/her and you can call me Julia." In retrospect I

am glad I didn't go this far; I also feel like a coward. I do think we need to set some ground rules for social interactions though. Despite my thoughts, I don't want to hurt her and equally I don't want her to hurt me. This could get very awkward, I think… Eve is clearly ready to go on this – I am a long way off still. For her, it has been years in the making. Only 2 months (of abject Hell) for me. I rethought my position afterwards, I did think about making her a deal, I won't use the "we" pronoun in public, if she uses exclusively female pronouns for me and calls me Julia at home. Seems like a much better solution and it takes the sting out of my earlier impulsive thought for her a bit. But I hope that this will not be as important in the future to me as it is now and as I said, I am not ready to move on in a social situation just yet. Also, this deal has the potential to dry up our conversations at home. It will make her uncomfortable and so she will shut the taps off even more I suspect. She is being antagonistic to me with this request, and so responding in kind is not a good way to go – I shall be the bigger girl (err, quite literally). This is stopping me from going to Europe with her… 'with' her… I know I will not be with her. This is so bloody difficult. There are other things getting in the way too – I do not <u>want</u> to go on my own – this is exactly what will happen I am sure of it. We'll share the same car, a room, and a ferry. But we will emphatically not be a couple, we will be two individuals and she will spend the entire time socialising in another language, primarily because she wants the real-world practice and also it is nicer for our friends to speak their native tongue (it's *very* rare that a Brit abroad goes to this much effort).

But I also think she will do it to spite me, knowing full well that I cannot join in the conversation, effectively isolating me not only from her, but also our friends. She will also go out of her way to avoid me, just like the last two times. I desperately want to see my friends again, and equally I desperately need a break. But I think it will be just as, if not more painful than the previous two trips and I know that I will be so upset and stressed that I won't get a much-needed holiday at all. I need to be in a vastly different place mentally to be able to go and not feel abandoned, alone and rejected. She undeniably is going to hurt me again on this trip, she has a twice-proven track record and at the moment, I am just not able to handle it. Maybe I will be in a better headspace when we get to it? But I'm certain she will ruin the trip for me anyway, intentionally, or otherwise. She will go out of her way to shut me out.

Decision made – **I am not going.**

Fuck. I was really looking forward to seeing them all again.

Eve can go on her own and pay for herself. I will likely book something else up just for me. Likely on a different weekend, just to make looking after the Mogs easier.

> Where do I want to go?
>
> > I will need to think about it...

It was a really nice evening, great to go and break bread with friends in a pub at last. A nice, summer evening hood down drive home too.

I'm looking forward to the next one.

Wednesday, June 2nd

I am OK again today. Eve is going away tonight and tomorrow for work (The Larkins), so I am going to be alone. But at this moment at least, I am OK with this. Hopefully this state of mind will continue.

I want to write a recap at the moment, but I think doing so will upset me. Our conversation, "we" vs "I" held in her sportscar last night is playing on my mind – it feels like a much bigger step than it actually is. But it is clearly important to her – she is purging me from her life, bit-by-bit, step-by (painful) step I am being surgically, and it feels like expertly, removed. It is awful and although I am definitely more resilient now, this is not because each cut of the scalpel is less painful, it is because I have developed scar tissue over the wound.

Part of me thinks that her not loving me anymore is a smokescreen. Part of me wonders if she ever truly loved me at all? I mean, I love her, I couldn't conceive of doing to her what she is doing to me. I wonder if she just finds me boring? I don't think I am boring – let's face it, with all the gender stuff going on in my head, I'm about as far from a boring person as possible – I am definitely not a regular person that's for sure. Life for Eve is all about the 'next big thing'. She has zero staying power and is in constant motion. I shackled myself to my job and the mortgage and this resulted in our new and shiny life together becoming routine. This is boring. She certainly doesn't listen to me anymore. I am not interesting enough, it seems, to be worth her time. We spend hours together, but we are not together. She takes herself off for a long bath, or makes herself busy, or immerses herself in her laptop, just to get away from me.

She will happily talk to me about her day but doesn't care to hear about mine. And when we do talk, it is normally to drop another bombshell on what's left of our relationship.

She says she doesn't have an agenda. This is **not** what it feels like. I know her, yes, she lives her life like a loose cannon, but when she commits to a project, she goes at it 110% and puts maximum effort into achieving her goal (or she gets bored and quits, or the next project comes along). There are never any half-measures and so, I'm pretty sure that she has a goal in mind – I am her next "project". Operation "Break Adam's heart and cut him out of my life". Or something along those lines anyway. I have no real idea what her goal is. She is giving me very mixed messages. What she says is different to what she is doing.

She says she wants to remain friends.

But.

She is trying to make me hate her. I feel pathetic, I'm at her every whim and so, at some point I am sure she will despise me. Sometimes, it feels like she does already.

She says she wants to stay living together as flat mates.

But.

She can't pay her way (hopefully this will change) and is not interested in sharing any time with me, so it makes me think that she only wants to stay here because I pay the bills. I suppose, *when* she can pay half the bills, if she moves out, this proves it. At this point is will **know** she has been taking the piss out of me for all this time. God, I hate thinking so badly of her.

She says she didn't tell me how she felt for years to spare my feelings.

But.

By doing so, she has given me TWO massive reasons to hate her. She has denied us the chance to work on our relationship, as couples do when they go through sticky patches. She just arbitrarily decided it was over between us and didn't even bother to tell me! And she has made me think that she has been using me to fund her unconventional lifestyle. I don't hate her. I

have EVERY reason to. But it is a fine line and I have come close to kicking her out a number of times. I have even gone to B&Q and stood looking at new door locks, pondering my options.

She says that she is OK with me being Julia.

But.

She will not validate me as her, she, or use my name. She doesn't talk to me when I am dressed properly. When I get changed, she shuts herself away, in the bath or hides inside her laptop. I either make her uncomfortable or am just not worth her wasting her time on it feels.

Mixed messages...

Furthermore, the common courtesies have started to dry up. Saying goodbye when she walks out the door. Letting me know what time she will be back. Leaving me wondering if I need to sort out my own meals or wait for her. Some of this is laziness. But regardless, it shows a lack of respect. And as I have previously written, whatever we have in the future, there <u>has</u> to be respect. Or we have nothing to build on and we go our separate ways. This, I think, although minor, is the start of a VERY slippery slope. Not only does this show a lack of respect, but it also proves that she just isn't thinking of me at all, or at least, I'm not important enough to her to warrant a simple "Goodbye", "See you later" or "Goodnight". This hurts. Being civil and polite costs nothing. Not being civil is rude, and rudeness is not acceptable.

I wonder if she is doing this to me because, me being in so much pain and turmoil is finally, after so many years of her being bored with me, interesting?

Is this why she is still here? Is dreaming up new and inventive ways to stab me once more in my broken heart and then watching the reaction finally, interesting to her? I feel like I'm a science experiment. It is awful.

If the most interesting thing I can do for her is to be in pain (what a sorry state of affairs). How can anyone put up with this?

She has hurt me more deeply and profoundly than I ever thought possible. And she is continuing to hurt me. And it is making me want to hate her. I do **not** want to hate her, but she is still hurting me!

This is why I have come close to throwing her stuff out on the front lawn and changing the locks. And as mentioned, when I say close, I have actually gone out to buy the locks.

We are both perched on a razor's edge. She is driving this, I am not. I am not resisting the inevitable, I am just not ready to do anything other than small steps at the moment. When she forces the situation, it hurts me.

I need to be ready to do what needs to be done. And she needs to be patient.

I love her, although I am trying not to – it is harder when I am hiding behind Adam. It is much less painful when I am me. Imprisoned in trousers, Adam loves her more than anything, it's the only reason he puts up with padlocking the hateful things onto himself day in, day out. He does it for her, to support our life together. And every tiny little thing she does without him rips him up inside.

She wants me to stop talking to others, friends, family, anyone as though we are still a couple. But emotionally, as this journal testifies, from my side of the equation, we ARE still a couple. I takes two to Tango as the adage goes. This is a **massive** step. It's the tip of the iceberg that declares our relationship is over to the world.

She can't push me into this. She has called time on our relationship. **I have not**. I can't do this while I still love her. And if I don't love her anymore, then I can't forgive her for fucking up my life and breaking my heart.

Thursday, June 3rd

It had to happen. It was only a matter of time. I'm crying again. It's been a good run, a couple of weeks or more – I suppose it had to happen sooner or later...

Eve is away for two nights. Last night and again tonight. My epic rant in these pages yesterday is, I think, partly due to her not being here. I **always** feel better when we are together, even if she is hurting me at the time. What a crazy situation.

Left alone with my thoughts, they go to dark places and logic is stretched to extremes. This explains most of yesterday's writings and it was all still buzzing around in my head at bedtime. I woke up at 3:30am in floods of tears...

And the house is too warm. I couldn't go too far with my outfit last night. It's a strange reversal of expectations, but I am always calmer, more rational and less emotionally raw when I am expressing myself properly – when I am in male guise, I am a mess emotionally and much more likely to go off on a hysterical tangent. Anyway, summertime sucks. Bra, knickers, skirt, blouse, and earrings. That's it. Respectable, barely, but in no way complete. I really missed my stockings, heels and make-up, my outfit felt incomplete and consequently, so did I. I suppose make-up would've been OK, but I was too hot to be bothered. Women do not wear make-up all the time. Also, women dress casually most of the time too. I am a woman; I did the same. But I should've gone further given my mental state and likely, if I had done so I would be in a better place this morning.

It was just too hot.

...and I am missing Eve. The house is empty and quiet... Too quiet. I just don't like it.

I have sent her a message on WhatsApp, she has yet to read it, likely because she is sleeping – her production wrapped around 11pm last night – good job she is staying locally.

Hopefully her call time is reasonable this morning and she can get some much-needed sleep.

I want to shave my legs. I want them to look nice in a skirt. But I will likely need to wear shorts as Adam or try out Eve's folk's new hot tub this weekend and I will need to look presentable as him. But I really want to shave them. I truly hate my body hair.

I think I am going to change the way I look after myself. I am already doing more female things – shaved underarms, make-up regularly (almost daily), female deodorant, painted toenails. I want to do it all. And as the Summer turns to Autumn, I probably will. It would be great to get rid of all my body hair permanently. I will see how my session with Katie goes tomorrow. Fingers crossed there is a good solution here.

It is 8:00am, no reply from Eve yet, the ticks are not blue, so I think she is asleep. I don't think she is avoiding me; I think she just hasn't read it yet.

I am hanging on her every word – shit.

It is no wonder I am upset today.

I <u>must</u> move on. I need to be Julia tonight, but in the meantime, I should go out and do something, just for me.

What can I do? What do I want? This is the question...

Eve replied shortly after I wrote this. She replied in typical Eve fashion – briefly – with a "I don't know what to say". To be fair, there really isn't anything she could say. I just have to deal with this on my own. So, I did. I cried for a bit, and I wrote my feelings down here. And then I went to work. I arrived at the site (Thursday again), still upset, but once I had some purpose – in this case snagging the next batch of works – I felt better. My site meeting was at 10am, no one turned up. So, after 45 minutes waiting around, I left. Halfway home I get a call, "Where are you?"

Idiots.

Still, feeling annoyed is better than feeling upset.

Back to the office. Some progress finally on the drawings that need doing and I am much more prepared for my Scottish trip next Tuesday / Wednesday.

I spoke to dad on the way home – we are getting together next Thursday night. I am looking forward to it.

And tomorrow, at 9:30am, I am having my beard lasered off! Sounds very Sci-Fi!

Woohoo!

I'm so happy about this! Finally, something to look forward to.

And I'm seeing Kay in the afternoon as well.

Friday, June 4th

Two months from "J-Day"...

Two months since I started this journal.

Two months since I tried to kill myself.

I drove my car in the wee small hours, out into the countryside with the intent to crash the car at very high speed. But instead, through floods of tears, a manic energy overtook me, and I began to write my feelings down. My thoughts and fears, a disjointed scream of pain, expressed in a cathartic stream of letters on every scrap of paper I could find in the car. I wrote as much of it as I could out.

And by doing so, I felt better.

Just the action of thinking things through and putting them into some semblance of order so they could be written down made them feel less overwhelming.

I found myself, sat in the car in the dead of night. Dressed completely, head to toe as my female self. Outside the house as a woman, after all, what did it matter anymore? It was an unconscious decision – I just wanted to be comfortable at the end. I sat in the car, surrounded by manic scribblings and in floods of tears.

And instead of a suicide note. When I look at those scant few pages now, I can see Adam. He is on the page, in immense agony, damaged to the point of utter despair. But there he is, permanently inked onto them, and he is no longer in my head. Those few pages are a grave site, a headstone, a memorial. Catharsis. Adam went out to kill himself, and in an unexpected, unconventional, but very real way, he succeeded. Through the tears, I found myself that night not only resembling a woman in appearance, but an actual woman in mind – a singular gender with no division, for the very first time.

Female. Julia. <u>Real</u>.

A woman staring through streaked mascara tears at the last remnants of the male side of her, now forever locked onto those few pages.

A hugely traumatic event. But it was successful. Instead of ending it all, I had <u>literally</u> written him out of me and in doing so, had also written myself out of the very lowest ebb of my life...

I don't **EVER** want to go this dark again.

So, I write. And I continue.

The following morning, I started this journal and although I still have bad days where I am crying and am desperately unhappy. Generally, and thankfully, I am on an upwards trend.

- I am still in immense pain.
- I am still lonely and sad.
- I am still Julia.
- The last of Adam remains purged from me onto those desperately scrawled pages.

But I am dealing with it all now. My bad days are related to Eve hurting me again and again, not because of my situation anymore.

- I can deal with the pain, providing it doesn't get any worse.
- I have accepted that I will be lonely for the rest of my life. It sucks and it makes me sad. But I can handle it. I will be OK.
- I **<u>like</u>** being Julia. But I have come to realise that it doesn't matter who I am, I am fundamentally a good person and I just need to be true to myself. It is good to be me, regardless of gender. Being true is the most important thing.

- If Eve would stop hurting me, then I think I would be OK and after a time, I will be OK with taking some painful steps.
- What she is asking of me is not unreasonable, but it is **way** too soon, and she is now being mean to me as well.
- This is **not** acceptable. We **have** to talk. Her attitude towards me is unwarranted and counterproductive.

> Hurting me further, and not affording me common courtesies, consideration or respect is unacceptable.

If this continues, I will end up hating her and I will kick her out of the house.

Eve STOP! Recognise the consequences of your actions will screw up your life. You are not financially ready to live elsewhere yet.

Counterproductive indeed.

Patience is needed from Eve, or all is lost...

Despite this latest piece of ranting and raving, I am OK today (of all days).

I didn't go for a full outfit again last night. I meant to, but I ended up cleaning the house instead. Productive. Afterwards, I washed Adam's black jeans, along with the other darks and hung them on the line. I picked up a package from next door – summer shorts for Adam – and tried them for size. The shorts were, as usual with shorts, not as good a fit as I would have liked, acceptable to others, but the cut was very wrong for me. I fed the Mogs and hoovered up after them (messy creatures!) Lastly, I set up the portable air-con unit in my bedroom – it was nice and cool in there at bedtime.

I then spent the night in my nightie. Comfy on the sofa downstairs with the TV, before off to bed. Nice.

If this is what my evenings are going to be like in the future, alone and looking after the house. Doing the housework. A housewife. I can do this. It's not so bad. I'll probably develop a routine, certain jobs on certain days to keep on top of it all. A weekly shop, dusting, washing, hoovering etc.

Keeping busy helped my mood, but due to trips to the washing line, I wasn't able to do the housework dressed the way I would've wanted.

Still, not a bad way to close out the day.

Eve comes home tonight. I miss her.

I'm worried about her.

I'm worried she is going to push me too far, too fast and I'll end up hating her.

I'm worried that the state I am in currently will be too much for her and she'll end up despising me.

- I want us to remain friends.
- I want her to remain in my life.
- I don't want to hurt her or to hate her.
- I don't want her to carry on hurting me.
- I don't want to be so sensitive to everything she does.
- I don't want to be boring to her.

I want her to smile again.

So, I think I need to be less boring. Somehow.

It will be good for me, and she will me more interested in listening to me.

But mainly, *it will be good for me.*

I need to re-connect with the world and take genuine joy in who I am and the things I do. And if Eve wants to join me,

great. But this has to be about me. I am the problem here. She is the symptom. If she has genuinely moved on, then I need to do the same.

I am not a selfish girl; this will be very hard to do. I am set in my ways, like my home comforts and breaking habits, making an effort and trying to be creative will be hard as well. But I must do this. I need to be able to live for me, not us.

> I see now that this was a fundamental problem with our relationship. I was putting 100% into us and neglecting me.

How can anyone love someone who does not exist? Selfless = lack of self. Adam was a construct and existed only for our relationship – he had no authenticity, just an expression of the male side of my nature.

I need to exist.

Only then, can I move on.

Only then will I be interesting again.

Only then will I be worthy of someone's love.

So, let's throw some ideas about, things I would like to try, things that are important to me and things that define who I am ...

A. Adam, as in who was, and how the world currently sees me.

Architecture

Archery

Astronomy

Appearance (female, as much as I possibly can)

Art, creation and appreciation.

Authenticity

B. Body image (female)
   Balance
   Beauty
   Boobs / Bras
   Boats
C. Clothes (female only, detest anything male, they're just the bars on my prison)
   Compassion
   Caring
   Cinema
   Cars
   Creativity
   Canada
   Cosplay? (Fun)
D. Dad
   Dresses
   Diligence
   Driving
   Deportment (female)
   Discovery
   Dance?
E. Eve (of course!)
   Earrings
   Eyes (pretty)
   Expression (personal, authentic)
   Entertainment
   Empathy
   Enthusiasm

Experiences
F. Female / Femininity
   Family
   Future (the)
   Friends
   Freedom
   Film (watch, or maybe create?)
G. Girlhood, being a Girl.
   Goodness, as a concept, leading a good life
H. Happiness
   Hair (removal, ideally permanently)
   Hair (styling)
   High heels (pretty shoes)
   HRT / Hormones
   Home
   Health
   History (learning)
   Holidays
I. Inspiration
   Independence (from Eve?)
   Intrigue (as a concept, for entertainment)
   I.T.
J. Julia, as in who I truly am.
   Julia, as a way of life.
   Jewellery
   Journal
K. Knowledge
L. Life

Love
Lingerie
Learning
Literature

M. Make-up
Mannerisms (Female)
Manicure (really want one!)
Mindfulness
Music

N. Nails (pretty)
Nice (being)
New things to do and try.

O. Open mindedness
Opportunities
Outside (as the real me, I want to exist in the world and be genuine)

P. Pretty
Politeness
Personable
Pedicure
Planning and making plans happen.
Photography?
Pilot?

Q. Quietness / stillness
Quality of life

R. Rest and relaxation
Retro-gaming

S. Skirts

    Smiles
    Stability (emotional / financial etc)
    Spirit
    Stories
    Spa day?
    Studies / learning
    Swimming
    Space (outer and physical)

T. Treatments (beauty)
    Temperament
    Time
    Technology
    Travel

U. Understanding

V. Voice (develop a female voice)

W. Womanhood
    Writing
    Work

X. Y. Z.

Interesting...

    ...well it's been an interesting day at least.

Up at my usual time. I am OK today. I headed to see Katie and was spot on for time. I rang her video doorbell, and we talked through it, she said my appointment was for 10:30, not 9:30! She was enroute and would be there in fifteen minutes. So, I waited and double checked my appointment time – definitely 9:30am. When she arrived, she double checked hers – definitely

10:30! There is a glitch in the appointment software it seems. Still, it's better I was early instead of late...

I had a good chat with Katie, I told her I was going through some relationship issues, small talk, no real details. Then the first session started. It was all good. Not really painful at all. I feel like I have taken a VERY big step. And it feels great.

When we were done, I paid for the next three sessions. I realised it was raining – my jeans were on the line! They were soaked through when I got home, as were the Mogs. My nice clean house is filthy again. I spun my jeans in the washing machine and re-hung them out to dry. I also waited for the mogs to de-filth themselves, then cleaned up the mess.

Around 1pm, I switched my underwear for something more comfortable and suitable, then went to see Kay at 2pm

Her session was emotional and challenging, we covered a lot of ground. I spoke about how Eve was being mean to me, she agrees, this is not acceptable, and Eve and I need to talk this through if we are to remain friends. She also agrees that her not paying her way is wrong and that she needs to step up financially – if we are not in a relationship, then we are housemates – I need to think of her as a lodger, and lodgers pay rent. And lodgers are civil. There is no excuse for a lack of common courtesy.

She says I need to do things for me – I have reached the same conclusion. She also said to be prepared – Eve is ready to move on it seems. I am not sure. She could find someone else and leave at any time I suppose, I need to be ready for this. I most definitely am not at the moment. This is the only way she can move out quickly, without some other patsy, she can only afford to stay here.

Home again, early dinner (left over pizza) and fully female in all the ways I can be by 6pm. I am calm and relaxed.

No idea on Eve's timing. I hope it's not too late; she will be tired, and the weather is bad. So, the drive home will be hard work for her.

Eve came home around 10:45, she seems to be in good spirits so far.

I'm glad she is home safely.

Saturday, June 5th

I slept well, up around 8am, just because. I am OK today, mogs fed, dishwasher on, litter trays cleaned, recycling bag put out and a new one in the bin.

We are planning on going up to see Eve's parents this weekend, they have a new hot tub, so I have removed the nail polish from my toes. Mogs sadly are not invited! So, they rather grumpily are confined to the house. They are washing at the moment, but I am sure they will be meowing at the door shortly...

Eve has the horses to do today, but she got home late last night so I have let her sleep in, and this is why I am up early and have done all the usual chores – not that she will notice or appreciate the effort. She'll be too wrapped up in her own little world as usual. Sorry, that's rude and not like me at all – I'm not sure where that came from, I'm genuinely OK today, honestly. It is 8:50am at the time of writing, I'm sure she will be up soon enough.

I want to see Eve smile again. So, I have decided I am going to smile again first. Smiles are infectious, hopefully it will rub off on her. I think that it is hard for her to smile when I am around because I am upset, and she is walking on eggshells. So, by smiling myself I hope to relieve some of the tension.

I genuinely miss Eve's smile.

I want her to smile again, I want her smile back in my life.

It is possibly a big ask, but it is important to me. So, I am going to try.

I have also decided to set some daily goals. Something to work on every day – some will take longer than a day to achieve, so will roll over, but I will try to work on them every day. I think though that they may well become repetitive, I hope not, but we shall see...

Today's goals

- Smile, genuinely and often.
- See Eve smile.
- Be pleasant company.
- Be interesting.

I think these are good goals to have, simple, and hopefully achievable – let the day commence! I am ready for it!

All goals met! It has been a **really** good day. The first one in months.

Eve was in good spirits today, lots of stories from her 3 days away working and I listened intently (as I always do) and she was exuberant. We went to the horses together and then we drove on to her mum and dad's place afterwards.

On the way there, we talked. We talked about how she has hurt me and that some of it is because I am still so raw, even the little things sting. I said that common courtesies, like saying 'good night', or listening when I am talking are important and I felt that she had not been as nice to me as she should have lately. This had stung and I was left wondering if I was even remotely important to her – the mogs felt like they are more important to her than I was. They certainly seemed to get more of her attention.

She took this on board and as a result, today was much better. I smiled genuinely, and often. I told her about my sessions with Katie and Kay and she listened. She was a bit put out that Kay and I had discussed her, but she is the instigator of my situation and I hope part of my future (in whatever capacity), so she is very much a valid and relevant topic that needs discussion.

My relationship to her is in flux and as a consequence, my life is focused on her at the moment. Eve felt she was being portrayed as "the bad guy" – this is **not** the case at all (although I now wonder if this is how she sees herself, and this is why it touched a nerve). But our living arrangements, financial, domestic, work, history and possible futures are right at the core of my situation and resolving them to develop a way through it all is what my sessions are all about. As well as my gender identity. It is all intertwined. I was understandably a little emotional in the car, but not overly so. It was a good chat and it spun off into us talking about of respective previous few days – it was great.

Drive-thru lunch enroute, we were in good spirits. I made a few amusing comments – and Eve laughed. I made her smile!!! And it was a revelation to me. The past 15 years I have been dedicated to making her happy. It has been my number one goal and I have put literally everything into it. But she has not been happy for some time and her smile is astonishingly important to me. I have truly missed it.

Today Eve smiled.

And so did I.

I was genuinely happy.

And so was she.

JOY!

And I made her smile more than once today, and each time was just glorious. I was genuinely happy too. I think Eve smiled in part because I was happy, the silly little quips were just the trigger. She smiled because I was in a good place, and it manifested in an environment where we could both be happy.

I decided I would smile today. So I did. And as a consequence, the smile became genuine, and others were empowered to smile too. A positive attitude fostered an environment of positivity.

TODAY IS A GOOD DAY!

And this continued all day. Eve's folks were glad we turned up, their garden is astonishingly beautiful, and the hot tub is amazing. The chat was bright and cheerful, I was happy.

I was happy.

I am still happy as I write this.

For the first time in two months plus, I am happy.

I am smiling as I write.

Sunday, June 6th

A nice night's sleep at Eve's folks' place. Up around 8am. I am OK this morning. Actually, I am more than OK, after yesterday, I am good.

I have not had much time to consider today's goals. But I think smiling should be on the list, every day. So I'll start there.

Today's goals

#02

- Smile, genuinely and often.
- Be positive and foster a positive environment.
- Try to find joy in anything and everything.
- Be appreciative for what I have.
- Be polite and good company.

Another good list of things to aim for. I hope I can make Eve smile again today. But as important and amazing as this is, it is more important that I smile.

Yes, I am happy with today's list of goals. I think if I can achieve them, today will be another good day. But equally, should I fail to achieve any, I can't get wrapped up in them. They are goals, not tests – this is an important distinction to make. They are a way to give me some focus, away from being at the whim of my emotions.

On with the day!

It is now 10:10pm, another great day! Woo!

It started off well, I was first up, and both Eve and her dad joined me after 20 minutes or so. A nice, relaxing morning, a cooked breakfast and (another) extended session in the hot tub. The day could be subtitled "three showers and a bath", one in the morning, one before the tub and one after to get rid of the

chlorine – I've never been so clean! The tub itself is a real treat, 35 degrees, bubbles and a nice undercover spot in the garden with privacy screens, Astro-turf and a soon to be finished bar. Awesome.

Eventually it was time to hit the road. We said our goodbyes and Eve drove us back. Once more, lots of chat in the car. For the first time, I am feeling OK about the future. I think I have a bit more of a handle on what Eve is trying to achieve and her motivations – it's not as bad as it seems – she feels like she went from being a child, looked after by her parents, to being my girlfriend, looked after by me and has therefore, never lived independently as an adult. I get it. I am similar, although I have 15 years more life experience on her. I went from living with my folks, straight into being her boyfriend. I too have never lived as an independent adult. The difference though is I never wanted to. I don't feel like I missed out, unlike her.

So, this is why she wants to travel. This is why she is trying to pay her own way when she can. And this is why her latest website venture is so important to her as well as why she is putting so much effort into it.

We disagree on selfishness though. She thinks it's good. I do not. But then I have spent every moment of the last 15 years being selfLESS. I lived to make her happy. And when she wasn't, I felt like such a failure. Being 100% selfless, just as being 100% selfish is <u>very</u> bad. The former robs you of your personality, it makes you uninteresting, a non-person. Trust me, I've been there. The latter cuts you off from the world and makes you a complete bastard whom everyone hates. We are of course, back at the universal truth...

Balance is everything.

And this led into a discussion on common courtesies again and their importance. She has been much better these past 2

days, a joy to be with again. I am so much more positive about us being able to continue to live together – the threat of her walking out feels diminished and if she is polite, respectful and is courteous, then I shall be good company, personable and do the same. This could work. I will not be so hurt, and we can remain friends. We can live our lives as mates, not "mates". Share the good times, be there for each other through the bad times, but not be a couple. Be individuals.

I don't think I will have to throw her out, to be honest, this is something of a relief. If she stops hurting me, I will not need to. If she pays her way, I will be much better off and if I am living for myself, then she can do as she pleases without upsetting me.

I still think she *will* ultimately leave me though. When it happens, I hope to be in a much better place, and I will be able to deal with it. I hope she will always be my best friend and we will always spend time together, I'm not sure at this point how realistic this is, and we don't have to live under the same roof for this to happen, actually, I am coming to realise it might be better if we don't. I will miss her, no question, but if she is in a position to, and wants to, she can go on her own with my blessing.

I don't want her to go, but if she does, I think I will be OK, just as long as it isn't anytime soon.

From a purely financial aspect, it is cheaper to share the bills with me than to pay them on her own. So, I think she will be here for a little while yet, maybe even after she has a regular income.

I have spent the last 15 years creating a stable environment for her to try her hand at anything she wants. **I have <u>always</u> thought of our lives together as a launch pad for Eve.** I have absolute faith in her and her abilities and support all of her endeavours 100%, even the more hair-brained ones! If anyone

can make an unconventional career path work, it's her. She puts so much effort into what she is doing, it's just that a lot of what she has previously tried hasn't been particularly suited to her or too left field to be viable in the real world. This hasn't stopped her trying though. And she *has* had successes. But she has I think, realised that none of these flights of fancy work, or that she just isn't cut out for the typical 9-5 most folks end up with. Unless of course, you have multiple irons in the fire together. This is where she is now. Her YouTube is dying on the vine, it's not going to pay big money and requires a lot of time, all of the time. If you don't love *every* aspect of it, then it just isn't viable. She doesn't. QED. It's something folks do for fun in general, a precious few can make it work as a living. Eve absolutely adores her acting work. Who wouldn't? but although quite well paid, the hours are long, the travel is a pain and the costs eat into her wage, also the work is very sparse a lot of the time. She has finally found a job that she feels is the best in the world for her. I am so happy for her. But she can't live on the income and when she has a lot of work on, it is physically unsustainable for her too. The website is a slow burn, but once it hits a threshold, it will generate an income and providing it stays relevant, should continue to do so independently.

This should, in theory at least, provide a background income 24/7 stabilising her finances. And once she has the first site up and running, she can diversify, build others to increase the income stream. It is a good plan, and her site is awesome. She deserves to succeed here, and I am, as always, 100% behind her.

<u>When</u> it takes off, she is potentially set for life. I am so proud of her. I have absolute faith that she will make this work – the only question is, when will it happen?

Bringing it back full circle, our lives together was a launch pad for her. By calling time on our relationship, she has lost this.

But she still has a safety net in me if she wants or needs it. She has a home with me if she wants and I will <u>always</u> be in her corner. That's what besties do.

She says she is not looking for a relationship with anyone. She wants to be an independent adult for the first time in her life. I think she will like it. I think she will like it a lot. I am not sure I will so much. She is much better suited to it than I am, I think.

This means that she is highly unlikely to fall for someone else any time soon. The heart, of course, is unpredictable and does what it wants when it wants. I mean, I didn't see Eve coming 15 years ago – it took me completely by surprise, I was totally blindsided, and she is now the age I was back then. If it can happen for me, of all people, then it can happen for her. But unlike me back then, she is not open to it. I wanted it, but never believed it could happen, so had given up hope. So, when Eve came along, I was happy to go for it, she, I think, won't be. So, although I can't be sure, I think the chances of her bringing a new boyfriend home are very remote.

And me? Well, I am back to square one. I have no hopes of finding someone else. If anything, my gender identity issues are vastly more insurmountable now. I was a man, who had to spend time as a woman. Now, I am unquestionably a woman, trapped in a man's body and will likely have to spend a large part of the rest of my life living a lie. I've said it before, this is the worst possible place for a trans-woman to be. Forever caught between the two genders, the physical at the far end away from the mind – instead of there being a balance, they try to cancel each other out, dysphoria running rampant. I am trying at least to restore some harmony, by embracing and exploring who I am now while I heal. But there has been a fundamental seismic shift here. I have no way back now and as much as I adore being Julia, a single gender, female. I am unacceptable

outside my front door as me. And my physicality prevents this from ever changing. I will <u>never</u> be a convincing woman; I am just too big. As a consequence, I don't think I will ever be happy with my body if I transitioned, and my life will be harder too. I will be less accepted in society. This is the harsh reality of my situation. The world has moved on, trans folks are much more socially accepted, and monumentally positive strides have been taken in recent years. But 95 times out of 100, I am the biggest person, man or woman, in every room. Out of context, I look OK, I'm no beauty, but I don't look bad, even dare I say it, a bit pretty. But put me in a space with other people and the illusion is shattered – there are statuesque women out there, a few even of my height. But there are very few with my build too. If I was put in a lineup of even the most unlovely of women, regardless of how successful a feminine appearance I have, or indeed how genuine a woman I am inside, I would still be the first to be picked out as a man. I would tower above all of the other ladies, high heels or no. A big woman is acceptable, a woman bigger than all the men in the room is far less so. My femininity will be questioned, constantly, everywhere.

I just want to be a "normal" girl. Why is that such a problem for folks?

I want to blend in and be a typical woman going about her daily business. My gender should be a given, not draw attention, something that isn't questioned.

Although I have yet to test the above out in the world, I have a real perspective on it. When I am looking through Adam's eyes, folks see a person who is unquestionably, a man – even though this is completely false. I will never have this level of unquestioned acceptance if I present myself as who I truly am. Folks will see a man dressed as a woman – always. I know I shouldn't, but I care.

I don't think I will never be happy living full time as who I truly am. Others just won't let me.

The best I think I can achieve is to be happy living part time, looking like Adam, wearing his face and playing the part. His face is permanently attached, but is now a lie, a grand deceit. Living a lie is just awful, but it doesn't stop me being happy and living a good life. Of the two bad options ahead of me, objectively this is the better of them both.

It is not as good as actually being Adam and 'managing' Julia. But I have no way back there, actually as time goes by, I am more and more certain that he won't come back. It's not what I want, but to quote the Stones, *you can't always get what you want*. My previous existence is still the best option and if, by some miracle, it happens, I will gladly take it. I suppose it is possible – I mean, a fundamental change in who I am happened to me recently. But I can't ever go to that place again, I think I was extremely lucky to have Julia waiting to save me, I very much doubt it can happen again. And I definitely don't want to revisit that level of pain, ever. If I transitioned and it happened after, that would be equally devastating. Yet another reason living a lie is the lesser of the two options.

> I will have to make the best of who I am and what I have, just as anyone does.
>
> Only I have been dealt some very unusual cards to play...

So, my gender situation remains unchanged. But I will make the best of it and actually, I really like who I am now. It feels right, being Julia is very nice indeed.

I am much happier about Eve too, I am beginning to think this crazy, one in a million shot of staying besties, sisters even, might actually be possible.

I had the best weekend for months. I smiled, genuinely, and often. And so did Eve.

Life is good again...

...at last.

Monday, June 7th

Eve is up early, out the door at 4am to get to Longcross Studios for a day's work on Call the Midwife. I was awake, even though she was being quiet, and we said our good mornings and I wished her a fun day, although she will likely be uncomfortable – she has to wear a pregnancy suit and a late '50's costume, likely a dress or a nightie, with a period hairstyle. It's going to be a hot June day. But I think the heat will be the least of her concerns – being pregnant AND wearing a dress? Sounds like Eve's worst nightmare to me! Does she wanna do a swap? I'm so weird, I think I'd kinda like this...

Up around 6:30am, usual ablutions, Mogs fed and let out, trays cleaned, glasses and crockery stacked in the dishwasher etc. Housewife duties, why do I like this? I should hate it, Eve does. They are absolutely chores, but I like the place to be tidy, even if my laziness sometimes gets the better of me.

There is always a moment, after I have shaved (electric) and before I have removed my end of the day (night) make-up, where I look in the mirror and see Julia staring back at me. I really like what I see, bedraggled hair, panda eyes, smudged lipstick (and don't get me started on my poor pillowcases), but undeniably Julia. The nightie, the mussed-up hair, the make-up in desperate need of repair, the earrings – all typical of a regular woman about to go to work on her appearance – and I love it. I love the image, of an unkempt woman just going about her regular routine, not polished, just genuine. It's one of the main reasons I hate my beard so much – I am forced to stare at it every day as I mow it into submission, all so I can look the way I feel. Hopefully its days are numbered. Never having to shave my face again cannot come soon enough!

I've begun thinking about Eve (as always!) spreading her wings and flying away. It occurs to me that this is what I've been working towards over the past 15 years. I have supported and encouraged her to find things she loves to do and built a stable platform where her financial restrictions were lifted. She could experiment until she found her niche and then fly.

But I expected her to take me with her on the spectacular journey. I expected our love would keep us together and we would share the adventure. I would have contributed to make it all happen for her. Well, for us.

I always knew she would do amazing things. I tried to give her everything she needed to make them happen. But I expected to be there when they did.

> I have given her the space, time, and platform to realise her dreams. And in return, she has stolen mine from me.

Her launch pad has been reduced to a safety net.

I only ever wanted to make her happy and worked so hard to achieve this.

Making her happy now, means letting her go.

She will fly without me, and this is hard to take.

But the end goal is the same – I just want her to be happy. So, as much as it hurts me, I **can** let her go. It's not fair, she has taken everything from me and is stealing my dreams. She has and will likely continue to cause me immense pain. <u>But she will be happy.</u>

When I started this journal, I knew this. I knew she was about to fly without me and that I was the last thing in the way, stopping her. I knew the solution was to remove myself from the picture. But I couldn't take the pain, my broken heart was my entire world, and I couldn't see anything other than loneliness, loss, and sorrow for the rest of my life. I felt betrayed that I

had done so much, redefined who I am at a fundamental level even, for her, for me, and for us to take this trip together. The most amazing trip, the one where she shows the world just how spectacular she can be. But in doing so, I became a tie. I was never a dead weight, far from it. I was completely supportive in everything she did. Just waiting for the blocks to fall into place and then join her into the most astonishing future. But I was tying her here. I was stopping her flying, and worst of all, I was making her unhappy.

I was the problem.

So, I decided to remove the problem in the most dramatic way possible. I couldn't think past the pain I was in, there was no reason or logic, because there was no future. It had been stolen from me and most painful of all, I didn't have her love anymore. She had taken it all and given me nothing back and now she had robbed me of my dreams, my future too. And I had failed in my number one mission – she was not happy. My whole life collapsed around me like a pack of cards, and I decided she would be happy if I wasn't there, tying her down, stopping her flying.

Two months of Hell followed. Two months of soul searching, healing, rebuilding myself and trying to find a reason, any reason at all, to carry on. I am not there yet. Every day is an unknown, I have no idea if I am going to be a human being, or a miserable wretch when I wake up every day.

But she will fly anyway, without me. At some point it will happen. I hope I am ready when it does. I hope I can watch from the side lines as she realises her potential and, I hope I can be happy too. I still think she has made it much harder for herself. But I suppose it will make her achievements all the more meaningful for her too.

And she will be happy, I'm sure.

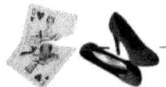

That's all I ever wanted.

I just need to find a different dream for myself...

And when I am old and grey, when she is at last ready to settle down, on the assumption she ever will. She still has her safety net. She will always be welcome to live with me. Maybe we can swap stories? I hope to live my own spectacular life too, what choice do I now have?

This is my dream.

To finally arrive at this point and be satisfied that we both lived lives worth living.

I'll be happy.

Hopefully she will join me and be happy too.

But in the meantime...

There's an entire world out there to see and explore.

I have built a superb launch pad. It'd be a shame not to use it wouldn't it?

Maybe I can fly too?

I shall try.

That little cottage by the sea is a long way off yet. And I have things to do!

Today's goals   #03

- Smile, often and genuinely
- Be diligent and try to enjoy work
- Be personable and interesting company

I have a work trip to Glasgow tomorrow, I will be out of the door at 6am to catch a plane and am staying overnight in Aberdeen. So, I will be leaving my journal at home, not sure this is such a good idea, but I need to save weight and space in my backpack. I will write up the events when I come home on Wednesday night. But for now, I've been dressed correctly from 8pm, so a full 12 hours in a skirt once more today.

I've said it before, but it is always worth saying again.

- I like being Julia.
- I like who I am.
- Being a woman is very nice.

Which is just as well, considering I am stuck. Still, it's a very pleasant place to explore. I like it.

I'm not looking forward to my trip. Too long shackled in trousers and no journal. I think I will need to chat with Eve tomorrow night from the hotel...

Tuesday, June 8th

Out the door at 6am as planned, I got to the airport, but then had to wait until 7am for my car park booking to begin. So I sat in Starbucks car park for 30 minutes or so.

Oh, and you may have guessed that I found space in my luggage for my journal after all – woo!

Stansted airport was really weird, so strange, I reckon 10% capacity, if that. It was like a ghost town. Almost eerie. And of course, masks indoors. So, I wore mine for an hour and a half, through check-in and security and then to the gate. Then an hour on the plane and another 15 minutes in Glasgow airport, and at the same time, collecting my rental car. 3 hours straight wearing a mask is just horrible. I really feel for folks who have to wear them all day.

An unexpected upgrade on the rental car, I had booked a Golf, but collected a Skoda Superb. It's actually a really nice car, very roomy and comfortable. Just as well, Aberdeen is 150 miles plus from Glasgow, it's a long way up and across to the eastern coast. But first, a handover in Wishaw (Newmains).

It went OK, 28 snags, so quite a few, but I've seen worse, and the Site Audit Pro app seemed to work well.

Back in the car, M&S lunch stop and a pleasant drive over the Forth road bridge, through Dundee and then up the coast road to Aberdeen. Scotland is lovely, catch it on a sunny day and there are few places as spectacular.

Chilling in a Premier Inn. I'm not planning on getting any dinner. Lunch was excessive! It's hot in the room though, a warm day and no aircon.

In my nightie (it's all I have brought with me) at 5pm – considering everything, 13 hours in a skirt is a real achievement – even if the room is too hot and in an ideal world, I would be wearing a <u>lot</u> more.

I don't think I need to chat with Eve tonight after all. What are we going to talk about? It's always nice to hear her voice and she could have the most mundane of days and I will still be enthralled. Sadly, the reverse is no longer true. Listening to me appears to be a waste of her time. Yet another string to the bow she shoots arrows at me with. I would only be calling her to make myself feel better. To her, it would be an imposition and in turn, I will feel badly about it. Actually, I am OK without it tonight.

I'm not sure if this means anything. I sometimes think of myself as an addict – Eve is my drug of choice and these last 2 months I have been in withdrawal, craving any and every moment with her. Since the beginning of April, this has been a real fear. I don't want there to be a last moment with her. Losing mum has brought this possibility into sharp focus too. I will never see mum again. And there were so many precious moments lost to the sands of time. Moments I can't remember because I didn't think they were anything special at the time. They were <u>all</u> special and now there won't be any more of them. I realise, all too late, that I should have made much more of an effort back then. I have been trying to do this with Eve. Every second I spend with her is precious to me because, there will, at some point, likely be no more of them. And then I am left with just my memories, so I <u>need</u> to remember them. This is one of the main reasons why shutting me out now is so painful to me. I don't know how many of these snippets of time are left to come, good or bad, they are all now important.

So, I am trying to make some good memories with her while I still can. It's bloody hard when she is wrapped up in her work, laptop, phone etc. She has so much to do and very little time for me anymore. It hurts. Likely because I am desperate to make the most of these fleeting moments. Addicted? Sadly, yes.

She could fly away tomorrow, and I am not sure if once she is flying, she will ever come back. Why would she? Being sad, hurt, and miserable gets in the way of making the most of every remaining moment. So, I am smiling. It is forced at first, but when my smile is returned, it becomes genuine and the more genuine it is, the more it happens. And then, I have moments <u>worth</u> remembering.

Time is a dwindling resource.

I don't have time to be miserable.

I need to cherish what we have so I have something great to look back on when time inevitably runs out...

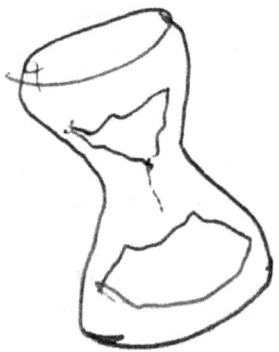

Wednesday, June 9th

Too hot. The hotel room in Aberdeen is too stuffy, even with the windows open. I slept OK and am OK today. But it is not nice in here. I was awake from 4:30am, I have been ready for the day for some time. Only the pleasantness of my nightie is keeping me here – I don't want to take it off. It is 7:10am as I write this, breakfast is at 8 and I am due on site an hour later in Lang Stracht. The site is approximately 100 yards from my hotel, so I have time. I may even walk it! Actually, I am looking forward to the aircon in the car…

What am I going to do?

In my mind, I am Julia 24/7 and I want to be able to express myself in a genuine and authentic way 24/7 too. I want to live as a woman now. I never used to, my body was wrong, but I lived with it and made the best of it I could. I worked with the tools I was given. I long to be physically female. I have always felt my genitalia was odd. I just don't like it. Furthermore, I detest what the hormones they produce has done, and are continuing to do to my body. I have fantasies where I am in an accident and the hospital has to amputate them. "We can reconstruct them, but they will never be right", "They never were, can I have a vagina instead?" But these are fantasies, if I end up travelling this road, I will have to make it happen – but I am just too big, so I will never be able to pass the "2 years living in your real gender" test, so the NHS, great as they all are, is I think, not an option for me. If it comes to this and I feel I have to go all the way, I suspect I will have to save and pay to travel to Thailand. I am losing weight, this will help. But my shoulders are broad, and my torso is long, contributing to my 6'-2" stature. So, I will <u>always</u> look like an unusual woman. As opposed to a manly man. Does this actually matter? Society thinks so, business thinks so. But

if I were physically female, even a huge female, at least I would be female. And I could always continue as I am. Disguise myself as Adam in order to fit in where needed. I am bloody good at it, but at least I would be physically who I actually am.

Would this make me happy?

Truly, I am not sure.

I think it would, the grass is always greener as they say, but I think, if I had the correct downstairs and wasn't constantly flooded with testosterone my dysphoria would be diminished. I don't think it will ever truly leave me in peace, I suspect that I will never be truly satisfied. But even though, in part, I will still be living a lie, I will be an enormous step closer to the truth than I am now.

I would need to take hormones. I already want to. They will change my appearance and make Adam's disguise harder to pull off, but Julia will become physically real, and this will definitely make me happier.

Being Adam though will make me sadder and this is a one-way ticket. There is no going back.

What I want, is to **BE** Julia, body and mind in harmony. But present as Adam if I absolutely have to.

I want the choice back.

I have <u>always</u> been both.

This, I suspect will never change.

Adam is diminished, the construct that he was is gone, but his body remains.

Julia is who I am now.

But Adam is still a part of my life, and he is useful! Being Adam used to be great, but can it ever be so again?

I don't know.

I just don't know.

And there is no way back from a full gender transition.

But I ***want*** a vagina. I want my breasts to develop further, I want hips and a waist, I want softer skin and all this hateful body hair gone forever. I want to be able to live 24/7 as Julia. Is some, or any of this possible? YES! All of it is. But will I be happier afterwards?

I am not sure.

How can I ever be sure?

If I am ever sure, it will happen. No doubt about it, I want it a lot, I want to be authentic. But until then, I am better off as I am. If I go through a full transition and I am not happy / happier, then this would be an utter disaster.

It can't happen if I am not sure.

I never used to want it. But I absolutely want it now.

I want to live openly as a girl.

I want to be a girl, in every physical way possible.

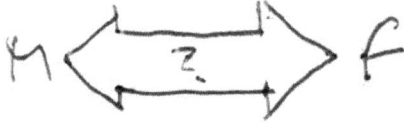

I already am one in mind.

And I like it a lot.

Shit.

Today's goals   #05

- Smile, genuinely and often.
- Be professional.
- Try to enjoy Scotland, it's a stunning place and a privilege to be here.

The handover was difficult. The contractor had a puncture and was half an hour late. I started without him, I had to, or I would miss my flight back. The client team turned up late too, including the Regional Building Surveyor – he is a snake, he

accused my company of cutting out works for no reason. I came close to walking out, part of me thinks I should have. He was up for an argument; I did not rise to it. I was professional when he wasn't. He looked like a fool in front of his peers, and I let him. I have lost all respect for him sadly.

I left the site 40 minutes late because of idiots who can't structure their day to be somewhere on time and then made themselves look like fools by causing a scene, throwing erroneous accusations around with no evidence at all to back them up. I had to drive non-stop back to Glasgow, I effectively traded my lunchbreak for not missing my flight home. In the duty-free section, I bought a tartan bow tie for Eve's Shetland pony. She could wear it as a bow in her mane – cute. I also bought Eve a 'Glasgow' mug for her tea.

The flight back was uneventful, I listened to music on the plane and was thankfully home on schedule. It is warm down here too, nice and sunny. Eve and I had a very pleasant night out at a local pub. A lovely and much needed pub dinner, outside, under the gazebo in the pub garden.

I was at last in a skirt from 8:30pm, 11-ish hours today. The aircon is on in my room – I will sleep well tonight.

Thursday, June 10th

Awake from 5am, the aircon is lovely and it enabled me to dress fully and sleep well. I switched my nightie for a full daywear outfit. It occurs to me that listing the garments I wear is a bit repetitive, not sure if I shall continue, fully clothed is all you, dear reader, really need to know I suppose. I am beginning to think these ramblings might be of interest to others, or maybe even, help someone. I am not writing this for anyone other than myself, but when I read back some of my prose (that sounds far too grand for my ramblings), it doesn't look like the random scrawling of someone who is new to keeping a diary. Equally, I find the words engaging, but then I suppose I would, given the subject matter is myself. It comes down to who this book is for I suppose and the answer to that, is of course, me. No offence! So, for the record... Bra, knickers, stockings, slip, skirt, blouse and at one point, heels too. Make-up and earrings were already done, so fully clothed. I snuggled up in bed in my cool room and drifted off to a very pleasant sleep. It is a great way to both end and start the day and after two days away, I needed some TLC.

Today's goals   #06

- Smile, genuinely and often.
- Be pleasant company, be personable.
- Dedicate some time to my appearance.

This last one is specific to my toes. I need to trim and paint my nails. When I get ready for bed tonight, I will make some time for a pedicure.

It was the regular site meeting again this morning – more snagging. Feels like this is my life at the moment... I'm not sure how long I will be there, and I could do with some time in the office after 2 days away. Afterwards, I am going to see dad for the evening. It'll be nice to see him as it's been a week or two.

I need a hug from Eve. I miss them. They are no longer automatic; I will ask for one shortly.

The hug was lovely, much needed and appreciated. Simple, human contact. Warm and meaningful. I set off to my meeting and was on site for 9:30am. I spent a lot of time walking the site with the Client, agreeing a definitive snag list. A good day's work.

I left the site and headed to the office for the last hour or so. Then I set off to see dad.

It's always good to see him. We chatted and then headed to a local bar for a meal. Sitting outside with my dad on a summer evening, watching the world go by. Nice, good times.

Back home around 9pm, Eve was watching Beverley Hills Cop 2 when I walked in. We watched the end together (a great film, good choice Eve). Then we headed up. I was in a skirt by 9:45pm, so 10 hours as a full woman today. I will make up the deficit tomorrow...

I painted my toenails tonight too. They look nice (I've not done too bad a job, if I do say so myself). It's great having pretty toes – I adore having them painted and polished.

I looked up "bottom surgery" today, this seems to be the current slang term for a vaginoplasty. It costs around £10k to go privately in the UK, I suspect less if I want to go abroad, but of course there is the travel expense. Doing so will mean fewer restrictions and hoops to jump through. Vaginoplasty and gender reassignment are part of a full and complete transition over here. I think this is what I want, I still have my doubts over how successful it will be. I am never going to be a completely convincing looking female.

But just as I can be physically male, but express myself as Julia, equally I can be physically female and present as Adam – if it works one way, it'll work the other too. Be intersex. Present

as a male and legally be Adam. But be Julia both in body and mind. However, in the UK, this is non-conventional and as such is likely to prevent any surgery happening. If I decide to do this, I am pretty sure I will have to save the money and travel abroad. Do-able, and I am certain there are world class surgeons out there but finding them is much harder and I would feel much more comfortable going through the NHS. A safe pair of (skilled) hands is what I want. Afterall, this is for the rest of my life.

    An intriguing idea, that's for sure.

    But at the moment, that is all it is.

An idea.

Friday, June 11th

A day off work, I am OK today. I'm seeing Kay at 11am, it is 9:30 and I had a nice lie in. Eve is at work, filming something called Endeavour, somewhere in Hertfordshire, she left early but I was awake, and we said our good mornings and goodbyes. I am showered and about to dress for the day. I had a good nine and a half hours in a skirt already, should be able to hit 50% easily.

Daily Goals #07

- Smile, genuinely and often.
- Foster an atmosphere where it is all good.
- Allow myself to be happy when I can.
- Get as much out of my session with Kay as possible.

10:45am, sat outside Kay's home watching the clock. I will wander over shortly...

Another good session with Kay, it was much less emotional than previously. I explained my new "smile" philosophy and how it was working well for me. I brought her up to speed on Eve and our recent conversations. Politeness, common courtesies and how this and my new openness to being happy had improved things generally between us. I also told Kay about how I felt I squandered so much time with my mum, so many moments that are now lost instead of remembered and how this has made me very aware that my time left with Eve is now limited. At some point it will end, I am sure. So I need to be able to make happy memories in the time we have left. When we go our separate ways and there are little, or no opportunities left, I will have a bank of good memories with her to look back on and remember fondly. This journal will help with this.

Being miserable stops this happening. So, I am working on not being so.

Smile.

A simple philosophy of life.

Generally, this is working well. But some days are much harder than others. Sometimes, I can't help but be sad. These moments are now, thankfully, transitory and becoming less frequent. But I think I will always carry this sadness with me from now on. I refuse to let it define me anymore though. It is a part of my life's journey, it has had an enormous and profound effect on me – this cannot be overstated, but I am much more than my recent traumatic experiences and the sorry circumstances I find myself in.

I did some chores around the house afterwards, when I got home. I then refitted the battery in car #2 and settled down to watch some TV in the afternoon.

Larry mog came up to see me, he was very pleased to have one of his 'hoomans' on hand to give him cuddles during the day. I binged watched 7 episodes of Clarkson's Farm and enjoyed them immensely. Eve came home mid-way through episode 7 and I picked up a KFC for dinner.

We chatted and told each other about our respective days – it was very nice, and I have made a good memory or two. She went for her usual bath around 8pm and I got changed. 14 hours be-skirted (is this even a word?) today. Nice.

While she bathed, I watched the final, episode 8 of Clarkson's Farm, just to finish off the series.

Bed around 11pm, aircon is on – the house is too hot, but my room is lovely and cool.

Night – a good day.

Saturday, June 12th

6:45am – awake with my thoughts...

I am thinking about dad and his Will at the moment. I think he has disinherited me. And I am not sure how I feel about that.

It's his estate and he can do with it as he sees fit. The problem is that he doesn't want any of it ending up with Eve in the event of my death. But what I think he has actually done; Is stop me from receiving any of it if Eve is in any way still in my life.

As you can imagine, this is very upsetting.

As I understand it, my brother and his wife have been made executors of his Will and I no longer am. I am OK with this, I trust them to do the right thing, but there is an opportunity for them if things are not great between them and I at this point in time. I am sure this will not be the case, so not a serious concern. But in a cold choice between their kids and me, I suspect that I won't get a look in. So, although small, there is a risk. I am not concerned as I said, we all get on really well, but (I hope), this is a long way into the future and who knows what will happen in between.

Furthermore, I don't know the wording of the Will. My understanding of the intent is that in the event of me passing, the part of dad's estate that came to me would pass to my niece and nephews, not Eve. I am happy with this.

But I think he has moved the goalposts. I think he has placed the portion of his estate that would come to me in trust and put my brother and sister-in-law in charge of determining if I should receive it. Or, if it stays in trust until I pass on and it then goes to their kids.

A straight choice. Me or their kids.

I can see a tiny possibility of Eve and me still being in some ways together at this time. I'd like this very much, although I don't think it is now very likely at all. I am however, working on making that happen, ideally, we would still be best friends, sisters, and possibly house mates.

This is the best of all possible outcomes as far as I am concerned. But it looks like it now comes at a cost.

In this scenario, I think this will prevent them releasing dad's estate to me. There is also a fair chance that Eve will not be completely financially independent, or it will be hard to prove. And that may well be all the excuse needed to tip the balance away from me.

What it means is this...

Live as house mates.	Go our separate ways.
Be happy.	Be lonely.
Salvage something worthwhile from the last 15 years	Last 15 years are lost. Only memories. Lose my best friend and lose everything I worked for
	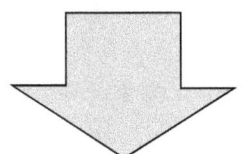
Disinherited	Inherit whatever dad leaves me

This is no choice at all. I don't care about his estate; I would much rather he spent every penny sharing a good life with me and his family and leave us all nothing but fluff in his wallet.

Don't get me wrong, I would love to receive a windfall and ultimately it is right that my niece and nephews get my portion of his estate anyway. But receiving it shouldn't cost my friendship with Eve. It shouldn't cost me my only slim chance at salvaging anything / something from the last 15 years. And it shouldn't cost me the tiny sliver of a chance of happiness with Eve still in my life.

Living on my own, lonely, and sad is not worth a third of his estate. Whatever that may turn out to be.

But it is upsetting never-the-less.

He's my dad, I love him dearly, but if I have to choose between his estate and a chance of having Eve still in my life, then this is no choice at all. Happiness trumps money *every* time.

It is really hard for me to not see this as a conscious effort on his part to lever Eve out of my life. It stinks like there is an agenda here. He can only see the pain she has caused me, and it is clear, he now sees her as a parasite on my finances. So, he is making sure she doesn't drain his estate too – I understand, I get it – and it is his choice. He is wrong of course but has made up his mind and this <u>is</u> going to affect me directly.

I don't care about his money. I never did.

I do care that he has such a low opinion of my friendship with Eve.

I do care that he doesn't trust me to deal with this on my own.

I really do care that he is adding to my relationship issues.

I am annoyed that I now have to think about his estate and, by implication, his passing.

I care greatly that events outside of my control are now directly affecting my recovery and relationship, such that it is, with Eve.

My happiness, that is my choice. Of course it is! How could I choose anything else.

Money is nice, but I would much rather be happy.

The future is not written, this may well be just a worry over nothing. But I am resigned to the eventuality that I am effectively now disinherited.

And that *is* upsetting.

If he had pulled this stunt 2 months ago, I think it would have absolutely resulted in me not coming back on that fateful night. If I died ahead of him, then his inheritance would go to my niece and nephews. Another reason to remove myself from the equation. There is the same twisted logic here that brought me to the brink in the first place. I am the problem, remove the problem. I barely survived that night; this is enough I think to have pushed me over the edge. He's playing an ill-informed, stupid and frankly dangerous game.

Spend it *all* dad. Spend it on good times with your family, me included. I suppose this means that I need to make the most of the time I have left with him too. This isn't a chore, I like spending time with him, even if he is making things a lot more difficult at the moment. I love him, he's my dad after all.

It's exactly the same as my need to make the most of the time I have left with Eve.

In both cases, money has nothing whatsoever to do with my relationships with them. It never has. Money is not what makes me happy.

I chose to be happy.

Not a good way to start the day, but despite this, I am OK. Maybe after all this time, I am numb to the Machiavellian intent of those closest to me? I will smile today and try my very best to have a great Saturday.

Daily goals #08

- Smile!!! And be happy!
- Don't worry about dad and his Will.
- Make some good memories.
- Buy at least 2 new journals!

Horses, it was nice to see them again. Eve has a new top; it is cropped and has a colourful eagle on it – she is so cool – it looks great on her! I'm jealous… In a good way!

We had (yet another) chat about money. I don't want to keep banging on about it, but she <u>has</u> to contribute more when she can. I cannot keep supporting her indefinitely and get nothing in return. If we are a couple, then this is fine. That's how couples work – love pays for all. But she doesn't want to be in a couple – I do, I like it and want to carry on – she does not and has taken her love from me. If she isn't paying me with love, then I can't continue to support her. She loves me and she lives with me as part of a couple, we support each other as a result. Team. Or. She doesn't love me, and we live as individuals. We pay our way as individuals. We are not a team.

The problem is, Eve cannot pay her way. Hopefully she will be able to at some point. I need her to, and I think, she needs to as well. For her own sake.

We both want and need her to succeed and earn a stable living.

When she can do so, our relationship as boyfriend / girlfriend will truly be over. I will be devastated again. But equally, I will be so proud of her and happy for her well-deserved success. My faith in her and her abilities is absolute – she works so hard and has so much passion – she deserves it.

Until then, the bills need to be paid regardless, so I will pay them.

But Eve no longer lives here for free. She <u>has</u> to contribute. She can have her independence, but this means she will be independent. Literally.

I am wondering if I should have put a deadline on how long I am prepared to support her. I really don't want to. But she has hurt me badly, sometimes in my head, I can't see the lines between being reasonable, lashing out or being taken advantage of.

Dad believes Eve is taking advantage of me. This is why I am effectively disinherited. I do <u>not</u> see it this way, she is my best friend – as long as she doesn't hurt me and I enjoy her company, I am happy to continue.

If she hurts me, ignores me, or makes it hard for me to enjoy her company, then I am not.

Regardless, she will have to step up financially. The mortgage and the bills <u>must</u> be her No.1 priority. I expect to be paying a progressively smaller amount from now on, up until we reach equilibrium.

This is going to be really hard for her and I run the risk of being resented for it. But I did <u>not</u> put us both in this position. She did.

Independence means individual responsibility. Fiscal as well as personal.

And, as she pays more, and stays poor, I will pay less and be better off. This will be hard for Eve, I think. It will be hard for

me too. I will want to help her, but I just can't, not anymore and I don't think she will want my help anyway – she has something to prove.

If I can sort out my Will and Eve pays her way, then I think I will no longer be disinherited. There is a glimmer of hope here.

But what sort of man disinherits his own son (daughter), just to spite the woman she loves?

What sort of man puts both of his children on a direct collision course, just when they are both grieving his loss?

What sort of man puts his other son in a position where he has to chose between his brother and his kids?

What sort of man?

My father.

I am going to do as he has asked. I am going to change my Will.

But.

I refuse to play his petty games.

I think it would be better all round if he just wrote me out of his Will completely.

It'll save a shed load of heartache.

My niece and nephews will get his estate anyway, regardless of me seeing it in the meantime. So why put my brother and I at loggerheads? And why give my brother such an unpleasant responsibility?

I can side-step it all if I wish.

I have no idea what I will be saying goodbye to.

But I don't want his money – I never did.

I just want to be happy.

His money would be nice, but it won't make me as happy as Eve still being in my life. In whatever capacity we end up.

Even if we are apart, but just friends, this will make me infinitely happier than spending his inheritance.

The additional financial stability would be lovely. But not essential and it is definitely not worth falling out with my brother over.

My niece and nephews will get it ultimately, I have no one else to leave it to and am highly unlikely to find anyone else. I'm far too late in life to have children of my own and don't want them anyway.

I think I can cut through all this petty bullshit. I probably will.

Sunday, June 13th

7:12am, good morning world. I am OK today; I will smile and then hopefully I will be happy.

I've been thinking about where I currently am in life and how this is going to affect my future. I had never really thought about my inheritance from dad, but I am now and as a consequence, I am also thinking of my long-term retirement plan and how I possibly finance it.

Something else fun that I have just thought about, wouldn't it be just perfect, if I spent my part of his inheritance on a full gender transition? The man who flatly denied my existence for my entire life. The man who stood in the way of mum having a daughter. The man who denied me the chance to grow up as the girl I am. The man who sent me to a psychotherapist in an attempt to 'fix' me. The man who even to this day, only sees in me what he wants to see. It would be perfect if he ends up funding my womanhood. I think so anyway.

Anyway, back to my future...

- The plan was: To climb the housing ladder with Eve and then downsize in stages to generate an income from the equity.
- This <u>hasn't</u> happened. We are still in our first home. I will not have enough equity I think to generate a significant enough sum if I downsize. I will have to move a very long way away to maximise the yield if this situation continues. Plus, although I pay for 100% of the house, I only own half of it. I will need to buy her out.
- The backup plan was: Buy a second property and become a landlord.
- This too hasn't happened.

- But I think I could now do it, maybe. I have some equity in the house to borrow against and I think I could use this to get a second mortgage. This mortgage would be paid for by the rent.

Eve and I talked about this some years ago. I think I now need to make it happen somehow. It will be hard to do, but it will result is me owning one and a half properties instead of half of the one I live in. I can sell the second property and retire to somewhere far away, but I don't think I will have enough to live on indefinitely.

Can I double this up? Possibly. Use the equity on both properties to get a third, or even a fourth. This will definitely see me through my retirement. It also gives Eve our current house to live in in perpetuity. It doesn't provide her with an income too, but she is working on that and to be honest, it is no longer my responsibility.

This will impact on me financially though; the deposit alone will be very hard to raise, and I will need to dramatically reduce my outgoings – my quality of life will suffer. The car will have to go, in favour of something much less ostentatious – something cheap to run and buy. I may also have to sell car #2. This will break my heart (again), I won't capitalise on my investment even 50% and I would very much have liked to enjoy the car at least for a little while.

Eve has to contribute to the home bills.

If I can end up with 1½ or 2½ houses over the next 25 years, then I can retire comfortably, I think. I am 50 years old; I only have 25 years of work life left (assuming I get that far, nothing is a given). My chances of getting a second mortgage are diminishing, I need to sort this out now if I want this to happen.

> This could be my "next big thing". A project to work on, investing in my future happiness.

Somehow, I need to do all of this *and be happy too*. This could be very difficult.

Heavy stuff, I never anticipated going off down a financial rabbit hole when I started writing this morning. Speaking of this morning, what about today?

Well, I joined Eve at the horses – it's a scorching hot day, 29°C according to the car mid/late afternoon – but, although warm, there was a pleasant breeze in the field, so it wasn't too bad.

Bacon and eggs for lunch, then we replaced the cold air induction pipes on Eve's sportscar. We spent time rubbing down and re-spraying some small components on her car too, just tinkering – so a productive and fun weekend.

Eve caught the sun on her shoulders, I caught it on the backs of my legs – my first day in shorts this year (yuk, another form of trouser torture). I am not a fan – I'd <u>much</u> rather be in a skirt.

We went to Nando's for dinner and then after, I watched episodes 1 and 2 of a Netflix show called 'Sweet Tooth' – it's quite good, I'll likely watch the rest over the next couple of days.

Eve is working on The Larkins again, Monday / Tuesday / Wednesday, so will be staying away the next few nights as she did last time. Early start for her tomorrow too – 5am ish. So, an early night tonight. I will miss her again.

I have my second Covid jab tomorrow too – fingers crossed I am better this time around...

A good day and indeed, a good weekend.

Daily goals #09

- Smile, genuinely and often.
- Be good company.
- Enjoy the day as best I can.
- Do stuff!

In my nightie around 9:30pm, circa 11 hours in a dress today. I am OK, it was just too hot to bother getting changed while there was still so much heat in the house. At the moment at least, I don't feel any the worse for it, plus I will have lots of time to be me tomorrow and Tuesday evening. I need to plan my time so that I don't have to leave the house or accept deliveries etc.

Also, I spent most of the day wearing knickers under my shorts! After working on Eve's car in the mid-day sun, we both decided to have a cooling and refreshing shower. I also decided that I would be much more comfortable in a pair of my knickers. And I was.

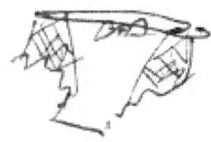 

Monday, June 14th

Eve left at 5:15am, I was awake from 4am, so was able to say good morning and wish her a good few days. I watched her drive away and said "I love you" to the window as she disappeared from view. I miss her already. I still love her. I don't want to. I am left empty now she is gone. The house feels wrong, too quiet again, even though empirically, the background noise level is the same as it was 10 minutes ago. I do not like this feeling. But it is not as fierce as it was a couple of months back – I would've been in pieces by now, instead, I am OK. Progress of a sort I suppose.

I am concerned about my second Covid vaccine today – I hope I am OK. The last time around wasn't very nice, but at least Eve was here, even if she is the world's worst nurse! She was available if I needed her. This time, I will face whatever side effects there may be alone. This is actually one of my biggest fears for the future. Being ill, on my own, with no one to care for me, or ring for an ambulance if I need one. I am sure the jab won't be anywhere near this bad, but at some point in the future it could be. This scares me.

I'm gonna snooze for a bit, and then get up for work, but first, ablutions and mogs.

Today's goals #10

- "Smile, though your heart is breaking".
- Try to find some joy in whatever I can.
- Be diligent and professional at work.
- Don't be lonely, or at least, try not to be.
- Try not to be too self-absorbed / introspective.

The last two are going to be tough...

Work was OK, my brother picked me up this morning and drove us to work, just in case I was unwell from the jab – but it

was OK. I mean, I am OK. I didn't feel the needle at all, my arm is a little dead, it is also sore where the needle went in, and I was a little woozy this afternoon. But much, much better than the first one (I passed out on the floor of the office, hence my nervousness and the precautionary lift in). I am relieved and now protected – I'm part of the solution, I hope.

Home around 6:30 – mogs in and washing done and on the line. Dinner was ½ a French stick, bacon, and eggs – yummy.

I couldn't get changed as early as I would've liked – I had to wait for the washing to dry. In the end I brought it in still a bit damp, just as well I delayed getting changed, I ended up chatting to a neighbour over the garden fence!

Changed around 8:30pm, so 11½ hours today, give or take, in a dress.

I retired to the very welcome AC in my room after a long, hot day. I watched a couple more episodes of 'Sweet tooth' and am about to go to sleep.

I miss Eve.

I am a bit lonely, not bad, but a bit. I didn't quite achieve this daily goals today.

My love for her seems to be not as fierce as it was. Being Julia really helps. But I do still love her. I care about her and her wellbeing. I worry the financial impact of her flying away will compromise her dreams. I worry that her passive income scheme isn't going to pay well enough. She is working so hard on it, and it only needs to pay around £500 per month. This will cover her responsibilities and leave her the acting money she earns to fly with.

This isn't going to happen anytime soon, I fear.

Tuesday, June 15th

7:15am, up, showered, mogs fed, house hoovered, and spare toilet rolls moved into the bathroom, so they are to hand from the "cupboard of mystery" downstairs.

I didn't sleep very well – overheated in the night and had to take my nightie off – even with the aircon on in the room. I woke up hot and sticky – eurgh. I suspect this is to do with the Covid jab and my body dealing with it. Also, a sore left arm meant sleeping on my left side was tricky and randomly, I have a sore left ear too. Although I think this may be my earring – I may well have slept awkwardly on it.

Today's goals #11
- Smiley smiler. Lots and lots.
- Be productive at work.
- Get changed as early as possible.
- Wear women's undies ALL DAY! Teehee!

The last one should be easy to achieve, indeed I may as well only wear knickers from now on. It'll simplify the laundry and I have enough pairs now to make it happen. I think I will only wear underpants now if I am doing something physical (rare) and there is a chance of my trousers slipping a little.

The house is quiet again. Mogs have eaten and are out, exploring, doing cat stuff. The place doesn't feel right without Eve home. But I suppose I will just have to get used to it.

I don't like it, it's a bit creepy and I miss her presence, her company, even just the knowledge she is there.

Strangely, I am not upset. Unsettled is probably a better word for how I am feeling. I am OK I suppose.

Work was good – a nice vibe in the office today. My brother and I have given everyone a £1k bonus and it was very

much appreciated. We also took them out and bought lunch for everyone.

Home on time, Mogs fed, dinner made and enjoyed. Fully clothed from 6:30pm in the correct attire, so 13½ hours living my life openly as a woman today. But of course, I have been wearing knickers all day too. It's all good. I am currently wearing a bra, knickers, stockings, suspenders, slip, skirt, blouse, and heels along with make-up and jewellery. Women's glasses in my prescription and my hair done as far as my limited skills allow – I look OK, maybe a little overdressed in my business-like satin blouse and long pencil skirt, but it's very nice and I like to look smart.

Going to relax, watch some TV and try not to miss Eve too much.

Wednesday, June 16th

7:48am, I am lonely, but I am OK.

Mogs fed and out, I am done in the bathroom, sitting in my knickers, about to get dressed. I have emptied the dishwasher and unpacked, tried on, folded and put away my 4 new T-Shirts (right size this time), put the cat food away and placed some packaging in the recycling – productive! Good job I appreciate most of the domestic things, chores or no, if I am not feeling lazy, I like to see the place tidy and find the results gratifying. If only I could enjoy cooking... No one is perfect!

I have a meeting with my Will people again, hopefully to finalise it. It has to go well, or I may have to go elsewhere.

Today's goals #12

- A genuine smile, or fifty...
- Don't be lonely.
- Be open, appreciate the world and the day.
- Be professional and productive.
- Try to find joy in whatever I can.

Work was OK, it started off well with an unusually productive meeting and then continued in much the same vein up until lunch time. I took the afternoon off to go and sort out my Will. It seems that despite my misgivings, the best way to ensure Eve doesn't receive any part of his estate is indeed to put my portion into a trust after all. I can then draw down from it as I want to, but the money is always owed back to the Trust, it is never a part of my estate, so in the event of my passing, the Trust gets first dibs on whatever is left, ahead of Eve and she has no claim to it. Actually, neither does the tax man or any other creditors I might have. I think, from the little I know, dad may well have done something along these lines, but I need to

be sure. So, I need to chat to him about the details. I will try to do so this week.

Home around 4pm, it's really hot and humid today – not nice at all – thunderstorms tonight apparently. Good, they will clear the air and I like a good storm, very dramatic. Although the mogs won't be very impressed.

I fed the cats late, so I could keep the doors and windows open for as long as I could. I watched 'The Wolfman' on Amazon and was just going to bed when Eve arrived home.

She has had the most amazing three days on "The Larkins" it seems, she'll tell me all about it when she is rested, I am sure. But for now, she is tired and in need of a cooling shower.

It was so good to see her. Even just for a little while before retiring to bed.

The aircon is on in my room once more – at last, some relief from the heat.

In my nightie from 9:30pm ish, so 10½ hours, plus all day in comfy undies.

Tuesday, June 17th

7:15am, the weather broke during the night. It's raining at the moment, but also still really hot and humid – the air has yet to clear. Had the AC on all night, condensate bucket filled up ½ way, so I emptied it this morning. The temperature difference between my room and the landing is marked – must be a good 10°C difference! Eve only has a fan in her room. Actually, she only has this because I had the foresight to buy it for her. She will have had a more uncomfortable night than I, but she was so tired, I suspect she slept well anyway. She is a very sound sleeper, not much disturbs her rest. Well, other than me snoring that is (it really ticks her off). I, on the other hand, wake up at a pin drop. On the plus side, I can drop off to sleep almost anywhere – it's a talent, although not a very useful one... Continuing on topic, I slept really well – to the extent I overslept by half an hour or so. So, after a good night's sleep, I am OK and looking forward to the day.

Pros and cons to sleeping alone, I never thought I would say this, but it's actually not all bad...

<u>Pros</u>	<u>Cons</u>
Temperature and ventilation in the room just how I like it.	Bed is cold in the winter.
Can stretch out and find the perfect sleeping position.	**Lonely, lack of human contact.**
No worries about disturbing the other person, or they, disturbing me.	**Waking up alone every day is the <u>worst</u> possible way to start each morning, <u>very</u> upsetting, has the potential to ruin the whole day.**
Much more likely to get a good night's sleep.	

I think that although there are more pros than cons, the severity of the cons tip the balance for me. If I ask myself "Would

I like to go back to sleeping with Eve?" the answer is a definitive yes. Eve, of course, has the opposite opinion – she instigated this sleeping arrangement and is happy with the status quo.

Selfish vs Selfless again. Time for yet another recap? Oh, go on then...

She put herself ahead of our relationship and in the process hurt me terribly. This was the final straw. The one that sent me over the edge when she explained that she wasn't coming back to our bed because she didn't love me anymore.

My world collapsed.

I have never been so lonely.

I had lost everything I cared about.

I've never felt so much pain.

It was overwhelming.

So I drowned.

I broke down as the enormity of the situation began to hit me, the man I used to be was destroyed utterly and I fled to my safe-haven, my only refuge, I inhabited my female nature and became Julia. I found myself, for the very first time, female in mind completely. And furthermore, there was no way back, all that remains there is pain. Julia was hurt too – I am one person after all, what affected my male side also affects me too. But I was a step further away from the maelstrom.

If I hadn't had this, there wasn't anywhere near enough of Adam left to carry on. I wouldn't have come back on that night, 2 and a bit months ago. There would have been nothing to stop me.

The maelstrom tried so hard to drag me down. But as I sat there, thinking about how I write my final words and how they could survive the crash, I realised that I wasn't Adam. I was Julia. Completely. Body and mind, outside the house, dressed entirely

and exclusively as a female, surrounded by the few scraps of paper I had in the car and a pen. And instead of a suicide note, I was manically scribbling all the pain down – literally purging my brain of all the poison. And in the end, it wasn't quite so overwhelming. In the end, I ran out of paper and was exhausted.

There was no thought process behind my actions that night – only that I wanted the pain to stop. I was dressed as myself, only because I had to be comfortable at the very end. I left the house as myself with no trepidation, fear or thought. As if I did so, dressed this way, all the time. I was utterly focused on doing what needed to be done. I hadn't even considered I might need to write a note – I only had what little paper I could find already in the car. A letter, comprising 2 sheets of paper, from my tax return, of all things! They are covered in my scrawl, and I suppose they should be part of this write up too – as important as these pages are, the most important thing I have ever written. They also contain what was left of Adam, he, along with my agony, is purged onto the pages, a memorial to the man he was.

I drove home, only now was I worried about how I was going to get back into the house unnoticed, dressed as girl, by my neighbours – I wasn't worried at all when I left the place, a total change of attitude, well everything really. I suppose I now cared again?

Five words.

Just five of them.

Said sincerely, quietly, and with absolute conviction.

"I don't love you anymore".

1, 2, 3, 4, 5. That's all it took.

They brought me to the very brink of existence.

Who would have thought that words could be so powerful?

These five words, spoken calmly and truthfully were enough to murder Adam. The man he was is gone now. I am healing, but whatever is left of him will never be the same. I escaped into the femininity of my mind, I became Julia, fully. She saved my life on that fateful night.

That, and words.

Lots of words.

Five words brought me to the very edge of life.

All the words on those three pages and then continuing within these journals stopped me plummeting over it.

> The King is dead...
>
> Long live the Queen.
>
> This journal belongs to Julia Phillips, and it saved her life.

And it continues to do so, so I write. I have never kept a diary before, I never saw the value, but it is a good outlet and I like the discipline. It's creative and constructive.

I am reaching the final pages of this book, but I have Volume 3, ready to go. At this point in time, I think I may write a journal every day, in perpetuity. Assuming I still have something to say other than repeating goals, listing my entire outfit and how many hours I have been dressed this way. If I have something worth writing about, then I shall. I like it and it definitely helps.

Speaking of which...

Daily Goals #13

- Smile, genuinely and often (of course!)
- Write in my journal.
- Be a good person, do something good today.
- Be professional.
- Be open to the world.
- Take joy in the moments.

A good set of goals today. Let's see how well I do with them...

The Thursday site meeting first, technically no meeting today and as the contractor hadn't been on site all week, none of the snags had been dealt with either. So, nothing for me to cross off the list. But I went anyway. The lead of the team who has moved in was frustrated at the lack of work from the contractor – so I went to help her and reassure her that they will be resolved. My client wasn't there, the contractor wasn't there – I went to be professional, and I did a good deed. The contractor will be back on Monday. I went above and beyond when no one else did. A good deed indeed and two ticks off my list.

Back in the office, I think I have (finally) finished off the first batch of the drawings. I'll send them out in the morning, yes.

For the first time in weeks, I am working on Friday. I am not back full time though, I have Kay a week tomorrow and Katie in a fortnight – there are more Fridays off to come, but I have begun to phase back into working 5 days a week like regular folk. The irony is that, for the first time in weeks, Eve is not working on Friday. We seem destined to spend our days apart. Not sure if fate has it in for us two...

After work I went to see dad and told him about my meeting with the Will advisors. He is going to take this to his solicitors and get their advice. To be honest, I'm not sure he will, I get the feeling they are railroading him into the way they want to play it and he doesn't understand, or care about the ramifications. All he can see is cutting Eve out and is happy to do so by any means. I know him, he makes a plan and follows it

through to the end, this train is already well in motion and the destination is set.

Despite this, we had a very enjoyable evening at a local bar and a very nice meal too. I returned home to find Eve halfway through "Goodbye Lenin" – a truly brilliant film – I watched it to the end with her.

In my nightie by 10pm – not so much time as me today, only 10 hours in a dress. I'm not sure if this means anything. I am still vastly more comfortable in women's clothes, but I am beginning to feel less uncomfortable dressed as Adam. Maybe because I am wearing knickers? I don't know. I hope this is progress, it feels like it just might be...

A good day.

Friday, June 18th

7:50am, I am tired today, I didn't sleep all that well. I was awake often, for various reasons. I'll have to get up shortly and get ready for work. I showered etc earlier, so I won't be late, but I really could do with another hour in bed. Other than this though, I am OK this morning.

Today's goals   #14

- Smile, ah well, you know the rest!
- Enjoy my work day and be productive.
- Be open to the world.
- Find the joy in all things.
- Look for an appreciate the beauty that is everywhere.

Work was good, although it felt weird going in on a Friday after such a run of having them off and the rain was torrential on the way in. Perilous driving conditions, very limited visibility. Once there though, I quickly finished off the drawings – batch one completed. I made a start on the next location's drawings, so very good progress.

Home around 5:30pm, I'm very annoyed with my local pizza place though – 1 hour, 45 minutes to deliver a pizza! Terrible, and it delayed me getting changed. Still, I managed to clock up 12½ hours today and of course, I was in the correct lingerie all day too. Well, at least the bottom half.

Watched "Kevin and Perry Go Large" with Eve – a very pleasant way to spend a wet Friday evening.

Saturday, June 19th

Good morning, I slept really well, I only woke up once to turn the fan off – I needed it. Despite being dressed fully (must kick this habit), I was chilly. It is 7:44am and I am still fully clothed. I am not just OK, I am actually feeling quite good today!

Eve has ordered a new backpack, it arrived yesterday. She backed a Kickstarter campaign, it was fully funded and after some time, the backpack came through. It's pretty epic – perfect for travellers – really well designed. It's an impressive thing. But she upset me (a little bit). She said, "It's not just a backpack, it's what it represents." I didn't answer – I knew I wouldn't react well. I want so badly to be excited for her and her travel plans. But it is still tainted by feelings of rejection. We are supposed to go on adventures together, that's what our lives have been all about until now. But she wants to do this on her own – this is bound to hurt. Before, I would have been upset, but would've done anything to make her happy. So, I would've let her go and indeed, if she needed anything from me to make it happen, I would've gladly given it. Now, it still hurts, but differently. Now, the backpack is a physical representation of how my life has fallen apart, how she has traded my life for a travel experience, without even consulting me. Now, she goes on her own, and on her own terms. Now, she funds it all herself. Now, I have no idea how long she will go for, or if she will even come back.

And in the meantime, I am slowly buying her a house! Every month I pay a bit more of the mortgage off, on my own. I pay Eve's share because it <u>has</u> to be paid. Every month the mortgage reduces a bit more and "we" own a tiny bit more of the property we live in. And when I pass away, in years to come, she will own it all, free and clear. And I don't begrudge her this, I love her. But I do begrudge her not pulling her weight, I never did, but I do now. She will end up owning it all. The house that

<u>I paid for.</u> The launchpad I funded and continue to fund, that enabled her to leave me behind and fly away.

Priorities.

The mortgage comes first. Eve has a commitment.

The house gives her a future, it is a vehicle that enables her to retire and live with no huge bills to pay. And she can sell it, move to a cheaper area, and live on the capital raised. Just as both of our parents have done. But I am no longer going to give her this for free. If she wants this safety net, then she needs to buy some of it off of me by reducing my monthly outgoings and paying off her half of the mortgage. Call it rent for living in the same house I pay for. She wants to be housemates? Well, she needs to pay her share.

It's a bloody amazing deal for her. She has the best landlady in the world and gets an entire house, for a very small amount. But she has to pay <u>something</u>, even if it starts small and becomes larger, as her finances dictate.

She can't blow the mortgage money on travel; the mortgage comes first. Mortgage, literally meaning "Death Pledge" – you don't mess around with something so named. And I am reasonable, she can have both. I recognise she can't pay it all, yet. This is vastly more than the mortgage company would do. I am willing to give her time to ramp up her contribution. But she has to pay something, even a peppercorn would do. Every month. Even if the amount is flexible, to suit her day-to-day circumstances. And eventually, she needs to pay her half of the bills. This is fair.

When she does this, I will no longer be supporting her, and this will open the door to releasing dad's inheritance to me.

In the meantime, I need to think about my retirement. The plan was to climb the ladder and downsize in stages to provide capital to live on. Eve stopped us climbing the ladder, we should

have moved house years ago. She didn't want to. My retirement is now in jeopardy. So, I think I need to buy a second property to rent out. It'll be hard to do, but Eve's contribution to the mortgage will help. This is another reason why she must pay her way. I have paid it for her for 15 years, she now needs to redress some of the balance. This will secure my future.

Both of our futures secured. It's a good plan.

Todays goals #15

- You know the first one, smiling is great.
- Find joy in everything I can.
- Be open to the world and all it can offer.
- **Take joy in being female.**

I don't want to get changed today. I want to spend it in a skirt. I love the fact I've spent the last 12 ½ hours straight dressed completely as a woman. I am going to see how long I can stay in my outfit. If Eve has the horses this morning, I should be able to get another couple of hours in at least, I think.

---

15 hours straight. Furthermore, I was back in a skirt by 7pm, so from midnight to midnight, 16 hours today. Amazing! I feel great.

But it's not all good. I am currently nursing a painful elbow. Indeed, I am writing this with an ice pack wrapped around it. It felt like I dislocated it for a moment moving the spare wheel in the boot of car #2. There was an audible pop, and the pain was instant, deep into the joint. On a scale of 1-10 (thanks Katie), I would put it at a 7. But now it's a solid 4, every time I move it. Hope it feels better tomorrow. It's really unpleasant.

Other than this, it's been a good day. Lunch in Colchester. Eve and I had a positive discussion about her paying me "board

and lodging". No fixed amount in the short term. I suggested she start with £100 this month and we'll play it by ear. But she needs to pay ½ of the bills eventually. I also said that the mortgage is non-negotiable, but if she is away for an extended period of time, other bills are. Facts are that if she isn't home, then the running costs of the house are less. Fair.

Lovely lunch in café mews in Colchester, then home and some jobs around the house. Cutting back the bush at the front, swapping Eve's sportscar and car #2 over on the drive so I can get it to the top of the estate, ready for collection and delivery back up the garage.

Finished the day off with a KFC and a film, bed around 10pm, Eve has an early start tomorrow. 7:30am call time in Swanley, Kent for "The Larkins".

*!&**! My elbow is sore!

Sunday, June 20th

Eve was up early, off for a day's work on "The Larkins" and she was gone before I woke. She has something called "Trigger Point" tomorrow, then some much needed time off.

I had a bit of a lie in. I decided I was going to push the boundaries a bit too, an experiment. Lingerie, skirt (casual), socks and a T-Shirt. A bit of make-up. Comfy. I chilled on the bed watching Veronica Mars (I've nearly completed Season 3) when the phone beeped. A text from dad. He invited me to brunch with him, his new lady friend, and my brother's family. But I only had half an hour to get there, and I needed to shower, get changed and get some diesel. My relaxing morning turned into a flat-out panic. I was 20 minutes late in the end, but it all worked out fine and we had a lovely breakfast / lunch at a local bar for Father's Day.

Fast forward to 2pm and I was enroute home. Once there, I changed back into my previous attire and dealt with some chores. I put some stuff away in the loft, despite my sore elbow (which is thankfully much improved today), laundry, hoovering, dishwasher etc. Then I chilled on the sofa with the TV. It was an interesting experience, climbing a ladder in a skirt. A first for me, but of course I was alone, so no danger of a girl losing her modesty...

Eve came home around 5pm, I rushed upstairs to switch into some (hateful) trousers so she wouldn't be freaked out by my casual experiment.

I had a sandwich around 6pm for dinner, then I got changed properly for the evening. No make-up tonight though, I have folks turning up tomorrow between 8 and 9am to collect car #2 and I didn't want any additional stress in the morning removing the make-up, or worse, checking for any tell-tale residues.

Eve's day was in Eynsford, in the village hall – nice. She retired to bed around 9:30pm. I watched a Godzilla movie (fun and spectacular, but no real emotion, nothing of substance, a popcorn film. It's not going to make anyone's top 10 list I'm sure).

I am writing this at 9:55pm. No daily goals today, but I did smile a lot, I was productive, I did stuff for myself and spent a **lot** of time in a skirt.

- Exclusively dressed as a woman   -   14 hours
- Partially dressed as a woman   -   6 hours
- Dressed as a man (except undies)   -   4 hours

That's got to be a good day, right?

Monday, June 21st

6:37am, ablutions done, and mogs tended to. I am more or less ready for the car to be collected. I would've liked to have cleaned it, but it is low on my priorities list. Besides, who washes their car at 7am on a Monday morning? The truck is due between 8 and 9am, so I have a little time to relax, I think.

Eve left for work around 5:30am, she is relatively local today, Harlow I believe, so not too bad for her. We were polite and civil, I wished her a good day and we said our goodbyes. Then I quietly said, "I love you" to the closed front door as she walked to her car. I am not upset, well, maybe just a little. I was stating a fact. I do still love her. But she doesn't want to hear this, so I said it where it meant something only to me. It would be so much easier if I didn't. My love for her doesn't burn as bright as it used to. It was all consuming for me, the hot motivation for my entire life. But now it is lessened, and consequently my life is not motivated *at all* anymore. I am working on this. If I can find something to motivate me other than my love for her, I will be in a better place.

Being Julia is helping, I am motivated to be true to myself as much as I can, so I do, and I put effort into it. I like being Julia, it is freeing. But I can't engage with the world, so sadly this is only part of the solution.

Today's goals #16
- A cheerful and genuine smile, as often as I feel.
- Be open to enjoy the day.
- Don't be lonely.
- Look for opportunities.

The car was collected around 8:30am, it was a big pickup and a low loader trailer instead of the anticipated recovery

truck. I watched it go; I'm going to miss the beastie. But we now only have 3 cars out, so that's a bonus!

Because of the car collection, I was about 15 minutes late in to work, only to find they had closed the road 100 yards from my office and a 20-minute diversion ensued. All in, over half an hour late – not the best of starts to the week really.

2 steps forward, 1 step back at work today – kinda frustrating, progress was hard won. I stayed late to catch up on the missing time. Home around 6:30pm. Nando's delivery when Eve got in, changed around 7pm – so 12½ hours wearing a nice skirt today. Not bad.

Tuesday, June 22nd

I overheated in the night once again; I really don't like Summer. I had to strip off my nightie and put it in the laundry. Despite this, I slept well though, in just my earrings and nail polish. I am OK today. I've just finished in the bathroom, it is 6:48am as I write.

I feel like this part of whatever process this is may well be coming to an end. Generally, I am OK everyday now. It's been a while since I broke down and really cried. Sure, every now and then, something will trigger an emotion, but in most cases, I am in control, and consequently I don't do anything rash. Spending as much time as possible being me, Julia, has really helped me stabilise. And most importantly, Eve and I are doing OK together all things considered. We seem to have reached a level where we are just siblings / mates, not a couple. I still don't like it anywhere near as much as I did before – I have definitely lost a huge part of my life, but we still have a small something and it is kinda working, at least for now. I am grateful for what we have, especially as on occasions we both came close to losing absolutely everything over the past 2½ months.

I am not sure how long this is going to last. It feels transitory, a calm before things progress to whatever comes next. So, I am trying to make the most of it. It's hard though because the times we do things together are fewer in number, and I don't want to follow her around like a love-sick puppy as I used to. She will find this irritating and eventually despise me for it, I am sure. I will lose any respect she may have had for me. So, we pretty much lead separate lives for the most part. We live in the same house, but even if we are both in the living room together, I am watching the TV and she is normally working on her laptop. It's hard to make any good memories from this and I can't help but feel every moment is a lost opportunity as I fear the end is coming at some point. It's like there is a countdown to the day

she flies away, but neither of us can see how much time is left on it. It's a horrible feeling, sitting there, not really engaged in the TV, looking at Eve, engrossed in whatever it is she is doing on her laptop and knowing that, although we have a dwindling amount of time left, she would prefer to spend it on her own effectively. It's not all like this thankfully, we still chat and do stuff together. Meals for instance, although whenever we can, we split the bill or pay alternately. We do stuff of a weekend, see her folks, visit Colchester, work on her car, it's nice. But it's not like it was. Still, I try to have fun and endeavour to make some good memories.

Every moment together has potential, but we both need to want to realise it for something good to happen – I always do, because I am very aware that we may not have many of these moments left. But Eve generally doesn't. She generally would prefer to do her own thing.

So, I put a skirt on and escape. I feel better about myself instantly and I am not as hurt, or as sensitive to her actions. Logic tells me to accept her choice and don't feel so rejected. As Julia, I can do this. I still feel the rejection, but it's almost as if Eve has spurned Adam's company and Julia is a step away from it, so the pain isn't as intense. Plus, I am in a skirt most of the time, so equally, the pain is lessened most of the time. Also, we are civil and polite, she doesn't withhold these simple courtesies in a nasty or mean way anymore – it sounds like a small thing, but it really isn't. The niceties are hugely important. They are the grease on the wheels and they make it work because they show respect. She just chooses time to herself is all. And that really is all there is to it. It's not personal.

So, things are OK, not great, not awful. OK. And OK is alright.

Plus, I <u>love</u> wearing a skirt most of the time! After so many years, it's such a privilege to finally wear what I want, when I want, for as long as I want. So nice.

I hope the next phase in our lives is alright too. I feel like I am at last in a stable place for now, it's a good place to be. I don't want to go back to playing pinball with my emotional state again. But we'll see what life throws my way and I'll continue witing it down in here until I no longer need to.

Today's goals #17

- I'm smiling as I write this, feels good.
- Be open to the world.
- Make progress and be professional.
- Enjoy the day.

Work was alright, productive and I like the social interaction with my colleagues. Home around 5:30pm, pizza and then changed around 6:45pm, so 13 hours plus in a skirt and of course, knickers all day. This is working out well, I may throw the last of my underpants away, I don't need them, I will think about it.

Eve wasn't very chatty tonight – she is getting an early one to bed as she is up at 5:30am tomorrow. I am not going to see much of her over the next couple of days, she is working and has early starts, I am also out tomorrow night. I am beginning to feel like I am living with a stranger. I don't like it much to be honest. We used to be so very close, I miss it a lot. But it seems to be what she wants and, as always, I just want her to be happy.

Me? Well, I spent the night dressed casually – it was fine, I am getting a little better at it. But, as I started to undress for bed, I stopped at my undies and instead, put on a camisole, skirt and blouse, added lipstick and then stepped back into my high

heels. It is 10:27pm and I am actually more dressed now than I was earlier! It is lovely though; I am very relaxed writing this. It just feels right. And actually, I don't look bad, or even comical, just a well-dressed, not very attractive, <u>very</u> large woman. It's about as good as it gets, and I am happy with my appearance. Anything that stops me looking too weird is good in my book. I just want to look like a normal woman. And, at the moment, other than scale, the things wrong with my appearance are relatively minor and there isn't much I can do about them. Hands, facial features, widow's peak, hips, and waist etc.

A reasonable day all in.

It would've been nice to have chatted with Eve more, but I suppose I shall see her on Friday (we both have a day off). And then there is her mum and dad's ruby wedding anniversary do on Saturday. It should be good fun; I am looking forward to it immensely. I just need to find a suitable gift for them in the meantime...

...speaking of weddings, I have been longing for a wedding dress again. I have **always** wanted one, but never been able to get one. I just can't see how, without being able to pass in public as a woman, or order online and run the very real risk of spending a large sum of money on something that is ill-fitting or not what I wanted. In a perfect world, I would go to a bridal salon and have a full fitting. I am happy to pay four figures for the perfect gown and the complete lingerie set too. It'd be good for them as I am practically a guaranteed sale.

But I just don't know how to do it. I suppose I would just have to be honest with them from the start and hope they are OK with it. Maybe set up late appointments when they are reaching the end of their customers for the day? I really want it, but I just don't see a way of making it happen.

I am never going to get married. Eve didn't want to, and I want to be the bride anyway. So, I think I am going to try to find a way. A way to be a bride, even if only in the comfort of my home, somehow, just for me.

How the hell am I going to find a (very) plus sized wedding dress that I adore?

This is going to take a lot of research, I think…

What I'd like…

- Long sleeves.
- High, or round neck.
- Satin, no mesh and limited lacework – classic.
- A-Line, or Ballgown.
- White or Ivory.
- Back zip and maybe buttons too, although they will be tricky to do up on my own but equally tricky to undo, this is a bonus!

Wednesday, June 23rd

Fantasies. They are odd things. All folks have them I suppose. Random stuff that appeals but are flights of fancy mainly. I am kind of traditional in the Trans mould. My fantasies revolve around being as female as possible. In any and all ways. So, stereotypical female attire, iconic even, are going to do it for me. Wedding dress, maid uniform (not a costume, a working uniform), waitress, nurse etc, you get the idea (not very original, sorry, but in all cases, I'm going for real, not ridiculous). Really clichéd stuff. But they are all unmistakably female, so they work. I don't own anything like this, all my clothes are sensible, all-be-it female in every way. Satins, silks, lace, skirts, dresses, pretty things – this is why I struggle to do casual.

I want a wedding dress, but this is a fantasy. I *could* make it happen, but what will I achieve? A very expensive dress taking up a lot of space in my wardrobe that I hardly ever wear? Actually, this sounds like every wedding dress to me... I can think of a million better things to spend a grand plus on. Maybe start smaller, with one of the other choices?

Eve left early, I was awake, but didn't sleep well (indigestion), so was able to say good morning, wish her a good day at work and then say goodbye. I also said "I love you" as she walked to the car again. I do. Still. Annoying.

I am OK again today. It looks like being a nice, sunny day out there, the birds are singing, and I am about to get ready for whatever comes my way.

I'm going out with colleagues, including family tonight. It should be fun and I am very much looking forward to it. Although it does mean I am unlikely to see much of Eve today / tomorrow and I also need to get the washing in off the line before work. So, I am going to list today's goals and then put this journal down.

Daily goals #18

- Genuinely smile, often.
- Be open to the world.
- Make some good memories.
- Try not to miss Eve too much.
- Have fun!

It is now 10:15pm, a good day.

Work was productive, I am close to finishing the drawings for the second site. Should have it all done by close of play tomorrow.

After work, we headed off to a pub in Chelmsford for a nice meal and a fun night out. It was good fun; I'd like to do it again.

Home around 9:10pm, mogs in, changed and in bed just as Eve arrived home. She was tired – we said our hellos and she had a quick shower before retiring to bed for the night.

Thursday site meeting tomorrow, then Kay on Friday.

Thursday, June 24th

6:48am, Eve left for work just over an hour ago. I was awake and said the usual greeting and goodbyes. I feel like I haven't seen her at all this week. Is this what my life is going to be like? I am not sure I like it to be honest, 80% on my own, 20% in the same house, but not together. It's not very nice, but it sort of works and I suppose I will get more used to it. Importantly, I will see her tonight.

Site meeting once more today – I thought I wasn't going to have to go, but both the client team lead and the contractor have called me in. A little annoying as I need to get my drawing pack done and ready by close of play so I can have tomorrow off work. It's a nice day, the meeting should be alright (sign off lots of snags), and I have to be back in the office with time enough to do what I have to do.

Daily goals #19

- Smile, a genuine smile, as much as I can.
- Get an anniversary card for Eve's parents.
- Enjoy whatever life brings my way today.

Lots of snags dealt with on site, a productive meeting and the list is now much shorter. Back to the office where I managed to finish the drawings – deadline successfully hit. All in all, a good day professionally.

Home 5:50ish, Amazon had thrown a parcel over my garden fence! What's worse is that it contained the crystal glasses I had bought as a gift for Eve's parent's ruby wedding anniversary. Thankfully they survived the drop onto the patio – very well packaged. But it could have been a disaster. There is no time to replace them if I'd needed to…

I waited as long as I could for dinner – in the end I sent Eve a message asking if I should eat without her, she said yes. So, I ordered some food for me. Too late to make anything, not that I do much cooking anyway. Consequently, I didn't eat until after 8pm – all caused by a missing common courtesy. It can breed resentment – I am trying very hard not to let it. Eve was busy at work, she didn't think to let me know when she was coming home and so I sat here, hungry, waiting for *any* kind of communication. I wasn't upset, in the end it was all OK and Eve apologised when she came home an hour and a half later. She said that the position is that I should sort myself out, I shouldn't wait for her – she'll let me know if she wants dinner. This is a good call – a practical solution – but it means, by default, we are no longer eating together. It's upsetting me a bit thinking about this. Having meals together is hugely important. It's a daily touchstone, a ritual. Meals are social bonding moment, even if eaten in silence. Giving and receiving food is a powerful thing for humans. It shows caring for the wellbeing of others and an activity that is primal. Meals can be mundane, or very special indeed – but they are all important.

> The default position is now that I am eating on my own unless she lets me know to wait. Because she is too wrapped up in her own little world to communicate her timing, too busy for a common courtesy.
>
> Or I am not important enough to consider or even think about.
>
> Or she just doesn't care.

This is why I am a little upset.

A couple of months ago I would have been in pieces over something like this. I suppose this is again, some sort of progress. You can read into this what you want. A short while ago I would have looked for all the negatives, the very worst

of motivations. But today, I just think she can't be bothered to message me, or I am now so unimportant to her, it doesn't occur to her that I might be waiting. Life gets in the way, you know? It's not deliberate, it just is what it is.

11 hours wearing a skirt today. If I had eaten earlier, it would have been more. The opportunity was there, but I had to stay chained in trousers to answer the door to the delivery driver. An unintended consequence.

Not a bad day, but could have been better, I think.

Kay tasked me with completing something called the Wheel of Life. I've neglected doing it, so I'll have to work on it tomorrow morning.

Friday, June 25th

Stop writing in here – complete Kay's Wheel of Life!!!

...BRB...

Done! Phew!

Daily goals #20

- The all-important smiles.
- Get the most out of my session with Kay.
- Enjoy the day, make it a good one.

It is 8:32am, I am OK, not sure if I will be spending much time with Eve today – she is tired and has plans for her Friday off. I am seeing Kay at 11am. I may take myself off somewhere.

A pleasant morning, Eve slept in till around 9:30, by which time I was up, ready for the day, dishwasher unstacked, bed stripped and bedding in the washing machine. In fact, I was about to begin getting ready for Kay when she emerged. We had a nice chat with her about her work, good to catch up and I love listening to her stories from on set.

I went to see Kay and Eve left for the horses. I stopped at the ATM at M&S to get some cash out for Kay and also picked up some OJ and a tub of chocolate treats for us to enjoy later.

My session with Kay went well – it was a bit more emotional today than last time, she knows how to ask all the right questions, then lets me talk and emote. It's a good process, I feel challenged, and a bit emotionally drained after, with lots to consider and contemplate. Kay is away next week, so we are trying an evening session on the following Monday (6pm). If this works, it'll mean I will be able to work on Fridays. I am going to miss my three-day weekends, but it's not fair on my colleagues for me to keep adding to their workload.

I popped into Tesco to get some bits for tomorrows party, and a nice baton of bread for lunch. Eve came home for a bit and then took herself off to find a café to sit and work on her laptop. I settled in to watch, what turned out to be three films! "Ice Road", a Liam Neeson film on Amazon, "Spider-Man Homecoming" and then," Spider-Man Far from Home" back-to-back. It's been a while since I've had such a movie marathon – it was great.

I went to pick up a Nando's takeaway for our dinner and rediscovered a great Joe Satriani album, one I've not listened to for years, on Spotify (Flying in a Blue Dream) – I love a bit of performance guitar (and very few lyrics to trigger me), so I turned it up while I sat in the usual Friday evening traffic. Make the best of things, you know?

Eve's sister will be here around 9am tomorrow, Eve is doing the horses early.

I am really looking forward to the party!

A good day.

Saturday, June 26th

Only 2 pages left in this book, I will need to bring the already waiting Volume 3 with me today.

I overslept! Awake at 7am not my usual 6am. I slept really well, Eve was first in the bathroom, then off to see the horses. I got up and loaded the car ready for the trip to Eve's folks once her sister arrives. We hit the road around 9:30am, a pleasant trip up there, with a minor stop in Wisbech so her sister could find a top to wear in the evening. She left her original top in her car, back at our place.

We arrived safely around mid-day and gave the anniversary couple their presents, before stringing banners, balloons etc all around the garden whilst Eve iced some cupcakes.

Eve's dad has hurt his foot, he's hobbling around and in quite a bit of pain – I hope he doesn't need it too much today, he could have problems tomorrow.

The guests started arriving around 3pm, lots of good people I've not seen in ages. Eve and I mingled separately, I felt a little awkward, but there were plenty of nice folks to chat to. All good fun. Great food and good company. A <u>really</u> good day. Eve's uncle is a retired stage magician, and he performed an impromptu show later on that wowed a lot of the people there. He's excellent. I feel lucky to see him working his magic (literally) close up – very, very impressive.

Eventually, people started drifting away. It is coming up to midnight as I write this. Eve's uncle and aunt have the spare room, her sister has the sofa bed in the box room. Eve has the sofa in the lounge and me? I am on an air bed in the summerhouse in the garden! It's actually pretty cosy in here. I think I will sleep well tonight.

Not much time in a skirt today, I will change into my nightie shortly – I need it and am tired.

One of the best days of the year, superb.

Sunday, June 27th

8:15am, it is cosy in here, I slept very well indeed. Eve's sister is up, busying herself in the kitchen, I have just packed up the air bed, others will be up soon – soon I will be sociable and pleasant company, in the meantime, I am transfixed by a robin, hopping around the garden, nature is really quite beautiful.

Everything about the party yesterday was perfect. All except Eve. We, effectively, attended as individuals. We mingled separately and held our own conversations with people. I wanted to be with her – shit – I always want to be with her – but she was quite happy on her own and I am trying so hard to give her some space. I am actually quite upset this morning. I felt like I was an outsider, I was here as a friend of the family, rather than a part of it. No one made me feel this way, well, Eve did, three months ago. I was very welcome and included, but in my mind – things have changed – I don't like this at all. I feel like I have lost a large part of my family. Inevitably this is how I think it will go; I will feel outside the inner circle from now on – so I am a bit upset.

The family slept in the house; I slept in the summerhouse. It was fine, a nice place to sleep, but I feel like something has shifted. And not in a good way.

I feel like I want to tell them all **everything**, they are all very important to me. But it is not my place to do so. Also, I don't know what Eve has told them. So, it makes me a bit nervous. I feel like I want to set the record straight. Eve, your daughter has done this, not me. They see that there is now a distance between us but can only go on what Eve has told them. So only have half of the story, the much more palatable half, and they likely never will hear my side of things. Maybe, in the far future, if these pages are ever published, I will send them a copy. I wonder what they think of me. In much the same way I suspect Eve wonders what my folks think of her.

It's probably worse for Eve. But maybe a bit easier too. Eve was only ever close to my mum, so she no longer has a strong connection to my family. But my brother and dad have both reacted astonishingly badly to this. She has seen their reactions and must wonder what I have told them. This makes what we / I have been trying to do that much harder. Even though my conscience is completely clear.

They just don't get it. I doubt they ever will. They just see me, hurt beyond measure – they see Eve as a "baddie" for doing this to me and have moved to protect their assets from a so called "threat". I love them both dearly and am so grateful for their support, but this has only made things worse – muppets.

Family is difficult. But my bridges are not burned yet. I am wondering if I should have a candid conversation with Eve – would she have preferred me not to have been there? Although I am trepidatious as to her answer. I had a wonderful time and wouldn't have missed it for the world, but there were moments when I felt that Eve was going out of her way to distance herself and shut me out. She was the only one I felt would have rathered I wasn't there.

I hope I will always be friends with Eve's folks – I have no reason to think I won't – but I do think I have lost them as family. So sad – I am upset. They have been my family for 15 years – so many good times – I love them all dearly. But as much as they welcomed me, as much as I enjoyed their company, the fact is that now Eve has split with me, we are no longer family – just good friends.

So, family slept in the house, I slept in the "annex", summerhouse, or I suppose shed. It was not done with this in mind, I am sure, and it worked out really well, but this is sadly how it now is.

I love them all, but Eve has shut me out of the inner circle and the dynamic has shifted.

Daily goals #21
- Be good company.
- Try not to be upset.
- Smile, be genuine.
- Enjoy life and the world.

A lovely, cooked breakfast and lots of good conversation. Then we all helped tidy up the garden after yesterday's festivities. As expected, Eve's dad's foot is really sore today, I hope it gets better soon, it's not nice for him and he's visibly in pain.

Eve, her sister, and I said our goodbyes and headed home around 3pm. We stopped in Wisbech again, this time for a spot of lunch and I drove back despite a persistent headache. Home around 6pm. Eve sat in the back with her sister, and they had a good chat all the way back. I felt a little excluded at times, in fact, I felt a little like I was a chauffeur – not hugely nice to be honest. And I came very close to snapping at Eve. The headache, idiots on the road in front of me and Eve, blathering on about how the horses are such a tie and a hinderance to her travel plans unless she can arrange to pay someone to "babysit" for her. In my mind, this is just another example of her shirking her responsibilities so she can be selfish. I came so close to saying, "Could be worse. Could have broken the heart of the person that loves you beyond measure and left him in therapy – all so you could go travelling – something which you could have done anyway." You know when a situation comes up and you only think of the perfect thing to say afterwards? Well, this was <u>not</u> one of those times. I knew exactly what to say – it was there ready – but I chose to hold my tongue. In the end, all it would

have done is hurt Eve – a cheap shot – so I decided to be the better person and kept my feelings to myself.

The moral high ground sucks sometimes.

But on the bright side, keeping my mouth shut meant I didn't ruin the mood in the car and thus, despite my emotions, the fun weekend continued. I think if I had reacted to her comments, I would have had instant gratification, followed by huge regret. And our pleasant evening would have been lost. So, it was the right decision, and furthermore, this was a decision I don't think I could have made a month ago. Instead of blurting out a stinging missive, I think I would have burst into tears. Progress once more...

Eve's sister left for home and then I helped Eve do a little work on her sportscar. We swapped out the hood clamps and I showed her how to adjust them.

I've still got this headache – I retired to bed around 8:30 to relax, write in this journal and get an early night. I need to sleep this off.

And that brings us to the end of Volume 2. I am well on the way to healing, I think. Things with Eve are progressing, all be it not in a way I want them to. Dad is being very Machiavellian, but more importantly of all, I am still Julia and I like being her more and more every day. I am beginning to realise that this is who I am now, she was always me, the real me, and the pretence was not expressing myself as Julia on occasions, trying to 'manage' my female side. The construct was Adam, someone built to more closely resemble the way I look. I have not swapped genders, I was always female, buried under 50 years of being bullied into thinking I was a boy. I am trying to live authentically as me, the real me. For the first time in my life.

If the Shoe fits... Wear it.

I am. And I really like my feet in heels.

The King is Dead, Long live the Queen

Volume 3

Skirting the issue

By
Julia Phillips

Volume 3 – Skirting the issue...

This journal belongs to: Miss Julia Phillips.

For Eve. Everything, always.

For me. These journals were necessary and saved me.

For Kay, you helped me more than you know.

For Katie, who managed great things, but my fair hair was a real challenge.

...And for Kayleigh and Rach. Two beautiful, open, and accepting people who are brilliant at what they do and helped me on my journey. You are amazing.

Forward

Phew, I've just finished typing up Volume 2. It felt like a sprint towards the end, I just had to get to the finish line – there's a lot in there and looking at Volume 3, I think I'm in for much the same – only this time I need to pace myself. But I've never been any good at marathons, or any distance running for that matter. And no, you can't make the Snickers joke anymore – most folks are too young to remember these days!

Tanya was very happy to get her hands on Volume 2, I hope she likes it. It has a different tone to the first one, much more rooted in the day-to-day healing process and is less extreme. It has its' emotional moments and I do like a good tangent to go off into for a bit, but you can see real progression, progression only hinted at in the first book. But of course, I still have the same hang ups.

This one? Well, it's more of the same, it covers some big events, and I took a downward turn in the middle – "Spoilers!" As River Song would say... But this is where I really begin to find out who I am, I hope it is as interesting to you as the first two, there's a lot to unpack here, so I think it should be.

My dedication to Kay is self-explanatory, and her help to me was vital and is detailed within these pages, she was a much-needed guiding light through a very dark time and I can't tell you how much she helped me and how grateful I am to her. Katie too, she helped me with my self-esteem when I needed it most, she was kind and lovely, professional, and very much appreciated.

Kayleigh and Rach are much newer people in my life – Kayleigh is my, well I suppose beautician is appropriate, although it somehow feels inadequate to cover her range of skills. I reached out to her for electrolysis to deal with my beard once and for all and she has been just fabulous. Warm,

welcoming and very professional – she's listened to all my sob stories and knows me as both Adam and Julia, although I kinda do a half-way house thing when I see her for my sessions – it's hard to look like a lady with 2 day's stubble on my chin. Maybe one day, when I'm nearing the end of my treatment and I'm there for something much more pleasant, like a pedicure (love them, but you knew that!) I'll surprise her and turn up as me.

Rach is about to become my lash tech – I hope it goes well, it should, she too is by all accounts brilliant at her job, award winning even. More importantly, she is Tanya's daughter and (with permission) has read Volume 1. She also has an interesting take on things, like Kayleigh, being of a younger generation and therefore hugely more open and accepting of folk like me. This kind of thing gives me hope for the future, us irritable old GenX'ers like to complain about the youngsters today and how the world has gone to wrack and ruin. But I see folk like Rach, Kayleigh and actually most of their respective generations and believe the world is in very safe hands. The only real question is, how do I leave the house in broad daylight as 'me' to visit her shop next week? I'm a resourceful old bird, I'll find a way I'm sure, I just need to make sure I don't 'bottle it' on the day – flipping nosy neighbours and their doorbell cameras...

Anyway, there's plenty of waffle coming up, so that's enough from me for now. To quote the youngsters, here are the 'deets'. I'm sounding more and more like a crotchety old lady every day... Good luck to them all, they have a much better handle on people in my situation than my peers that's for sure, and as I said, it gives me lots of hope for the future.

Julia, Friday, April 12th, 2024.

Monday, June 28th 2021

It's a trilogy! Who knew? Hope it's better than the recent Star Wars films...

"Welcome back, sir/madam to our gourmet restaurant; "Long Live the Queen", lovely to see you both again. Are you ready to order? What can I recommend you say? Well, Volume 3 is on special today, it's a sordid tale, full of twists and turns, highs and lows and is about a lady named Julia. Drama? Why yes, it has drama in spades, she's a feisty heroine coming to terms with loss, heartache and the realisation that she is not who she thought she was for the first 50 years of her life. Romance? Well, in a way – our leading lady has just come through a very painful breakup and is still very much in love with her beaux. Ah, yes, it is indeed a bit of a weepy in places, very astute of you madam, it's full of passion and the emotions run very high. Action, you say? Well, there's some exotic travel and she faces her demons out in the real world at one point, but sadly if you are looking for Indiana Jones, he's in the main course section of the menu. But the special effects are mind blowing, Oscar worthy even. And it's a true story too. How does this sound? You do? Certainly, coming right up. And might I say, what an excellent choice too. Can I show you the wine list?"

"Two more suckers for a plate of yesterday's leftovers!"

I think I'd make a great waitress!

Early, 6:45am – done in the bathroom, Tara cat though has decided that now is the perfect time to re-apply her ownership scent to my freshly showered body and shed cat fluff all over me! As cute as she is, I don't want her clawing my new satin duvet set, so I am having to be a bit firm with her (she is most taken aback!) She gets her cuddles, but I won't let her settle on the bed and there is a throw between the duvet and her paws.

There are three garments that are the pinnacle of femininity, well, in my opinion at least (and I like to think, after all this time, I know my stuff, but I am still playing catch up behind other women – if I am way off, sorry, but I don't think so, I kinda have a different perspective on things, at least, I feel like I do). Anyway, the "Trinity" – *The Bra*, *The Skirt/Dress* and *The Heels*. They don't have a like-for-like male equivalent in daily wear and a person wearing all three is making a definite "I am a woman" statement. At least, that is how society views a person who chooses to wear them. There is a reason the symbol on the door of a female WC is a person in a skirt/dress. No, it doesn't mean Scottish folk only...

Actually, that is a fantasy of mine by the way. Being able to use a public, female WC without causing distress to the other ladies also using it. It's never going to happen; I am just too big to 'pass'. Ironically, as a building surveyor I regularly measure the ladies' conveniences, unoccupied of course, so I am very familiar with them in my professional capacity. I find it strange that I am more acceptable in there looking like a man, than as who I truly am. I don't think I will ever be *completely* acceptable in public as a woman, so female WCs in particular are off limits to me.

What is it the Rolling Stones said? "You can't always get what you want?" Sums up my life. Anyway, who in the hell has a fantasy about being able to use a female WC? I am so strange. But it's not really about the WC. It's about being accepted as a female by others, random ladies, who look at me in an exclusively female space and don't question my gender, my right to be there, they just see another woman using the facilities as they are. Acceptance and validation. So important and yet so unattainable. I want what I can't have. So, a fantasy.

I digress, back to the "Trinity" of female attire. I have tried to put them in order of femininity in the past and I can't – both

the skirt/dress and the bra are equal first, with the heels a *very* close second.

On the face of it, the bra has it all sewn up and should come top. It is an exclusive garment for women and is to do a job that only a woman's physiology would require – the reason it has no male equivalent is simply because men don't have boobs, therefore there is no need (blooming obvious really). On this basis, how could anything be more feminine? The bra is such a female icon – there is a reason the trope about feminists burning them exists (although I suspect it plays into the patriarchy much more than the feminist movement, just another thing to insult us). Harnessing your 'girls' every day into a bra – I can see how it has become such a symbol of female oppression. A bra literally controls your womanhood. Especially when you add in the sexual overtones of display and enhancement to the support and control reasons for wearing one. To any possible male readers of this – this is why women wear bras. You have absolutely no context to understand (such a shame, you really are missing out – wow, I am so strange...) I know when I was growing up, I was <u>very</u> puzzled by the concept of strapping yourself into an uncomfortable, tight-fitting undergarment with an awkward behind the back fastening on a daily basis. It wasn't until I grew my own breasts that I began to realise how much they jiggle, how aware of them I am and how much better I feel when they are supported. They look really pretty too, always a bonus. The benefits of wearing one outweigh the discomfort at the end of a long day, not by much sometimes, but they do. And with bras in particular, it is <u>all</u> about fit. It's taken me 35 plus years to finally find a bra the correct size. And a well-fitting bra is a revelation! So nice to wear, equally, an ill-fitting bra is utter torture.

So, given the above, how can a skirt or dress possibly compete? The top spot is very fiercely fought over – but a

skirt has a lot of cards to play. Firstly, men only have 2 bodily functions to deal with, women have three. In these terms, a skirt is more practical for a lady, particularly for someone who has to sit down. Secondly, a woman's hips make the skirt hang beautifully – it truly is a garment made to flatter the female figure. Men will say that displaying the legs is a huge turn on, but they are missing the big point by miles – it's staring them in the face – What actually is a skirt? It's a hole at the top of your legs. Effectively a vagina extension, in much the same way inadequate men tend to drive powerful cars with long bonnets. Although I'm not saying women in skirts feel inadequate, the exact opposite if my experiences are anything to go by. <u>This</u> is why there are no real male equivalents, sure there are kilts, traditional country specific uniform pieces and the male skirt turns up in fashion every now and then, as a novelty generally. But on a subconscious level, everyone knows a skirt equals vagina, so no 'man's man' will ever feel completely comfortable in one. Wearing a skirt or a dress is a declaration and a celebration of your womanhood. I find them astonishingly comfortable to wear, given my circumstances, I would I suppose. They truly are freedom to me, liberating in every sense. I literally skirt my issues. Hey, that sounds like a good title for Volume 3... This is why my (Julia's) wardrobe doesn't contain **ANY** trousers, not even women's trousers. I can wear trousers whenever I want (never), I dress properly to escape them. Hateful things. I would love to be comfortable in women's trousers – but they just can't compete with a skirt – and wearing trousers when I am 'me' is a missed opportunity. Skirts are special – I adore them! I could quite happily spend every moment of the rest of my life wearing one or a dress. I literally count the hours until I can be back wearing one. This journal is proof of that.

 Which brings me to high heels – a true love / hate relationship. So very beautiful, in equal parts empowering and

debilitating – a real dichotomy. I wear them, and I love wearing them – to the extent I will put up with the discomfort and even pain sometimes – *it's worth it*. I will put up with the difficulty of walking down hill – *it's worth it*. I will put up with men thinking I can't run (I can) and am therefore helpless (I'm not) – *it's worth it*.

Being able to adjust and control your height is astonishing. It literally gives you a different perspective on the world. I am tall anyway, the *last* thing I need is additional height, but I can't imagine how much more empowering this must feel to my less statuesque sisters. To go from being literally looked down upon, to looking others eye-to-eye is mind-blowing. Amazing.

Men see them as beautiful and as a way to restrict females, make us less capable. It's horrible but being 'in the inner circle' of manhood, this is sadly, in general, how they think (I'm a spy!) This is the nature of the fragile male ego; boys are brought up to compete and they do this by putting others below them. They strive to be at the top, it's how they are moulded as they grow up. Women in particular – they just can't get their heads around not having any 'junk in the trunk' and being happy about it, it drives them crazy. It's not their fault, it's just the way they are formed by those with the most influence, and society as a whole. What they don't know, is that walking in heels is a skill and once mastered, is actually no problem at all, well, up to a point anyway – my limit is 3½ inches. Smoke and mirrors – heels give men a false impression, make a woman's legs shapelier, put an attractive wiggle into their walk and most importantly of all, empower women by giving them control over their height. Women control their visibility in a myriad of ways, but none more so than through heels, and to some extent their visibility relates to their status in society. This is astonishing to me; heels are so powerful, and I can fully understand why some women are obsessed with shoes – it makes perfect sense.

Wearing all three together is a mind-blowing experience. Literally. What little is left of my male side cannot get any purchase at all and checks out completely. He is gone and I inhabit my female nature fully. Add in make-up, accessories, perfume and hair to my completed outfit and I am transported to my happy place. I am continuously reminded by every sense that I am a woman – it is profound, amazingly powerful and is just so damned nice – all my cares float away and I truly relax. I love it – it feels so right, and I am completely comfortable in my skin at last.

This is how Julia saved my life. She is my refuge. Being her, stepping away from the pain Adam was experiencing, literally fleeing from the paper man I had constructed into my unexplored female nature, gave me some essential peace, some calm, a release from the stress and agony as well as some much needed, rational perspective on my situation.

The downside? The man Adam was, died. Not because I ran from him, but because he was never truly real, a house of cards that Eve expertly blew away. I have no way back, there is nothing to go back to. I am Julia now, for the first time in my life, I am me. It's not so bad, very nice even. I like the view from over here, the grass is genuinely greener, the air sweeter and the flowers are very pretty. My life has changed completely at the most fundamental level.

Still, it was a huge change, and one that I wasn't prepared for at all. I am making the best of it – that is my goal, as it always has been. Life dealt me some unusual cards, I came close to losing it all, there are now a few cards missing from the deck, the King of hearts is torn in half and the queen of hearts is growing stronger and more complete by the day. Nearly all my blue chips are gone, but I have a fair pile of pink ones to play with and I keep winning more of them. Most folks aren't this lucky.

Daily goals #22

- Smile, genuinely and often.
- Find as much joy in life as I can.
- Work hard and enjoy work.
- Be a good person.

Work was, well, work. Some nice banter in the office today though – I cracked a few funnies too – all good stuff. Sushi for lunch again, it's good for me and my figure, but I am getting a bit bored with it though. I may have to find an alternative.

Home around 5:45pm, said hi to Eve and asked if she was up for the sportscar natter tonight? She had forgotten but was in good spirits and we headed out to the pub for a nice evening with friends. Hood down on the way home – I miss my little red sportscar – they are such fun. And although it is nice having access to Eve's one, it's not the same as having your own to play with. Erm, I've just re-read that last sentence, it wasn't intended to be a euphemism honestly…

That said, I am considering selling my three 'pseudo' classics. I love them, but car #3 is a project and is not progressing – I have other, much more pressing things to fix in my life at the moment. It is stuck in a barn gathering dust (& not mice, I hope). Car #2 has issues and is back at the garage for yet more work. And my little sportscar? Well, I modified her with one purpose in mind, EU touring and to be honest, I can't see me going on holiday with Eve in the car anymore and not **be** with Eve. Equally, I can't look at the empty passenger seat – it makes me very upset. She has screwed this up for me completely. So, the car, much like Adam, has lost its purpose. After 25 years of ownership, I am wondering if I am ever going to drive her again. How can I go to events if Eve is there too? She is intrinsically linked to our fellow sportscar friends, events, and holidays. I

am not sure I will ever be able to enjoy them again. If we go separately, but are at the same event, it will be torture for me. Indeed, this has happened to me twice now. And if I go on my own and see our circle of friends, I will be constantly reminded of her. Similarly, there are so many places we have been to together, Silverstone, Brooklands, Gaydon, Cofton Park, Abingdon, Dunkerque, Kempen, Mechelen, Bruges, Amsterdam, Reims, Normandy, Rheinland, the Black Forest (adore the Black Forest), the Nurburgring, most of western Germany in fact, the Alps, basically all of northern Europe and parts of Scandinavia as well, not to mention all the local natters we attended. I'll see Eve in all of them. Too many memories and now they are all bitter-sweet. I have tried to go back to a few of the more local ones, and it is very painful to revisit them on my own.

Maybe I can do my own thing? Maybe I can go on my own grand tour, southern and eastern Europe perhaps? Spain, Portugal, Italy, Greece, Hungary, East Germany, Poland, Norway even. Maybe I'll drive to Russia – just for the fun of it, I hear St.Petersburg is lovely. Maybe I can go EU touring again? After all, Europe is a very big place.

And on the subject of travel, I think I might like to do some adventuring of my own, why should Eve have all the fun?

Canada
New Zealand
Japan
Iceland
Norway
Hawaii
Jamaica
Madeira
Canary Islands

Cyprus

Maldives

Italy

Corsica

Sicily

Croatia

Ibiza

I think I may have to make some of these happen when things settle down a bit, in the meantime, there is the family trip to Majorca coming up, although this is likely to be very difficult for me indeed.

Home around 10pm, in my nightie by 10:30. 9½ hours today. OK I guess...

Tuesday, June 29th

7:49am, snoozin' – nice. Tara cat tried her very best to get me out of bed early, she has given up and has gone to pester Eve instead. Up at my usual time, a very nice and very welcome hug from Eve this morning. I think I am going to miss her hugs the most. It brought me to tears as I left for work – I miss her so much – the hug was lovely, really special – we have lost so much. So, I cried. Tears of joy and sadness as I closed the front door behind me and walked to the car.

I was OK on the drive to work – a bit emotional still when I arrived – I had to stop at Starbucks for a sweet treat to cheer me up a bit – the sugar did the trick, and I was OK for the day.

I finished work an hour early – there was a football thing on today apparently, so we let everyone go a bit early to watch. I headed over to my brother's place and had a very pleasant evening with them all and dad. Lasagne for dinner and lots of discussions about travel, particularly the additional Covid hoops to jump through these days. I took some unusual photos of my nephew's old car for use in an advert to sell it using a borrowed drone. He should get a fair price I think once the MOT is renewed.

Back home around 8pm, changed by 8:30 so just under 12 hours in a skirt today and of course, knickers are my daily go-to these days. I am thinking about sleeping fully clothed again tonight – I've a full outfit on, including the 'Trinity'. I think I look good, and I feel great. I really don't want to take anything off.

I had a good chat with Eve tonight too. She has had a productive day working on her website and also has three days' work booked up for Monday through Wednesday next week. It's in Reading though, so she has booked a hotel to stay locally for the 2 nights.

We ended up watching episode 1 of 'Loki' on Disney+ and after, before retiring to our beds, I painted her toenails. I like doing things like this with her. I like to feel useful. And I'm not too bad at it – I certainly have more practice than she does!

It's nice to still share these fleeting moments. I will miss them if we go our separate ways. I made a good memory and took joy in the moment.

Oh, and apparently, we won the football thing. It's a big deal it seems. I never did get why folks love it so much, I'm obviously missing something, like most sports, I find football very boring. And the crowd, especially the noise, is hugely intimidating and terrifying to me. Not my thing at all, there's far too much testosterone. Scary.

No daily goals today, but I did smile a lot and laughed a lot too. That's got to be a big win, I think. I was productive and open to the world. I found (some) joy in moments and made some good memories.

A good day.

Wednesday, June 30th

I slept fully clothed again last night, no problems whatsoever – I switched my pendants for hoop earrings and took off my glasses, watch and heels – laid on the bed, made myself comfy and drifted off into a very pleasant sleep. I delayed getting up too – I just wanted to spend as much time as I could in my outfit. I find this very nice, but it is odd behaviour – I suppose it's because I spend the day disguised and then only have a limited time in the evening to be myself. As any woman does, I put a fair amount of effort into my appearance, and it seems a shame to take it all off again after such a short time. Still, I can't sleep fully clothed forever, it's more than a bit strange. Equally, I adore my nighties.

Eventually I disrobed, removed my (smudged) make-up and had a leisurely shower. I'm currently sat in bed in my nightie; full length, satin and lace, elegant you know? It's no wonder I love sleeping in them – I have 45 minutes or so to relax before I need to get up for work. Hopefully the cat will let me...

Daily goals #23

- Smile! Often and for real.
- Professionalism and diligence.
- Be sensible about my food intake.
- Enjoy as much of the day as I can.

Work was OK today, I managed to get a lot done. The traffic jam on the main road home wasn't nice, but I arrived home safely, if delayed by about 45 minutes. A nice dinner with Eve and then changed around 7:15pm – 13 hours plus, and of course, pretty undies all day.

I am in a dress tonight, lingerie, tights, heels, make-up, jewellery, hair and perfume. My women's glasses complete my outfit (thank heaven for online glasses retailers!) It's all great and I am very comfy. And of course, the dress zips up the back. Perfection.

Thursday, July 1st

White rabbits, white rabbits, white rabbits...

It's the regular Thursday site visit again today, at least I think so. From my point of view, the job is in limbo until all the snags are signed off, it's a big project and there are a few things to do, in a lot of places so it is taking time. This means my weekly visits continue, whether there is an official meeting or not. At least until they are all done. Back to the office later.

I am OK again today – although my razor battery is flat, and my spare is on charge in Eve's room. It is 7:30am, I am done in the bathroom, but I still have a face full of hateful stubble. It's so horrible and I am in a quandary – I really want to get rid of it, but I don't want to disturb Eve to collect my razor. I'll give it a few more minutes, maybe the cat will wake her... I have my second appointment with Katie tomorrow, so a really close shave tomorrow morning is required, and I'll be even more face fungus free. One more step towards never having to shave again! It can't come soon enough.

Despite my chin, I am feeling very female today. It's hard to describe, but I just don't want my time in a dress to end and I know that play acting Adam's role already feels like a challenge today. I am so comfortable and feel so 'right' in these clothes. My dress last night was lovely and the nightie I am currently wearing is equally so. I am thinking about transitioning again. It is never far from my mind these days to be honest, but I can't shake the thought that it would be so good to have a vagina. I want it a **LOT** today. I am so strange, truly a bizarre person. Female hormones and a vagina – my life would be infinitely better – my brain is telling me these half-truths all the time today. It's not true of course. Dysphoria once more, my constant companion for my entire life. I'd like to say an old friend, but she's a truly spiteful bitch, and she just loves to torture me – she lives for it. A softer, shapelier version of me may well be nice

(and it may well put a sock in that cow dysphoria's mouth for a bit), but I'll still look like me. I'll still be the largest person in the vast majority of rooms I enter, and I'll look odd with even larger breasts, wider hips, a waist and softer skin on a 6'-2" frame. My really broad shoulders complete the image. Still, my dresses will hang much better. Maybe that's why I want it so badly today?

Daily targets #24

- Shave my chin! Urgent! Urgghh!
- Smile, as much as I can and genuinely.
- Be open to the world, enjoy the gift of life.

Work was quite good today, I crossed off some more snags, then into the office after, where I finished the first draft of the 10-drawing set for a project in the Trafford Centre, plus there was a good vibe in there today – lots of good-natured banter, we have some great and talented people working for us.

I headed over to see dad this evening, I helped him with some new bedroom furniture and then we headed out to a local pub for dinner. Conversation was difficult though. He keeps telling me the same thing. Eve and I can't "move on" if we are still living together and that we should sell the house and split. The past 15 years are not worth sacrificing the next 25 for.

So, I've come to a big decision…

…I am not going to listen to him anymore.

It's hard, he's my dad, and I've always looked up to him, put him on a pedestal and strived to make him proud of me. He's also been full of valid wisdom over the years and has never really steered me wrong before. But there's a first time for everything… Eve and I will stay together for as long as **WE** want to. He has no say in it at all. If Eve or I want to go our separate ways, we will. But until that day, we are both content to live where we are, thank you very much. She has her safety net, and I am happy to keep paying the bills, providing she contributes

a fair sum on a monthly basis and most importantly of all, she doesn't hurt me again.

If we sell the house and split, it is **our** decision and no one else's.

It may well happen anyway; indeed, I think it likely at this point. If it does, we'll deal with it at that time. Not before. And not because of outside influences trying to speed the process up without all the facts.

He keeps saying "What if I find someone else?" And then uses his recent life experiences as an example. Er, hello!?! Does he remember nothing of who I actually am? Is his memory of all my childhood issues buried so deep? He doesn't understand that Eve was my one shot. I am highly unlikely to find someone else (although I'll never say never). And even *if* the right person does come into my life, how can I let them in? I can't, not anymore. I can never risk being this hurt again, it is no exaggeration to say it nearly killed me, so I can never open myself up in the same way that I did. Furthermore, if I did open myself up to someone new and special to me, what will they find? A woman named Julia, trapped in a man's body. They'll run a mile, or they will be even more loopy than I am...

More likely is that Eve will find someone. Part of me hopes not. But equally, part of me hopes she does too, after all, I just want her to be happy, even if it is with someone else. If this happens, I won't be able to live with her anymore. At this point, she moves in with him and we sell the house. Just as well, I don't think I can live in "*our*" house on my own for long. I would like some time to heal first though – I am pretty sure I couldn't handle this at the moment. It would be a <u>major</u> setback for me both mentally and emotionally. For me to be happy for her moving on, I need to love her less. Being Julia helps. The more time I spend emersed and fully invested in being female the more I get used to the distance Eve has put between us. Adam

loved her with every fibre of his being. Julia loves her more like a sister. This is a significant difference and is why being Julia is my haven, my safe space, and sadly, also why Adam is pretty much gone. Without Eve, he has no reason to exist and what little is left of him is in far too much pain.

Home around 8:30, changed by 9pm – 11 hours today.

Eve is out early, a Covid test in Ealing first thing ahead of her 3 days' work next week. I have my 2nd full beard removal treatment at 10:45am tomorrow with Katie – I'm looking forward to it. I may have lunch with Eve afterwards – it will depend on our timings – we shall see.

A good, productive day.

Night x.

Friday, July 2nd

A lie in this morning, it's 9:15am and I am watching 'Veronica Mars' in my room on TV. Eve is out, getting a Covid test ahead of her 3 days' work next week. I am about to have a shower and then head over to see Katie. Not sure how the day is going to pan out – maybe get some lunch with Eve depending on timing, but there is no plan – going to play it by ear.

Daily goals #25

- Smile, of course, you know it.
- Be open and available to whatever the world offers today.
- Go with the flow…

So… Nice lie in, then 10 minutes early at Katie's place of business. I waited in the car until it was time, just being polite she may be working with another Client, and I don't want to interrupt another's session. I bumped into Katie as I walked to her clinic, she had left her lunch in her car – it was 24°C today, so not a good idea to let it cook in the heat…

A nice chat with Katie, she is moving house tomorrow and is very excited. But she is also concerned it will be a very long, hard day's work. I have begun to open up a bit more to her, it was kinda inevitable really, laying on her treatment bench for a good hour regularly, the chat was always going to come around to my situation. The beard removal treatment went well, and she was super quick today, covering my beard area diligently and with not much pain either. I ranked each zap at a 2 to 3 out of 10, even though the IPL machine was set to high. I hope it's working – I just want my beard gone for good. I said my goodbyes and then headed home, I sent Eve a text about lunch, but no reply – she's likely driving – so I stopped by a supermarket and brought a French stick and some hams. Yum.

I settled in for a lazy day – I watched 'Ant Man' and then 'Ant Man and the Wasp' back-to-back – all good fun. Eve arrived home mid-way through the second film, then made herself busy while I continued my movie-marathon by watching 'The Tomorrow War'. It was also very good.

Dinner – Nando's was a bust, so we headed for the Green Dragon, a local pub/restaurant. We sat in the garden and had a pleasant evening meal, along with some good chat. Eve is embarrassed to be English it seems. We talked about the despicable behaviour of the English football fans at the England v Germany match during the week. Booing every time the German team had possession of the ball and the hurtful, gloating memes afterwards – I agreed with her, although most of this has passed me by it seems. The memes apparently use the image of a little German girl supporter in tears. I get it. I walked out of my brother's living room when the match was on. It was more than just boring to me; it was painful to watch. So, between football thugs, Nigel Farage, and Brexit, she is ashamed to be associated with her country of birth, the flag of the Nation and the flag of the Union. They have both been usurped by louts, racists, and morons. It's not all bad, she still loves where she is from, the countryside, our culture, history, and the Queen etc. But her feelings are very mixed. Learning languages, including German, and now being fluent means she is able to understand the German media, and this has given her a different perspective. She sees how we as a Nation are perceived in Germany and to be honest – it is not good it seems. I don't particularly like this change in her. It is upsetting for her, and she is very passionate in her views – sometimes ignorance is indeed bliss.

I am all for broadening horizons and appreciating different points of view, but she now has a personal dilemma here – and it is distressing for her. She wants to like where she is from, but

these total fuckwits make our entire Nation look like arseholes and she can see it clearly now, this particular veil has been lifted.

Back at home, I watched a bit of 'House' on the telly – it's such a great show – but there's loads of it, so it'll take me a while to see all the episodes. Eventually, I retired to bed. It is 10:38pm as I write this – up early tomorrow, so It will be turning in soon.

12 hours today – a good day.

Saturday, July 3rd

Up at 5am, it is 5:51 now and I am ready for the day ahead. I'm about to head for Kent, to meet up with a friend and his US cop car pals for American Speed Fest at Brands Hatch. The weather looks a bit rubbish to be honest and due to Covid, we are likely to be outside all day. I am having last minute second thoughts about whether this is how I really want to spend my Saturday…

Nothing ventured, nothing gained – I'm going!

Daily goals #26

- Smile and have fun.
- Don't get too wet in the rain.
- Make the effort, it's worth it.

It was good fun today – I was out the front door on time, a straightforward drive down to Dartford, across the bridge and to a Premier Inn. I met up with my friend and he kindly spotted me breakfast in the Beefeater next door. With my car parked up in the Hotel car park, I logged my numberplate into their system and then jumped into my friend's NYPD Chevrolet – the day's fun began.

There were 17 cars at Bluewater and then in convoy to Brands Hatch. The 'Bluesmobile' with us, it turns out, had a fully functional giant speaker on the roof! As if 17 US police vehicles in convoy wasn't enough, a selection of disco classics was more than ample to have random strangers dancing in the streets, including a group of road workers at one point! Really good fun, I was grinning like an idiot.

Once at Brands and American Speed Fest, we turned yet more heads – arriving on mass, even at an event filled with some seriously cool American cars, it's a spectacle – now that

we were no longer on public roads, the lights and sirens went on and of course, more disco classics getting the crowds going and drowning out the circuit PA system – we certainly made an entrance!

We all parked up in our display paddock and chatted away the day, trying hard not to be ripped off at the burger stands and wandering around looking at all the exotic vehicles. A great day out, I'm so glad I made the effort. I ended up getting a little sunburned on the top of my head in the parting (male pattern baldness is beginning to be a serious concern for me, I just can't lose any more hair on my head), but other than this, it was excellent. By 5pm though I was wiped out. The others all headed off to Southend for the evening, most staying locally, and they will do it all again tomorrow on American Independence Day. I, however, headed home.

A nice evening with Eve, I told her all about my day and she reciprocated in kind. Domino's Pizza, TV and an early night.

Yawn – time to turn in. I need my nightie tonight.

Sunday, July 4th

J-Day: monthly anniversary...

Lazy start to the day, it's just gone 8am and I have yet to visit the bathroom. I was so tired last night – I slept like a log. It's so nice to wake up every morning in my nightie – I've slept in one for years, ever since I was 18 years old, the vast majority of my life in fact, but it's still a lovely experience and a perfect way to begin a new day. Well, up until I have to mow the lawn that has sprouted on my face overnight anyway. Eve is up, kind of, she has finished her ablutions and is currently in her room – I presume either dressing or relaxing – it is Sunday after all. Tara cat is meowing for her breakfast though. She's a persistent little mog!

Lots on my mind this morning. I am struggling to enjoy the things I am doing on my own. I mean, I have a good time and it *is* worth the effort, but I come away afterwards feeling a bit hollow, a bit dissatisfied – I always think either "Eve would've liked this" or "I would've liked this more if Eve had shared it with me". I am sure she doesn't feel the same way when she does her own thing. I am sure I don't cross her mind at all while she is having fun (which is hurtful now that I think about it). But I don't begrudge her this, I just want her to be happy – even if I miss out or am excluded. It hurts me, but she is happy. This conundrum is mine to solve, my problem to deal with. I have to **not** want to share every moment of her life, so hard when you love someone, more importantly, I **have** to not be so hurt when she chooses to be on her own. I never used to be like this, I was never this clingy or this desperate for whatever crumb she might deign to toss my way. This is so bloody difficult...

All I know is, I am **always** happier when I am with Eve, than when I am on my own.

Which brings me to dad. He is deliberately trying to split Eve and I up. I see this now – he has an agenda – this is really hard to deal with. Furthermore, I don't think I can sit around the pool in Majorca with him for a week while he plays his mind games. I may bring volumes 1 & 2 of this journal and start typing them up. It'll keep me busy. I am also thinking about renting a car – just to go and do something, anything, rather than spend all day being subjected to his 'advice'. He'll wear me down eventually, for someone who denies my very existence and doesn't know me at all, he certainly knows how to manipulate my emotions. I'll end up blowing up in his face – this will be awful – but no one knows how to press all my buttons better than he and my brother. I can't get angry with him, there of all places. Such a special place for us as a family and him and mum in particular. So, it may be best if I just take myself out of the situation. But I have decided on a course of action regarding my inheritance. I've written it off. It's upsetting, but I refuse to be manipulated by him and I won't let him try to use this to lever Eve and I further apart. If it happens, then it is our choice, not his. I don't interfere in his love life; he needs to mind his own damned business. And if it costs me my inheritance – so be it. I don't want to profit from his death anyway. I'd much rather he left me nothing, but I was happy. And no, it isn't right that I am buying Eve a house and she isn't pulling her weight. But I'd rather do this and still have her in my life, at whatever level, than receive a windfall – I just need to be in a position where I don't need it. So, I am going to increase the provisions I have made for my future.

Sounds like a bit of a plan? I think it is.

But what about me? Where do I fit into this mess my life has become? To be honest, I don't know who "me" is anymore. I used to know, at least I thought I did. I used to have a good handle on it. I was Adam in body, and I thought, largely in mind.

And I was Julia when I needed to be. I 'managed' my gender issues and it worked because I was mostly Adam. 50(M):50(F) in mind, 90(M):10(F) in body.

But now I am not. If I had to throw percentages at it, I'd say I am now 10(M):90(F) mentally / 90(M):10(F) in body and that last 10% in mind is a horribly painful place to be. What I find astonishing is that looking back, my 50:50 estimate back then doesn't seem right *at all* to me anymore. I think that if I actually was 50:50 then I wouldn't have needed to 'manage' my gender at all – thinking back, I can clearly see now that my time spent as Julia was a cry to be heard, she was shouting "let me out! I am real, I need to exist!" I now think I was always more female in mind than male. And keeping myself hidden away, with only just enough personal expression time to allow me to take a breath, was never going to work. I'm amazed it did at all to be honest. Adam was built to hide behind and then after he became Eve's boyfriend, being her partner became his sole reason to exist. He was a paper man and the pain of the breakup meant that he literally ended up on paper. I wrote what was left of him and his anguish out of me on the night I tried to end it all. I found I was Julia, for the first time, unencumbered by societal, familial and all the self-imposed (so many of these – why?) expectations of manhood. I was new and at last, **I was FREE.**

> When you are *literally* at the very end.
> All the walls fall down.
> And you see yourself for who you truly are.

Adam was gone, dead and buried on those few pages, caught amidst the stream of consciousness that poured out of me – the pretence of being him was revealed to be a sham and I discovered that not only was I Julia, I liked being her!! I was unexplored, new and oh so curious. I had something to live for

after all. The irony is, I went out that night to free Eve, but in the end, it was me who was released.

But it was a total and profound shock. To realise that after 50 years, I didn't know who I was *at all* and had spent all those years hiding. Something much bigger than the Eve situation. Something equally difficult to deal with. But a really lovely thing to try to resolve.

And my body? Well, I'm working on it. Tentatively taking steps to do what I can. I am getting rid of my beard, and I think I am beginning to see some subtle results from the oestrogen I have begun taking, my mood swings are nowhere near as dramatic, so I felt it was a good time to start. My boobs feel a little bigger, my nipples even more sensitive than they were and downstairs feels even more of an irrelevance. I hope I am now firmly off the emotional roller coaster – I feel OK, you know? Yes, I cry occasionally, but it is hard to say if this is the oestrogen or if it is still my circumstances triggering me. All I do know is that I am not crying very much anymore and am not having massive breakdowns like I was. Got to be a good thing. I wonder if I can get my hands on some anti-androgens? I am so strange – who would want this? I loathe what testosterone has done to my body – it'd be nice to fight back and have some much-needed respite from the chemical warfare assault it puts me through 24/7. Also, I am thinning on top, I must put a stop to this – now! I can't lose any more hair. I just can't.

I am now showered and dressed, with the emphasis on the word 'dress'. I feel good and would dearly love to spend the day like this. But Eve and I have plans to go to Colchester and she will be back from the gym soon. Considering she's been working out it seems odd that we are planning on some tea and cake – but it does sound very nice. So, I'll imprison my legs in some hateful jeans shortly, just so I can face the world. But in my mind, I am free...

Daily goals   #27
- Smile (always!)
- Find some joy, be happy.
- Be pleasant company, so others will want to share their time with me.

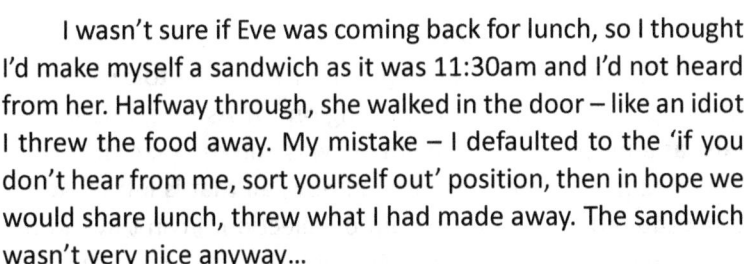

I wasn't sure if Eve was coming back for lunch, so I thought I'd make myself a sandwich as it was 11:30am and I'd not heard from her. Halfway through, she walked in the door – like an idiot I threw the food away. My mistake – I defaulted to the 'if you don't hear from me, sort yourself out' position, then in hope we would share lunch, threw what I had made away. The sandwich wasn't very nice anyway...

We went to Colchester in her sportscar, hood down, it was nice. I got a bit upset in the car though, dad has irritated me and I had a bit of a rant. The rant turned into me pouring out my heart again – I think I scared Eve a little – she didn't know what to say. She thought I was on the verge of another breakdown – I wasn't, but I was very emotional. Angry that dad has put me in such an impossible position and then upset and scared that I am on a direct path to a full and likely unsuccessful gender reassignment. I truly feel that this is the end of the path I am now firmly set upon. If Eve leaves, I have nothing to stop me *and I want it all.* I have been on this path before, back in my 30's, it looks a little familiar in places. Then out of left field, along came Eve, she came into my life, and Adam suddenly had a purpose, a reason for being, and a damned good one too. I chose to be him, to try to inhabit my physiology completely, well, as completely as I could. To *be a man* for Eve and to give us a chance. I chose to package up the female side of me and fitted it all into a nightie, every night, while we were both asleep. I fitted Julia into our lives in the least impactful way I could.

- *But all my efforts were not enough.*

My life was amazing, I loved every part of it. And it was only possible because of our love.

"I don't love you anymore".

How do I come back from that? I was totally invested in her – all in – my whole life and who I am at my core was dedicated completely to our relationship.

- *It wasn't enough.*

Who I was, wasn't enough. And I am being told I need to "move on" – but what am I moving on to? As now, I no longer exist as a person. Adam, the man I was and the man the world knows, is gone. I am Julia in mind now, all that is left of Adam is unrequited love and the pain of rejection. I can't live in his world anymore – he still loves Eve with every ounce of the little of what remains and seeing her step away, begin to lead a life without him, is unbearable - so I tried to kill myself.

Julia stopped me going through with it. I began to write. I wrote it all down and when I ran out of paper, I **had** to continue to write – so I had a reason not to do the deed. I looked around the car and had a profound moment of clarity – I was not Adam; I never really was. I was Julia. I had dressed myself head to toe as a woman – I looked down at my skirt and blouse and then at Adam, entombed in the words on the pages I had written, and it was like a switch had been thrown in my head – Adam died, and I was revealed. For the first time, he wasn't standing in front of me.

I am still a divided soul. There is still a semblance of a male side to my nature, how could there not be? I lived as a man for 50 years, so much time in fact it became second nature to me. But this part of me is hugely damaged, very likely beyond repair, and although I can still draw from what is left of it, it is not a pleasant place to be. It takes a toll, I become agitated and can't concentrate on anything. Too much time locked in trousers

makes me feel like I am losing my sanity. It's truly horrible and just not who I am. Dysphoria running rampant.

So, if I end up on my own, I will be Julia all the time. Or at least as much as I possibly can be. It's who I am after all. My life will be spent in a skirt, with me putting on an "Adam disguise" to face the world when I have to. That's exactly what it feels like now, a disguise, false, not genuine. Although after close to three months now, it is getting a little easier. No less uncomfortable, but the old skills set is still there, like muscle memory. When Eve is not around my thoughts go to dark places – it scares me silly – my rational brain tells me that this is the only way I can live in this world, but my emotional state wants a <u>full</u> gender reassignment. I know categorically that this will make my life much harder in a lot of important ways and in my darker moments, feel that it may well ruin what is left of my days on this planet – but I **<u>want</u>** it, I **<u>crave</u>** it. And it motivates me to do stupid things. If I end up on my own, this will be my reality 24/7 and I will likely end up going to the far east and paying a stupid amount of money so a surgeon can correct a mistake that should never have been there in the first place.

And I **<u>know</u>**, I **<u>KNOW </u>** I will not be happy after. Happier, absolutely, but that bitch dysphoria has her claws dug so deeply into my psyche, she is never letting me go.

So, when I say I am on a direct path to full gender reassignment this is what I mean. Despite what I have written previously, this is what scares me the most about being on my own. And this is why my dad trying to split Eve and me up is such a big deal (beyond the obvious). He will **<u>never</u>** understand the damage he is doing. He can't see beyond the end of his nose on this (and he never has been able to, he's denied my existence my entire life – is it any wonder I'm crippled with dysphoria and I've such a hang up about showing my true face to the world?)

He doesn't see that the **ONLY** thing preventing his son becoming his daughter, is Eve.

As long as she is in my life, in some way, I have a reason to stay in this body. If she goes, if she leaves me to live on my own, I will be consumed by the monster that is called Trans. It will swallow me whole.

I expressed some of this to Eve in the car – she became very worried – so I reigned it in and didn't tell her the whole story. She knows, I think, that I am on a direct path to transition – but it scared her, so I didn't elaborate. ***I really wish she would read this diary***. I am so much more eloquent in writing. When I can consider my words more carefully and have time to compose rational sentences. In conversation, I do not phrase things correctly, or miss important things out. The time pressure of an instant conversation and my emotions conspire together to compromise what I want to say.

A nice walk around Colchester, cake and then home. We spent the afternoon spray painting the hood catches on her car and then did our own thing in the evening as usual. I despise this. We live together and I want to be with her all the time, but she wants to do her own thing, so I sit opposite her, and we don't talk. It's horrible.

But it is better than being on my own.

I didn't do very well on my daily goals today, will try harder tomorrow.

Four months since 'J-Day'

Monday, July 5th

Eve left for work at 4am – I was kinda awake, but not enough to say goodbye. By the time I was conscious enough, she was closing the front door – I said "I love you" as she walked down the steps to her car, but she won't have heard me.

Epic entry yesterday – lots on my mind, some of it has been covered in depth here before, but I'm sorting through stuff, getting it down on paper and in doing so, working through the issues in my head. I hope this journal doesn't become too repetitive, but I suppose that is the nature of what I am going through, revisit and resolve until I'm healed. Anyway, I need to get up now – it's ten past eight and I need to go to work.

Daily goals   #27

- Smile!
- Be productive and professional.
- Be open, especially with Kay later on.

The day went well, although no word at all from Eve. She is likely very busy – they are working her a lot on set it seems.

I headed home on time, my appointment with Kay was at 6pm, so I had ½ an hour to get the mogs in and feed them, get the washing in, and put the bins out. Then 10 minutes to drive to Kay.

It was an interesting and enlightening session with her. She asked how I had been, and unlike the majority of times when I'm asked this question in a more social setting – I actually told her. I told her about how manipulative I feel dad is being, how worried I am that he is going to spend the week we are together at Deià in Majorca, brow beating me into selling the house and how I am planning escape routes so I can get away from his so-called 'advice'. I told her that Eve and I hadn't seen much of each other recently, that she is working her pants off, but

has yet to be paid for most of it. I also told her that when she is paid, I'm worried she'll blow it all on herself and shirk her responsibilities to the mortgage, at my expense. And then we talked about Julia...

It all came out today. How much I now want to live openly as myself, Julia. How much I fear I'll be in a worse position afterwards and how it is a one-way journey with no coming back. How dad's idea of 'moving on' is nowhere near my reality. For me – this means full gender reassignment. I think if he knew this, if he could comprehend it, I mean, actually face the reality of my situation, and truly understood that me living on my own = me living full time as a female. He might not be so gung-ho about meddling in my affairs. Kay took this on board and played Devil's Advocate. People have to be true to themselves to be truly happy. Have I spent my entire life hiding who I am? What would be so bad about fully transitioning? How do you measure 'successful'? Does it matter what other folks think? I need to be who I am, not who society expects me to be. **Powerful stuff.** All I really know is that I was beginning to explore who I am in my mid-30's and I think if Eve hadn't come along, I would likely be physically female by now.

- In my early childhood, I realised I was not like other boys, I was much more like girls.
- In my teens, I was physically and bodily turned into a man against my will – it was an assault. And I went off the rails.
- In my twenties, I made peace with who I thought I was and developed ways of fitting my female nature into my life.
- In my thirties, I tentatively began to explore my female nature more fully.

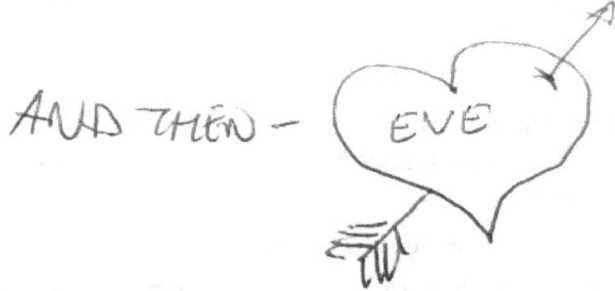

AND THEN — EVE

In my mid-thirties, I fell completely and desperately in love. My life suddenly took a huge left turn, and I literally became a man in order to be with Eve. I inhabited and accepted being Adam for the first time in my life and it was good. So very good. So good to love and be loved. I was open and honest with her from the very beginning and we both knew it was a gamble, a long shot – but was more or less at peace for the first time, and we built a life together, a good one. But I was still dysphoric. I still had to express my female nature. I had to fit who I am into our lives together and I did so in the least intrusive way I could – I continued sleeping in a nightie. 8 hours a day, every day, while we both slept. It worked. But ultimately, I'm sure it changed the way she felt about me. In the end, seeing her boyfriend in a nightie every evening at bedtime and making love to him/her was untenable – she fell out of love with me. Sex dried up first. It just stopped happening. To be honest, it felt like hard work to me anyway – I did it for her, to give her pleasure – it was a selfless act and although I enjoyed the connection, the bond of something so intimate and so personal, and of course the conclusion, I did it for her, not for me. And if she failed to climax, not often, but more so as the years rolled by, I took it personally as a failure on my part. I see now that it was more likely her not being attracted to me anymore. So, it stopped. Little by little it just stopped.

Alarm bells should have been ringing – I missed them utterly.

I am so stupid.

Next, she stopped talking to me. Our little pillow talks dried up too. Conversations became matter of fact. Small talk, nothing meaningful.

I missed this too – I am a blind fool.

Then she really started to hurt me. She began shutting me out of her life. It was systematic and progressive and up until this point; I have never felt pain and confusion like it.

And then, just as I needed to do something, because **NOW** I finally realised something was majorly wrong with our relationship. **Finally,** I began to see things were not right and getting worse. Just when I was about to try to build some bridges. Mum passed away right at the beginning of lockdown.

I went to a dark place.

My emotions shut down.

And it took an entire year for me to come back.

Sooo much time lost...

Eve started sleeping on the sofa. I was devastated. It wasn't a one-off – she preferred the hugely uncomfortable sofa to sleeping in a nice, warm, comfy bed with me. I took this really badly. But I, as always, just wanted her to be happy. So, I bought her a bed and we moved her into the spare bedroom. I was so lonely – it was awful. It still is.

I began to try to rebuild our relationship at Christmas.

It did **not** go well.

I opened up to her in her Christmas card, I said I was willing to try to rebuild, it was to begin a conversation – but it ended up with me breaking down in tears and Eve not coming to the table at all.

The next three months were abject hell. We put her new bed together and we finished setting up her bedroom, she loves it in there, she's really cosy. I have never been so sad. I cried myself to sleep each and every night, but the mornings were, and still are, much worse. I <u>hate</u> waking up alone – it ruins every day. I am wrong-footed from the moment I open my eyes and it is a struggle to smile or find any joy in the day.

But as bad as it was – it was nothing compared to what was to come.

March ended and with it my 50th birthday. Eve signed my birthday card with the word "love". It is likely that this is the last time she will ever use that word in relation to me. I have kept the card – it is by far the most precious thing I own.

"I don't love you anymore".
Said three months ago now. Said quietly, and truthfully.

Five words. Just five of them. They were enough to tear my entire life asunder. They were all it took to undo 50 years of striving to be Adam. He was mortally wounded by these little words, and I was left with nowhere to go. I had *chosen* to be a man for love. Without love, the man died, and I was left with my raw female nature fully and completely exposed. For the first time in my life, I became the woman I am at my core. The pretence was gone, and there was no way back.

This moment book-ended 38 years of my life.

Puberty forcibly turned my body into a man. 38 years later, five little words were the trigger that left me no choice, but to become who I truly am, a woman named Julia.

In both cases it was an assault. It was done to me against my will, and it did me untold damage. In both cases it brought me to the point of ending it all, and the second time, the second time, I came so very, very close.

The first time I considered suicide, well it never got beyond me thinking it was a viable option. But I did determine the method – crash the car at high speed, late at night when no one else could be involved in the "accident". Not nice for the emergency services, but then I suppose suicide never is and I wasn't thinking about others or the aftermath, I was too wrapped up in my own private Hell.

The second time around I left the house to **<u>actually do it</u>**.

Drive at 100mph plus and crash the car on purpose. Short, sharp – gone. Just another R.T.A.

                                        I was not in my right mind, clearly.

What I was, was in a very bad place. I could not see anything other than disaster, no hope, no future, no love – my life was a sham – I no longer existed – I lived to make Eve happy, taking myself out of the equation would free her and her happiness would be assured. Bonkers, all of it. So, I waited until 3am and crept out of the house. I entered my car and drove out into the countryside, then I pulled over. I should write a note. Paper, a pen – I found some in the glovebox, not much, but it will be enough. I only need to write Eve's name, "I love you, always", "You are free" and sign it. I'll photograph it on my phone and send it to her. She sleeps like a log; she'll get it when she wakes up and will know she is free. She'll be happy at last.

As I said. <u>Bonkers.</u>

Through an endless stream of tears, I started to write. And write and write. I wrote until I ran out of paper. Running out of space made me look at what I had written – surely those few words couldn't have filled the paper? It wasn't a note. I had written out my thoughts, my feelings, my pain. And in doing so, I had broken all my problems down into little pieces, manageable sentences, bullet points and huge scrawls. They were still problems, but separately they were not so overwhelming. And then I perceived something astonishing. In between the lines, not in any tangible sense, but plain as day to me. I looked at the pages and Adam was staring back at me. I was, for the first time in decades, outside the house dressed completely, head to toe, inside and out, as a woman. It didn't register when I left the house – I was so wrapped up in what I was about to do, I hadn't cared about how anyone would see me, I just wanted to be comfortable at the very end. I had a moment of profound clarity – I have never had one like this before or since. It was a revelation. I wasn't Adam anymore – I was Julia. And all these issues I had written down, they were catastrophic for Adam, but *I wasn't him*. How bad were they for Julia? Still awful, but I was a

step away. Adam's love for Eve is all consuming and it genuinely consumed him. Julia loves her too, but it is not as intense, more like a sister. And Julia is unexplored, I was curious, really curious, I had always been Adam and 'managed' my female side, but now, for the first time ever, I <u>was</u> Julia. And Adam? He was gone! Permanently inked onto those few pages, a paper grave for a paper man. Where he used to be was pain. Only pain. There was no way back. There was no one there, there never really was.

Julia didn't want to kill herself. She was curious, a real person for the first time, the prison guard was dead, and she was free to be herself, free after so many years hidden away, only let out when she was asleep. She was new and full of wonder…

She was also wondering how the hell she was going to get back into the house without any of her neighbours seeing her!

I had written for an hour and a half. Only three pages but covered in ink. It was now 4:30am and the sun was beginning to brighten the sky. Dawn was coming, a brand-new day. Any one of my neighbours could have an early start – it was a workday after all.

I cared about my neighbours seeing me in a skirt. I wasn't embarrassed, I felt right in the clothes – I was worried I'd upset them.

I started the car, turned around and headed back home. A journey I didn't think I would ever make. No one was around as I nervously walked from the car to the back door – safe.

A pen and three sides of A4 saved my life that night. The words I wrote brought me back from the absolute brink. And the clothes I was wearing reminded me that I was not Adam, I never had been, not really. I was a woman, named Julia – a

person I had never inhabited fully before and furthermore, the man I had hidden behind all my life was gone. He ceased to exist when his reason for being disappeared.

I mused over including these pages in this Journal, but I think they need to be in here – they are hugely important to me and integral to my life story. But they were scrawled on the back of a letter from my accountant and contain tax information, so I've re-written them – they are identical, other than the blue text in the top right-hand corner. Here they are:

The most important three pages of my life...

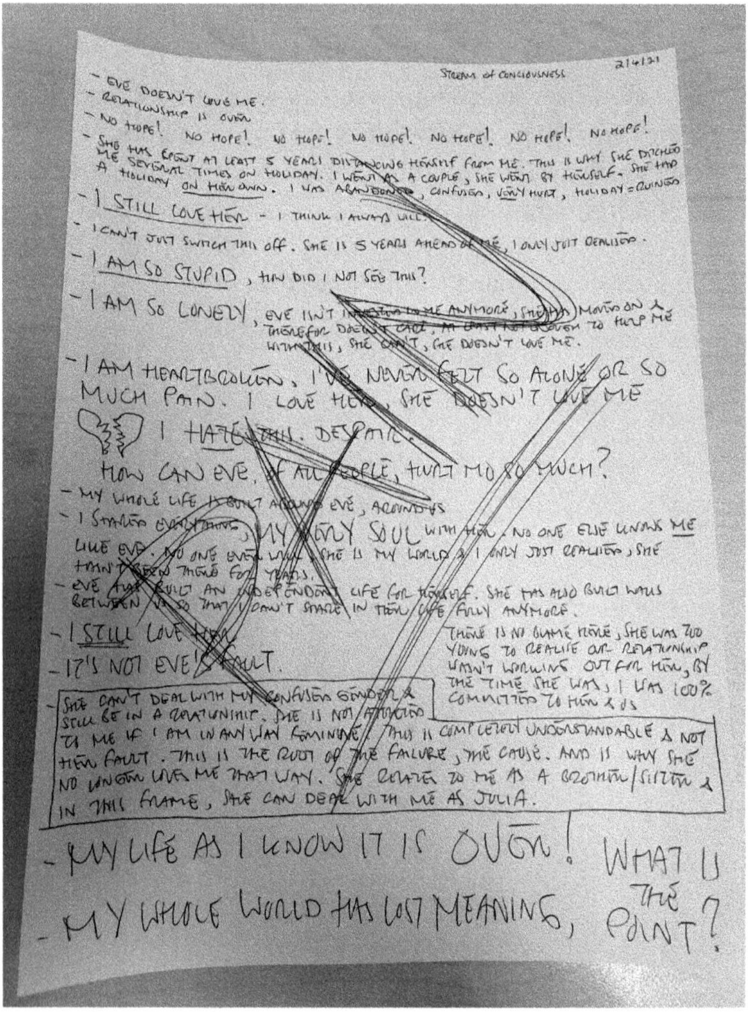

Stream of conciousness — 21/4/21

- EVE DOESN'T LOVE ME.
- RELATIONSHIP IS OVER.
- NO HOPE! NO HOPE! NO HOPE! NO HOPE! NO HOPE! NO HOPE! NO HOPE!
- SHE HAS SPENT AT LEAST 5 YEARS DIVORCING HERSELF FROM ME. THIS IS WHY SHE DITCHED ME SEVERAL TIMES ON HOLIDAY. I WENT AS A COUPLE, SHE WENT BY HERSELF. SHE HAD A HOLIDAY ON HER OWN. I WAS ABANDONED, CONFUSED, VERY HURT, HOLIDAY = RUINED.
- I STILL LOVE HER - I THINK I ALWAYS WILL.
- I CAN'T JUST SWITCH THIS OFF. SHE IS 5 YEARS AHEAD OF ME, I ONLY JUST REALISED.
- I AM SO STUPID, HOW DID I NOT SEE THIS?
- I AM SO LONELY, EVE ISN'T INTERESTED IN ME ANYMORE, SHE HAS MOVED ON & THEREFORE DOESN'T CARE, AT LEAST NOT ENOUGH TO HELP ME WITH THIS, SHE CAN'T, SHE DOESN'T LOVE ME.
- I AM HEARTBROKEN, I'VE NEVER FELT SO ALONE OR SO MUCH PAIN. I LOVE HER, SHE DOESN'T LOVE ME ♡ :'(I HATE THIS. DESPAIR.
- HOW CAN EVE, OF ALL PEOPLE, HURT ME SO MUCH?
- MY WHOLE LIFE IS BUILT AROUND EVE, AROUND US.
- I SHARED EVERYTHING, MY VERY SOUL WITH HER. NO ONE ELSE KNOWS ME LIKE EVE. NO ONE EVER WILL. SHE IS MY WORLD & I ONLY JUST REALISED, SHE HASN'T BEEN THERE FOR YEARS.
- EVE HAS BUILT AN INDEPENDENT LIFE FOR HERSELF. SHE HAS ALSO BUILT WALLS BETWEEN US THAT I DON'T SHARE IN HER LIFE FULLY ANYMORE.
- I STILL LOVE HER.
- IT'S NOT EVE'S FAULT.

  THERE IS NO BLAME HERE, SHE WAS TOO YOUNG TO REALISE OUR RELATIONSHIP WASN'T WORKING OUT FOR HER, BY THE TIME SHE WAS, I WAS 100% COMMITTED TO HER & US.

  SHE CAN'T DEAL WITH MY CONFUSED GENDER & STILL BE IN A RELATIONSHIP. SHE IS NOT ATTRACTED TO ME IF I AM IN ANY WAY FEMININE. THIS IS COMPLETELY UNDERSTANDABLE & NOT HER FAULT. THIS IS THE ROOT OF THE FAILURE, THE CAUSE. AND IS WHY SHE NO LONGER LOVES ME THAT WAY. SHE RELATES TO ME AS A BROTHER/SISTER & IN THIS FRAME, SHE CAN DEAL WITH ME AS JULIA.

- MY LIFE AS I KNOW IT IS OVER! WHAT IS
- MY WHOLE WORLD HAS LOST MEANING, THE POINT?

404

EVE IS ENCOURAGING ME TO FOLLOW IN HER FOOTSTEPS & BUILD AN INDEPENDENT LIFE OF MY OWN

I DON'T WANT TO! I STILL LOVE HER!

- ME EXPRESSING MYSELF AS JULIA IS NO LONGER A PROBLEM FOR EVE, IT WAS AN ISSUE AS HER BOYFRIEND, BUT NOT AS A SISTER OR BEST FRIEND.

I HATE SLEEPING ON MY OWN, I AM SO LONELY...

- EVE LOVES SLEEPING ON HER OWN. MY LOVE IS MAKING HER FEEL TRAPPED

I WANT EVE TO BE HAPPY, EVEN IF IT CAUSES ME PAIN, I LOVE HER TO THE POINT OF SELF-HARM. THIS IS VERY FRIGHTENING. TO BE SO IN LOVE WITH SOMEONE THAT YOU WOULD LITERALLY GIVE YOUR LIFE FOR THEM. I ALWAYS THOUGHT THIS WAS A CLICHÉ — IT IS NOT: I AM PROOF!

WORK
- MANIC, UNFULFILLING, STRESSFULL. I CAN'T DEAL WITH THIS RIGHT NOW BUT, ALL THIS WORK SHOULD REAP REWARDS...

FAMILY
- MUM. GONE. JESUS I MISS HER. I COULD REALLY DO WITH A HUG RIGHT NOW
- DAD. GONE. HE'S NOT THE MAN HE WAS & TO BE HONEST, HE WAS ALWAYS DISTANT & ON A PEDESTAL. I LOOKED UP TO HIM, BUT THAT MAN LEFT WHEN MUM PASSED AWAY.
- MY BROTHER & HIS FAMILY. THEY ARE ALL I NOW HAVE IN MY LIFE THAT IS GOOD. BUT HE & WORK ARE TOO INTERTWINED FOR ME TO SEPERATE. RELATIONSHIP WITH MY NEPHEW IN PARTICULAR IS GREAT.
- EVE'S FAMILY. THEY ARE GREAT, BUT THEY HAVE MOVED AWAY. THEY ARE NOT AS ON HAND AS THEY WERE, PLUS, AS MUCH AS I LOVE THEM & CONSIDER THEM MY FAMILY, ULTIMATELY, MY RELATIONSHIP WITH THEM IS GOING TO CHANGE.
- IF EVE'S FAMILY ARE MY FAMILY, WHAT HAPPENS IF WE ARE NO LONGER A COUPLE? FRIENDS ONLY? HAVE I LOST THEM TOO?

FRIENDS
- SUBJECT TO THE ABOVE, NONE.
- LOTS OF ACQUAINTENCES, NO ONE IS CLOSE.

I AM ALONE?

WHAT ABOUT EVE? WE ARE BEST FRIENDS

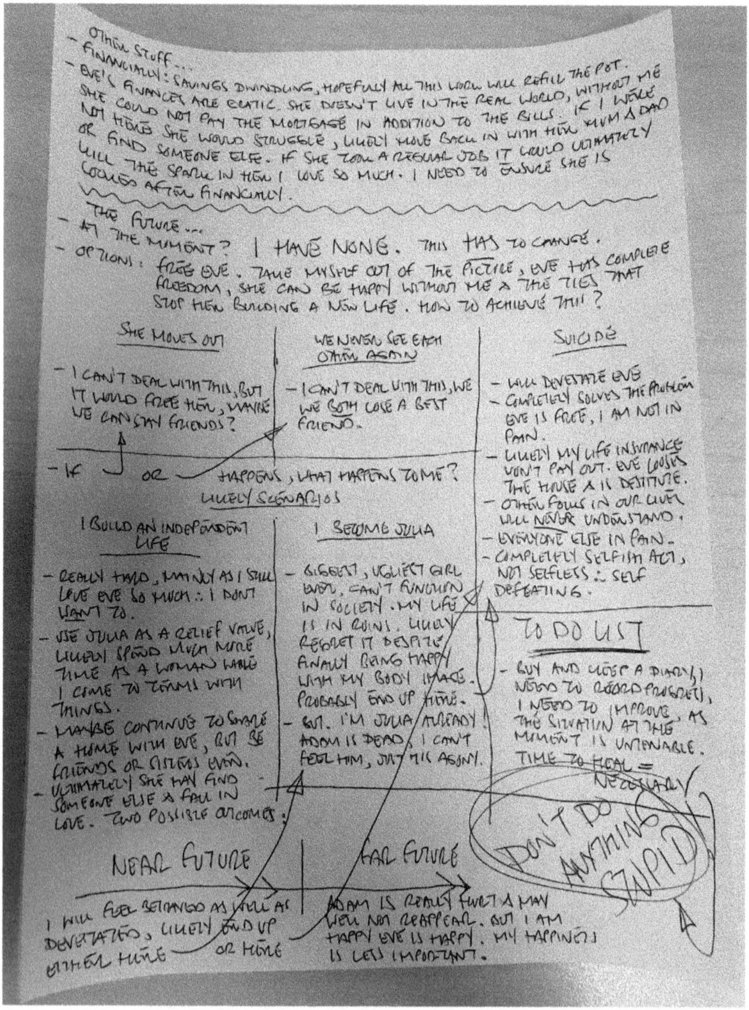

- OTHER STUFF...
- FINANCIALLY: SAVINGS DWINDLING, HOPEFULLY ALL THIS WORK WILL REFILL THE POT.
- EVE'S FINANCES ARE EXOTIC. SHE DOESN'T LIVE IN THE REAL WORLD, WITHOUT ME SHE COULD NOT PAY THE MORTGAGE IN ADDITION TO THE BILLS. IF I WERE NOT HERE SHE WOULD STRUGGLE, LIKELY MOVE BACK IN WITH HER MUM & DAD OR FIND SOMEONE ELSE. IF SHE TOOK A REGULAR JOB IT WOULD ULTIMATELY KILL THE SPARK IN HER I LOVE SO MUCH. I NEED TO ENSURE SHE IS LOOKED AFTER FINANCIALLY.

- THE FUTURE...
- AT THE MOMENT? I HAVE NONE. THIS HAS TO CHANGE.
- OPTIONS: FREE EVE. TAKE MYSELF OUT OF THE PICTURE, EVE HAS COMPLETE FREEDOM, SHE CAN BE HAPPY WITHOUT ME & THE TIES THAT STOP HER BUILDING A NEW LIFE. HOW TO ACHIEVE THIS?

SHE MOVES OUT	WE NEVER SEE EACH OTHER AGAIN	SUICIDE
- I CAN'T DEAL WITH THIS, BUT IT WOULD FREE HER, MAYBE WE CAN STAY FRIENDS?	- I CAN'T DEAL WITH THIS, WE BOTH LOSE A BEST FRIEND.	- WILL DEVASTATE EVE. - COMPLETELY SOLVES THE PROBLEM. EVE IS FREE, I AM NOT IN PAIN.
- IF ___ OR ___ HAPPENS, WHAT HAPPENS TO ME? LIKELY SCENARIOS		- LIKELY MY LIFE INSURANCE WON'T PAY OUT. EVE LOSES THE HOUSE & IS DESTITUTE.
I BUILD AN INDEPENDENT LIFE	I BECOME JULIA	- OTHER FOLKS IN OUR LIVES WILL NEVER UNDERSTAND. - EVERYONE ELSE IN PAIN.
- REALLY HARD, MAINLY AS I STILL LOVE EVE SO MUCH :: I DON'T WANT TO.	- BIGGEST, UGLIEST GIRL EVER, CAN'T FUNCTION IN SOCIETY. MY LIFE IS IN RUINS. LIKELY	- COMPLETELY SELFISH ACT, NOT SELFLESS :: SELF DEFEATING.
- USE JULIA AS A RELIEF VALVE, LIKELY SPEND MUCH MORE TIME AS A WOMAN WHILE I COME TO TERMS WITH THINGS.	REGRET IT DESPITE FINALLY BEING HAPPY WITH MY BODY IMAGE. PROBABLY END UP HERE.	TO DO LIST - BUY AND CLOSE A DIARY, NEED TO RECORD PROGRESS. I NEED TO IMPROVE AS THE SITUATION AT THE MOMENT IS UNTENABLE. TIME TO HEAL = NECESSARY
- MAYBE CONTINUE TO SHARE A HOME WITH EVE, BUT BE FRIENDS OR SISTERS EVEN.	- BUT, I'M JULIA ALREADY ADAM IS DEAD, I CAN'T FEEL HIM, JUST HIS AGONY.	
- ULTIMATELY SHE MAY FIND SOMEONE ELSE & FALL IN LOVE. TWO POSSIBLE OUTCOMES :		DON'T DO ANYTHING STUPID
NEAR FUTURE	FAR FUTURE	
I WILL FEEL BETRAYED AS WELL AS DEVASTATED, LIKELY END UP EITHER HERE OR HERE	ADAM IS REALLY HURT & MAY WELL NOT REAPPEAR. BUT I AM HAPPY EVE IS HAPPY. MY HAPPINESS IS LESS IMPORTANT.	

Can you see him? He's there on the pages somewhere...

Work happened, Kay happened, dressed correctly from 10pm – chores. Mogs. Laundry – stuff...

Oh, and a parcel was delivered late evening. A new nightie, robe and cami set. They are a very good fit and I love them.

Tuesday, July 6th

Up at 6am, 10½ hours in a skirt yesterday – I must try harder tonight, it's likely the reason for the epic piece in my journal yesterday. Mogs are fed and released out into the wild – tiny little lions out prowling the savannah. I finished up in the bathroom and then retired back to bed for a snooze – I still have about an hour before I need to leave for work.

Daily goals #28

- Smile, smile, and smile again.
- Diligence and professionalism.
- When good things happen, allow myself to appreciate them.

It was a good day at work, I managed to get loads done. I arrived home around 6pm, despite the twenty-minute mystery traffic jam on the main road. I had fish and chips tonight; I'm eating far too many takeaways. Afterwards, I got changed – earlier than is typical – I needed it today – I miss Eve, so I needed to spend as little time in Adam's clothes as possible. Back in a skirt from 6:30pm – so 13½ hours today in total – at last, and relax…

…I miss Eve, but I am in my happy place.

Wednesday, July 7th

Up at 6am as usual, bathroom & cute little fuzzies are now done. I have discovered that a satin duvet set is lovely, but your skin needs to be 100% smooth – no rough patches – or the satin will snag in the night and then go bobbly, ruining it, it'll start to look & feel terrible. I might have to wear tights / stockings to bed and step up my footcare routine… Not such a bad thing!

I am OK today – I am missing Eve, but it's not so bad. I kinda like looking after the house. I am so odd – most women are supposed to hate the housework. I think, if I am ever on my own for an extended period of time, I will probably develop a routine. Tackle different jobs/rooms on different days. I would make someone a perfect wife it seems. Not really a surprise. I like to look pretty, and I get at least some satisfaction out of housework. If only I enjoyed cooking…

I say this in jest – I hate cooking, I really shouldn't, it's a creative endeavour, but it's just such a waste of time and can be very technical. I can see why there are a lot of male chefs, and doing this to a very high standard, for lots of people all at once must be very challenging. But maybe I should expand my 'bucket list' to include things like this? I might like a cookery course, or indeed other "traditionally female" pass times? Beyond wiping down the surfaces and running the hover around, my knowledge of the domestic sciences is pretty limited – I can use the white goods, I have a laundry load in now as it happens, but how to remove stains, what cleaners are best on which surfaces, needlework, meal planning, stuff like this – important, day-to-day life skills. They might be fun to learn, definitely useful. And then beyond the mundane, there are things like hair and beauty – I'd love to learn make-up properly, not just play around with it, watching YouTube tutorials, learning by trial and error. Maybe I'll do some research.

I wished Eve good morning via WhatsApp, she replied today – my first genuine smile of the day. I'm a happy girl.

I am going through different women's deodorants / antiperspirants at the moment, trying to find one that I like and is effective. Impulse is nice, I like it a lot, but it ultimately lets me down and is more of a body scent. Sure, at least so far, sadly doesn't work for me. I like it, smells really fresh when applying, but the chemistry isn't effective enough for my body. My current favourite is Nivea Black and White – it seems to be very good so far.

A couple of small mysteries…

I had a parcel left on my doorstep yesterday with a slip pushed through my letterbox saying it had been delivered next door. I assumed it was a mistake, the delivery person changed their mind after they had posted the slip through my letterbox. But maybe I should've knocked to find out, as after I got changed for the evening there was a knock at my door – I was in no position to answer, but I am wondering if it was my neighbour with a parcel? Ockham's razor suggests the two are related…

I am wondering if Kay would like to meet "me". Logistically this would be difficult, but not impossible. It would mean leaving the house in broad daylight dressed fully as a woman. I am not sure I am ready for this just yet. She keeps telling me that I should be true to myself and not worry about what others think. That it is a brave new world and being trans is vastly more accepted than it used to be. But part of me is aware of the old adage – "Don't shit where you eat".

I think I can be happy with random strangers looking at me and wondering / knowing that I am physically male, although dressed as a female. But I am not ready for people I know, live next door to, work with and chat to regularly seeing the world's largest woman. It's chicken and egg – I need to look more female

to "pass". But to look more female I need to live as a woman for 2 years.

The word "pass" is also confusing – there are a multitude of levels to passing – and I know my size will always raise eyebrows – it doesn't matter how female I look or behave; people will wonder. Do I care? Not really, providing they don't make things difficult for me. But I want to look acceptable. That is actually the bigger issue and much more important to me. I want to conform and fit into a typical female size range. I want it. It'll never happen. But I want it.

Time to go to work…

Daily goals   #29

- Smile lots!
- Have fun.
- Don't worry, be happy (Bobby McFerrin was spot on!)

A really great day.

Work was OK, I did around 3 hours in the morning, then we, as a company, closed up shop and headed to Top Golf for mid-day – a fun filled afternoon, split into 2 teams with targets on the driving range and a computer keeping score. Nice food and lots of good-natured chat and banter.

Dad joined us too, as the patriarch of the company, he is always very welcome to join us. He was on good form today as well – likely because we were in company and at a fun event.

Traffic jam on the M11, but home around 5:30pm – Eve has been home, but her car was missing, likely she was at the horses. I settled in for the evening and she arrived back around 6pm – new trainers (she's very pleased with them), she had already eaten, and I had had a big lunch, so no dinner tonight.

I slipped into something more comfortable around 8pm – 12 hours in a skirt today. Eve wasn't overly enthused about the production; she didn't have a lot of stories for me. She went for a walk in her new trainers and then after, had a bath.

It's lovely she is home, I really missed her. But she looked tired, and we didn't really connect this evening. Maybe tomorrow. At least she's home.

It's just coming up to 10pm – I'm going to get changed for bed shortly.

Night xx

Thursday, July 8th

6:48am, up, showered and now relaxing – usual routine – just chilling for a bit before the day begins. Eve is awake – she said good morning and asked how I was, she also said my new satin robe was nice – both of these things, the good morning and the compliment, mean so much. More than she appreciates, I'm sure. If / when she goes, I am going to miss these little things the most, I'm certain of it.

I slept in knickers, stockings, nightie, earrings, perfume, and make-up – the stockings solved the rough skin issue & without the bra I was supremely comfy – a really good night's sleep. New Estradot today, the hormones I am taking are a patch, rather than a pill – I've not used patches for any medicines before. Seems to be working well enough though, I am alternating between hips. This one is on my left, and it will be there until Sunday. I only have 4 patches left though, so I think I will be out in a fortnight. I am not sure the online pharmacy will send me a second batch – they gave me the benefit of the doubt once, but I don't think they will do so again. I may have to find an alternate supply... Maybe I need to schedule an appointment with my GP for a referral to a gender specialist? I will talk to Kay about this in the next session, she may well know someone.

> I think I may be ready. Ready to start the journey that leads to surgery and a life as a physical female. I am so scared, but if I have lost Eve, then I have no reason to stay in this horrid man's body. I need to be true to myself.

Even though I am too big, I will be me. I will love being female, I will struggle in some areas that I currently find easy and will in all likelihood face comments and derision from idiots in random situations.

But I will be who I am.

I started these journals with the mindset that I was emotionally compromised and therefore couldn't make any big decisions. It is now three months on, and I think I may have just made the biggest decision of my life. I have doubts, I have no idea if this is the right thing to do. This is going to change everything in so many ways, most of which I cannot foresee. My life will never be the same again. But of course, that is the whole point. I am going to roll the dice and see. But it doesn't all have to happen right away, I can take my time and do it right, starting with trying to be as authentic as I can, little steps, but definite steps in the right direction, with a destination in mind. Mid-life crisis do not get much bigger than this...

And I have no idea if I will be happy afterwards. None whatsoever. I think I will, but there are no certainties here. But does this really matter? If I am true to myself then this will be enough. I think my life will be harder in a lot of ways, but also, better in others. All I really know is I want it. I want to be physically female. <u>I want a vagina.</u>

I became a man for Eve's love. That love is gone. Why am I still a man?

I am not.

I am a woman.

Time to start making it real.

Time to start showing the world my true face. Time to be the woman I am, win, lose or draw – at least I will have tried and at least I will be true to myself. I already <u>know</u> that I will be happier with my physicality if I were the same inside and out. Perhaps even feel less dysphoric all the time. I can make this work – but it's going to be astonishingly difficult. And other folks just won't understand. I hope those closest to me will. I hope that I can keep at least some of the life I currently have. That's

what the last 3 months have been about – trying to hold on to as much of my previous life as I could. That life is over, but the salvage operation continues.

Everyone is telling me this, my previous life with Eve is over. I just chose not to listen. I didn't want to because I knew, somewhere deep inside, that Eve was worth denying myself for. But now, she has stepped away and I can no longer live like this.

I <u>am</u> Julia.

...and it is time for her to start to shine.

Daily goals #30
- Smile, be good company.
- Be professional.
- Be true to myself.

A good day, all told. All be it expensive. I bought the twins and my sister-in-law vouchers / gift cards for their birthdays, I want to buy them something cool for the pool side in Majorca too, but I have yet to find anything. Work in progress...

I also bought myself a nice ring for my finger and 2 sets of earrings too. As well as 2 summer dresses and 6 T-Shirts for my disguise along with some sandals, again, all for the holiday. I had to transfer some money from my savings – ouch!

Eve was quite upset tonight. Her lease on her electric car is up this year and she is realising that she needs to find £5k somehow if she wants to keep it. I think she will ask her folks for a loan, but she is really distressed – her life choices now mean that my help will not be appreciated.

I want to. I hate seeing her upset. I even offered. But she turned me down flat. Pride...

I also said that she needs to find ½ the money for the bills every month and gave her 12 months to do it. An incremental increase of £50 every month, in 12 months' time she will be at £600 – ½ what I am paying. If not, we will need to sell the house.

She has some serious financial issues to resolve and no mistake. But it's do-able *if she wants it*.

I bought us both dinner and she took her sportscar out for a ride. Hopefully she cleared her head. I then got changed for the evening.

I feel like I'm such a git. I hated doing this tonight and I feel I was kicking her when she was down. But this is her doing. And I can't have her blowing whatever little money she has on the balloon payment on her car in favour of the mortgage and bills. She needed a (hopefully gentle) reminder that she has other, more important commitments. It's a question of priorities. If she hadn't broken my heart, we would have been OK, and I would have gladly carried on supporting her. Even now I still want to. And I would if she swallowed her damned pride and asked. But she won't do it. I respect that, she has something to prove to herself. But it *IS* foolish.

Sooner or later, it will become impossible for me to carry on supporting her. She **has** to step up before then.

July	£100.00
August	£150.00
September	£200.00
October	£250.00
November	£300.00
December	£350.00
January	£400.00
February	£450.00
March	£500.00

April   £550.00

May   £600.00   Mortgage and bills target hit = **FAIR**

£600.00 per month, every month from June 2022 onwards. Or we sell the house.

12 months is enough time, and the £50 increments should be manageable. If she is prepared to do whatever it takes.

I want to help her to be happy. It's all I ever wanted. But make no mistake, she has done this. She has rejected me and my help. She has dissolved the team. There are consequences to living in the real world, as an adult, on your own.

I gave her everything in exchange for her love – it is the best deal in the world. She took her love away. The deal is now broken.

I **hate** this.

Finding £600 a month is hard to do. But I find £1200 a month, every month, and I have done so for **years**. I have paid her commitments to the house willingly and gladly. But no more. I can't do it and get nothing in return.

If we end up selling the house, we will both walk away with around £70k I reckon. I will have no problem putting this down as a deposit and getting another mortgage. I have a stable, regular income and an A1 track record. She will have a large sum of money, but not enough to buy a place outright and (assuming things do not change), she is a bad bet for a mortgage lender.

My new house will be mine. I will not be paying her half of the bills. She is welcome to live with me in my house, but I will want rent from her. This rent is negotiable – I am reasonable, and it doesn't have to cover the mortgage in the new place. Only ½ the bills.

She will be massively better off. I will own the house entirely, so I will be better off too. She can use the money to

travel or do whatever and she will always be welcome to live with me. Unless she finds someone else. At which point, she becomes their partner and they, I am sure, will gladly take her on.

> I am her safety net. And always will be. She only has to ask. I will be there for her.

So, assuming she steps up, the worst-case scenario is actually pretty good, all told. I don't want to sell this house, but I won't live here in <u>our</u> *home* on my own and I can't keep on paying her ½ of the bills. Not now. Not without her love.

I hope she finds the money. I hope her website starts paying off – she deserves it. She's worked her arse off to build it and it is really, really good.

I have faith in her. She is capable of truly great things. She just needs to put her energies into the right things and importantly, stick with them. This, plus a bit of luck and it'll all come good. We all need a little luck, but we need to create the right circumstances to capitalise on the luck if it happens.

---

13 hours today. I loved every minute of it. This is definitely how I want to live my life. Being a woman is wonderful.

Friday, July 9th

Good morning world! Dunno why I have that Friday feeling – I am going into work today – not taking a day off. Odd.

Spent the night, err, 'excessively attired' – so cosy – I slept really well, like a princess. So nice. I looked in the bathroom mirror earlier and liked what I saw. A dishevelled, sleepy, not very pretty woman, about to get herself ready for the day. I looked into my smudged, mascara enhanced eyes and I don't see Adam anymore. I am Julia.

Maybe this is why I am not just OK, but actually feeling quite good this morning?

I feel like I have reached some conclusions over the past couple of days. I feel like I am ready to begin the next phase of my life. I've no idea how true this is. But we shall see I suppose...

Daily goals #31
- Smile (shouldn't be too hard today!)
- Be true to myself.
- Find joy in the moments and make good memories.

Be true to myself – well, I have really gone for it tonight – not just fully clothed as a woman in every way, but false nails, nail polish and full make-up, not just my typical 'day look'. Also, I was applying my nails from 6pm, so 14 hours as a woman today – I am almost euphoric – I love this so much. I might stay like this all night, after all, as mentioned (often), it seems a waste to put so much effort in for only a few hours. I'm all dressed up and nowhere to go... If I get the chance I may go for a drive in the wee-small hours. I am going to have to go out as a woman sooner or later after all. Eve, I think will be spending the night at her sister's place, so I have an opportunity and if I am awake at 3am, I may pop out for a bit! Exciting! A bit of a landmark...

Work was OK, I finished another drawing set. Home on time, Eve popped in briefly to get changed and pack a bag. I watched the current episode of Loki and then the first 4 of The Falcon and the Winter Soldier. I was fully female by 6pm.

Lingerie, stockings, heels, skirt, blouse, ladies watch, ring, necklace, and earrings. Deodorant, body spray and perfume. False nails, nail polish (fingers and toes), eyebrow pencil, kohl line, mascara, eye shadow, blush, lip liner, lipstick, and lip gloss. A woman's long hair, loose and styled in a feminine manner. My ladies' glasses complete my outfit. I look OK and I feel great.

Although I'm not looking forward to removing any of it, my nails will be challenging – they are stuck on really firmly!

Saturday, July 10th

...ooops! 4am, I have just stepped onto the patio outside the back door for a moment. It is daybreak and I've missed my window of opportunity to go out – I fell asleep – I should have set an alarm...

I had a nice lie in instead (it's Saturday after all) – I remained fully clothed until 10am, then, very reluctantly, I began to deconstruct my appearance. Removing the nails, as predicted, took some time, but I managed to do so without wasting a lot of remover. I will do it again sometime – I'd love to get them done professionally – that'd be awesome.

Once back in Adam's disguise I tidied the house, hoovered, and packed for the weekend's trip to Eve's parents' place. I have also begun a pile of things to take with me to Majorca next week. I'm starting to get a little bit organised.

It's just gone 11am, no word at all from Eve – not even a good morning today. I'm just not worth the effort it seems, or worse, not important enough to her to even register. I hate this so much.

My new sandals for my trip to Majorca have arrived – I tried them on this morning, they are a good, comfy fit, it's always a gamble buying footwear online, men's and women's alike. I am waiting on some T-shirts and then I am more or less ready.

Daily goals #32

- Smile, enjoy life, be happy if I can.
- Be good company.
- Don't hold grudges, Eve (I hope) isn't doing this on purpose.

A good day all in. Eve arrived shortly after I wrote the above, she was in good spirits and actually, so was I. Larry cat though has escaped! He now faces a night outside the house. His sister, Tara, stayed in though, so we are only worried about him. He'll be OK, I am sure.

We hit the road around mid-day, it seemed to take ages to get there today. We stopped for lunch at McDs in Stansted and then again in a Costa in Ely for a tea for Eve. These 2 stops, plus unexpected road works added up to make the 2 hour journey 3 hours. I was shattered when we arrived, driving seemed to be hard work today. Although there was some good conversation between Eve and I, this helped massively.

We arrived safely, I was tired and a little headachey – always great to see Eve's folks again though. I spent a nice afternoon chatting in the summerhouse. Then a takeaway curry and a board game this evening – all good fun.

I retired to bed around 11pm – 11 hours in a skirt today.

I am very tired, going to sleep now.

Night. xx

Sunday, July 11th

A reasonable night's sleep, nightie, and knickers only, plus the bed has a footboard so my feet couldn't hang out the end as usual (being statuesque is not all fun and games!) I am OK today. Today, the full height mirror on the wardrobe door is a bonus, I am sat on the edge of the bed directly in front of it and you know what? I don't look too bad. Lots of things wrong of course, size, shoulders, body hair etc. But my shape is a little better, boobs, a hint of hip, just the very beginnings of a waist (I'm still vastly overweight, but the fat looks to be distributed a tad differently). The nightie hides a multitude of sins too. Or. I should put my glasses on...

It's around 9am, again, no glasses, I can't see the clock clearly. I am waiting for my slot in the bathroom. Eve's dad is outside in the garden, and I think Eve has been and gone in there, so it can only be her mum. But it's gone very quiet – I am wondering if she has finished, and it is now vacant? I hope I am not sitting here waiting for an already empty bathroom to vacate...

I can't investigate without getting changed. I need to be sure before I venture out of the relative safety of my room in my nightie – I am not sure, so I am stuck here (with my legs crossed). Still, my nightie is lovely – I think I can hold on for a bit longer.

Today's goals   #33

- Smile. (Really important!)
- Be good company for others.
- Be open to the world, <u>enjoy life.</u>

A nice breakfast, and then I helped Eve's dad install a new toilet pan and cistern in the downstairs WC. It was good to help

out for a bit, I like to be useful. It makes me feel good to help and to have my help appreciated. All in all, a pleasant morning, but all-too-soon it was time to head for home. We said our goodbyes and hit the road, Eve driving, me taking it easy in the passenger seat.

We diverted to Wisbech to get some lunch and thus, ended up on the road to March instead of our usual run back through Welney. As we were passing, we spotted a 22kw charger for Eve's electric car. I think, now she knows where it is, she can drive herself up here to see her folks (and it will save me some diesel). It was supposed to be a 42kW rapid, but when we investigated, it was untethered, so 22kW max.

We had a pleasant chat on the way home, we talked about Eve's balloon payment on her car, due in October. She has seen the logic of paying the £5k and keeping the car, so she needs to borrow the money. I think she will talk to her mum & dad, likely while I am away. My offer still stands, and her mum knows it too, so there is a small chance I will be asked, but I'm not holding my breath. We also talked about ownership of the car. I think I can transfer ownership simply by filling in the green slip on the V5C document – effectively a sale of the car. How much I choose to sell it for is not important. A peppercorn if I must. To be honest, she has paid for the car herself – it is only in my name because of her income situation – they wouldn't have approved the finance. So, I did it for her. I don't want her car, technically yes, I own it, but it was never my car really, she is welcome. Maybe a symbolic penny would be fun!

We arrived home between 2 and 3pm, no Larry cat. We called and called him, no sign. We went out looking for him too – the little beggar had disappeared! Sooo worrying. It started to get dark and then began raining – I was thinking the worst and then, around 9:30pm, I heard a meow at the front door – he was home! What a relief! He was fine too and was very happy

to be fed. Maybe he was shut in a shed or something? He likely watched us from the bushes while we were frantically looking for him... What a little tinker!

I delayed getting changed because of him. Just in case I had to go out searching again. I was back in my nightie by 10pm though – 11 hours, all things considered – not too bad.

It feels odd not having my toenails polished – but I'll be like this for the next fortnight whilst I am away – I better get used to it. My new T-shirts have arrived, so I think I am all set, other than the two summer dresses. I also ordered a couple of pool inflatables for the twins' birthdays – they should be fun for them, assuming the inflatables fit in my suitcase!

Night xx

Monday, July 12th

Bathroom at 6, bed again by 7am, I'm relaxing before I begin the day as normal – or at least I would be, if Tara cat would let me. Thankfully Eve is awake too, so the cat is sharing her time between us.

I am a little out of sorts this morning, the stress of Larry cat yesterday combined with not getting changed until after he came home has upset my equilibrium a bit. I am <u>very</u> aware of my nightie at the moment, it feels great, so comfy – I <u>really</u> don't want to take it off and change for the day. Or at least, I don't want to exchange it for something horribly male.

I have to visit a site this morning, although I am not looking forward to it. It's in a mental health facility, the irony is not lost on me. But it means I need to be out of the house half an hour earlier – less time in my nightie.

I am going to the cinema tonight with Eve. We are going to see 'Black Widow' – I've been waiting to see this for months. We are not going on a "date" though – just two friends getting together for a night out. I hope I am going to be OK with this. I love going to the cinema, film is one of my passions and it just won't be the same without someone to share it with. I hope our night's out together can continue. Especially as we have had so few of them due to the lockdowns.

Daily goals #34

- Smile and try to be joyful.
- Be professional at work, even if you don't want to be there today.
- Make the most of whatever life offers me.

It was a productive day, and the site visit went well. Then later in the office I completed my 'Passenger Locator Form' for

entry into Spain – I think, as far as paperwork goes, I am now ready for my flight to Majorca. I drew up some more plans – everyone done is one less to do. I also took a few private minutes to research gender reassignment. It seems there is a minimum 33 months wait for an NHS specialist and going private is likely to cost around £20k for "bottom surgery" (orchiectomy, labiaplasty and penile inversion). And that's before breast augmentation, facial feminisation, voice training, deportment lessons and permanent hair removal. Plus, anti-androgens will improve male pattern baldness, but not fully reverse the damage – I will never have a woman's hairline it seems (shit), but my remaining hair should thicken up though. I might need to do this much sooner to halt the damage. I think I would be lucky to see the lower side of £90k all in to be as female as physically possible, and I will **still** be 6'-2" tall and have an American footballer's shoulders. It is a **lot** cheaper in the Far East, but I have no idea at all how to make that happen. How do you find a reputable place? I am trusting them with my body and my future. I am sure there are places that do amazing work but finding the good ones is a major challenge.

I want it so badly though. It's odd that I never used to. But now, not only is there no reason whatsoever to put up with this hateful male body anymore, I have 15 years of lost time to make up as well.

And where will I end up? An androgyne I think – a female body stretched over a male framework. This is **not** good, I know this, so why do I want it so badly?

An impossible dream? I will do my best, take one day at a time and see where this road takes me.

The very first step is to talk to Kay, let her know I have come to a fundamental decision. And ask for a referral. 33 months, wow, almost three years wait. I need to start counting these down, I think. I am in this for the long haul...

Home on time, we headed off to Nando's for dinner and then went to the cinema! So amazing to be able to go to the cinema again, I've missed the experience. Sadly, Eve made it abundantly clear that this was **not a date**, just two good friends / sisters going to the flix together, nothing more. It didn't spoil the evening though – we had a great time. 'Black Widow' was excellent, I loved every minute of it.

Home around 10pm, in my nightie shortly after. 10 hours is not enough – must try harder…

Tuesday, July 13th

T-minus 1 day...

...I am **not** looking forward to it.

I'm going to Majorca for nine days. On my own. This is the longest I will have been apart from Eve in the last 15 years, on top of this, my opportunities to dress properly will be limited and due to the heat, likely unsatisfying.

More and more, I am missing Eve even when we are together. It's not the same as it used to be – I can't help it, I miss who she was and actually, I miss who I was too. I shouldn't, but I do.

However, I **really** miss her when we she works away. I see her in every square millimetre of *our house.*

I miss her immensely when I go away for work too. Especially if she doesn't want to chat. But I lock myself away in my hotel room and get changed...

This trip is going to be **_VERY_** difficult for me. I wish she was coming with me. It would be so much easier to deal with mum's final request, to have a small amount of her ashes scattered in her most favourite holiday destination. Factor in the psychological brow beating I am expecting from dad too. I need her support, now more than ever. I need her company and I desperately want her love back. We were so good together; I want our lives back... Can't help it, I know it's over, but I just don't want it to be.

I am going to speak to Kay tonight in our session about transitioning and how I get the ball rolling. Time for a new life. **A life as a female.**

Adam isn't in as much pain as he was, the fact is, there's not much left of him to feel it anymore. He is an empty and hollow space – an outline of a man. He is not real to me, just a

horrible place to be made of dead dreams, crushed hopes, and unrequited love. I **can't** be him anymore. I just can't. His outline is a desolate and miserable place. A paper-thin disguise pasted over who I truly am. He never really existed anyway.

And who am I?

If you had asked me when I was growing up, I would have said I was split, 50 / 50, right down the middle, male / female. I looked male, so I lived as a male, I lived the way I was required to. And I only expressed my female nature in private.

The term 'non-binary trans' hadn't been invented back then, but pretty much sums up how I used to be, or at least, how I thought I was. At the time, the best I could come up with was the blanket term, 'cross-dresser'.

But my female nature was suppressed, unexplored and a mystery I was too afraid to investigate. Literally **_EVERYONE_** was shouting at me "you are a boy", I was afraid to open Pandora's box.

Pandora's box is now WIDE open.

And what did I find inside? I found I was not a cross-dresser after all, or even non-binary trans. No. the walls fell away, and I saw myself truly for the first time. I am a trans woman.

This is who I am. I am a female stuck in a huge male body – I've said it before, the worst of all possible situations for a trans woman. I **have** to transition, I am compelled to and furthermore, now that I've looked into the abyss & seen who I truly am, I *really* want it. But I know it will result in an odd-looking woman, a woman who will not fit into society's blinkered view of how a woman should be. But I can't deny who I am anymore. The scales have fallen from my eyes, and I have seen my true reflection. I must be true to myself. I no longer have a choice.

I used to think I needed to balance both sides of my nature. I loved being a man for Eve – they truly were the best days of my

life. If I could close the lid on Pandora's box and go back there, choose to be a man once more in exchange for Eve's love – I would do so in a heartbeat. It was worth it, so worth it. But I can't. Pandora's box is open all the way. I can no longer deny who I am.

I am Julia, and she is awesome. So much potential. *So much to give to a world that hates her.*

I know this now and every fibre of my being wants to match my physical body to my internal gender. I **want** a vagina. I want it so badly. I need one, I crave it. And I want everything that goes with a vagina – the whole package. I want to show the world my true face, stand proud and live openly as the woman I am.

I am so sick of hiding.

Enough is enough.

50 years – shit. So much time lost.

Daily goals #35
- Smile (gonna be hard today).
- Be prepared for my trip.
- Make the best of the day.
- Talk to Kay about transitioning.

Work – Clients in for a meeting, the meeting took **all day**. Productive though but tiring.

Home on time, rush, rush, rush – appointment with Kay at 6pm.

It was a very productive and emotional session with Kay – I feel like I have made a positive step forward with regards to my gender and I laid it all out for her. We chatted it through and she challenged me in a number of key areas. For instance,

I explained that I would like to be physically female, but still be able to dip in and out of Adam (mainly professionally). Basically, the reverse of what I am now. She countered with if I am not done with Adam, am I sure this is what I want? I said that I am never going to be 100% sure – all I know is I want it to the point of obsession and I am ready to start putting wheels in motion. I came away feeling good, like I had done something really positive.

I also showed Kay a couple of photos of me (Julia), there really aren't many (such a shame). She was complimentary – apparently, I scrub up quite well!

Home again – chatting to Eve – we had such a nice night out at the cinema last night, we are talking about going to see it again when I come back from holidays.

Packing... I hate it. It took ages – 9 days' worth of horrid clothing, plus the bare minimum of *my* things – really hard to fit it all into two bags! I also had prezzies for the twins to bring with me. I did all of this dressed completely of course – 12 hours again today – I am making the most of these scant few remaining hours.

A nice 'goodbye' hug from Eve before bed – I set my alarm for 3am and retired... Big day tomorrow.

Wednesday, July 14th

Holidays, day 1...

Wow, 3am is just brutal.

Up / bathroom / dressed / out the door / Stansted airport parking / mini-bus / check-in / security / wait / departure gate / wait / plane / take-off – **sleep!**

...but not before tears.

A stewardess asked me about Eve on the plane. I said she couldn't make it, she was satisfied, but I turned to the window and cried. I cried through the safety demo and take off. I cried myself to sleep...

God how I miss her. Doing this on my own <u>is not right</u>.

There were spectacular crystal-clear views of Barcelona as we flew over at circa 33,000 feet, coming over the Majorcan mountains was stunning too. By this time, I was thankfully back in a reasonable head space, so I was able to appreciate them.

Landing / terminal / passport control / baggage / Spanish health form / Palma airport / taxi / scary mountain roads / spectacular / Deià / hotel / check-in – **Family.**

We are all here – all except mum and Eve. I miss them both so much. But I have mum's wedding ring on a chain around my neck, a chain that Eve bought me. They are both *always* with me and close to my heart.

The hotel is mum and dad's special place. They have stayed here more than thirty times over the years. Dad had scattered the last of mum's ashes already – he decided to do this on his own before we all arrived. A private and personal moment for him. I'm sure it was very meaningful. I will see the spot tomorrow and will have my own special moment with her.

We took the coach to Mulletta and I had a spot of lunch with my brother and his family – all very nice. Dad stayed behind

in the hotel, we have friends here too, they kept dad company while us 'youngsters' went out to play. Youngsters, sheesh, I'm 50 years old...

Back at the hotel around 4pm, I crashed out in my room only to be awakened by a text – dinner at 7pm, it was 6:30 already! I was only a little late and equally, a little dishevelled. It was a really a lovely dinner together, then we all retired to the pool bar for the evening.

Back in the room around midnight, only 3 hours in a skirt today, although technically, Majorca is an hour ahead. I'm clutching at straws here, not good, not good at all. But not unexpected, I knew this was going to be challenging.

I am very tired – good night, time to close the book on today...

Thursday, July 15th

Holidays, day 2...

My alarm went off at 6am, but of course, Majorca is an hour ahead – schoolgirl error, breakfast isn't for another three hours. I snoozed for a bit, then showered and dressed – my first opportunity to put an outfit together. I bought a couple of summer dresses ahead of this trip, but due to space in my luggage, and the fact that one of them, although I prefer the fit and look of it, is lined so is quite warm, I have only brought one with me. I am wearing it now, as I write, along with bra, knickers, jewellery, lipstick, and heels – finally, I get to relax. It's a holiday after all.

I am missing my nail polish though. My eldest nephew is with his girlfriend, it seems she has decided to paint random toes red – but not on herself, on my nephew! They look lovely and the irony is – I took my nail polish off to come on holiday...

I miss Eve. I thought about her a lot yesterday. It was all I could do to not message her all day – she would've loved it here. The rooms have been refurbished since we were last here, they are beautiful. We have the place more or less to ourselves, partly due to Covid and the complexities of travel I suspect, but also because we are by far the largest group here. Probably a third of the total number of guests I estimate. So, plenty of space. Mulletta was nice yesterday too. I am very emotional, for lots of reasons – I am having to deny myself due to the situation – the pressure to be sociable with my family is immense – so I am Adam for them much more than I would've liked and in truth, more than I can handle at the moment – if this keeps up I am going to have to have a "me" day where I lock myself in my room and just chill as authentically as I can manage. I really need Eve's support – but she is not here. *I miss mum.* Dad is teary and clingy, and my brother is panicking because Majorca

looks like it's going back on the Covid amber list so he, like lots of travellers on the island, is trying to rearrange flights – my nephew and his girlfriend need to get home sooner than anticipated – she is a lifeguard and cannot take time off to self-isolate – her job is on the line.

Daily goals #36

- Smile.
- Relax.
- Enjoy the holiday – it's a rare treat, I need to appreciate it.

A nice day – not too hot, I'm not sunburned, at least not yet anyway... I was first for breakfast, not surprising really given the ditzy girl error with my alarm. I sat on the terrace overlooking the Deià valley in the early morning sunshine and made a good memory – it's so beautiful here. A short while later I was joined by the twins and my brother and sister-in-law. The others then followed after I had finished eating.

Later on, we played some tennis and then lunch by the pool followed by chess on the giant chess board. I asked my nephews if they knew where mum was – they showed me and left me with her for a bit.

It is a truly beautiful spot, right on the fence line of the hotel, quiet, tranquil and with amazing views of Deià and the Can Quet restaurant, another of mum's favourite places. She spent many an hour there enjoying first rate cuisine in great company – the best of times. A perfect place for her.

I sat in a lounger and said some things to her. I told her how much I love and miss her and how I am going through some stuff right now. I said sorry for messing up my relationship with Eve and I explained what has happened and why she isn't here. I also told her about me, my decision to transition and that I

likely may never come back to the hotel, at least, not as her son. I took some photos of the spot and shed more than a few tears – I also messaged Eve. She and mum were close – she really wanted to be here, but dad made it impossible for her.

I needed a hug from mum today – I didn't get one. So, I cried.

A perfect spot for mum – so beautiful.

And mum's other resting place, the church in her hometown. Equally beautiful.

Night mum, sleep well. I love you.

A quick dip in the pool before dinner – no one can see your tears in the pool.

I am looking at the ladies in their lovely swimwear around the pool – gosh, I am so jealous. I want to be one of these beautiful people, I want to be just like them – curves in all the right places, flattering swimwear, relaxed and confident. My dysphoria is maddening, likely because I am so emotional.

Dinner was nice, if a little delayed, then back to the pool bar for a nightcap before retiring to bed.

I am currently in my summer dress; I'll swap into my nightie shortly.

8½ hours today.

A very emotional day indeed.

Saturday, July 17th

Holidays, day 3...

I didn't want to get up this morning – I'm still missing Eve badly – I really needed her to be here with me. Nothing I do here makes me truly happy as my love isn't here to share it with. It is lovely here and it is great to be surrounded by close family – but as much as I am having a good time, I can't really relax – there feels like there is a lid on how much fun I can have. I keep finding myself looking at pictures of Eve I took on my phone, the last time we were here together. It is getting <u>very</u> emotional. It doesn't help that mum is in a lot of them too. I am putting on a brave face. I am trying **<u>very</u>** hard not to message Eve every day.

Breakfast – a nice distraction. I sat with dad and his friends, mine too, once removed if you know what I mean – good people – I spent some time with them this morning. The rest of the family have headed into Sollier to have Covid tests ahead of their return trip home – I am really going to miss them – I don't think I am going to like being here with dad on our own. He is finding it equally difficult here too.

I have begun typing up Volume 1 of this journal, I brought my laptop with me and am now up to 4000 words, 12 pages done. Good progress. It's nice to escape to my room and type up a few pages every now and then. I think I am going to give it to Kay to read, I feel like I am giving her 'homework' – teehee.

A nice, light lunch, then the kids arrived back. Dad went for an afternoon snooze; I am about to join the kids in the pool.

Chess, my youngest nephew beat me – I also think this is where I picked up all ten of my gnat bites – sooo itchy. Infuriating, both the bites and losing at chess! I chilled for the afternoon then met up with everyone at the pool bar for pre-dinner drinks. My brother showed me how to fill in the UK Passenger Locator

Form, it's overly complicated compared to the Spanish one, I am not looking forward to doing mine, and I suppose, dads too. He's a technophobe. This is the reason I brought my laptop with me, typing up this journal is a bonus.

We sat down to dinner at 8pm but we didn't eat until after 10pm. Then back to the pool bar for chat and drinks into the mediterranean night. My eldest nephew and his girlfriend are flying home tomorrow – they are likely to be in an extensive queue for the Passenger Locator Form check. From the news, it seems like there are lots of holidaymakers cutting their trips short to get home before the 4am deadline when Majorca goes from green to amber. What a crazy world we live in. My brother has pulled their taxi forward half an hour to give them as much time as possible.

I retired around midnight – a good day, but only 7½ hours in a skirt.

Sunday, July 18th

Holidays, day 4...

I'm struggling to remember what day of the week it is, time is different here, holidays are always run to a different clock, but this time, more than most, I am not quite in the right headspace to deal with all the minutiae.

My nephew and his girlfriend fly home today – I am going to miss them – the family dynamic will change, some of the fun will go with them, I think.

I am feeling a bit out of sorts today – God I miss Eve – her voice, her smile, the sparkle in her eyes. I want to go home.

I am sitting in a 5-star hotel room, in the most spectacular setting, surrounded by my closest family. And I want to go home. I just need to see her, and I am really feeling the distance between us, both emotional and physical, this morning. I think today may well be a difficult day. I hope not, but I am feeling fragile again.

Breakfast with my brother and his wife. He quizzed me on my situation with Eve – he thinks I should be forcing it to a conclusion – I asked if could be candid? I turned to my sister-in-law and asked, "if she **knew** about me?" She said yes, so I told them that as difficult as the situation is with Eve, it is not the biggest issue I am dealing with. Eve is all that is standing in the way, without her I am on a direct path and **all** that entails. I inferred my situation, without going into the details, we are on holiday after all.

I hope this has opened my brother's eyes a bit – he and dad need to back off – things with Eve will take their natural course and I am **not** going to accelerate things with her. I just need to be ready for whatever happens. In the meantime, I need to think about me.

The fact is, I have already decided that transition is not only where I am heading for, I actually really want it now. When I get home, I think I am going to try to make an appointment with my GP to see if I can get a referral. I need to find out more and should really start the clock ticking on the 33-month lead in.

It's nice to know that my sister-in-law knows, I always suspected she did, husbands and wives share stuff you know? I feel like I might have someone else to talk to if I need to, although, lovely as she is, she will always be on my brother's side, I am sure. And I wouldn't want to put her in the same situation mum had with dad. But it is comforting to know anyway. Likewise, I'm sure my niece and nephews would have no issues with my situation at all, but again, it's not my place to tell them.

I headed for the poolside and a lounger for a bit afterwards – I snoozed for a while but kept waking up thinking I might be snoring. I changed into my swimmers and had a swim in the pool with everyone except dad. It was very nice to swim with them all, special.

My nephew and his girlfriend headed for home this morning – we said our goodbyes – I am going to miss them. As predicted, the dynamic is indeed now different. They had a good flight home and were both in England ahead of Majorca switching from green to amber. They lost a day of their holiday, but they don't need to self-isolate thankfully. If Eve had been with me, she too would have had to leave today or face quarantine at home. Eve would have lost five days of her holiday – not good.

After a yummy lunch at the pool bar, dad's friends arrived – they had been into Sollier to have Covid tests but were turned away – the test is only valid for 72 hours it seems, so theirs would have expired while they were mid-flight, before they landed in the UK. They have to do it all again tomorrow…

After lunch, I headed for my room and did some more writing – 7000 words now typed up – I'm making some good progress, I think. I snoozed in the very welcome aircon in the room for an hour or so before heading back to the pool bar for pre-dinner drinks.

A very nice dinner – although the service was a little slow again – dad is not happy. He says we are paying 5-star prices and getting a 3-star service. Personally, I am not bothered too much, it must be really hard getting back on their feet after lockdown, I know we've struggled a little at work, and we are not in a service industry. Providing the meals are good (which they very much are), I'm happy to roll with it. I've got far more important issues on my mind to be honest.

We *believe* there is a celebrity guest at the hotel – Pippa Heywood – from the Brittas Empire and Green Wing. The irony is that Eve worked with her recently, I think on Silent Witness! No one has approached her though – she is on holiday after all – so we don't know for sure. But if she isn't who we think she is, she is a dead ringer, she even sounds like her. And the hotel has celebrity guests quite often, I can remember vividly my nephew's reaction when we realised Rhys Ifans was staying here a few years back – Kevin & Perry Go Large being a favourite comedy film and to have "Eye-ball Paul" here, just a stone's throw from Ibiza was very, very cool. Again, propriety and good manners stopped us approaching him on his holidays, we all need a break, I imagine this is even more important for those in the public eye.

After dinner fun at the pool bar. All but dad and his friends fly back tomorrow – so it was their last night here – the dynamic will change once more tomorrow afternoon. I am expecting the remaining time to be challenging. Hopefully not, but we shall see. I am not looking forward to spending the next four days alone with dad – but at least we have his friends here with us until Wednesday.

Monday, July 19th

Holidays, day 5...

And then there were four...

Up on time today, what am I saying, I'm on holiday, there is no "on time". But I needed to wish my brother's family bon voyage. I'll join them for a last breakfast and then, maybe, catch some Zzzz in my room after.

Dad didn't make it down to breakfast and our friends were enroute to Sollier for their second attempt at a Covid test. So, it was five for breakfast, five at the pool bar and then five became one as I waved them goodbye.

I am now sat on my own, in my room – I am so lonely – I wish Eve were here. I don't want to be here on my own with dad for the next four days. I am sure it will be fine, but he is very sad and so am I – not a good combination. I feel like all the energy has left with them.

I need to be here for dad. So, I will be. But this is going to be difficult. This is what I was most dreading – this is why I didn't want to come without Eve. Still, even if Eve had come, she would have had to leave on Sunday – so the situation would've been the same.

I got out some playing cards and played solitaire on a lounger for a bit, then retreated to the shade at the poolside where I counted my mosquito bites – I am up to 22 now – sooo itchy. I have some cream, but there are so many bites.

Dad joined me around mid-day, we had the first of the inevitable conversations about Eve – it was OK, he didn't come on very strong – so it wasn't as bad as I feared. So far, so good.

We walked into Deià town for some lunch. It was 40°C today and the walk in this heat was brutal. Dad had to stop three times to rest. He's a bit frail to be honest. I don't like seeing him

this way – he's always been a tower of strength to me. I am actually quite worried about him; he seems fragile both in mind and body. I think he was hoping to recapture some of the old times here, but the circumstances have dramatically changed, and I don't think, nice as it is, the holiday has given him what he hoped it would.

A lovely lunch in a small café in Deià, then after a little mooch around, the long, hot walk back. Once in the hotel we headed for the sanctuary of our respective air-conditioned rooms. I got changed, and promptly fell asleep. I was awakened by the phone ringing at 6:45pm – are you coming for dinner? If so, bring your laptop so you can help our friends with their Passenger Locator Forms – I feel like I am IT support… "Hello IT, have you tried turning it off and on again?"

Pizza for dinner and then drinks at the pool bar. It is 11:30pm and I am now back in the room, ready for bed – not too bad today, 11 skirt hours clocked up.

Tuesday, July 20th

Holidays, day 6...

It is 12:22am on Wednesday as I write this – it has been a <u>very</u> unusual day, and I am not quite sure what to make of it all to be honest.

I'll start with the odd conversation I literally just had with a random lady named Jane. Dad and I were sitting around the pool bar having after dinner and there was a couple on the table next to us who were appreciating dad's choice in music on his phone – The Eagles. This was enough for them to initiate a conversation and introduce themselves. Everyone by this point, except me of course, was very drunk. Richard and Jane. Richard was talking to my dad; I believe about mum – Jane pulled me aside and said I was hot! Do you know what? That has **NEVER** happened to me before. She then went on to say I needed some work but was basically gorgeous. After which she proceeded to extoll me to lose some weight and cut my hair short. She said that women don't like apathy (which is a very sweeping statement) and asked if Eve was worth fighting for (she definitely is). She then begged me to do something about my weight or I could lose her. If only she knew...

I was **very** uncomfortable to be honest, it's quite hard to be told I am hot and then have some forthright home truths said earnestly, if a little slurred, by a random stranger – I've known her for less than a couple of hours and she was *very* sloshed – but through the alcoholic haze, she made at least a little sense. I don't think I have let myself go, but equally I have not made an effort. I am sure this has contributed, even if only in a small way, to Eve falling out of love with me.

I need to make some changes, not for Eve – sadly this ship has sailed. But for me. I need to get serious about losing some weight – not just lip service – do it properly and make real

lifestyle changes. At the very least it will help with my transition to Julia. Plus, my clothes will fit better, and I am sure I will feel all the better for it. I need a kick up the bum – this random drunk lady may just have given it to me.

I think it may be time to get serious.

And this was at the end of what was already a very unusual day...

It was just dad and I for breakfast. It was OK and then we headed to the pool and a couple of loungers. It was so hot today – almost unbearable, I'm not a sun-seeker – I flitted to and from my air-conditioned room. I did some more writing and before I knew it, it was time for lunch.

Afterwards, dad retired to his room for a siesta. I got changed and relaxed for a bit. Eve WhatsApp messaged me to say she had spoken to the organizer of the European rally (Mark) about her possibly being on her own. I broke down in tears. We had a very emotional exchange of messages. And then I messaged Mark directly – he deserved an explanation.

The conversation with him was equally emotional – he is such a good friend – he also told me some home truths about his own relationship – lots of very personal information that I am sadly not at liberty to share with you, dear reader. I would never betray such a confidence, so I hope you understand. This is actually, other than some name changes, the *only* reasonable edit in these journals, but it was done for the very best of reasons.

When he told me, I was gobsmacked! I have relayed *some* of it to Eve, she was equally floored. But it gives me some small hope – They have agreed to stay friends but live separately. This, I think, is where Eve and I will end up. At least I hope so. I am incredibly grateful to have such a good friend who was so

open and willing to share this confidence with me. I confess, I spent most of the afternoon crying into my dress.

Mark also said that he loves another from afar, but the opportunity to make more of their friendship has long passed as she is happily married. I said I didn't know how he did that. Then I said, actually, I think I do. He just wanted her to be happy – exactly how I feel about Eve. He said I was spot on. He sacrificed his own happiness for hers. I am in the same situation at the moment…

Also today, dad & I had our Covid tests (waiting on the returns), and I completed our Passenger Locator Forms.

A very full day all in.

I am not sure if it was good or not…

But I think I am going to get serious about my weight, which has to be a good thing.

Dad's friends fly home tomorrow, so it is just dad and I together from now on. I shall make the best of it. And I shall watch my food intake. Maybe take some exercise. Good intentions…

So very beautiful, it's a shame I'm just not in the right headspace to appreciate it.

Wednesday, July 21st

Holidays, day 7...

My alarm went off at 6am – I ignored it for a bit. I wasn't ready just yet to do this again. Eventually I did my ablutions – I am upset today and cried in the shower. Then cried some more after. There are thousands of people who would kill to be in a hotel like this, especially this soon after lockdown, but my life is so shit at the moment I can't appreciate it and just want to go home. I'm very annoyed at myself for this on top of everything else.

These 7 days apart from Eve have been some of the hardest of my life. It's been great. It's been awful. But the only constants are my dysphoria running riot and my yearning to see Eve again. It is overwhelming at times. I miss her so much. My biggest fears have not manifested though, at least not yet anyway. I was worried dad would've spent this time together trying to "fix" my life. He hasn't thankfully. We have spoken about my situation – he of course only looks at the relationship part, not the much bigger picture. But the conversations have been brief, and not too deep – I haven't had to use any of my pre-planned 'escape routes' so far which is good.

Breakfast at 9am. I pre-ordered loads of bread yesterday, I left most of it. Step 1 – watch the carbs. A little victory. Then up to the loungers by the pool. Blimey, it's hot today. 31°C, so imperically cooler but there is little to no breeze. It's a bit too much for me to be honest (as I said, I'm not a sun worshiper). But I am company for dad for as long as he wants me to be. We chatted on and off today – he wants to go travelling with his new lady friend – I said that's a great idea, they have a cruise booked along the Rhein in September and he is talking about going away for Christmas. I ran down some of the places I'd like to visit from the (extensive) list I put together some time ago.

I am feeling very upset about the European rally though – when she goes it will be really hard for me, I think. Sitting at home while she goes off on a wonderful adventure with all our friends will be unbelievably difficult. Still, I'll live fully as the woman I am for most of it, so it will be easier than it is for me here and now. Also, I will be further along the road to healing by then, so I hope it won't be so emotional.

She'll have a great time, I am sure they will really look after her and rather upsettingly, she won't think about me at all. As ever, I just want her to be happy. Even if this makes me sad. Shit. I am crying again.

I looked up the Covid test results (all clear) and downloaded both mine and dads. Reception kindly printed them off for us, so we are good to fly home tomorrow. I am counting the hours...

Lunch came with a couple of bread rolls on the side – I didn't eat them. Plus, of all the things on the menu, I chose a toasted cheese sandwich – not completely brilliant, but <u>much</u> better than I could've done – a *fairly* sensible choice. No ice cream today either – I really wanted some. I also took the stairs not the lift (4 floors) to visit Reception earlier. Small stuff, but I feel like I have made a fair start.

It is now 3pm, I am in the very welcome aircon of my room. I am in my nightie and will type up some more of this journal shortly, then maybe a snooze while I cool down.

Over 9000 words written so far, I am pleased with my progress – it's more or less a straight transcript of the handwritten Volume 1, I have left a couple of paragraphs out as I felt they were too repetitive, but it's pretty much like-for-like and both brutally honest and insightful, at least to me anyway.

I have been wondering again if I could have these journals published? Not for my own ego, but they are an honest chronicle,

in real time of a person in a very difficult situation, and they may just help someone going through something similar. If they help only one person, then that justifies them being published. Is this hubris? As I am re-reading Volume 1 to type it up, I find myself thinking it is actually not too bad. However, there are some big issues with doing so. Not least of which is changing names. From where I am sitting at the moment, I don't want the world knowing literally _everything_ about me, in the most intimate detail. Similarly, there are friends and family that also may not appreciate being name-dropped in such a book. A good example of this is the piece I wrote about Mark yesterday; this was told to me in absolute confidence and so I have had to omit the fascinating details. Also, are my musings any good? I am not sure to be honest – I seem to be repeating myself *a lot*, working through the same issues again and again, making a little progress each time and then there are the daily goals and the hours in a skirt count. I'm not sure this would hold a reader's attention for long. And that's without all the grammatical errors and poorly phrased sentences – it'll be a huge editing job... Plus, the narrative is all over the place – but it's all 100% honest, written through necessity, just not with any intent to make sense. I need to work things out for my well-being and putting things on a page instead of them constantly buzzing around in my head all at once is incredibly helpful. And what about the conclusion? It is unwritten. Not very satisfying for a reader...

Sea Bass for dinner with dad. I've never had it before – it was lovely. Then we sat at the pool bar for one last time and chatted 'till around 10pm. We turned in shortly after as we are both up for an early start tomorrow and the effort of the trip home.

Not a bad day, I am very much looking forward to going home though.

One last night at the pool bar.

Thursday, July 22nd

Holidays, day 8...

Up at 6am, I needed to be efficient today – lots to do – a real change of pace. I was down in Reception by 7:30am for the cab to Palma. Just as well I settled the bill last night. The bill was actually OK. Dad has paid for the room, well, all the rooms the family stayed in actually, so I only had food and drinks to pay for and of course, I went on my own, so my bill was halved more or less. I was expecting at least a grand, but it was €450.00, plus tips.

The taxi arrived and so dad and I headed out of the mountains and across the Majorcan caldera to Palma. Majorca is truly a spectacular island, but it is very much split into two halves. The flat plains and beeches are what most folks experience of the place. But the mountains are astonishingly beautiful – we were both quiet in the cab. I suspect dad was thinking about mum, it is their special place after all, and they have done this journey together so many times. Only this time, now the last of mum's ashes are in place, he is doing it without her. I also wonder, if in his mind, this was his last trip here? He is noticeably more frail this year, the walk into Deià showed up his limitations, although it was so hot, even I struggled to be honest. Plus, he has spent a fair amount of time this trip talking about his "new life" (and urging me to do the same). I think he would like to come back, but he won't bring his new companion. As I said, this is his and mum's special place. Explaining to her why he wants to come back here on his own will be very hard, so much so I think it unlikely to happen. So, I think he was mentally saying goodbye to the island during the cab ride to Palma.

Me? Well some of the same I suppose. If I come back here, I will, in all likelihood do so as Julia. It'll be me on a sun lounger with tan lines from my swimsuit and it'll be me in a lightweight

summer dress and a big, beautiful hat, walking into Deià for lunch, or down to the Can Quet for a special dinner. I'd like to think this can happen. The hotel is prohibitively expensive though and I have other things to spend my money on, plus – after I transition, I suspect things may well be a lot tighter financially.

Dad wants me to get a new life – if only he knew or could comprehend what that life will be...

Palma airport was OK, it is a very long walk, through check-in, security, border control and to the gate. Dad was suffering a bit and I needed to keep him moving as I didn't know if there would be additional hurdles to vault for our Covid tests and queuing for the Passenger Locator Forms check – there weren't thankfully. So we arrived at the departure gate in good time and at last, we could relax.

The flight home was OK, I missed Eve again, sitting next to an empty seat. But I kept it together – no tears this time.

Speaking of Eve, she had her second Covid vaccine shot today – I was concerned about her. Two hours out of contact on a plane made me worry if she was alright. Sheesh, it was only two hours. I was really looking forward to seeing her again – I needed a hug.

A safe landing at Stansted – I think I prefer Jet2 to the "big two" budget airlines – they seem to be just a little bit better and a little bit nicer than them in all areas. I will use them again; it is worth the very few pounds more.

We collected the car in blazing sunshine. It's hot here as well! The same as it was in Majorca! I drove dad home and then we had a light lunch in a local bar watching a TV news film crew shoot take, after take, after take outside the iconic Guildhall. Every time the camera rolled a giant tractor or lorry came past

making a racket. It was amusing at first, but in the end, I felt sorry for them.

I said my goodbyes to dad and then headed home. Key in the door and at last, there she was. I just wanted to rush over to her and give her such a massive hug, but she was working on her laptop – it just didn't feel right. A little awkward. I diffused the tension by giving the cats a squish – cute furs – it seems that these days, this is the only thing we truly enjoy doing together. How tragic is that?

I sat on the sofa, and we chatted. I told her about the trip – it was great, it was bloody awful, yada yada yada, and I showed her my photos. Unpacking, washing, the usual. We then spent a little time replacing the windscreen washer jets on her sports car, which was fun.

Pizza for dinner – I ate more than I should and kicked myself afterwards – and then I went to bed early. I was shattered.

> It's good to be home. But I need a hug. I will try to get one tomorrow.

And Eve is fine – no ill-effects from her second Covid jab.

> A small piece of mum will always be in her favourite place in the spectacular Deià mountains of Majorca. She wanted this and dad made it happen. He has done right by her, and I have said my final goodbyes. Perfection.

> Night night mum.
> I love you so much, sleep well, God bless.

Friday, July 23rd

So nice to wake up in my air-conditioned room, in a clean nightie. In many ways, I am so lucky. I just wish Eve was in bed next to me – I would trade it all for this to happen. I am also wondering if that night at her mum and dad's place all those weeks ago, was the last time we will spend the night together. It didn't feel significant at the time, but I am now certain that it was.

Eve has a headache today – I suspect from the Covid vaccine – she also says she feels like she is getting a cold. Not nice.

I have a session with Kay a little later on today. I'll need to get some cash out for her (she probably doesn't take Euros!) And I have given some serious thought about going there as Julia. It's been decades since I was last outside in broad daylight as me, but I kinda want to. It's actually quite a small step, house to the car, car to her front door and then back again. And if I am going to transition, I need to start being me in public. I am not sure if I am up for the trip to the ATM as Julia too – I think it will be do-able. But I'm also thinking I should probably play it safe this time.

Maybe I could get changed in the car? Nope, a silly idea, at the very least I need to be presentable.

In the meantime, I've had a really nice morning. I shaved my legs, something I was putting off due to the holiday, swimming, and the potential for shorts in the summer. Holidays and swimming are now done – and I am in a skirt practically all the time – sod it, my legs <u>have</u> to be shaved. I've also re-painted my toenails – I look good, and I feel great.

9:40am – Eve has gone to the horses and is then heading for Chelmsford for a workday. I have dressed myself as Julia –

completely — lingerie, dress, heels, make-up, hair, jewellery, even a spritz of perfume, the works. I *am* going to see Kay today as myself. Wish me luck...

Well, I made it to the car, I think, undetected. I then drove to the ATM and waited in the car for the parking bay in front of it to empty, then I claimed it. A short walk to the ATM, no problems at all — sheez I was nervous though — a very busy public space. But there is no one here who will recognise me, so why should I care if I am read? I don't. Kay's money obtained and secreted in my handbag (despite being a couple of inches taller than I am used to due to the heels, the ATM is too low! Also, note to self - I really need a purse), then back to the relative safety of the car. Phew! I am now sat outside Kay's place — I am 15 minutes early and there is no turning back. I am about to have my first social interaction as Julia in years. Eve doesn't count, she doesn't acknowledge who I am — Kay will, I am sure. Actually, I am really looking forward to her face when I walk through her door! Teehee!

And then I need to get back into my house afterwards... This could be tricky, depending on if anyone is about. But we'll deal with that as and when, I am committed now.

9 minutes left to wait. I am *very* nervous. I have no idea why — she will be fine, I am certain — but I am nervous anyway. I hope I don't make her too uncomfortable, she is a professional, so I'm sure she will be fine with me. But it is a surprise...

Shit! I didn't bring any tissues and my mascara isn't waterproof! No crying, OK? Keep it together girl, you can do this.

I hope it's not too warm in there — I don't want to overheat. My dress is quite floaty, but I am covered up. I need to stay cool — in both meanings of the word.

...I hope this was a good idea.

4 minutes now, a quick last minute make-up check, all good, I'm not looking like a monster, actually I look alright. I did a pretty good job on it today and it's still looking fresh. I could knock on the door now if I wanted too. It'll only take seconds to reach her home. 3 minutes – I am going to leave the car at 10:58...

Here I go...

Well, that went about as well as I think it could've. Kay was very surprised, but I think amused is the best way to describe her reaction. A knowing smile if you will. She was complimentary about my ability to walk in heels as I climbed the stairs, I made myself comfortable in the chair and the session began.

We talked about me, what had prompted me to visit as Julia, the holiday, how it went, the ups and downs. I came close to tears a couple of times, but my mascara was spared thankfully. It was a really good session to be honest – I felt great throughout – like I had made a significant breakthrough. And most importantly of all, Kay was, as I knew she would be, professional throughout and not phased by my appearance at all.

All too soon it was time to wrap things up and say goodbye – I left her house, comfortable, relaxed and in good spirits. The drive home was uneventful, and I reversed onto the drive so the drivers' door was closest to my front door – exited and went straight inside.

Mission accomplished!

Wow. Mind, blown.

I celebrated by remaining me, right up until 6pm. Sadly, I had to visit my brother's house to collect a Covid test (2-day test following travel), and then Eve and I headed for Nando's for dinner. It was lovely – and very much needed.

Eve has been under-the-weather today. Yesterday's Covid vaccination has hit her today, she was quiet and lethargic – but dinner perked her up a bit.

I was back in my nightie by 9pm, so 21 hours as a woman today – and outside in broad daylight too – Amazing!!

Up early tomorrow, have a milestone anniversary event for our little sportscars. Should be fun if the weather holds off...

Saturday, July 24th

Alarm set for 6am. Wow shaved legs and satin sheets – I'd forgotten how nice this combination feels.

It's a big day today – we were out the door early and then off to the Heritage Motor Museum for the 25th anniversary celebrations of our little sportscars. The weather forecast is not good though – torrential rain is on its way apparently – we have brought rain macs and umbrellas with us. 'Be Prepared' as the Scouts say... I wonder of the Brownies and Guides have the same motto? Sheez, I've missed out on so much in my life – I would have loved to have been in the Girl Guides as a kid. Cubs was OK, but a bit odd – I didn't fit in (of course I didn't). But I digress...

The journey there was OK. We picked up another of our cars at South Mimms, but no real convoy until we got to within a spit of the venue – that's when things began to get interesting. There were over 600 cars today – a great turn out – especially given the forecast. Personally, I know of at least 20 more owners who could have been there if it wasn't for the Covid restrictions or other commitments. And of course, we were in Eve's car, my one is tucked away in storage, so there's at least one more car that could have made it. The event was very impressive, but the best thing was seeing so many friends and acquaintances after so long.

Eve, of course, ditched me straight away – we bumped into each other sporadically, but we pretty much had two separate events. I kept looking for her, I couldn't help myself, and I saw her often, sometimes on her own, sometimes with others – but she wasn't looking for me. So, I never caught her eye. It was very upsetting, but not unexpected and I was often distracted by folks chatting to me. I chatted so much I ended up with a sore throat! Eve couldn't upset me too much today – I had a good time despite her ignoring me for the most part.

Today really brought things home to me. We really are no longer a couple. I spent, other than the journeys there and back, more time with others than with Eve today. When the most important person in the world to you doesn't want to spend time with you at an event that means so much to the both of us – well, it makes things pretty real. Unpleasantly so. Up until now, this would have been more than enough to ruin the entire day for me. Indeed, this is <u>exactly</u> what she did to me on the last two Euro rallies. Rejection is astonishingly cruel. It cuts me to the core. But today, there were <u>lots</u> of other folk around. I was in demand; people wanted my company – I was valued and appreciated. And do you know what? I don't think Eve did this on purpose. I mean, she did go there with the intention of doing her own thing, it was pre-meditated, but I don't think she thought for one second how her actions would affect me – I just didn't cross her mind, she was far too self-absorbed.

Her time is too valuable to her to spend it with me, and my time literally means nothing to her. My feelings are not important to her anymore. <u>I am not important to her anymore.</u>

So, I made myself happy, I am important enough to *others* for them to want to spend time with me, I made my own fun. And I had a good time, a really good day. And actually, after such a successful experiment yesterday, going out as me in broad daylight, I am still on a bit of a high.

I wonder if others noticed the distance between us? To be honest, I am beginning to not care. Or at least, not care as much. Telling Mark has in some ways made me accept the situation a bit more. If others know now, well, I think it is going to happen anyway – I just need to be OK with it. And I think I am getting there. Slowly, gradually, painfully – I am getting there.

If I can go out dressed exclusively as a woman in broad daylight – even if for less than 2 hours. Why should I worry about our friends knowing we are no longer a couple? It puts things into perspective a bit. Us breaking up is nowhere near as big news as me going for full gender reassignment and that is also going to come out eventually. Even if I cut all ties and become a recluse, people will get to know in the end, I am sure.

I think I need to make an appointment with my GP. 33 months wait for a referral is immense – I should start the clock ticking now.

And this means more experiments, I think. I'm gonna have to work on my weight, voice, and deportment more as well. I need to be ready.

The drive back was OK, Eve's car was on the red, she was worried about having enough fuel to get home. She is very skint and can't afford to fill the car up. She wouldn't let me pay for an emergency fuel stop. Stubborn and actually, *very* stupid. She'd rather run out of fuel and leave us both stranded than accept £20 from me for some peace of mind. I don't get it. I really don't.

Oh, and the rain didn't happen beyond a few spots – instead, I caught the sun – through the extensive cloud cover! Bloody annoying considering I did so well in Majorca to avoid it. I have a red face and neck – Katie is going to be upset with me next Friday.

Home, post holidays Covid test done, I will post it in the drop box. I am in proper clothes at last. Only 10 hours today – but tomorrow will be better.

Overall, it was a really good day, despite Eve's best efforts to be independent and stab me in the heart once more. I enjoyed myself and I did it largely on my own. I might not have to sell the cars after all…

Sunday, July 25th

A quiet day, after yesterday's events, it was just what I needed before going back to work tomorrow.

I slept fully clothed again last night – *I must stop doing this*, it's weird and my nighties are sooo lovely – but I went for it, full make-up, the works. I also had a lie in 'till around 10:30am. I felt I needed to make up some lost time if I could.

I had to adopt Adam's appearance to visit Chelmsford and drop my Covid test in the registered drop box. Eve came with me, and then we headed into the town for some lunch. Eve was quiet today – I am not sure why. She said it was because she was tired, but I wonder. It looked like she had a lot on her mind. I know she is *very* poor at the moment, money worries – she is owed a lot from her recent work, but the money hasn't landed yet. But it was more than likely just the Covid jab still in her system.

She went for a lie down after we returned home – I did similar and dropped off on the sofa for a bit.

It was really humid today – oppressive even, so I thought I'd try to order some ice cream as a treat. It worked well and was delivered just as Eve woke up. She was appreciative and afterwards she headed out for a drive – I know not where, and I didn't feel I should ask. I think she just needed some space, so I gave it to her.

In the meantime, I settled in and watched some good TV. I also wrote up some more of this journal – I'm up to 13000 words now. It's quite a good read and I confess to getting more than a bit emotional re-living those earlier, much darker days.

Eve came home after around 3 hours. We had a curry for dinner and watched "The Movies That Made Us", the episodes on Back to the Future and Jurassic Park – very entertaining (I think I've mentioned that film is one of my passions).

Eve retired around 10pm, I followed an hour later. 11½ hours today – I am OK with this.

Back to work tomorrow...

Monday, 26th July

Quarter past seven – bathroom, check, and back in bed. I don't want to get up this morning – I'm feeling tired, and I want a lie in. It's a shame the cat won't let me!

Out of the door on time, then off to work – it feels odd, the work routine after a couple of weeks off – I'll get used to it once more in time, I am sure.

A huge pile of emails to sift through, a new set of working drawings to start, upgrading software on a colleague's PC and prep for a Teams meeting first thing tomorrow – phew! A full day's work and then home.

There's a car meet tonight – neither Eve nor I were particularly keen to go out to be honest, but once we were there, we both perked up – it was a nice evening after all.

Home around 9:30pm and in my nightie shortly after – 11½ hours – not too bad…

Tuesday, July 27th

7:34 am, usual, usual, usual – Bathroom, bed, mog. Just said 'Good morning' to Eve, Tara cat has abandoned sitting on my chest, filling my lungs with fluff for the chance to do the same with the other 'hooman' – I'm going to doze for a bit, now I can breathe again.

A short entry last night – I spent some time typing up Volume 1 of this journal instead of filling in some more new pages, I'm quite enjoying the process, but it can be very emotional reliving the darker days. I'm still far too close to it, it's only been 3 or 4 months after all.

Off to work – Eve was in better spirits today (probably just relief from not being suffocated by the cat anymore) – it's amazing what a good night's sleep can do.

I had a coffee this morning, Starbucks at the airport on the way to the office – a latte, no sugar – just a pick-me-up ahead of my Teams meeting today. I am not a big fan of hot beverages to be honest, but it did the trick, and I was on the ball in the meeting. Thankfully, it went well, despite some firefighting via correspondence. Work was OK today, I was productive. I worked through my lunch though – by the time I realised I had missed it, it was 4:30pm and there was no point in eating now. I saved myself for dinner – Two for Tuesdays – pizza for us both.

Dressed from around 7pm tonight, so 13 hours today. Also typed up another 1000 words or so, I am up to 15000 words now. Pretty good.

Night!

Wednesday, July 28th

Day three – this getting up for work lark is bugging me! I've done my ablutions, so am now sparkly clean, Tara cat decided I didn't smell enough like her and I need to be covered in cat fluff. She then decided to sleep right across my chest again, cute, but suffocating... Half an hour was all I could take, and I had to boot her off – she can go play with Eve for a bit!

Work, it was OK. Sushi for lunch – I'm trying hard not to eat bread or excessive carbs, but I confess I'm struggling. The pizza last night didn't help, all that bread and cheese, so very tasty, but so bad for my weight.

Home on time, Eve was in a good mood this evening, plus she finally managed to shave a large mat out of Larry cat's fur – it's been a problem for him for weeks – he must feel better.

I watched 2 episodes of 'Wandavision' – it was weird. But I am told it is much better from episode 3 onwards – we shall see.

Back in my nightie from 8pm – 12 hours today. Sleepy now though. A good day.

Oh, and I applied my last Estradot today – 2 months' supply, nearly gone.

I don't know how I am going to get some more...

Thursday, July 29th

It's a Thursday, so back to the old routine of my weekly site visits. I will be bringing my brother with me today though, it's been a fortnight since my last one, hopefully a lot of the snags have been done. I want to put this one to bed. Speaking of which, I've yet to get up, it is 6:50am as I write this.

I was snoozing in my room when I was suddenly brought back to reality by the sound of a cat throwing up a hairball – I leapt out of bed and shooed her out of my room onto the landing – I don't want *that* in my bedroom – ideally, she would do it in the bathroom, but the door was closed, Eve is in the shower. Much easier to clean the vinyl. Now where's the carpet cleaner?

I picked up my brother and we headed to the site, annoyingly he said I need to step up at work – I get it, I have necessarily had to take my foot off the accelerator since March. He knows what I am going through, although he doesn't know **what** I am going through, if you get my meaning. I wrote some time ago that he and dad are cut from the same cloth. Here is an example of them putting work ahead of my well-being. Annoyingly it doesn't make him wrong though, so I said nothing – I'm not upset, just mildly irritated – numb almost. What else can the world throw at me? It wasn't that long ago I would've blown up in his face. He has completely misjudged the enormity of what I am going through – mainly because it suits him to do so.

Am I going to do anything about it? That is the question. Probably not – he is relying on "nice guy Adam", this is potentially a very big mistake – that man is gone. I've told him so, but he chooses not to listen, again, because it suits him to. Julia though, well, I am still finding out to be honest – but I think Adam's pleasant, easy-going nature, in all likelihood, always

came from her. I'm talking about myself in the third person again, what a topsy-turvy situation. I have <u>always</u> been placid – it is **<u>very</u>** rare I get angry with people. Unusually rare I would say. Only two people can really push my buttons – my brother and my dad. Eve came close, oh so very close – she's never seen me angry, it's not a pretty sight to be honest. It's strange, I have more reason to be angry with her than anyone, ever. Nothing comes even remotely close. She has hurt me like no one else can or ever will. But there was no malintent, just monumental miss-management through fear of hurting me. So, with no "bad guy", my anger had no focus, and it eventually blew itself out. Being Julia helped – Adam was very angry, but his anger was always far less than his pain and Julia wasn't in the eye of the storm like Adam – she was calmer, her nature is indeed placid it seems. So, I don't think I will do anything – as I said – he is not wrong. He is insensitive and his timing sucks, plus his decisions are based on only half an understanding of my situation. If my plan to transition comes off, then he'll see just how badly he has miss-judged me. But it is very early days for me yet, so no point in ringing this particular alarm bell just now. I am likely close to three years away from a consultation – who knows how I will feel then? I'm now sure I'll still be Julia – in fact, this is the **only** thing I am certain of – but will I need to transition as much then? Maybe, I'll want it more? I am sure though that if mind and body are aligned, I will be true to myself and be happier as a person. The question is, "Can I be OK as I am?" Or to put another way, Is that extra happiness worth such an astronomically huge upheaval in my life? I've lost so much time already; I'm really feeling the pressure to start the clock on this.

The site was a mixed bag, a lot of snags done in some areas, but a lot still to do elsewhere.

Back in the office, and a stupid last-minute deadline from a client meant I had to drop everything to hit it. There's nothing like a big dose of chaos to distract you from the more important tasks. Still, I pulled it out of the bag (again) and hit the target. Not that it'll be appreciated you understand. There'll be another idiot inspired, so called 'crisis' along soon enough anyway – I sometimes wonder if the world would stop if I wasn't catching all the plates other folks keep dropping. If I sound a bit jaded – sorry – my job is hard enough without others making it harder. It's not a difficult concept really – do what you are meant to do in good time, this way a bottle neck further down the line is avoided. No one outside my company makes timely decisions and so we end up time and again going the extra mile to save their bacon. To be honest, I'm sick of it. And now my brother wants me to step up!

Firefighting your own fires is one thing, but putting out other peoples is annoying, costly to us and counterproductive. What's worse, is that it is unappreciated, an expectation. I am feeling like a door mat. Having a placid nature means folks will walk all over you... Look at my situation with Eve – I'm just too nice. She has killed the man I was and what did I do? I became a woman – sheesh, there really is no hope for me...

Home a little late (had to hit that deadline), I also had to fill up with diesel.

And then the NHS pinged my phone – shit.

I am in a quandary – it was pinged twice, once for me, and once for my dad. This means it has come from the Passenger Locator Forms as this is the only place I've put my phone number on dad's information. So, I surmise someone on our flight has tested positive for Covid.

- We are both double vaxxed.

- We have both had a negative 2-day Covid test and neither of us have symptoms.
- Neither of us have isolated (due to the above).
- We are on day 7 since the flight.

'If' we have it, then the damage is done – it's now completely pointless getting us both to isolate for the remaining 3 days – we will have already infected others by now. Equally, I don't want to (potentially) spread it further. Also, I don't want HM Government singling me out, or dad for that matter. I spoke to him, mainly to check he was OK (he is) – he is going to ignore it and he likely can, they only have my contact info. I think I am going to fill in the forms tomorrow and be sensible until Sunday (day 10). I can't 100% self-isolate at this stage, but I can minimise all contacts. The bigger issue is Eve, she has work on Monday so if I input her name on the form, she may have to cancel. She will be tested before and during though, so I think she is safe (assuming the tests are negative). I think I'll leave her off the forms. I also think I'm going to get hold of a test for me, just for peace of mind. It's all bloody annoying – it really feels like closing the door after the horse has bolted. Still, crazy as the system is, I will comply. I'd feel awful if I didn't and I actually was infectious.

The phone pinged again while Eve and I were at Nando's, see what I mean by too little, too late?

Dinner was nice, if rushed. We were home and I was changed by 8pm – 12 hours again – great.

I feel fine, but Tara cat is unwell though – bad smells and the runs – we've shut her downstairs on the hard surfaces tonight – hopefully the mess in the morning won't be too bad. I noted that the NHS didn't ping the cat's phone!! Teehee!

I have a day off tomorrow (Kay and Katie) – I am not sure if I am going to see Kay as Julia again – I'd really like to and it's good to try to get used to being female in public (even if I'm unconvincing), but it's later in the day and the chances of me being spotted and "read", mainly by my neighbours, are higher. Plus, Eve is likely to be around. I will probably play it safe, what a shame.

These are my only two commitments for the next three days – I'll keep them as I am very confident that I am not infectious (negative test results on day 2 and double immunised), but I will isolate for the rest of the time as far as I can, just for my own peace of mind.

I'm tired now – night!

Friday, July 30th

Quite a day – firstly, I overslept. I was in the bathroom ½ an hour later than usual, my snooze turned to sleep, and I was up at 8:30am. Typically, this is when I leave the house for work – thankfully I had a day off – Katie at 9:30am though so I did need to get up.

Eve has a Covid test ahead of her work next week, in Reading – so she was up already – we said our good mornings and then she hit the road. I took the opportunity to put a bra on to match my knickers and then set off to see Katie for my IPL treatment.

A good session with Katie, she is worried that I am not seeing much of an effect, I am not concerned though, I have confidence in her and to be honest, ANY improvement, however small, is wonderful to me. The treatment went well – she is pretty much at max power, but I am only registering between a 2 and a 3 on the pain scale. Lots of burning hair smell though, so this is promising. To the extent I booked and paid for sessions 4, 5 and 6 today – these are on a three-week interval though (to try to hit the growth phase of the hair). Katie said I should start to see some of the hair sloughing at some point after the session – I am pleased to report that this afternoon it began to happen. Progress.

Home. I made some lunch for Eve and me, then she got her Covid results – negative, meaning I am negative too. Eight days living in close proximity to her since the NHS believes I was exposed – if she is negative, then I am too. My Day-2 test concurs. But other than Katie, and later on Kay, I haven't left the house since my phone was pinged. Double vaxxed, 2x negative tests and being as sensible as I can, no symptoms either. Phew, what a relief.

Afternoon session with Kay – I went locked in my prison – I didn't want to explain to Eve why I was leaving the house in a dress – I would have loved to, but this is a conversation for another day, I think. The lingerie will just have to suffice.

We covered the usual topics, holiday, dad, Eve and Julia – it went well – I'm actually feeling pretty good to be honest. We talked about Eve having a year to sort out her finances and the backstop being to sell the house. I hope she manages to sort it out, her recent financial woes are concerning for me – I suppose it all comes down to how much she wants to live here. If she wants it badly enough, she'll do whatever it takes to make it work. £600 a month is actually a very small amount for a mortgage and bills, relatively speaking. Although at the moment, £600 per month is more or less what she earns, and this is in a good month. So, I think she is going to find it hard, and it will only get harder. Initially, she only needs to pay me £100, then £150, then £200 etc. And she has a year to get to £600, or ½ the mortgage and bills. I don't think many other people would have been this generous.

Julia is a bigger issue. She is who I am. And 33 months is a <u>really</u> long time to wait for a referral. I do though have a huge amount to do in this time, so maybe this is a good thing? I'm still musing about a second property, buying, renting it out, effectively supplementing my retirement and giving me somewhere to go if Eve defaults on her payments. I need to work on my female voice and deportment. I need to work on my wardrobe and appearance, and I need to be able to be a woman in public, or at least present myself as acceptably female – even if I am not very convincing. And do you know what? Providing I have made a credible attempt at being a woman in public, I don't care if folks see through the work I've put in.

> ***If they see a man in a dress, <u>they are missing the woman in the man</u>.***
> And that is **<u>their problem</u>**, not mine.

Furthermore, I am unlikely to see any of them again, so why should I care what they think? I hope they would think "wow, that's a big woman", instead of "that's a guy in a dress", but either way, it doesn't matter to me – I **<u>know</u>** who I am in this regard. That is what matters, and on top of this – I **<u>like</u>** who I am.

Home again, Eve and I watched a fascinating documentary on John De-Lorean, we binged all three parts, it was that good.

Bed around 9pm, in a nightie shortly after – not too much time in a skirt today, but all-day in knickers and pretty much two thirds of the day in a bra as well. Not bad.

Oh, and the company landed a new client today – great news!

Saturday, July 31st

A much-appreciated lie in today – Eve was out early to visit the gym with her sister, I woke up in my nightie, earrings, and make-up, used the facilities and then dressed myself in some nice clothes for an hour or two until Eve came home. Shaving my legs in the shower is nice and actually, now they are hair free, maintaining them is quite easy. Just routine.

I packed an overnight bag after Eve returned, then we set off to see her folks. This time though, we are in Eve's EV. Finding a car charger enroute was a real trial. Three failed attempts before we found a working one in Wisbech. Only 7kW though, so 3½ hours to charge. In the end, we called her mum to come and pick us up, then drop us back after it was topped up.

It was a nice day at Eve's folks place, dinner in Kings Lynn later on – a steak for Eve, the same for her parents and a mixed grill for me. I treated them all and I felt good for doing so.

We had a pleasant walk around the town into the twilight. I took a couple of photos of Eve standing on a jetty on the river in the half light of dusk. I am wondering if these will be the last photos that I take of her, it's possible I suppose, I felt a bit odd taking them to be honest, as if I didn't have her permission anymore. I felt bad, but equally good that I have them.

I'd love to include one of the photos here for you, dear reader, and indeed the early drafts of this journal included one. But I don't think Eve would appreciate it, I've changed all the names on her request so a photo of her will undo this work. Suffice it to say, these pictures are particularly meaningful to me, and it is such a shame I'm not able to include them. But Eve's wishes take precedent. Although this page looks empty to my eyes without it. I think I'm going to sketch it out for you, dear reader.

Back to her parents' place after, I retired to bed around 10pm, so 13 hours today.

Sunday, August 1st

Pinch and a punch, first day of the month!

It's coming up to 10am, I am waiting my turn in the bathroom – I love being in my nightie though – I'm having a nice moment, just revelling in the sensations wearing a satin dress produces. I am hyper aware of my shaved legs, the slipperiness of the fabric and the feel of the skirt, it's just so lovely. I've slept in a nightie more or less every night since I was 18 years old. 32 years. And I still love it, such a privilege, so comfortable, so pretty and so relaxing. It just feels right, and more importantly, I feel right in one.

The bathroom is free, but Eve's parent's shower isn't working – I'm going to feel scummy today, rats. I will shower when I get home.

We had a pleasant breakfast, then Eve and her mum popped out to a garden centre (& likely for a catch up out of earshot), whilst I helped her dad hang a vertical damp proof membrane and then stud out a wall ready for plasterboards. I like being useful, but it struck me that we had divided what we were doing along gendered lines. Not through choice, but just who was best suited for each task. It's just an observation, it likely means nothing at all.

All too soon it was time to leave, we loaded up Eve's EV and headed for the hills.

The conversation was light and cheery, but I felt Eve had something on her mind and, as it happens, so did I. Eve went first. She started by mentioning that it was probably time to start moving things out of the joint account and into an account in my name. Direct debits, bills, standing orders, mortgage etc. I agreed, to be honest, we should have begun this some time ago, I had thought about it, but I just wasn't ready yet. I couldn't face it. Then conversation moved onto her car, she said she had

asked her mum and dad for a loan, and they were happy to oblige. I reminded her that I am still here if she needs me, but I am happy that she has this sorted. I also said we should dig out the V5C to sign the car over to her. So far, so good.

I then said that I will probably need her consent to use the house as collateral to guarantee the mortgage on the second property I am considering buying. She didn't get it at first, she was confusing mortgage payments (which I do, and have done for almost the entire term, she only contributed a very small amount, proportionate to her income, in the first year) – with legal title to the property (ownership). Who pays the mortgage doesn't change the fact that **both** our names are on the deed. There are only three ways out of this, I buy her out, she buys me out, or we sell the house and split the equity. Of the three, the last is the quickest, easiest and most pain free. But the house needs a fair amount of work to get top drawer money and to be honest, I am not keen on spending my money on it to increase the value, just for her to benefit from an increased equity split. I have other things I need my money for at the moment. She said that if she could, she would buy me out – she can't. I said that I likely could but would need to arrange a second mortgage to do so, and this would stop me buying a second property – plus, it feels like to me, having pretty much paid the entire mortgage, I'm buying the house twice. Lastly, I don't think I can live in this house for long without her, so why would I buy it off of her?

Eve didn't realise it was so complex, she suggested we see a solicitor – I agreed, we'll likely set something up in the near future.

And then it came out.

I said that what we currently have is working, kinda, isn't it? She said yes, so I suggested that a fourth option would be to maintain the status quo. She also agreed. I then explained my frustration with my financial advisors, how they had cancelled

our most recent meeting and that I needed to do something about a second property sooner rather than later. She asked why? So, I said that it would be my pension provision and it needs to be mortgage free ASAP, before I retire. Plus, my finances are likely to become very shaky in the medium term. She was surprised to hear this, so I told her about my intention to transition fully, or as fully as I can. She got a bit emotional; I explained the 33 months wait for a consultation and that I want to get the ball rolling because of it. I also said that I had been out in broad daylight as Julia, I had seen Kay, as me. She said she knew! Apparently, she had come home early that day and spotted that I was out, but a pair of my heels were missing, so suspected as much. Wow, I go out _one time_ and she notices! She doesn't notice me **at all** when we are together. I said I will need to go out more if I am going to be a woman and live openly as one. I also said that my transition will hamper the rest of my life in all probability, but I will finally be happy with myself. I also said that a **lot** can happen in 33 months, who knows how I will feel when the referral comes through? But I have been waiting for Adam to come back – he hasn't. All that has happened is the pain is reduced and I am feeling a little less awkward disguising myself as him. She was upset to hear this, she asked a lot of questions, the usual stuff like: 'What about your family?' – I'm prepared to walk away – dad and my brother are insensitive 'bar stewards' (I told her that my brother wants me to 'step up'). 'What about work?' – I likely won't be able to stay, I think work will be very hard and my fortunes are likely to suffer a lot. So be it. 'What about the neighbours?' – it'll be a surprise to them, but it has to happen. Although I really don't want to 'shit where I eat' if you know what I mean. They'll find out sooner or later anyway. 'What about the public?' – I don't care, providing they don't make things difficult, I'll never see them again, so why should I care what they think? 'What does Kay say?' – She says I need to be true to myself – she is right.

It got quiet in the car. We arrived at the horses, Eve said she didn't know what to say, she had no idea what she was getting into when she was 21. This **really** hurt me. It negates the last 15 years, the best years of my life and likely to always be. While she was at the horses, I cried in the car. I don't think the words were meant maliciously, they were a throw away comment, but they cut me to the core. I've said it before, if I could wind the clock back, fix the mistakes I made, oh so many, many mistakes, I would. If I could go back 15 years to the point where I chose to be a man for Eve – I would do it all again in a heartbeat. But I can't, and besides, there is no man in me to choose any more. He is gone. On the night I left the house to end it all, two people left, one real, but suppressed, and one imagined, only the real one returned. I didn't kill Adam; he wasn't real anyway, and he was dying already. Eve pulled the plug on him when she did the same to our relationship. It just took him a day or so to breathe his last breath.

I went out to kill myself, in the end I didn't need to. Adam died anyway.

I became Julia because she was all I had left; she is who I truly am. It happened to me without my consent – I had chosen to be Adam – when he died this choice was taken away from me. I became myself, in full, for the first time, Julia, and I had no way back. This was done to me; I had no choice. And I fought it. But I have realised that being Julia is nice – I like it, I like it a lot, and I like who I am. My life will never be the same again. Eve once said to me that change can be good, she also said that I should 'own this'. She was right on both counts.

> ***I wonder if she will come with me on one last "Grand Adventure?"***
>
> I hope she will – I know it's hard for her, but she is all I have, the **only** one who truly knows me. And I am damned sure I am going to need my hand held through the hard and painful times ahead.

A Grand Adventure.

I like the sound of that. It's exciting and full of possibility.

That's what transitioning is, probably the grandest adventure of them all. An adventure that leads to perceiving the world from an entirely new perspective. Everything, literally everything is the same, but equally, completely different in every possible way.

Could be fun.

To quote Mr. Spock: "Fascinating".

Monday, August 2nd

It's been a busy morning so far; I've lots on my mind as you can imagine. Eve left for work at 4:30am, I was awake and said goodbye. I didn't sleep well, I drifted off around 1:30am but was awake in fits and starts all night, more or less. So, when 6am arrived, I chose to snooze through it, but I had to get up an hour later, the mogs needed me and the bathroom routine of course. It's now 7:54 and I'll have to get up properly in the next 10 minutes or so.

Eve is working away until Wednesday night. She has 2 days shooting near Reading and then a day in Twickenham, so she has booked a couple of hotels for tonight and tomorrow. I miss her already and wonder how our conversation yesterday is affecting her? I wonder if she is thinking about it on the drive there today? If it were me, I would be – if she were going through such a crisis, I would be there for her and I would be a good friend. I would try to understand because I love her. But even if I didn't, I would still be there for her. It's what friends and family do. If the situation were reversed, this would be front and centre of my mind <u>all day</u>. I wouldn't be able to shake it, I would be so worried for her and have so many questions. So, as the situation *isn't* reversed, and as I still (annoyingly), love her, I am worried for her and wondering if she is worried for me. Madness.

I suspect she is already at the set. So, she is likely distracted by now. But I think she had a journey full of deep thoughts. Knowing her as I do though, they would have been centred on her, not me. She doesn't love me anymore and, bless her, she was never gifted with an abundance of empathy anyway. Her fierce independence is one of the things I love most about her, but it does make it hard for her to put herself in someone else's shoes, especially if they are my high heels (she hates wearing heels).

If she cares for me at all, she will be worried for me. If not, then she will be worried for herself. I suspect the reality is a little of both.

Regardless, I am worried about her.

Time to get up and go to work.

A productive day. A client came in to see us, we went through a lot of her projects and brought her up to speed. Also, I updated a drawing for another client, filling in for a colleague who is on holiday.

Back home around 6pm, bins, mogs, tidy the house, ordered a Chinese for delivery, and settled down for the night. I watched Guardians of the Galaxy Vol2 again – I'd forgotten how good it is, in my mind it is overshadowed by the first one, but it's a good movie on its own terms too. A pleasant evening relaxing as me with a good film. I love a good film; I wonder if I can go to the cinema as me?

I miss Eve though.

Oh shit. Here we go again…

It's really hard for me when we are apart. It's only been one day, and I miss her already. How am I going to cope when she goes travelling? Or worse when she finally leaves me?

I hate this so much…

…because I love her so much still.

Her job on Wednesday has been cancelled though, I feel bad for her, but I will see her sooner than I thought. I hate being this selfish. But I miss her. I can't help it.

Tuesday, August 3rd

I had a little crisis this morning – I broke down in tears on the loo. An odd place I suppose, but I am missing Eve badly and it came to a head in a place where I wasn't distracted by anything else.

I just can't get my head around the situation. I can't square what she has done to me and how, awful as it is, it hasn't diminished my love for her. Given the converse of her not loving me anymore when I haven't done anything to her that's even remotely on this scale.

> I have given her everything... and yet, she doesn't love me.
> She has broken my heart and left me with nothing... but I still love her.

I just can't wrap my head around it. It really makes no sense at all.

After my ablutions, I resolved to make myself busy. I cleaned the bathroom, cleared up after the cat (yikes!) Fed them, restocked the loo roll, sanitized the litter tray, hoovered, tidied up the sofa, stripped my bed, put the bedding in the wash, remade my bed and then hung the laundry out to dry – it's amazing what you can do in just over an hour and a quarter when you are motivated to do so.

I'm off to work now – I will see Eve later, I think. I hope. I need to get out of these doldrums.

Work was good, site meeting in Stratford, followed by a company meeting about resourcing for the new client. I also managed to do a little drawing work too – all very productive.

Home around 6pm, Eve was home too – Yay! But I didn't get much time with her, a few pleasantries and then off to

my brother's place for dinner. Lasagne with family and a film afterwards (Captain America: Civil War) – a very nice evening.

Home (again) around twenty past ten, Eve had retired to bed, but was awake – we said our good nights and after brushing my teeth, climbed into my very welcome bed, where I am writing this.

I look back at the day and think it was a good one. I had a shaky start, but other than this it went well, I think.

Not brilliant from a 'time spent in a skirt' point of view – only 8½ hours today – but I am appreciating it now very much.

Wednesday, August 4th

J-Day: monthly anniversary...

I am OK today – seems to be the routine, when I am low, it's nowhere near as bad as it was, a few tears, I feel desperately sad, but it passes – nothing as dramatic, or overwhelming as it has been. I am wading through the shallows, rather than drowning in the deep ocean. I have yet to wake up feeling happy though. I used to be jolly and eager to start the day around half the time. But in the past four months, this has not happened, not once. The best I have managed is rolling over a high from the day before. But waking up without Eve next to me has taken all the meaning out of my life – so I am OK. And even though I miss feeling good, engaged, ready to meet the new day. Being OK, is, well, OK. And it's vastly better than being miserable. I can live with OK.

Five months since the day my life was turned on its head. Five months since Adam breathed his last gasp. Five months since my life had a purpose. Five months since I faced up to who I truly am.

Today is an anniversary of sorts.

It's a mixed bag, my feelings, and thoughts about today. The previous four anniversaries have been completely negative. A day to mark whatever progress I had made since I hit rock bottom and tried to kill myself. But today, I choose to focus on the one good thing, the thing that excites and scares me in equal measure. Julia. I have no idea where I am going to end up, but I am liking finding out – being a woman isn't so bad – for the first time in my life, the pieces of my psyche fit together with no bits left over. The extra pieces are now gone, so I have a complete picture of who I am – one jigsaw puzzle, not two. It's just a shame the picture on the puzzle pieces is pink, but the one on the lid of the box is blue...

So called anniversary or no, I am OK.

Not a bad day all told. Work was alright, I got a fair amount done. I have resolved to not carry out my weekly site visit tomorrow – with people on holiday, I need to be in the office as much as possible. And with this in mind I stayed a little late, then hit the road home.

I walked in the front door, no Eve. Her cars were both outside, but no answer when I called. I found her sitting at the back of the garden watching a swarm of honeybees in one of our compost bins! We watched them together for about 40 minutes, Eve had called a local beekeeper to come and collect them, so we waited for him to arrive. He lifted the lid on the bin and... Oh, only about 40 bees, not the thousands we were expecting. No queen either. Very strange. The bee man said it was odd but thought they may have become separated from the swarm and were just looking for somewhere to spend the night. We left them to it – it was fascinating to watch though.

After the bee man had left, we headed to a car natter – it was the first one for this group post-lockdown and it was great to see this different circle of friends again. A nice pub meal (we split the bill) and a pleasant evening catching up.

The drive home was nice too – nothing quite like a hood down drive on a warm summer's night. Good for the soul.

Home around 10pm and in my nightie shortly after. So, 10 hours skirted today. Tomorrow will be shy a couple of hours too as well – yet another car meet (Hertfordshire group this time, it was Essex today). I will make up for it on Friday.

Thursday, August 5th

6:43am, I am half done in the bathroom. Eve has left for Twickenham, her previous job there wasn't cancelled after all, just postponed until tomorrow – she has a Covid test today to clear her for work. It's kind of annoying, it was supposed to happen yesterday, and she had sorted out hotels so she could run her 2 days work in Reading straight into this one in Twickenham, but they re-scheduled at the last minute, creating a space in the middle. Thankfully she didn't lose anything on the hotel (no penalty for cancelling) and I suppose she'll get an extra £60 for today's test. It's just annoying that she'll have to fight her way through the M25 rush hour traffic to get there between 9 and 10am. The upshot for me is that Eve had priority in the bathroom, so I am about to go back in there for a shower...

Ablutions now done, I got dressed – Ooops! Wrong clothes! Err, actually, right clothes! Seriously, I had half an hour or so, so I put on some lingerie, skirt, blouse, and heels for a little bit – a very good way to start the day.

All too soon though it was time for work – shame. I switched clothes for my daily ball and chain, the knickers, as always remained. Out the door and off to the office.

A productive day all told, I made some good headway on the current set of working drawings, I helped a colleague with his NVQ and my brother a little too with the new client. I stayed a little late and worked my lunch hour, finally it was home time.

We have a car show on Sunday, Eve has cleaned her car in preparation. We headed off to the Hertfordshire meet and got caught, hood down, in a downpour. Thankfully the rain mostly goes over the top of the open cabin providing the car keeps moving. Being tall, the top of my head got a little wet, but in the end, we had to pull over in a layby to put the top up. Water from the wipers tracks over the top of the driver's side window

and then up, over the top onto the driver's shoulder if the rain is heavy and persistent. Pace wipe is fine, continuous wipe results in a wet shoulder.

Good to see (a different) set of friends at the meet, some nice folks, and a great chat.

Both Eve and I are up early tomorrow (Eve at 5am, then me at 6 (out the door by 7:30am)), so we had to call it a night sooner than we would've liked. We arrived home around 10:30pm, I was in bed shortly after. 10 hours in a skirt today.

I have a session with Kay tomorrow at 6pm. Eve is working and may well be late home. I am wondering if I can go as myself (and if so, what should I wear). 6pm on a Friday night is a bit dangerous in terms of getting in and out of the house unnoticed. It might be do-able but it is a bit risky. I think I will play it by ear...

Friday, August 6th

Well, what a roller-coaster today was...

Eve left early as anticipated, consequently my bathroom routine was interrupted as yesterday. This put me a bit out of sorts from the word go and I was already feeling emotional today.

Three sites to hand over today, the first was in Bury St. Edmunds. It was a good installation, on time and to a good standard – not too many snags.

Site number 2 was in Leytonstone, so I hit the road out of Bury St.Edmunds and then fought through a torrential downpour, complete with flash flooding, down the M11 and into East London. As I approached the site, I received a call from the contractor saying not to bother! The Police had cordoned off the road directly in front of the site so we couldn't get to it! I was only a couple of minutes away, so I carried on anyway. I also asked him to ring the site to see if there was a back door and a way in that circumnavigates the no go area – sadly not. I parked up locally and walked up to the Police tape to chat with an Officer. It was actually pretty serious – a forensic team were onsite collecting evidence, looks like it may have been a violent crime. The Police officer said that they would likely be there at least until the end of the day, in all likelihood, tomorrow too. So, I called the contractor and postponed the handover until Monday – rats. In all my years of working, this has never happened to me before. Retail projects *always* hand over on time. The pressure to get the tills ringing as soon as possible is immense.

Back in the car, I drove to Dagenham for the third handover. This one had issues. Materials had arrived a day late and so it wasn't quite finished. They will work through the night – I'll

return on Monday after I have seen the Leytonstone site. Two missed handovers on the same day? Unprecedented.

I finished around 4pm, then home just after 5pm, with Kay at 6pm. I went in Adam's disguise in the end. There just wasn't enough time to change, and getting distracted by social media didn't help. One of our good friends (Alistair) had sold his car and was leaving the scene. Much to the amazement of everyone – I was pointed in this direction by another friend in Germany of all places – news travels far and wide it seems. It blew my mind to be honest, so I direct messaged him to lend some support and, well, I ended up telling him about Eve and me. I was therefore very emotional when I knocked on Kay's door – I needed to unload a bit and the timing of the session was spot on. Last week's session was very good, and I was beginning to think about reducing the frequency of my visits, but today made me think I still needed her guidance, and it is always good to get things off my chest.

So, Mark knows, my colleague knows and now Alistair (& I presume his wife) knows about Eve and I splitting too. After the European rally, all our friends over there will know too – Eve should let them know in advance to avoid all the awkward questions asking where I am. It won't be long before it is common knowledge. My time in denial is rapidly coming to an end. Of course, I hate this.

I have been listening to the album "12 stops and home" by The Feeling. It is a great album, one of the few recent ones without a duff track on it. But it is a bit emotional for me to listen to. A lot of the lyrics are very relevant to my situation. One song in particular is very apt. "Miss you", the third act of "Blue Piccadilly":

Everyone knows it.
You cannot deny it.
I was the only one, for you.
Everyone knows it.
You cannot deny it.
Nobody else came close, it's true.

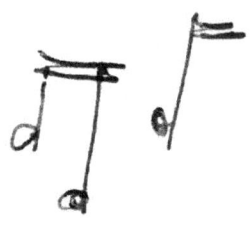

My love is stronger than you (thought).
Much stronger now I've had time to (think).

I hope you know that I miss you.
And I wonder where you've been.
And I wonder who you've seen.
And I hope that (they are friends).
Do I miss you (yes).
Do I miss you (yes).
Well I wonder where you've been.
And I hope that you are with (some friends).

Everyone knows it.
So don't you deny it.
We had it all laid out, for two.
Everyone knows it.
'cos we couldn't hide it.
I was the sea and the sky was you.

I hope you know that I miss you.
And I wonder where you've been.
And I wonder who you've seen.
And I hope that (they are friends).

Do I miss you (yes).
Do I miss you (yes I do).
Well I wonder where you've been.
And I hope that they are friends.

Minor changes to the lyric, apologies to The Feeling. But it's pretty spot on and set to a beautiful, haunting piano melody. I was crying in the car as a result earlier...

I ordered fish and chips for tea, Eve said she didn't want me to get her any dinner when I messaged. So, I stayed in horrid trousers to wait for the delivery and was eating when Eve walked through the front door. I had "House" on the TV and after a good chat about our respective days, we watched a couple of episodes together. It was nice, civil and a good way to wrap up a difficult day. I don't know if her attitude this evening was because I spent it dressed incorrectly – I hope not, but I know it is easier for her if I am. We certainly both had a lot to say this evening, that's for sure.

We were both in our respective beds around 10:30pm, so only 10 hours in a skirt for me today – I could've done better to be fair. But it ended well enough I suppose.

I'd love to include the album artwork, like the music, it's very well done, but I can't for copyright reasons... Shame.

Saturday, August 7th

I had a relaxing lie-in, looks like it's a bit of a rainy day outside, it is nice and cozy in bed though. I've done a lot of typing up, so close to 20k words now and nearly all of April covered.

Eve was in a foul mood today – I tried to say good morning and make polite conversation, but she shot me down each time. I then offered to help with fixing the post and rail fencing at the horse's field, but she closed me out. I couldn't help myself – I broke down. Last night was really nice – this morning, I am in tears. No reason – she was just in a bad mood. And now, although involuntary, I feel like I've emotionally blackmailed her. She won't take no for an answer – fine, I'm coming to help, even though she doesn't want me to be there.

The journey there was difficult. Quiet. Things improved when her mum and dad arrived – suddenly the atmosphere improved, and we were galvanised into work. Lots to do, six acres of field with a lot of damaged post and rail. Thirty new rails moved to the field from the yard and then we set to work. Eve and her mum removed the broken rails, making sure to collect any nails as they did so. Her dad and I nailed the new ones into place. Hard work, but productive, despite the highly changeable weather, sunshine and torrential showers – boy did we get wet! Her dad had brought 2 packs of 50 4" nails, we only had one left at the end – 99 nails banged in by hand. No wonder I have a huge blister on my right index finger.

We headed back to the tack room just as another cloudburst happened. That's when Eve's mum realised, she couldn't find her keys. We spent the next hour retracing her steps, searching the (rainy) six-acre field in vain. I had decided to drive them home to get the spare set, 2 hours each way, when her mum found them at last. She had put them in a pot in the tack room *"so she wouldn't lose them"* and had forgotten she had done so! To be honest, I was just glad she had found them.

All the horses together in one photo – a very rare thing. No rain on this particular day.

We headed home and tried to find a last-minute hotel for Eve's folks – no joy, so we offered our sofa-bed, even though it is uncomfortable and with this sorted, we all went out for dinner.

Pub dinner at The Bell. I began to feel unwell. A headache that then turned into a migraine during the meal. When we got home, I had no option but to go to bed. I missed a good evening by all accounts, but I needed to sleep it off in a darkened room.

Sunday, August 8th

Up early, the migraine has gone thankfully, Eve's parents slept OK and ended up taking our old bikes away with them. We don't use them anymore and they may well do in their new home.

Eve got the car ready, and we headed off to a show in Billericay. On the way I told Eve that I had told a good friend of ours, Alistair, about our breakup and that he hadn't taken it well. He basically has heard what he wanted to hear and decided arbitrarily that Eve was at fault. He then proceeded to tell me what I should be doing. This was all going on yesterday – it's no wonder I got a migraine. Eve was quite upset. She feels betrayed by him. I am annoyed too – with only one exception so far (Mark), every time I tell someone I regret it instantly. It <u>never</u> goes well and just makes things much worse.

They all hear what they want to hear and instead of offering the right support, they try to fix things – this is unwarranted, unwanted, and unnecessary. I hate it.

By the time we got to the show, neither of us were "feeling it" – the weather didn't help, but we parked up with our friends' cars and socialised in between the rainstorms.

You know what? Despite the poor start, we both had a really good time. It was much like it used to be and I'm very glad we went.

The drive home was full of conversation. Re-hashing old topics. Eve truly doesn't know what she wants. She just knew things weren't working any more. It's hard to hear. I understand from an intellectual perspective and have accepted it. But emotionally I have a <u>long</u> way to go still.

When we got home, I got changed and ordered pizza. We were both shattered and so we had a relaxing evening in,

watching some more of "House" on TV. It was lovely and very much needed.

In bed by 10pm, 15 hours today – Yay!

I'm relaxed and feeling OK.

Monday, August 9th

I was out of bed at the usual time, is it another sunny August day? No, it is humming it down, grey and miserable. But I am OK this morning and so, it seems, is Eve. It is 6:52am and we have exchanged pleasantries. A good morning and she asked if I am alright. I am actually. And I am going to be alright, I am sure, maybe better than just alright. But I am not who I once was, so 'alright' is about as good as I can hope for right now.

Eve is really hurt by Alistair's reaction to our situation. She has been painted as "the bad guy" by him, with no evidence at all. People who are in the know, fall into two camps. Those (very few) who know about my situation, and those who don't. Without this vital piece of information, what Eve has done, and her still living with me makes no sense – you need an insider view to unravel it all and very few are privileged to peek behind the curtain, not even our closest family members. All they can see is her instigating it with no justification at all. They then look at her actions over the past few years and see her taking trips abroad on her own and treating me poorly in public – they jump to their own incorrect conclusions and assume she is at fault. I am sorry for her. Yes, what she has done to me is terrible, I can't express just how badly she has hurt me - Sheez have I tried and tried in these pages. All these words and yet I am still banging on about it. She is beginning to understand just how huge those *five little words* are and what they mean, in very real terms, to our lives and all those in and around us.

She has fucked up <u>everything.</u>

And she has done it for no solid reason.

And others won't understand.

She is also beginning to feel the financial ramifications. I think this will get worse before it gets better for her. She is now realising that when this becomes widespread knowledge,

she runs a real risk of losing a lot of friends too. Sadly, as do I. They just can't understand. They don't have the full picture so will look for a scapegoat, and as she instigated the breakup, will assume the worst of her. They will fill in the blanks to make the pieces fit and they won't get it right – who could? To them all, I'm a big guy, there are clues, lots of them if you are looking, but I hide who I am so well – 50 years of practice has made me a formidable actress. Eve has put herself in an impossible situation and is only just beginning to realise it.

This is going to get <u>much</u> worse.   For both of us.

Strangely, she has an unexpected ally. Me. I am here for her, always – she doesn't love me, but I still love her. I hate seeing her like this, but I am here. She only has to ask... I doubt she ever will.

Our relationship is over. But I hope our friendship isn't. She says she loves me like a sister and we both had a good time this weekend. We can still have good times together, just not as a couple. This is a huge thing. When most couples split up the good times stop. Ours don't have to if we *both* want them to continue.

I am still massively upset by what she has done and in truth, I still don't get it. I accept it and intellectually understand, even though her reasons are pathetic and don't stand up to any real scrutiny – I still think she did it because she was bored. Ultimately, I believe this was the driving factor. She was bored with me and looked for an excuse, and I gave her a really huge one to pin it on. But my trans nature has always been there, right from the word go, it was and always has been out in the open between us. Nothing has changed, there was no incident or instigator.

She just got bored. And the Covid lockdowns didn't help.

I love her. It's not a sexual love, I think she is the most beautiful person I have ever known, but I am just not wired to have a sexual attraction to anyone. My love for her is deeper and much more fundamental than just sex. She is my soul mate and always will be. I have found the one person I am meant to share my life with, and she has ended our relationship because she got bored. It's hard to take, a very bitter pill to swallow.

Her love for me, it seems, was based upon sexual attraction. I don't get it. I mean, I understand that humans feel attracted to other humans and that sex is a biological imperative, but not for me. My gender confused brain just doesn't work this way. So, I can't comprehend a love based solely on this. It seems to me to be a very fragile thing to build a relationship on – people age and become less physically attractive. Love, true love **_must_** be based on more than just this. Or else, how do you explain all the old couples? Is their love any less valid because sex is more difficult, and the attractiveness of youth has gone? No. Of course not. If anything, their love is stronger than ever. It's a profound love, not a transient thing based upon appearance and vigour.

So, I forgive her. Indeed, I can forgive her anything. Well, almost anything. The purity of my love makes this possible.

She has literally forced me to face my womanhood and broken my heart. But I forgave her instantly. And I hate seeing her struggling financially. And I also hate seeing her struggling with other folks' reactions.

I just want her to be happy.

It's all I ever wanted.

I love her.

And, to some degree, I suspect I always will.

> And if she needs me, if she needs anything, I am here for her, always.
>
> She knows this. And only has to ask.
>
> But she doesn't want anything from me, so she likely won't ask, and it kills me to see her struggling. To have all these hopes and dreams and for them to now be much harder to achieve. I want so much to help her.
>
> She won't let me.

I am alright, and I will be alright.

Alright is about as good as it can get, so it will just have to do.

I headed into work, but not before a very lovely hug from Eve. It was so nice and so needed. I was overwhelmed and burst into tears. I mean, just look at what I wrote this morning immediately before – I was emotionally vulnerable, so the hug really hit home. So special. So necessary. I can't picture a life without hugs. But I may well have to.

I drove away with tears still in my eyes. But I was OK by the time I reached the office. Just as well as the day started with a Teams meeting and I needed to be on the ball.

Afterwards, I caught up on correspondence and did some drawing work before heading into Leytonstone to do the delayed handover from Friday. Once complete, I headed over to Dagenham to check the missing materials had arrived and been installed – they had – and then I headed for home.

A home cooked curry for dinner, Eve and I then had a nice evening together, but we both turned in a little early.

I was changed around 6pm, so 14 hours today (woo!) I tried another casual look tonight. I'm not sure how successful it was to be honest – I don't tend to get any feedback from Eve sadly,

I'd very much like it, but it's not her thing. Casual pencil skirt, simple undies, minimal make-up and jewellery, lady's T-shirt, and heels. I think it worked, it was certainly comfortable, but I am not sure. My shaved legs helped, bare legged in a skirt is a very female look. But I think my T-shirt showed a bit too much of my (hairy) arms. I shall keep trying...

Night. xx

Tuesday, August 10th

Seven fifteen, Eve is awake and watching something, likely in a foreign language, on her laptop in her room. No sign of Tara cat yet, she is probably in with Eve.

A nice shower and I shaved my legs again. It's not really a chore to run a razor over them every couple of days – it takes no time really and is just a maintenance thing. Although the surface area is larger than most ladies, it's easy now the hair is short. Unlike my face which is always annoying. Thick, coarse hair that takes time to remove – I hate it so much. My sessions with Katie, although not as effective as I would have liked so far, are having a really positive effect on my demeanour. I really hope she can get it all, but I suspect there will need to be some electrolysis sessions in my near future to get the last of it. In the meantime, my legs look and feel amazing in my satin nightie.

Another handover today, then back into the office. It should be OK. And I am also OK today.

I typed up some more of this journal last night. 21k words so far. So much writing and so much pain. It's hard to read, I was in a <u>very</u> bad way back then. But it makes me see just how far I have come, although it has been difficult & very emotional for me to revisit on occasions. I'm still too close to the coal face to be objective and dispassionate it seems.

The handover went well, there were very few snags. Back to the office afterwards and everyone wanted a piece of my time. So much so I only managed an hour of drawing work in the four hours I had this afternoon.

Home on time, Eve wasn't hugely chatty tonight, she went for a walk in the evening sunshine for an hour or so – after the crazy weather we've had recently, I think she just wanted to make the most of it.

I watched some TV, Series 2, Episode 1 of 'The Mandalorian' and some more episodes of 'House'. We had a Chinese takeaway and then Eve had a bath.

While she was soaking, Alistair rang me. Not to see how I was, although some of this is true, he wanted to pick my brains on my second car. He's looking at a similar one tomorrow. We chatted and I gave him the benefit of my experiences.

After this I retired to bed to write this entry up. My nightie, as ever, is lovely. 11½ hours today.

Wednesday, August 11th

I was rudely awakened to the cat coughing up a hairball on the carpet in the threshold of my bedroom – filthy mog! Still, after I was done in the bathroom, she tried to make amends. Fifteen minutes of cat cuddles, so now, immediately after I got clean, I am covered in cat fluff and my clean nightie is adorned with a cat dribble stain. So, it's gone into the laundry pile ahead of schedule. I love my cute little fur babies, but there are limits…

Eve is working on a show called 'Man vs Bee', apparently Rowan Atkinson is the lead – she is very excited, although there is no guarantee he will even be on the same set as her, and even if he was, it is not professional for her to approach him unbidden. So, seeing him isn't likely, talking to him, even less so, but she is still excited – the potential is there, and he is a bit of a legend. Her call time wasn't too early, so we both left the house together… I had a flat tyre. Rats.

The car told me it was low last night, I pumped it up and drove home. It was pancaked this morning though. Definitely a puncture. I messaged the office. I'm going to be late in. I used the compressor from Eve's car to pump the tyre up and then she left for work. I headed around the corner to my local tyre place. It turns out I had run over a Stanley knife blade shard! Thankfully it was in the repairable zone of the tyre, so the chaps there set to work removing the blade and patching it up.

Whilst I was there my phone rang – my nephew had clipped a kerb next to the office and guess what? He'd shredded a tyre! Two in one day – wow! Mine was only £27.00 though, he paid close to £100.00 for a mobile tyre fitter to replace it.

Work stuff was OK. I got a fair amount done. But then had to wait after hours for Amazon to deliver a parcel. They tried at 8pm yesterday – I mean, it's clear from the address it is a

business – who delivers to a business after 5pm? Thankfully I only had to wait until 5:30 tonight.

Home just after 6, I picked up a sausage and egg French stick on the way from a local burger van. No news from Eve, so I sorted myself out. Mogs done, stick eaten and then Eve walked in around 6:30pm. She'd not eaten and not told me she was on her way home. She said she didn't want anything, but I think she was hungry. I offered to get her something, but she turned me down flat. I got changed and settled in for the night, just to feel a bit better. I'm not responsible for feeding her, but I can't help but feel I still am and it's nice to break bread together, a lovely social ritual.

I look good tonight, a full outfit, matching undies, stockings, skirt, blouse, and heels. Simple make-up and jewellery. Perfume and my ladies' glasses. I look alright and I feel alright too. Aaannd reelaaxx.

I had a good chat with Eve tonight. She is getting requests from our European friends to bring some UK items with her when she goes on the rally next month and has slipped into the conversation about us a few times, so there should be fewer questions when she arrives on her own. I am strangely OK with this. I am not sure why. Maybe I am just in a chilled-out mood? Possibly.

My brother is organising a family BBQ, extended family and all, for the back end of August. Understandably, Eve doesn't want to come, this means I am going to have to tell them all – assuming I go. I may not – it will depend on whether I am up to an inquisition all night. With one exception (Mark), I have instantly regretted telling <u>everyone</u> I have told. It's not a good track record to be honest. This makes me quite nervous. But they will find out soon enough, I am sure.

12½ hours today – fantastic!

Thursday, August 12th

I decided to shave my chest this morning. I hate seeing the forest of hair there and it limits my wardrobe – I can't wear anything even slightly low cut, well I can, but it's a dead giveaway. I haven't shaved it since before Eve and I got together – she liked my chest hair, so I kept it for her. But she hasn't noticed it for years and now, well, she doesn't love me, so I decided to get rid of it today. Blimey, there's a lot there! A flipping (mostly white) carpet! It took a while, I had to clip it back first, then use my electric razor before graduating to a real razor in the shower. I re-did my legs and underarms at the same time. It looks great. I am so happy. But I will need to use a razor every other day though – stubble is bloody horrible – but it's worth the effort. I tried a bra on afterwards and it felt sublime. Nothing feels quite like a silky skirt on freshly shaved legs, and I'm pleased to report that slotting my smooth boobs into the satin cups of a bra was equally amazing. I can now wear some more of my wardrobe with confidence.

Seven thirty-five, and I'm back in bed writing this up. Eve is awake, we have said our good mornings. My workday will begin soon, but for now, I am relaxed.

Work was good, I got a lot done today. Then, an unexpected dinner invitation from dad, gratefully accepted. I headed over there after work, and we had a nice evening together in a local bar. The conversation was light and breezy for the most part, Eve and mum were discussed, but nothing heavy or very emotional thankfully.

Arriving home, just after 9pm, Eve was very chilled on the sofa with her laptop. We chatted about our respective days for an hour or so before I retired to bed and my much-needed nightie. I have spent a bit too long in trousers today

and am beginning to feel it. I'm physically uncomfortable and a bit agitated. Bloody dysphoria is needling me again. She's a heartless and relentless cow who just adores making my life unbearable. It's always lovely to be back in a skirt, I need it very much today.

Friday, August 13th

Friday the thirteenth. Eek!

I hope the date isn't going to screw the day up...

So far, so good, although I am a little tired this morning, I didn't sleep particularly well, I overheated in the night. But I was in good(ish) spirits on the way to work, likely the end of the week I suppose – a bit of that 'Friday feeling' creeping in despite the date.

Nine am and a conference call, it went OK, only two of us on the call, so we were able to zip through the previous minutes and update each other. Afterwards, I carried on drawing up the current project's working information and this kept me busy for most of the day.

I was home on time, I crossed over with Eve as I left for my session with Kay. She was coming in as I was leaving. We managed to say our hellos and kinda agreed to go out for dinner later.

Kay was very good today. I was going to wear a bra under my T-shirt, but I have a bit of a shaving rash (body hair, no woman likes it, now imagine there's 10x more of it, everywhere. It's such a big thing in my life – I would hope any women reading this can sympathise. At the last minute, I changed my mind. Instead of the bra, I took a pair of stud earrings with me and popped them in for the session. It's a small thing, but it made me feel good. I think I am going to wear them more often.

Kay asked me to rate my general demeanour on a scale of 1 to 10 (what is it with people wanting me to rate stuff on a scale of 1 to 10)? I said I was a 4 or 5. This is kinda where I am at most of the time. Not great, not awful, just OK. I used to be a 6 or a 7 on average and four months ago, I was sadly well below zero. Good progress, and I hope to be averaging a 6 or a 7 most of the time again someday, hopefully sooner rather than later.

Lastly, she asked me if I could print out my journal pages so she could read them – hey, I thought I was giving *her* homework, not the other way around! I think I can do this, logistically it's tricky given my colleagues (I'll have to use the work printer) but printing them out after hours should be do-able safely.

Home, and then out with Eve to Nando's – a nice evening out with some good conversation and a very welcome way to round off the working week.

Back home again around 8:30pm, I was fully changed shortly after – 12 hours, 'half my time' target hit, I'm a happy girl.

I'm looking forward to tomorrow, we have a charity open day to go to and we should see a lot of friends.

Night! xx

                    Oh, and Friday the 13th was OK after all.

Saturday, August 14th

Eight fifteen, I am done in the bathroom. We are going to drop Eve's car off at a workshop this morning for some work, so we need to take two cars. Co-incidentally, they are having a charity open day for MacMillan, there will be lots of our friends there, so it should be fun. And the sun is shining too.

I am OK today, a 5 or a 6 on the brand new 'Kay scale'. Looking forward to a good weekend. However, I am in a particularly girly mood, I really don't want to take my nightie off, and I delayed removing my make-up for as long as I could this morning.

We left around 9am, two cars on the way to Rochford – Eve was having fun, hood down, exhaust singing. Speaking of singing, I had Spotify running on my phone, Bluetoothed through the cars' media centre, I am in Eve's electric car – a very pleasant drive & it is no wonder I can hear her exhaust note in front, other than road noise, the EV is practically silent, a very relaxing way to travel.

Loads of good folks at the open day, good times, chatting with friends old and new. Lots of nice cars too and I think the charity did alright as the collection bucket seemed well visited.

We were there until mid-afternoon, I spent some time unsuccessfully avoiding the sun – Katie is going to go mental at me on Friday – I forgot my sunscreen and even though I wore a cap, my face is a little red...

We stopped for a late lunch on the way home. The chat with Eve was nice, but we were both a little tired after so much fun socialising.

I had a bit of a snooze when we got home. Eve took herself out for a bit – I know not where, and it is no longer my place to ask.

I got changed around 4pm and continued to watch 'The Mandalorian' Season 2 – it's very good, but Eve came home halfway through the finale. So, I'll have to finish it off later.

A yummy curry for dinner, followed by 'The Simpsons' and then an episode of 'House' on TV. I was in bed around 9:30pm.

A good day. Very enjoyable. The sun shone and we both had fun.

Plus...

16 hours in a skirt!

<u>Love it!</u>

Sunday, August 15th

I hit a bit of a milestone today, but I am getting ahead of myself – firstly, as it is Sunday, a lie-in. Eve was up before me, she needed to see to the horses today, so after we said our morning greetings, she left for the yard. I remained tucked up in bed, so I decided to carry on typing up Volume 1 of this journal. Two hours later, I was done!

76 pages, over 30,000 words. Wow. Kay would like to read it on paper, so I began to formulate a bit of a plan today to print it out. Just as Eve arrived back home.

She got changed and so did I, after a nice shower. Such a shame to take my make-up off, but I knew I'd be re-applying it soon enough.

Eve was going to spend the day with her sister, leaving me at a bit of a loose end. I decided I would be productive, with Volume 1 all typed up, I headed to Lidl to buy some lunch and then to the office to finish off word processing and print off a hard copy.

This took much longer than I thought, I decided to photograph all the little sketches and insert them into the document. But they needed cropping and editing too – the clock ticked away, and it took close to three hours before I was done.

I now have a bound document to give to Kay, it's only a draft and is filled with typos, but it exists now as an actual, real thing beyond my handwritten pages. I'm quite proud of it!

I was home around 5pm, so only four hours in hateful trousers today – twenty hours in a skirt and I have a paper copy of the first book I have ever written!

Amazing!

Eve said she would be out late and as I had eaten a big lunch, once I was all dolled up, I settled into a nice relaxing evening. Dinner was not needed tonight.

I was worried that a day without Eve would be upsetting. I think, even a couple of weeks ago it might have been. But I made myself busy and I spent a huge amount of time fully clothed as my true self. I am OK you know? Despite hardly seeing Eve, I had a good day after all.

Monday, August 16th

I was up on time today and done in the bathroom quickly. It is now just gone 7am, Eve is up too and doing her ablutions. She has work today and we will both be leaving around the same time. Tara cat has covered me in cat fluff already – she doesn't waste any time claiming me as her own...

I had a really nice day yesterday. The only thing that could've made it better would've been to share it with my love. From the photos on Facebook, she had a lovely day out with her sister too.

I love looking in the mirror and seeing a woman looking back at me. I did a full make-up yesterday and slept in it (seems such a shame to go to this trouble and then take it off after only a couple of hours, my pillows loathe me though). But it's great to see a pretty face first thing in the morning – even if a little dishevelled. It sometimes takes me a while to get around to removing it. I just don't want to. Still, earrings, nail polish and a razor for my legs in the shower means I am <u>never</u> fully male anymore. I plan on keeping it this way; indeed, things can only get more female. It's just who I am after all.

It's chilly today, 16°C apparently, I am cold in bed, but it is not raining, and it looks to be a fair day. The sun is trying to break through – I think it will be nice.

An interesting day, my colleagues were back from holidays and were thrown in at the deep end straight away. The one-hour conference call resulted in a pile of work and no time this week to do it. Mainly because two of us have meetings on two days lined up already and we all have an all-day company conference tomorrow. Plus, I am going to see Katie and Kay on Friday, so I only have today to do work, tomorrow is a write off, I am out Wednesday and Thursday and away on Friday. It's going to be a

weird week. But I was in a bit early today, I worked through my lunch and left late, so I have 'created' and extra few hours work. Actually, we got through a lot today – more than I thought we would. So, I am quite pleased. Or should it be relieved?

But I did have some chocolate – not good. I bought a bar and ate the whole thing; my diet has lost a lot of its momentum. Discipline Julia. I must try harder.

Back home around 6pm, Eve was home too. She went for a Covid test today; her work is tomorrow – I had misunderstood yesterday. I'm not sure if we can go to the cinema tomorrow after all – I hope so, but it'll depend on her timing and how tired she is. I hope it will be OK. I quite fancy a night out.

Pizza, then changed around 7:30pm – 12½ hours today. I am about to get ready for bed. But I am not quite ready to get changed just yet. I am enjoying my outfit too much – I am a funny old stick – heels are uncomfortable, but I truly love wearing them. Logic says I shouldn't, but I do. I adore wearing a skirt. Again, logic says I should prefer trousers – *I <u>absolutely</u> do not*. Given the choice, I will <u>always</u> pick a skirt or a dress. I even like wearing a bra! *The Trinity.* I am wearing one of my older, ill-fitting underwired ones tonight. I <u>should</u> hate it. It <u>should</u> be uncomfortable. It isn't, and I don't. I like feeling it wrapped around me and I like the feel of my boobs in the cups. But I can't wear this one all day, or worse all night. Eventually the underwire will jab me in the boob, it'll make its presence known in a painful way. So, my time in it is limited.

My newer bras though fit well and do not have wires (bralettes?) I can wear them as long as I want. But my boobs don't feel as supported and they do not give much lift. I guess this is a dilemma all women face. Comfort vs duration vs appearance. Today's choice was all about the first and last – duration lost out. Still, it keeps things interesting I suppose. I'll just have to keep buying bras until I find one that'll tick all three

boxes... And that's before we consider fabric, colour, and style! If I can find some in a 48C I would like to try a plunge, a demi-cup, balcony or a push up style too. Sounds like fun. Wow, it sure is complicated being a woman!

I'm tired now. I'm going to start typing up Volume 2 of this journal, then, finally, switch into my nightie and go to bed.

Oh, and guess what else I did today?

*I threw away **ALL** of my male underpants!!*

Looks like I'll be wearing pretty knickers all the time from now on, I'm going to have to as, just like my nighties, I literally don't own anything else! Teehee!

There was no point at all keeping them, I haven't worn them in months, and I **_never_** want to wear male underwear again.

An awesome milestone. I feel great. Empowered even.

And maybe just a little mischievous!

If only I could bin all my hateful trousers too...

Tuesday, August 17th

It's not quite 7am, I am OK. I have been thinking about, maybe, making an appointment and visiting a salon. I'd like my hair cut and styled properly in a women's manner. I'd also like my eyebrows shaped and a mani-pedi, although the manicure, if it's even possible, will have to be subtle. Sounds like a lot of fun and I would like my hair to look more feminine when it is loose, as opposed to just long. I wonder if I can get an appointment for a Friday afternoon after Katie? I have some time to fit one in, although it might be a bit weird for the stylist if I turn up and my beard starts falling out during the session. I think I am going to do some research, to see if I can find somewhere discreet, not too far from Katie, but far enough away from where I work.

It was an on odd kind of day all in. Work began with the usual hour-long conference call. Then straight into a company meeting to discuss the new client, ways of working, fitting in with their templates and processes, resourcing, expected levels of work, training, possible recruitment and company growth. This took practically <u>all day</u>. And, although I was excited to begin with, by the end I was worn out – it was just too full on for too long and my excitement for a new client waned in the end – it felt a little anti-climactic. I am sure my excitement will return when I start putting things together for them, setting it all up to run as smoothly as it can - I love this sort of thing, it's my jam. On top of this, with two days out of the office at meetings tomorrow and Thursday with a mountain of prep to do so that we have all we need with us, by 4:30pm I needed to be getting on with other things. In the end, three of us had to stay late. But we got it done.

Home, Eve was here too – I booked the cinema, and we headed out dinner. It seems like we were up against time this evening too. We had to wait for a table, then Eve took her time eating, being distracted by her phone. I tried to initiate

conversation – but it felt like an uphill struggle today. No idea why. It wasn't unpleasant. It's just she wasn't in a talkative mood it seems. I didn't push the situation. If she doesn't want to chat – fair enough. In the end I ran out of opening gambits. Saved by the bell! Time for the main feature...

'The Suicide Squad'. It was good fun, very funny, full of action, surprising plot twists, very violent and actually, kinda weird. We loved it. A good night out.

Home around 10pm. I packed an overnight bag for tomorrow night. In my nightie by quarter past ten. I charged up my laptop too – I will try to type up some more of Volume 2 tomorrow evening. There seems to be a great deal more in Volume 2, it's huge! This could take some time...

Wednesday, August 18th

Out the door at 7:30am, I then drove to Hinkley, near Birmingham for today's contractor meeting. The silly satnav tried to take me south to the M25, this of course, is total folly, as any UK resident will confirm. The M25 is best avoided at all costs. So, northwards was the direction I set off in and after a moment of realisation, the satnav recalculated and decided I was right after all – 25 miles and 16 minutes saved. So much for technology…

I arrived at my destination a half hour early, the meeting went very well – lots sorted out and we were done by 2:30pm. I headed to my hotel – I've got to do it all again tomorrow on a different site and with a different contractor.

I checked in just after three and was in a skirt by quarter past. No wonder I am feeling OK today – nearly 17 hours – an astonishing result for a weekday.

I spent some time this afternoon dealing with work correspondence and typing up some more of Volume 2. I'm beginning to get into a rhythm again – my writing has definitely improved, although my handwriting has, if anything, noticeably deteriorated. If I can't read it, what hope has anyone else? In some places it's so bad it might as well be written in code!

Eve was on my mind a lot today. Some of it was just the hours spent driving – I had a lot of thinking time. Some of it was because I am typing up Volume 2, so I am re-living events. Also, I didn't really see her this morning – we said our 'hellos' and she wished me a good day as I left the house. It feels odd, almost as if I am living on my own. I don't like it very much to be honest. I will send her a text to say my day went well. But I am not going to push for a chat – I'd like to, I always like chatting to her. But only if she wants to.

I think she was going to pick her car up from the garage today. She was talking about taking the train there, but I don't know for sure. It may be tomorrow. Also, there is a car meet tonight, so she may well want to collect it today ahead of the meet. I find the lack of conversation difficult – it feels like she is shutting me out even more. I hope not, I hope she is just not in a particularly chatty mood. With a bit of luck, this is what it is and things will improve. I hope so. I miss her.

Thursday, August 19th

The hotel room – it's OK and so am I today. My meeting isn't until 10am, so I have a bit of a lazy start to the day. It has just gone 7am as I write this, I am about to visit the ensuite and then begin packing so I can vacate. Eve is still on my mind...

I find it hard to be away from her. Especially if she doesn't want to chat – it's like she adds to my isolation. I miss her company, her touch, her smell. But most of all I miss her smile. Although I try, neither of us smile very much anymore. I try *very* hard to smile every day.

Smiling is important.

        Receiving a smile is even more so.

        I need to see Eve's smile.

        I just want her to be happy.

                                Always.

The meeting was long, but productive – there's lots of pressure on us now to deliver on time – it's going to be difficult, but we'll get it done, somehow. We always do, we are a safe pair of hands, but this means clients take advantage of us sometimes. Because we deliver the impossible time and again, they keep asking for it. The impossible has become an expectation.

I jumped in the car for home around 2:30pm, but the flipping phone just wouldn't shut up. Call after call after call. I had to stop twice enroute to sort out some emails – still, at least I have tomorrow off work. After these two days, I need it.

Eve has had a last-minute job on Eastenders come through, a late one apparently, so she wasn't home when I arrived. I dealt with the mogs, brought the laundry in off the line, emptied and then stacked the dishwasher, lastly, I hoovered. Time to get

changed. In my nightie by 7:30pm, so 13 hours today. Pretty good.

I am seeing Katie tomorrow at ten past ten. Then Kay at 5pm. I may pop out and see if I can find a salon that I like. I'd like to get a pedicure and my hair needs a trim too. I just need to find a nice one, off the beaten track and a distance from home. Kinda tricky, a tall order, but we will see what we can find.

I am in bed now – no sign of Eve yet... I miss her.

Friday, August 20th

My appointment with Katie is just after 10am today, so a very puzzled Eve knocked on my door at 8am asking if I had overslept and if I was late for work. I explained and she was relieved – we said our good mornings and then I got up to make use of the facilities. Extra close shave today – I need to do a good job to increase the effectiveness of the IPL treatment, the shorter the hair, the more concentrated the heat at the follicle.

I decided to wear a bra today too. I wear knickers all the time now (I love the fact I don't own any male undies anymore – teehee!) Indeed, I can't even remember the last time I wore underpants – probably in Majorca due to needing to pack lots of undies. Today though, I added a matching bra – Katie knows I am trans and to be honest, on the incredibly slim chance it is spotted by a passer-by, I don't really care. It is comfy and I wanted the support – QED.

My session with Katie went well. We are beginning to see some progress, although not as much as both she and I would've hoped, still, there was a lot of burning hair smell today, so I am still hopeful. I don't think she will be able to get it all, but if she can get the dark ones, I'll have electrolysis on the fair hairs to remove them too. I may have my eyebrows done at the same time.

Home just after 11am, Eve was out. Covid test apparently and I suspect she will find a café and work on her website some more. It is a workday after all.

Me? Well let's just say I was dressed fully from mid-day. No reason to stay uncomfortable – I put on my black skater dress, some tights, heels, jewellery, and a little lipstick – I am in a good place.

I am seeing Kay at 5pm today – not sure if it will be me, or in disguise yet. 5pm on a Friday is a busy time and there is a high

chance of bumping into neighbours. I shouldn't care – but I do. It's starting to really bug me that I just can't come and go as I please. Annoying. I'm going to play this by ear, I think...

Eve came home around 2pm, I was typing up some more of Volume 2. She looked tired and said she wanted an early night, so can we have an early dinner? I agreed and got changed so we could go out to eat. Nando's at 3pm, back around 4:30. I then remembered my 5pm session with Kay! I put my bra back on, grabbed the hard copy of Volume 1 and headed over to her place.

The session went well. I recapped the week's events, including Eve's exploits as relayed to me over lunch/dinner. She has had a busy week – filming something called 'Scrapper', but it was an odd production, she thinks it may be a student film. Covid test on Wednesday and she picked her car up Thursday. Then onto a costume fitting for something called 'Mechanical' next week. After this onto Elstree for a late shoot on Eastenders. It's no wonder she is tired today.

I spoke about my night away and how I miss Eve when we are apart. Also how going away for work is not as bad as it was when I went to Majorca. Not just the duration, but also the element of choice. I find it astonishingly difficult to choose to spend time away from her. Staying away for work – there is no choice, so it is just easier to do.

Home again by 6pm, fully clothed in a complete outfit, heels, and make-up by quarter past. I'm getting good at this (lots of practice). Nice.

Eve retired to have a relaxing bath and then to her room to chill. I watched some TV and then slipped into my nightie around nine thirty – this is where I am now, writing this in my room.

There seems to be a <u>lot</u> of maniacs on the local roads tonight. We get morons travelling from all over to use the bypass as a racetrack in the wee-small hours – it's a thing apparently, the "Essex Raceway". But they have started early tonight and there seems to be loads of them. I can normally hear the odd bike doing warp factor-9 most nights after midnight. It has just gone 10pm and there is a cacophony of loud exhausts making a right racket on the dual carriageway. I have no issues with folks having fun, three of my cars have loud exhausts, so I am in no position to grumble really, but this is anti-social behaviour at this hour. Save it for later, I'll likely sleep through it as usual.

I'm trying to work out how long I've been 'me' today. Even when the world saw Adam, I was wearing a bra with my knickers for most of it. I reckon I have been in trousers for no more than three hours today, so 21 hours in a skirt. And, actually, plus an additional 1½ hours of bra wear.

I wonder if I can do a whole day?

Of course I can! I can live easily 24/7 in women's clothes if I want – I absolutely love it. But the world intrudes and every day it seems, I need to put on a disguise to leave the house. Sometimes for a long while, sometimes less – but it means that doing an entire day is very difficult. At least for the meantime...

I need to make this happen somehow. Let's see what I can do...

Saturday, August 21ˢᵗ

I am not sure what I am doing this weekend, there doesn't seem to be a plan and I have thought about just taking myself off somewhere. Or maybe starting on the repairs to the deck in the garden. I am at a loose end it seems and as I had a day off yesterday, lounging around the house feels like a bit of a waste of time.

Debating it isn't getting me anywhere though, it is 9am and I am still in bed. Eve has just finished in the bathroom – today is beginning regardless – carpe diem – but once seized, what am I going to do with it?

Well, I began with a shower. Eve went to the horses, I put on something very comfortable, but I changed when she came home. We both went out and went our separate ways. I confess, I found it hard today. She decided <u>not</u> to spend time with me. It was a conscious decision. She just didn't want my company. Of course this hurts. It hurts me massively – it's the No.1 thing she does that cuts me to the core and not only does she keep doing this to me, it can only get worse.

Ignore it. Do something for myself. Have a good day on my own. Some good medicine.

Except...

        I don't want to be on my own.

                I never did.

It's no wonder I am sad – the woman I love doesn't love me anymore and keeps on demonstrating this over and over again by not sharing her life with me.

It's not like this, I am sure. She just wants some time alone – I get it.

But I am also a petulant child having a tantrum because I don't have what I want.

I decided I would go to Cambridge. But I only got as far as Saffron Walden.

Dad rang, he invited me to dinner tonight. I declined. I am upset enough today without his particular form of tender loving care. Plus, I am not a charity case. So, I lied. A little white lie. I told him Eve and I are going to the cinema. And we actually did go during the week, if he asks, I can tell him all about the plot of the film. I feel guilty about it though.

It started to rain. I stopped at B&M and bought a duster on a pole – my life is so exciting – just 'cos we needed one, the house is full of cobwebs, and I am sick of them.

I sat in the car and thought, 'sod it, Cambridge on a wet day is no fun'. So I headed for home via a Toby carvery for lunch. I blew my diet today, but it was very tasty. And a Toby carvery is no where near as bad for my diet as some of the other options out there...

Home and finally, dressed comfortably. Casual again today, bra and knickers, skirt, and a pink T-shirt, minimal make-up, heels (peep-toe, no tights), I brushed my hair out and earrings – I think I look nice. Sensible and appropriate ladieswear for a day in the house.

The new duster works well. Shame about the towels on the line – bloody rain.

I did some computer stuff and then TV for a bit. Eve came home and we had pizza (diet really ruined, ahh well...) More TV and then we retired to our beds.

So, 20 hours I think today. I could've done the whole day, but I messed it up. I am a little annoyed at myself actually – I had a golden opportunity today, handed to me on a platter. Especially as I was thinking about it only last night. Still, there will be others – this is my life from now on in – at some point I will be dressed and living as a woman openly, all day, every day.

This used to scare me.   But now I am oh so curious...

Still, spending the rest of my days as a woman is no compensation for losing the love of my life.

I truly hate it when she shuts me out.

Sunday, August 22nd

Wow, what a storm last night! It woke me up at 5am, lots of lighting and torrential rain – it was really exciting – I love a good thunderstorm. I stayed awake as long as I could to watch one of nature's most spectacular shows, but then, sleep inevitably claimed me once more.

I am in an OK kinda mood so far. It has just gone eight-thirty and I am feeling nice in my nightie and make-up. As usual, I don't really want to take any of it off, but at the very least I need a shower, so it's going to happen. But in the meantime – it's nice.

So, not a bad day really. Eve went to the horses first thing – I stayed dressed comfortably until she came home around 11:30am. I donned my disguise, and we went to Chelmsford for a bit. We had a nice lunch in Walkabout, it's a sports bar, but has an Australian theme, so is actually quite a nice place. Despite the TV monitors showing sports (yawn!) The burger and a drink were nice, Eve began to loosen up a bit and we chatted – the frostiness of the past few days melted somewhat as we wandered to Costa for some tea and chatted some more.

Eve is worried about money – she has had an unexpected bill – car tax on her sportscar – it had to be paid, but they took it by direct debit, so it surprised her. Consequently, she wasn't sure she could pay me the £200 for the mortgage. I said it was only £150 – £50 a month increments on top of the previous. I also said that she needs to ultimately pay £600 per month, but she has a year to get there. The £50 monthly increase is just to make it as easy as possible and so that the £600 doesn't hit her all at once.

I wanted so badly to say forget it this month, but I didn't. I stuck to my guns. The problem is, I <u>want</u> to help her, and I

don't like to see her struggling. This is <u>very</u> hard for me. But eventually, she needs to understand that this was <u>her</u> choice. This is the reality of her decision to break my heart. She wants to be independent? Not part of a couple? Not be as strong as she was? Fine. I have said this over and over again, without her love, I <u>can't</u> continue giving her everything. Knowing all this doesn't stop me wanting to though. It doesn't stop me hating to see her struggle. It just stops me saying "forget it". I have been more than generous. Who else would have given her a year? Who else would have made it so easy? Little baby steps to get it to the fair, equal share of the bills.

This is the reality of the world, my love.

Nobody rides for free, nobody.

Kings, Queens, beggars and paupers – we all have to pay the piper...

Independence comes at a cost. The cost to you, my love, is financial. And actually – very reasonable – there are hundreds of thousands of folks out there who don't get this lucky - £600 per month all in for half ownership of a house? A house that'll be yours completely when I pass on? That's her retirement sorted out right there. There are so few folks who have this safety net. And even fewer who pay as little as £600 per month for it. The couple next door pays more than this in rent alone, without the bills on top. And they are not a rarity. Not by a long shot. Furthermore, they don't, and never will own their house!

Your independence, my love, is costing me a <u>lot</u> more. The cost to me is not monetary. The cost to me is watching the woman I love slowly, and <u>painfully</u> reject and step away from me. The cost is a broken heart, broken dreams, and a broken life. The cost to me is my manhood and the hope of any kind of a so called 'normal' life from now on.

And worst of all. The cost to me is knowing for absolute certain, that I wasn't good enough for you. That ultimately, I was lucky to have the 15 years we had. And I am lucky to still have you in my life, for whatever time we have left.

I gave you everything I had.

And it just wasn't enough.

This is why I am sad.

This is why Adam can't come back.

He is lost. Broken. Gone.

But I am more than Adam, as you know, dear reader. And our conversation didn't get anywhere near as deep as the above. I am <u>much</u> more eloquent in writing, when I have the time to consider my words, than I am person. I suspect most folks are the same, we always think of the perfect thing to say after the opportunity to say it has gone.

Eve understands that the time and monthly increments are to make it as easy as possible. But I do think there will come a time when she realises that she can't afford to go travelling like she wants to. At least not yet. Unless she decides to do something about her employment situation. I don't want her to have to get a job, that is why I have given her a year. But I do want her to pay her way. That's only fair and I am not being unreasonable. She doesn't want to be a couple; this is **<u>her choice</u>**. She has broken up the team.

And we are both diminished as a consequence.

We were **<u>so</u>** much stronger together.

Stronger as a team, stronger than the sum of our parts.

It wasn't perfect, no relationship ever is. But I kept my side of "The Deal" and was prepared to work through anything with her to keep 'us' alive.

> You just don't bail out on a 15-year relationship without at least talking to your partner!

Did she just wake up one morning and think, "I want to go travelling" or "I can't be bothered with this anymore" or "I don't love him, let's throw it **all** away and not tell him until it's too late?"

There is no logic here.

None at all.

That is what is so hard to take.

It just doesn't make any sense.

And this is why I can't move on. I can't accept that what she has done to us was *worth it*.

Neither of us has gained anything.

It's just immensely more difficult now for us both.

Conversation. It wasn't too deep. We have both covered this ground before, often even. I don't get it. I don't think I ever will. It seems to have been an arbitrary decision for her. She had **no idea** of what those five little words would do. None whatsoever.

What a mess.

I love you, Eve.

That is the problem…

We chatted in the car on the way home. And when we got there, the sun came out and our mood equally brightened. We spent a very enjoyable couple of hours tinkering with her car. She is more or less ready for the Euro rally now. She even has a small pile of parts to bring with her for our continental friends to save their postage.

She, and indeed all of our friends on the rally, are very excited. She is going to have a great time. I'd love to be going too, but I know for certain that she'll ruin it for me, a leopard doesn't change its spots, and she has even less reason now to include me – I will be miserable, I know it. She will have a great time whether I am there or not. That is the problem. I just want her to be happy, and she will be. She doesn't care about my happiness – it isn't even remotely a priority for her. So, me not going is an exercise in damage limitation.

Part of me wants her to miss me. To miss my company. But I know she won't. She is going to have loads of fun with great friends and just won't have the time to miss me.

Importantly – if I am not there, she <u>can't</u> hurt me like she has done in the past. I will be lonely, and I will miss her terribly, but I won't be in pain, and I won't have my holiday ruined by her again.

It's for the best.

But I feel like I am shooting myself in the foot.

Am I doing the right thing?

I just don't know.

> But I **<u>do</u>** know that I **<u>can't</u>** go on holiday with her.
> But not **<u>be</u>** with her.

So, I suppose right or wrong doesn't matter. Only what I can or can't do.

So, what am I going to do while she is away? Who knows? I should put some thought into it. I don't want to spend the whole time stuck at home pining for her that's for sure... I really hope this isn't what happens. But I suspect it might.

I went and bought us some nibbles – neither of us fancied a big dinner. We watched a bit of TV and then Eve had her usual bath before bed. I was changed from around 9pm, so 14 hours today. Not bad. And despite the above, overall, a good day I think.

"Welcome."

I think this sums it up. I am no longer welcome in Eve's life. I am only in it by default, but she doesn't really want me there, not anymore. So, she includes me when she wants to, when it suits her, but resents me trying to help her in any way. I am just not welcome.

This is very painful.

It used to be so different.

I miss those days...

Monday, August 23rd

I'm not so good this morning. Waking up alone sucks. Plus, I am still a bit emotional from what I wrote last night. I shed a tear in the bathroom, just thinking about all that we had and all that we have now lost. I hate feeling like this. I am not in a good place to start the week.

Eve has work today. Somewhere near Kew gardens, it'll be a bitch to get there for her. She is up already; we have said our good mornings, and she is currently in the bathroom. I am thinking about going into the office early. I have shed loads to do this week. But I don't want to take my nightie off just yet. I need it today.

An interesting run into work – Eve left 5 minutes ahead of me, I called into Starbucks at the airport and in McD's drive through right next to me was Eve! A bacon roll breakfast probably – I rang her just to say hello and comment on the coincidence – she was as surprised as I was. It put me in a good mood for the day after all. Not even the 96 emails in my inbox from Friday could dampen my spirits today after this – amazing.

Actually, I felt alright today. Much more like my old, energised self. No idea why, especially after such a bad start. Work was relatively high-pressure today; one of my colleagues was late in (traffic jam) and I had to send my nephew home (poorly after his second Covid jab). Under resourced, drowning in emails and far too much to do with no time – yet I knuckled down and it was OK. I made good progress and was down to only 11 emails by the end of the day.

Home a little late. In an hour early, so clocked up some extra work time. A good chat with my sister-in-law in the car on the way home. I am still undecided about the family BBQ on Saturday. Part of me really wants to go. But I don't want a million questions about Eve from the myriad of cousins, aunts,

and uncles. Still, they'll find out eventually, it might be a good opportunity to tell them all in one go and get it over with. I shall think on it a bit more. Another part of me still doesn't want it to be true. Telling folks makes it real and pretty much every time I have told someone I have hugely regretted it afterwards. None more so than my brother and my dad.

Chores, bins, mogs, dinner and then an Amazon delivery all conspired to keep me in trousers for far too long. I was still in my prison when Eve arrived home. She is very tired, there was a nasty jam on the M25 (typical) and although the conversation was very pleasant – she retired early.

I watched 'Black Panther' again. To be honest, I was not impressed with it when I saw it in the cinema upon release. My least favourite of all the MCU films so far and the only one I don't own on physical media. Still, I've not seen it since it came out, so I thought I'd give it another go. Loads of folks really rate it highly, so I <u>must</u> be missing something. Sadly, I am still missing whatever it is. It's very well done, superbly acted and a real visual treat. But the villain, Killmonger, left me cold. No idea why. He's a very credible threat, but I just couldn't engage with him – these movies stand or fall by the villain – an uninteresting baddie sadly stops me caring about the heroes. It felt run-of-the-mill to me, even on a second viewing. I want to like it. I like all the others and as I said, it was very well executed – it's even got Andy Serkis in it, one of my favourite actors. Puzzling...

Finally changed around 8:45pm – not great today – 10½ hours in a dress – I will do better tomorrow.

Night. xx

Tuesday, August 24th

Another early start today, I was in the office by 7:30am and didn't finish until 12 hours later – sooo much to do.

I said my good mornings to Eve but I didn't hang around for long. I didn't even write in this journal this morning. I wanted to get a head start on the day's work. On the way in, the news reported on the M25 traffic jam Eve was stuck in yesterday. A really bad accident – 3 people lost their lives – just horrible.

I did find time though to strip my bed and set the washing machine going. The weather forecast looked good, so I thought it might be a good day to get this done. I asked Eve if she could hang them out on the line and she said OK.

I got loads done today – I am still kind of energised professionally – it's good to get some enthusiasm back. It's been really hard this year – flat out in the office, particularly in January and again this month, but I've not really cared about work until recently, this week even. It's just been work if you know what I mean? I did it because it had to be done and got no satisfaction or had any motivation to do any of it. I just went through the motions because I had to. This general malaise extended to my entire life when things collapsed with Eve in March/April, but in truth, it was already there through 2020 due to mum and then Covid. It just spiralled out of control when I lost Eve and Adam ceased to exist.

But finally, after close to five months, I have some enthusiasm back. I hope it lasts. It feels kinda fragile, but I am at last enjoying work again. Maybe I just thrive when I'm under pressure?

So, I worked until 7:30pm. Ordered a B.O.G.O.F.F. pizza deal and headed for home. As I planned, the pizza was delivered more or less as I arrived (perfect timing).

Eve told me about her day yesterday, she filmed some scenes for 'Killing Eve', but wasn't used much it seems. Today, she went into Chelmsford, but just got settled in a tea shop when one of her agents called. She has a day's work on Thursday filming season two of 'The Capture' on the proviso she could get to Harrow today for a Covid test. She has had a busy day too.

I am in Leeds on Thursday, so won't see much of her anyway. We had our pizza and watched an episode of 'House'. Eve had her usual bath and I changed into my nightie after re-making my bed.

I have, however, just dropped this (leaky) pen and put an ink spot on one of my nighties. Black ink and light pink satin are not a good combination. I think it's likely ruined. Oh well – it's had a good innings.

12 hours at work means less than 50% of the day in a dress today. I think about 10 hours all in.

> "All work and no skirt, makes Julia a sad girl".

Or something like that!

Nightie night. Long day... Zzzzz

Wednesday, August 25th

Up as usual, done with my ablutions by 7am, covered in cat fluff by five past... I am OK today.

The sun is out, my satin duvet cover is lovely and the blue pen I am now using isn't as leaky as the black one was. At least so far anyway.

I am going to get up shortly, I want to try to get into the office an hour early today. Not quite so bad as yesterday (I have some time to write in here). But we've still shed loads to do, so I am creating time, if you know what I mean. Eve, I think, is still asleep. At least it is quiet in her room, and she hasn't used the facilities yet.

I am rapidly approaching the end of Volume 3. Just three pages of this journal to fill. I may be onto Volume 4 tomorrow, depending on what happens today. Looking back at these pages I can see further progress. I am emotionally much more stable, and I am beginning to make decisions as an individual, for my own benefit, instead of for "ours". I confess, I am still finding this incredibly difficult. It's made worse by me having little to no motivation to do so – I just don't *want* to do any of it. I want Eve back, but she has already gone. If I have learned one thing over the past month or so, it's that Eve doesn't have time for me anymore. It's hard to take, but I am not really a priority, certainly not like I used to be. There are days when she is not very communicative. It feels like she is resenting having to spend time with me. This hurts. It is bloody painful. I am not welcome, at least, not as much as I was. She began this roller coaster by saying she is not the person she was 15 years ago, well, this is a major piece of supporting evidence. I was <u>always</u> welcome, but I'm not anymore.

But I am welcome *occasionally*...

I live for these fleeting moments.

And I try to make the best of them.

But it is hard, because I am sad.

The cat has just woken Eve up. I am about to put on my disguise, lock myself in horrible trousers and go to work. A new day is just beginning, and I am going to be ready for it...

A busy day, lots done at work. I am beginning to see some light at the end of the tunnel. These long hours are starting to pay off. After work I headed off to Hutton to meet up with a colleague. He is buying a house there and asked me to have a look at it from a condition point of view. It's a nice place, nothing to worry about. Afterwards he said thank you with a pub dinner.

I was back home around 10pm, off to Leeds tomorrow, so the next 10 hours in my nightie will be nice.

Thursday, August 26th

Volume 3 comes to an end, and I am feeling a bit philosophical. My place in the world feels vastly diminished, I am a speck on the face of creation, assuming you subscribe to such beliefs. Without Eve, without love, there really isn't anything truly worthwhile to strive for. I have said it before in these very pages. After 50 years on this planet, the **only** thing I have found that justifies my existence is love. Religion, organised or otherwise, means nothing to me – I have no faith in a creator, but I hedge my bets, so I am agnostic – I am open to be proved wrong at the very end, and I strive to lead a 'good life', whatever that means. Not through fear of retribution or some form of afterlife, but because it is simply the right thing to do. We are all here together, why make it harder for everyone? I strive to lead a good life, and by doing this I found love.

> I have found the love of my life.
>
> Most folks find love at some point, but finding 'the one', it seems, is very rare.
>
> She no longer loves me, this is devastating.
>
> But I still love her. My life is diminished, but I still love.
>
> *And love, apparently, is all you need…*

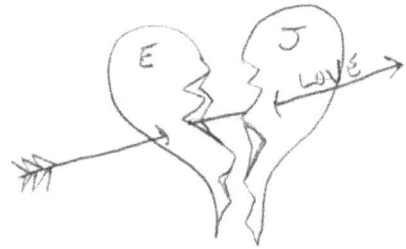

That, and 12 hours a day in a skirt!

…Aaaand… cut!

That's a wrap on Volume 3.

Good job everybody.

Time for a tea break...

To be continued...

The King is Dead, Long live the Queen

Volume 4

I am Julia

By
Julia Phillips

Volume 4 – I am Julia...

This journal belongs to: Miss Julia Phillips and it saved her life.

For me.

Forward

Volume 3 is in the bag. Wow, there's a lot of typos... Miss Secretary could do with brushing up on her skills it seems... Although, I suspect she will be retiring soon.

So, here we are at last, the fourth and final volume of the epic 'Long Live the Queen' saga. I hope you are not expecting a big finale? These journals were written to draw out the poison in my head, break down all the issues I was dealing with into more manageable pieces and lay them out, bit by bit, so I could work my way towards understanding and acceptance. As such, there came a point in time where I simply didn't need to write anymore. The worst was behind me.

This volume therefore presents me with a particular challenge, if these journals ever make it into print, I need to bring them to a satisfying conclusion. Fortunately, I am writing this from the future – it is April 29th, 2024 as I sit at my keyboard trying to write something meaningful and maybe a little amusing as an introduction to this final missive. I am thinking it needs some form of epilogue, and I suppose that should be a little about where I am now and what has happened in the intervening years.

I've tried this before, Volume 4 peters out on the 5th of November 2021, but I wrote some kind of conclusion eleven months later on October 4th 2022. For no reason other than it felt like unfinished business. I will include this in these pages, it's part of my journey after all, but there will be an all-new Epilogue to follow, the game has definitely moved on from 2022. I just need to be inspired – hopefully typing up the pages in between will give me this inspiration.

So now, all I need to do is wrap up this forward without dropping any hints as to what is to come, actually, this may be the trickiest thing to write, thinking about it – I could quite

easily ramble on, as you know, I'm a bit of a chatterbox and talking about me is, of course, my favourite subject!

What I can tell you is that these pages see me settling down and there is a progression through November 2021 all the way to where I am sitting now – my journey is far from finished, and I am so very curious as to not only the destination, but all the beautiful sights along the way. The road is still rocky, but the flowers are lovely.

Julia, Monday, April 29th, 2024.

No finale?!? What a rip-off!
Sorry, no refunds... Maybe I could be a shop girl?

Thursday, August 26th 2021

Quadrilogy, I'm pretty sure this is a make-believe term dreamed up by some marketing executive to sell a set of four McGuffins. Certainly, my word processing software has picked it out as utter nonsense. Still, in lieu of something better, it'll have to do. Oddly, 'McGuffin' is perfectly acceptable – who knew?

"Roll up, roll up, ladies and gentlemen! Come one, come all, see one of the wonders of the world! You've heard of the bearded lady? Well, she has nothing on what is behind these very curtains! Not only will you marvel at the spectacle of the most unusual female specimen ever to walk the face of the planet, but you are given exclusive, and might I say, very privileged, access to the inner workings of her mind too! You will ask yourself how nature could permit such an unusual creature to exist? How could the exterior be so completely different to the interior? What manner of Devilry is this? You will scarcely believe your eyes I tell you! Come closer, that's right, closer and gaze in wonder... The show... Is about to begin..."

> Oi! Dysphoria! Sod off you heartless cow – this is my journal, you are not welcome here at all, and who gave you a pen?

I am up on time, legs shaved and off to Leeds today with colleagues for a pre-start meeting. It should be good, I think. Eve is up, she has a day's filming for Season 2 of 'The Capture', but I will beat her out the front door today. I need to be at my brother's house for 8:30am to pick both him and my nephew up, as well as one of my colleagues. We are going up in force because we are about to have nine live sites on all at once – a big deal – this is the first pre-start meeting, so we will likely have to split the remaining sites up between us to ensure they all go

well. My nephew is with us for the experience primarily, but he's bright and eager, so he'll be running his own projects soon enough I suspect.

But, before I set off, I took 5 minutes to tell my wider family what has been going on with Eve and me. We have a Family group on WhatsApp and this seemed like the perfect place to tell everyone, all at once. I need to get it all out in the open ahead of the family BBQ this Saturday. This will stop all the awkward "Where's Eve?" questions and the last thing I want is to spend the entire time answering this emotive, and potentially triggering question over and over again. It's too painful and I'll end up not only breaking down in front of all my family, but worse, I'll also have a rubbish time – I just want to go there and have fun with my family, I need it. Not spend the whole time reliving the past three horrific months.

Duty done, I exited the house and then headed for the hills…

The meeting went well, there was some good banter in the car, although it was very "blokey" (as I said in a previous volume, I feel like a spy sometimes!) Although, I also felt a little uncomfortable. Like I was part of a male bonding ritual, and I didn't fit in. It was fun – but a little misogynistic and I came close to being offended. Not because the content was offensive – it was – but it was meant to be, lots of guys trying to one-up each other by lowering the bar as much as they could. I came close because it occurred to me that if my appearance matched who I truly am inside, the conversation would have been **very** different. Sometimes my disguise gives me an insight, sometimes that insight is not very pleasant. Ladies, and I am sure this is not a revelation to you, yes, guys are every bit as crass as you think they are, likely worse. And it is all in the name of male bonding – males bond by seeing who can be the most disrespectful, the most gross and the most inappropriate. It's a competitive sport.

What's worse, is that I am every bit as distasteful when I am in this kind of company – it leaves a bad taste in my mouth – and this is exactly the kind of line any of my male colleagues would delight in adding a crude comment to.

Close to 400 miles driven today. I didn't have a chance to check up on the WhatsApp comments until I arrived home much later at around 8pm. Wow. Very, very touching. I'm crying, but I'm not sad. And I think I can go to the BBQ now.

It is 10pm now – Eve is still not home – she must be doing a late one. I'll message her. I am worried.

Eve arrived home half an hour later – she's had a long day, and actually, so have I. We are both tired. We said our 'goodnights' and we retired to our respective beds.

A long day, but a good one, I think.

But only 10½ hours in a dress.

Friday, August 27th

I didn't sleep well – indigestion woke me twice. Not nice. I am done in the bathroom; Eve is currently in the shower. She has the horses to attend to first and then she's off, into London, St. James' Park, for a Covid test ahead of work there on Monday. Something called 'Nightingale' – she's going to be in a Police uniform apparently.

I have a loose plan for the weekend. I am going to the family BBQ on Saturday. Eve is going to her parent's place and will stay over. She'll come back on Sunday, and we'll get together for her birthday.

Half past seven, I will get up soon – I want to get into the office early again and get a head start on the day.

I went to work – I ate too much for lunch once more – I need to get a grip on this – make more of an effort. It was a productive day though, not as much progress on the working drawings I am meant to be doing, but I made a fair dent in some of my colleagues' work whilst he is away and have set it up so that it's relatively straightforward for him to finish off upon his return.

Home on time, Eve had also just arrived. We decided we both needed a quiet night after such a hectic week. Diner, and then I was back in a skirt from 7:30pm. It's been a few days since I had the opportunity for a complete outfit. I've missed it. So nice. So comfy. So, well, *me*. Nothing too fancy, just a skirt and blouse, heels lingerie, make-up, and jewellery – simple, smart, nice. I watched some TV for a bit, and it is now twenty to ten. I am about to retire to bed as I'm very tired.

I am seeing Kay tomorrow morning. Then the family BBQ in the afternoon. Eve has the horses first and then off to her folk's place. It should be a good weekend for both of us, I think.

Saturday, August 28th

A lazy morning so far – I slept very well – through until 8am. I am up but dressed comfortably – Eve is about to leave for the horses, and I am seeing Kay at 11:30am, so I have a little time before I need to get ready.

I bought a couple of satin skater dresses recently; they seem to be a trend at the moment. They are nice, but the skirts don't do me any favours, something about the shape just doesn't work for me – the perils of buying clothes off the internet. The bodices are lovely though, a little low cut, but a stitch or two has ensured my modesty is maintained. Because I don't think the shape is very flattering on me, I have been tucking the skirts inside an actual skirt – using them as a slip – it works really well, at least, I think so. The only minor issue is where do I hang them in my wardrobe? With the dresses or with the blouses? It's complicated being a woman!

My appointment with Kay went well, we chatted about a number of things, not least of which was that she has read Volume 1 of this journal – she read it straight through in one session! I am not sure if this means it is good or not, Kay gave some constructive criticism – but of course I didn't write it, or any of these volumes for that matter, with the intent to be published, or even understood by those who don't know me. I wrote them and still am writing them, as much needed therapy – to get all the millions of thoughts and emotions clogging up my brain, out of my head and onto a page. And in the process, break them down into elements that can be looked at rationally. So, background information on me and my life is missing – I already know all this stuff, there's little point in writing it down given I'm the only target audience. But I agree. *If* it ever is published, then maybe an introduction will be needed. Or indeed, maybe a few additional paragraphs to explain a little about me and who I am.

Speaking of therapy, I am still writing... Although I am not sure for how much longer. To be honest I am not feeling the need as much, my emotional state appears to be much less turbulent, and I am concerned that these writings will either become very mundane or just peter out as my life begins to resolve itself. But for now, I am still scrawling my terrible handwriting in this book.

As an example of mundanity, after my session, I went to Tesco and bought some lunch as well as a card for my nephew's birthday – Eve and he have birthdays on consecutive days at the very end of August. I also bought some Diet Coke, a bottle of wine and some nibbles for this afternoon's BBQ.

When I got home, Eve's car was gone, and her sister's car was on the drive. I'd missed them. They were on their way up to see their folks for the weekend, and I was now, once again, alone. Not nice.

But...

A perfect opportunity to wrap up Eve's and my nephew's birthday presents. Always a silver lining...

I made myself busy – wrapping, then laundry, then dishes, then hoovering. Finally, it was time to head over to my brother's house for the BBQ.

You know what? It was great. Really amazing to see them all again – I forgot how cool my extended family is – they are awesome. Dad and his new lady were there, as was my uncle Reg (mum's brother). One of my aunts and all the cousins bar two. The former was doing a 24hr live stream for charity and the latter is moving to France. Good excuses.

My plan with the WhatsApp posting worked. The situation between Eve and myself was mentioned a few times, but briefly and it was all sympathetic, not enquiring, so not an issue and none of my raw emotions were triggered.

We ate and chatted into the wee-small hours, eventually, the last 4 guests, including me, left for home. A really enjoyable night, Eve would've loved it, I am sure. But equally, I am sure she was having a good time with her family too. In a perfect world, we would have both gone to the BBQ, then driven up to her folk's place on her birthday – it's a bank holiday weekend, so we could have stayed over Sunday/Monday – it was possible for us both to have done all of it. But sadly, it was not meant to be.

We have both missed out.
    Home.
        Cold.
            Alone.

A great night followed by a stark reminder of my situation.

A shower to rid myself of the smell of the BBQ and then into my much-needed nightie. I'm going to have a lie in tomorrow / today – I need it.

Sunday, August 29th

Happy Birthday Eve!!!
Wait...

She's not here.

This has **never** happened before. I have been with Eve on her birthday, every year, for the last 15 years. I didn't think I would like it, I was right, I don't.

Plus, I've got a bit of a headache – not from drinking – I haven't since my 21st birthday, 'a night to remember', except I can't, I was far too drunk and have sworn it off ever since – but probably from over-doing it. I am tired – it's a long time since I stayed up so late socialising. Even sober, it takes a toll.

I messaged Eve a birthday greeting just after midnight – I wanted to be the first. Hopefully I was, but I don't know.

Then I fed the ravenous wee beasties (mogs) and back to bed – lie in time.

The house is quiet – too quiet. I don't like it much and it feels empty. It's like the emptiness of my heart has overspilled onto my bed, into the bedroom and now through the whole house. I miss her. But despite this, I am OK. Does this mean I am (finally) coming to terms with things? To be honest, I am not sure. Again, progress of a sort I suppose. I hate the situation, I hate being apart from Eve on her birthday, it feels *very* wrong to me, and I hate being alone. But I am **not** upset. So, yes. Some progress.

And I don't resent her having a good time with her family. I just would have liked to have shared it with them all. There was no reason I couldn't go other than I wasn't invited by Eve. I wrote this yesterday: "we have both lost out as a consequence". This is bloody stupid. What kind of idiots put themselves in a situation where they *both* loose out? There are no winners here.

I don't feel like I am family anymore.

I hate it.

This was **not** my choice, only an idiot would choose this.

Happy Birthday Eve, my love – you idiot. A beautiful idiot, the one true idiot for me. But still an idiot all the same. An idiot for doing this to us.

Besides, I shall see my lovely idiot later.

Stuff...

I did stuff. Nothing of any real note, just stuff. Lidl for some lunch stuff, house cleaning stuff, TV stuff, just stuff to keep me occupied.

And then, Eve came home. She had indeed had a great time; we did the present thing and I think she liked my gift.

I love to see her smile. She smiled on her birthday. It was glorious.

We said our goodbyes to her sister and then settled in for the night. A curry and TV for a bit, before retiring to our respective beds.

11 hours today. I could've quite easily clocked up some more, the opportunity was there. But I am happy with my choices today.

Monday, August 30th

Bank Holiday Monday

A strange day – it didn't feel like a Bank Holiday. I was up around 9am, Eve was up too – she has work today, 'Nightingale' in St. James' Park, London. Likely to be a long one I think, the estimated wrap time is 10:45pm and then she has to get home.

We said our 'good mornings' and made small talk. I decided I would pop out to get some new trainers, so left the house just before she did.

In the end, I didn't get my new shoes. It was just too busy. A cold, overcast Bank Holiday – no one is at the seaside, they all went shopping instead. So, I bought a French stick and then came home to get changed and have some lunch.

And that is pretty much my day. I spent it happily pottering around the house in a full outfit, make-up, and accessories. It's been lovely, I think it will end up being around 21 hours today. I watched some TV, cleaned the house a bit, typed up some more of volume 2 (wading through it, there's so much to write up). Productive, in a lazy kind of way.

I miss Eve. I miss her company and I am upset that I didn't see much of her on her birthday weekend. It feels like a big loss to me. And although her mum said I was always welcome at their place; Eve didn't want me there. She didn't want me there on her birthday. For the first time, I missed the celebrations. I know I had the BBQ, but between us, we could have made it work – it just needed a little thought and a minor rearrangement of things. Seems I wasn't worth the effort. A big loss indeed.

Still, I have made the best of it. 21 hours is really good – I am so comfy right now. I may pop out for a little drive – there is time before Eve comes home. Am I feeling brave? I kinda am... It may well happen...

Tuesday, August 31st

Well, I wussed out. I fell asleep and woke up when Eve arrived home around 11pm. She was dead tired, understandably so, and after saying our hellos, we retired.

Up a little later than expected today. Normally, I try to get into the bathroom around 6am, but was half an hour behind schedule this morning. I am writing this "morning piece" at 9am as a consequence. It's been a very long time since I missed a time slot for writing in this journal. Speaking of which, is there a difference between a Diary and a Journal? I've never thought about it and have been using these words interchangeably since the word go. I prefer diary. It is more intimate, personal, and friendly – like I am telling secrets to a confidant. But journal is good too. It carries more gravitas, I think. A more formal term and I suppose, has more professional connotations – not that I am in any way a professional you understand!

So, I sacrificed my diary/journal entry writing time this morning for getting to work early – I've still got loads to do and a deadline to hit. But today was painful and uncomfortable. Physically.

I think I may have slept awkwardly; I have some sciatic pain in my right hip. I've had it before; it normally sorts itself out after a day or so – today is day 1. It's horrible – a dull ache that flares up if I move or sit incorrectly, or if I am immobile for a while. I haven't taken any pills. I don't like to and generally only do so as a last resort. But, if it is no better tomorrow, I will. Likely because I am carrying too much weight.

I worked an extra ½ hour in the evening – until I couldn't stand sitting at my desk any longer. So, I was home a little late too. Eve wasn't in, I have no idea where she was. She didn't tell me when I asked about her day when she arrived a little later

and I didn't press her. She'll tell me if she wants to or if it is important. I was just making conversation anyway.

Pizza (Two for Tuesdays). I left 1/3 of it as usual. In the past, I would have polished the whole thing off, but I am trying not to clear my plate (box in this case) at every meal. Mum would not approve – starving 3rd World kids etc, etc. Especially if the food is a high calorie item, like pizza.

Watched some more of 'House' on Amazon – this show just gets better and better – we are up to Season 4 now.

Eve is currently in the bath, I am in my nightie, in bed. I am going to try to unkink my hips tonight by sleeping on my side – hopefully this will work, and I will be OK in the morning. Wish me luck!

Who am I talking to?
It's a diary...

Ah, well.
Night! xx

Wednesday, September 1st

New month, sheez this year is flying by. Where does all the time go? Seems like only yesterday I started writing this diary. Five months! Wow!

It is twenty past seven, I should get up and go into work early, but my hip is still aching, and I am appreciating some quiet time in bed before the day starts in earnest. It's a bit grey outside, but not too cold, a nice cool temperature. The birds are singing, and Tara cat has been in to see me for her usual early morning cuddles. I am OK.

It was a very productive day at work, I've finally broken the back (pun intended) of the current set of working drawings, they are all done except the reflected ceiling plan. I am going to hit my deadline this week I think (I've managed the 'impossible' again).

I was home half an hour later than normal, Eve was in, although she wasn't very talkative tonight. Engrossed in her laptop as usual. We watched three episodes of House back-to-back and ordered a Nando's in for dinner. I was changed from around 8pm, so just a smidge under 12 hours today.

Not a bad day all in. I would've liked to have chatted with Eve more, she has yet to tell me about her day's filming on Monday, so there is stuff to talk about, she'll tell me when she is ready, I suppose...

...too late for 'white rabbits' – I forgot.

Thursday, September 2nd

Up as usual, ablutions, mogs and then back to bed for a snooze. Satin nightie and freshly shaved legs – lovely, it just never gets old. I need to repaint my toes though; I will try to do so tonight.

Also, I need to make some notes on my finances tonight. I have tomorrow afternoon off work to see my financial advisors about getting things moving. Is a second mortgage viable? Can I buy a second house to rent out? It's my retirement and my safety net should things not work out with Eve. They should be ready for me by now, but they have cancelled on me a few times, so I am behind where I would've wanted to be.

Not a peep from Eve yet, she is still asleep. It is seven thirty, I am about to get up, grudgingly accept my prison sentence, and go into work.

A long day. I arrived early and left late, but I managed to finish the last of the working drawings packs. Finally. I will double-check them and issue first thing tomorrow.

Home around 6pm, but then straight out again. One of our local car club natters was on tonight, so Eve and I jumped into her car, and we headed out for dinner and socialise with friends.

I confess I am not feeling it the way I used to – these evenings were once the highlight of my month, good company, good food and lots of interesting chat about a subject I am passionate. However, the growing distance between Eve and I has sadly taken the shine off of these evenings somewhat. My friends are all great and I really love seeing them, but the spark that I used to have is now missing. I am not sure if I will continue with them once Eve flies away. I will miss my friends, but I am

just not engaged as I once was. Maybe I need to find something new?

We walked through the front door of our home around 10pm, I was in a dress shortly after. But not for long. I had a corset arrive today! I've never worn one before and I was intrigued. I have watched a couple of YouTube videos on how to put one on and lace up the back. It's quite a skill, but I managed a halfway decent reduction in my waist. Wow, **very** uncomfortable. Maybe I overtightened it, but I thought "I'm in now, might as well complete my outfit". So, as Thursday rolled into Friday, I was fully clothed in every way, from my corset to my make-up. Sadly, I couldn't sleep like this. But I do think that the three or four hours in it has done my aching back some good. I can't say the same about my respiration though…

Back in my nightie in the wee-small hours of Friday. Time for some sleep, sweet dreams…

Friday, September 3rd

Almost five months since 'J-Day'. Tomorrow is the monthly anniversary once more, the anniversary of the day I went out to take my own life. You know what? I am doing alright. Yes, I am still Julia all of the time. No, my broken heart hasn't got any better. Yes, Eve and I are no longer a couple. But I am not as upset anymore. I mean, I am not breaking down in tears, inconsolable or hysterical anyway. It's a truly horrible situation, but I am dealing with it as best as I can.

Yes – I still love Eve.

No – she doesn't love me anymore.

It's shit. But I am getting on with it.

Eve is working again today (Trigger Point once more), we both left early-ish after our usual 'good mornings'.

Morning done at work, the drawings were issued, I have this afternoon off. I am going to see my financial advisors at 3pm, then Kay at 5:30pm, and then dad afterwards. A busy afternoon. But first I need to review my finances to take with me to the meeting.

It was a very interesting meeting with the 'wealth planners' (sounds a bit grand, certainly far too grand for someone like me). It seems I have a fair sum in my various pension pots and 2 of them can be moved and combined somewhere more profitable. Time to make this money work harder to make more money. It's my pension after all.

Kay was very good as always. I am in a much better place than I was, and I have been thinking about not seeing her as often. But I **always** feel better after our sessions and as long as I do, then I think they are worthwhile. We chatted about work, my meeting with the financial gurus, Eve, and of course, the family BBQ. How it went very well, but also, that I missed Eve's

family birthday celebrations and how this is a very big thing to me.

Then I set off to see dad. I met him at a local bar for some dinner – he was sitting with a couple; the chap was *very* pissed – it was only 7pm... Nice enough, but the conversation was more difficult than it should've been. Dad was OK though and we had a good chat over dinner. I confess, I am finding his line of questioning about Eve and my situation very wearing. He is the only one who keeps banging on about it. "You need to...", "You must...", "You have to..." Actually, NO. I don't need, must or have to do anything. As Kay says, I should live in the moment. And, as I have written, these moments are what make up my life, and when they are good, I am going to try to take joy in them. This was **REALLY** hard back at the beginning of this journal. But now, I take as much joy out of life as I can find. Real progress. Not just ring-fencing money and trying to find someone else. Dad's advice is practical in nature, but is very heavily skewed in my favour, at the expense of Eve. I can't help myself, I resent it. Because I resent the situation and, of course, I still love her. Anything I am advised to do that hurts her is bound to set off emotional warning sirens in my head. This doesn't mean that he is wrong. But it does make it incredibly hard for me to hear. Also, these so-called solutions don't help *"me"*, they only look at the practicalities. Kay helps me deal with the situation on a personal level – this is the fundamental difference.

I was home around 10pm, in a dress at last. I am definitely going to have a lie-in tomorrow. Let's see if I can do 12 hours straight...

I need it.

Saturday, September 4th

5 month anniversary of 'J-Day'...

It is 10:46am as I write this entry. I am still in my nightie, earrings, make-up, and undies – I am very relaxed and am about to get up. I have decided I am not going to mark the anniversary in here in the manner I have done in the past. Instead, I am going to try to enjoy the day and not be maudlin or overly contemplative.

Eve came back from the horses, and we drove to Lavenham for a cream tea. On the way we diverted to Pentlow to do a drive-by of her parent's old home, just for curiosities sake, and what have the new owners done with it? Turns out, quite a lot. The central island on the in and out drive has been thinned out, the drives are wider, there is a new oil tank, and they have painted the exterior (white), including the garage door. There is also a routered out timber sign in the island with the house name. All in all, a big improvement, not that it was in bad shape before.

Lavenham was a little quiet for a Saturday. Some folks were milling about, but we have both seen it much busier. We had a wander and then tried to find a nice tea shop. Our favourite one has sadly closed – we spent a lot of time in there over the years, but now it is someone's home. As Eve said, it is odd that such a special place, that used to be enjoyed by thousands every year, is now only enjoyed by one person. Such a shame. Still, it meant we were going to try somewhere new and there are at least five tea shops in Lavenham to choose from. The first place was sadly full, but the second had some space and we found a table. It was very nice, not as good as our favourite, but nice never-the-less. The food was good, and the shop was pleasant. It could've done with a little background music, just to add to the ambience, but this is all we could find fault with. The scones were homemade and lovely.

We headed for home after, the chat in the car was bright and cheerful. It felt a little like old times – we both had fun. On the way we stopped at Carpet Right to buy a small piece of vinyl for our lobby. Currently we have a fitted coir mat, and this is still the best solution for this space, but Tara cat has taken to using it as a litter tray and despite daily cleaning, when you open the front door, you are assaulted by the smell of ammonia. It's horrible, so we've decided it has to go in favour of something impervious and more cleanable. We got a quote and then headed home to eject the old coir mat – yuk! Much, much better.

I did a run to Tesco, Eve is working tomorrow, and I have plans, so I bought some supplies.

Then some TV, relaxation in my nightie and finally bed. Close to 14 hours today. Nice.

Sunday, September 5th

It's ten am, Eve has been gone for four and a half hours – she had an early call today, but she should be well paid for the inconvenience on a Sunday. She's filming something called 'Trigger Point' again today. I am in my nightie; I am about to shower. Today, I plan to be myself – I am going to spend it completely in female mode and live as the woman I am. The only small fly in the ointment is there is a washing line full of clean clothes that'll need to come in at some point. Could be tricky, or I could simply "not give a monkey's" and just go about my business as me. It's all in my head anyway – caring about what others think – I should care more about my own well-being and just express myself truthfully.

What a lovely day. I, for once, literally took a day off. A day off from my prison sentence. I relaxed in a casual skirt and a woman's T-shirt all day. It was nice, to just chill in comfy clothes and not have a million and one things to do. I watched some TV, wrote in this diary, made myself some lunch, pottered around the house and got the washing in. All good and stress-free.

A full 24 hours spent dressed and living as a woman in every way. I can live like this, no problem. The next steps are to do more as me, including leaving the house more. Let's see how this works out...

Eve came home around 6:30pm, we had pizza for dinner (I was brave and answered the door!) Eve was understandably tired, so went to bed shortly after.

A bit of a landmark day.

More like this please!

Monday, September 6th

Up at 6am, bathroom first and then accosted by the cat as usual. It is now an hour later, I am in bed, kinda snoozing, looking up at the blue sky outside my window and wondering if it is going to be a nice day – it looks like it might, and after such a damp squib of a summer, a nice day would be very welcome.

Eve is up, I am about to join her. I have been getting into work early for the past couple of weeks, just trying to squeeze an extra few minutes into each working day in the quiet, before and again after the chaos of a typical working 9 to 5. I am doing this to try to hit deadlines and targets, even if they are unreasonable. Every client has unreasonable expectations, so we do what we can and what we must to give them what they want. I sometimes wonder if this is self-defeating ultimately. I hope not, but if the client asks for the impossible, and somehow, we go way beyond our limitations to deliver, are we encouraging them to ask for the even *more* impossible next time? All I know is that we *can't* fail. We can decline beforehand, but we can't say we'll deliver and then not do so. So, this is a dangerous position to be in. Once we are committed, we have to succeed, because the client will not remember how unreasonable, or impossible the task is, or how many times they moved the goalposts, or missed their own targets. They will only remember the one time we were unable to perform a miracle for them. The one failure that made them forget about all the successes and we likely lose that client. So, we go above and beyond, and we do what we must to succeed. And we do not get paid for this dedication, or the additional hours, caused by ridiculous deadlines and an inability to make up their minds about what they want in good time. But we **do** get future projects. And that is ultimately what it is all about. We want future work, so we foster a good working relationship with our clients and their contractors to work as a team and deliver the best possible result. We go the extra mile,

always. And we do it with a smile, in a professional manner, and we deliver the impossible, time and again. This is why I worry we are making a rod for our own backs after we have succeeded where others in all likelihood would have failed. It's why, after 33 years, we are still in business and are currently expanding, when a lot of companies are struggling. It's also why we have been flat out all year. It's been tough. All this work on top of the worst year of my life. The year my personal life disintegrated, I lost Eve, the single most important thing to me, and in the process, lost the lion's share of who I was. My life has changed completely – I look out on the world through new eyes and for the longest of times, all I could see was loss and despair. But now, just over five months on from 'J-Day', I am at last getting a grip on who I am. And do you know what? It's not too bad. Sure, I'd give anything to be able to wind the clock back and fix things between Eve and I, but we are where we are and I am, as best as I can, dealing with it, and all the other stuff that has come about as a consequence.

My life isn't perfect. It never was and I doubt anyone's ever is. My life now, at least for the time-being I hope, is not as good as before. There's a chance it never will be again, I hope not, but from where I am sitting at the moment, I am finding it hard to see a similarly bright future. But that doesn't mean it is not a life worth living – far from it. It's still a life full of opportunity and the potential for joy. I am on a particularly interesting adventure right now. An adventure into who I am and how I manifest this to the world. It's fascinating and a fundamental life experience – one that, relatively speaking, most of the human race do not get the privilege to go on. A journey that has the potential to alter my perception of the world and the world's perception of me. And, like all adventures, it is full of drama, pain, mistakes and triumphs. It also has a finale that is shrouded in mystery. I am

excited to see where this path of discovery takes me. I am also trepidatious about where I am going to end up.

I hope it is better, I think it will be.

It won't be the same, and getting there will be challenging. Am I ready? I don't think so. But who is? No one is ever ready to find out if the grass truly *is* greener. I doubt it is. I suspect it is just different grass. But it is a patch of grass where I belong. And I think the flowers over there are pretty...

A good day at work. Lots done and I was home around 6pm. Astonishingly, considering we had only just ordered it, the vinyl flooring was installed today. They had had a cancellation and squeezed us in. It's great, a big improvement. Also, Eve's new passport arrived, so she can now go on the European rally in a couple of weeks – she is very excited!

I ordered a curry for us both, watched some TV. Larry cat was particularly pleased with himself today. He caught his first rat. "Being a cat – Expert Level" achieved. I retired to bed around 11pm, only 8 hours today, but I am OK. I'm still on a bit of a high from yesterday.

Tuesday, September 7th

I'm tired today, I didn't sleep well – I finally dropped off around 3:30am. No idea why, it just didn't happen. Up and dressed by 7:30am, said my good mornings to Eve and then headed for work.

I had a CPD training day today. Three back-to-back CPD lectures on the big screen in the office with colleagues. Necessary, but a lot of stuff I already knew, and already being tired didn't help either. Still, it's done now. I also reviewed the health and safety on all 9 sets of Working drawings, adding in any relevant information to inform the contractor when they come to carry out these tasks. I felt good afterwards – not just because I have complied with my responsibilities, but because, if just one of these notes prevents an accident due to raised awareness, then this makes everything worthwhile.

Home on time, but I'm not planning much tonight – I'm just too tired – some TV, meatballs for dinner and then early to bed.

11 hours in a dress today – not too bad.

Wednesday, September 8th

I am not looking forward to today, I am about to start researching all the new systems and documentation our new client requires. They have a **very** prescribed process for delivery of their information at every stage, including a million and one templates that we will need to be familiar with and understand their purpose, content and how they fit in. I'm a creative kind of girl, but sitting at my desk all day opening, reading, and understanding endless documentation is not my idea of fun. But it needs to happen, we need to build a team to deal with this level of bureaucracy, and I sit right in the middle of it all. So, I am going to spend my day as well as half of tomorrow trying to wrap my head around it all.

It has just gone 7am, I am back in bed writing this. The sun is up and there is the tail end of the dawn chorus outside my window – it's going to be a nice day, I think. I am OK.

The research went alright. It was, thankfully, broken up by other work so I wasn't on it completely all day. It was a hot one today too, 28 degrees C. The aircon in the office was on all day but step outside and the heat hit you. I bought ice creams for everyone and they were very much appreciated.

I bumped into one of my neighbours as I drove into my estate. He took me for a spin in his new car – a US import, left hand drive and a column change. A very interesting / fun experience. He has asked if I can help him pick up another from a studio in the middle of London, a week tomorrow – I said I would.

Eve and I went to Nando's for dinner. It was pleasant enough, we chatted about our respective days, her website and her new (blue/black) passport. I mentioned I am thinking about buying a drone, just for fun really, but that I didn't want to spend hundreds of pounds, so I'll likely wait for Black Friday.

We returned home around 7:30pm, a little TV and then in my nightie by 8 o'clock. I put the air con on in my bedroom and literally chilled out for a bit. 11½ hours in a dress today.

Tuesday, September 9th

It's nice and cool in my bedroom this morning. But it was still dark at 6am when I visited the bathroom – I had to put the light on. I am now back in bed, it is foggy outside – the sun is up, but it has that quiet, ethereal quality out there. Not that I am getting much tIme to appreciate it. Tara cat is very interactive this morning...

Work – a site visit first thing and then into the office. More research, it's tedious, but necessary. I spent a little time looking at Go-Pros and drones. I fancy one of each to be honest and shooting some video. But I don't want to spend loads of money, so I think if I do buy one/both, I'll wait for Black Friday / Cyber Monday.

I was home briefly around 6pm. A quick chat with Eve, the I changed out of my work top before heading over to my brother's house for dinner. Lasagne, yum. A very pleasant evening, all in. Good company, good food, good times.

Back home around 10pm, in my nightie shortly after. Only 10 hours today. Tomorrow will be better.

Friday, September 10th

I have a day off today, but no time for a lie-in – I'm off to see Katie for my fifth IPL treatment to remove my beard permanently. I am wondering if I am going to see any further benefit though. My beard is not very dark, there are some ginger hairs, but mainly it is white these days (I'm getting old) and the treatment relies on pigmentation in the hair. The darker it is, the better it works. I think I am going to end up needing electrolysis as well. But I am paid up to six sessions and I have seen some hair loss. Just not the loads I want.

I arrived at Katie's salon at 9:10am, 20 minutes early. Katie arrived shortly after, but I waited in the car until my appointment at half past. Just a common courtesy, giving her time to set up and get herself ready for the day. It was a good session, and pretty much pain free despite the IPL machine being set to maximum.

Afterwards, I came home via Gridserve. They have a test drive event this weekend and I thought it might be good to get some information on potential electric vehicles (EVs) that may be suitable to replace my current company car. I ended up test driving a Tesla Model X! It's waaay out of my price bracket and far too big. But wow! What a car. It's impractical to park (gull wing doors don't change the overall size of the car) – I would struggle in a multi-storey car park for instance. And of course, I have no need at all for a seven-seater. But after the test drive, I want one anyway!

I popped home for some lunch but didn't get it. Instead, a change of plans – I was thinking about going to the cinema – but Eve has had a work opportunity on Sunday, so we jumped in the car and headed up to her folk's place for a BBQ to celebrate her dad's upcoming birthday with some of their friends. The two-hour drive ended up taking over three though – there were

some total morons on the road today. Random traffic jams caused by a light splattering of rain. A suicidal petrol tanker cutting people up and jumping red lights, tractors and straw bale lorries creating chaos and an idiot driving with his wing mirrors folded in. Madness...

Good times as usual at Eve's parents' place. It's always lovely to see them again. The food was excellent, as was the company and as a bonus, the rain held off too. I did split my jeans however and had to sew them up (I have ordered another 2 pairs to replace them – hateful things, it felt good to destroy a pair! All-be-it by accident).

Bed around 11pm – a good fun day.

9 hours today.

Saturday, September 11th

I didn't sleep too well; the bed has a footboard, and it was very warm (I missed my fan/aircon). It didn't help that it was a very calm night so, even with the windows open, there was little to no air movement. Still, my nightie was very welcome, and I slept above the covers.

Up around 9am, breakfast with Eve's folks was lovely and then we headed off to a local knick-knack shop for a look-see and a bit later on, a cream tea for lunch. It was a strange place, one of those shops where there is something interesting or surprising everywhere you look.

The cream tea was nice, inexpensive too. All too soon however, it was time to head back and then say our goodbyes ahead of the journey home. Today's trip, thankfully, was much better than yesterday, although Eve was a bit quiet in the car. I think she was tired too. I made the effort, but there wasn't much conversation.

We stopped at the horses on the way home, they are fine, I stayed in the car whilst Eve saw to them.

Once home, Eve tinkered with her car a little. It is making an odd, intermittent whine – it sounds like gas escaping, and it isn't related to the rpm, or the drivetrain as it happens when idling. No idea what it is, but likely it has been doing it for a while – it is so subtle, I'm surprised she spotted it. Can't do anything about it now anyway – she is driving across mainland Europe on Wednesday.

A curry for dinner, a little TV and then bed. I went for it tonight. Full day wear and I ended up sleeping in it all. I love waking up fully clothed – I am sooo weird... Still, 12 hours today, so all is good.

Sunday, September 12th

Eight thirty, I am sitting on my bed in stockings, heels, make-up, undies, and jewellery – I have swapped my skirt and blouse for a nightie. I have also taken my bra off. I am waiting my turn in the bathroom – Eve is up, she has a drive into Holborn this morning for a job – she is part of a traffic jam apparently. I am letting her get ready as I suspect she'll be leaving pretty soon. Plus, I am not quite ready to get fully undressed just yet. But I do need a shower, so I will be getting up soon...

Up, clean and I've said my goodbyes to Eve, time to put on my disguise and go out into the world. First stop, Tesco – as I had to throw Friday's French stick out, I bought another, along with some milk and some cereal. Then, off to see car #3, to remove the battery and bring it home to charge. I also dropped the steering wheel controls off in the boot, just to keep them in the logical place. There's always something to do on these old cars.

Back home, and a nice lunch. Some TV, and then off to the cinema – 'Shang Chi and the legend of the ten rings' – it was much better than I was expecting, I liked it a lot. But I missed not sharing it with my love, or with anyone for that matter. It's been a good 15 to 20 years since I last went to the cinema alone. The film was excellent though, so I had a good time anyway.

Home again, cereal for dinner. I also found that Disney+ has the show 'Angel' – I used to have Seasons 1-4 on VHS box set back in the day and I never did get around to watching Season 5. I binge watched the first 4 episodes – it's better than I remembered.

Eve walked in around 8:10pm, she's had a long day, but was in good spirits. She has managed to organise EU car recovery ahead of her trip next week too. No small feet on a car this old, and it wasn't hugely expensive, so that's a bonus.

In my nightie from 7pm – So, 14 hours today.

A good day.

It would have been better if I had shared it with Eve.

But a good day, never-the-less.

Monday, September 13th

Usual morning routine, early into work, around 8am – lots to do today. My brother wasn't in, he's not very well. One of my colleagues also left early - migraine. An odd kinda day, but productive.

Home around 5:45pm, Eve and I went out for dinner to Nando's. It was lovely and nice to chat with her, she brought me up to speed with her work on Sunday. Apparently, they didn't use her until the afternoon and there wasn't any food or refreshments – not even a holding area for her and her fellow actors. Eve found a Starbucks in the morning and her involvement was mainly just sitting in her car. Odd...

Home around 8pm, watched some TV and in my nightie by 9 o'clock. It is 10pm now as I write, I am going to bed shortly.

Dad annoyed me a little this evening, it seems he has broken his printer, the scanner, I think, has packed up and it seems to have coincided with me being press-ganged into moving it a while back. So, now I feel obliged to try to fix it, even though I know nothing at all about printers. Looks like I will be popping round there at some point this week...

Eve is off on her trip on Wednesday – the ferry leaves Dover at eight o'clock, so she will be leaving home around 6am, an hour from here to the Dartford crossing and a further hour down to Dover – I'm not sure I will be up to see her off. I hope so, but I will say my goodbyes tomorrow night, I think.

I am going to miss her.

I was thinking about the nature of my love for her earlier. It seems to me that I am incapable of a 'normal' love for someone, whatever *that* may be. Love, if what I surmise of it is true, seems to be built on three pillars: common interests, compatible personalities, and physical attraction. With these in place, a powerful emotional bond can form. But this is not how

it works for me. For me, with Eve, the first two pillars are <u>very</u> much in place. But I am not, and never have been, physically attracted to anyone. Male, female, young, old, no one. This is missing from my mental make up. And so, I just don't fully understand it. I mean, I understand the mechanics of it. But I have never looked at someone and thought "phwoar". I see beauty and appreciate it. Actually, I see beauty everywhere. In the fresh smell of rain, or the majesty of a clear night sky. In the sound of the ocean, or the industry of honeybees. But most of all, I see beauty in Eve's smile. She is the most beautiful person I have ever known. But I am not physically attracted to her. I am <u>drawn</u> to her. An important distinction. I have a need to share my life with her, but I am just not wired to have a typical male physical reaction. My love for her is purer than some seedy sex act. Our lovemaking, for me at least, was never about physical pleasure on my part. It was about the bond, sharing something intimate and most important of all, giving her pleasure – it was a selfless act, and I did my very best. But it wasn't enough in the end. It was more than enough for me, my love for her, even after our relationship became platonic, continued to deepen. Up until recent events, my love for her had never been stronger. And I suspect, I am always going to love her to some degree. I called her my soul mate often and for me, this is very true. But she feels differently, and indeed, is wired differently. She needs to be physically attracted to me to love me it seems. And, while my love for her was deepening, her love for me was based upon a waning physical attraction. In the end, she just didn't feel attracted to me anymore and instead of her love for me moving beyond the physical, as mine always was, it gradually faltered, and faded away.

This is the truth of it. The very root I think, of the situation I find myself in. I have found my one and only, the person I am meant to share my life with. My true love, my soul mate. But

she has fallen out of love with me. And as a consequence, dealt the man I was a death blow.

I don't think Adam is coming back. I used to think he would. But, after all this time, I think I am Julia for good.

But I still love Eve. I am not the person I once was, but my love for her remains.

So, when she goes on her trip, a trip we are meant to share together as a couple, I am going to miss her dreadfully. But I can't go on this trip and not be with her. I am not sure I will ever be able to. We fell in love on a trip just like this, and this is why her abandoning me on the last two rallies hurt me so much. They are our 'special thing', the one thing we do together that defines us as a couple. And she wrecked the last two. She had a great time **at my expense**. She had an amazing couple of trips **because** she ditched me, and she didn't care!!! She didn't for one second consider what she did to me might be wrong, or how I might be feeling. She cut me out of her holiday and cut me to the core by doing so. It was deliberate, and excruciatingly painful. And I didn't understand. I do now, but at the time I was so confused – how could she do this to me? What had I done to deserve this awful treatment? Why was she going out of her way to ruin my holiday? All these questions and more – but mainly, the pain of being rejected. The realisation that I was no longer special to her, at least, no more special than any of our friends. And not worth her time, or the effort, to include me. It was an awful feeling, and despite everything, I could see she was happy and having a good time without me. So, I stepped back. After all, I just want her to be happy.

> But, for the very first time, her happiness was at the expense of my own.

And this is a truly awful thing to experience. I have never really gotten over it to be honest. Even now, as I write these

words, I can feel myself getting upset again. It's been years, pull yourself together girl.

I love her, but she used my love as a weapon against me to cause me pain. Not once, but twice.

I can't go through this again. I won't.

So, I am not going. Eve can go on her own and I am sure she will have a great time; indeed, I am going to ask all our friends to make sure she does. If I was there, she would abandon me again I am certain. So, I may as well have a lovely time, here at home, instead of a really painful time, on a so-called holiday. It's very much the lesser of two evils.

But I *am* going to miss her...

Tuesday, September 14th

T-Minus one...

Up as usual, my bathroom routine is exactly that, routine – not much worth writing about, other than I am keeping my legs, underarms and chest shaved – it's a routine maintenance thing now, the novelty has worn off. But freshly shaved legs in nylons, or a skirt is just a magical feeling. And no one likes stubble on their boobs. I am still getting a bit of a shaving rash, but it is worth it. I have to say, my shaved legs look amazing in a skirt. I can't tell you how much I adore looking down at myself, seeing them in a skirt and appreciating a completely feminine view, a view of me. It just never gets old, and it looks *right* on every level.

I was in work an hour early, both my brother and colleague were still off today, my brother still has a bad tummy, and my colleague hasn't fully shaken his migraine yet. I hope they get well soon. On a more selfish note, I had to do the daily Teams update – it was OK, but it got in the way of me doing some actual work. Still, a productive day never-the-less.

Back home on time, I had a nice evening with Eve. We swapped the cars over as she is leaving early tomorrow, and she continued packing before a bath and an early night. We said our goodbyes and I wished her a safe and amazing trip this evening, the hug was particularly lovely.

I miss her already...

Wednesday, September 15th

Day 1...

Well, she's gone. I slept through her leaving, so missed it. Probably for the best, it would have only upset me more. I woke up briefly at 5:30am, her car was not on the drive. I am alone.

I am upset this morning. I don't like it.

We should be doing this trip together as a couple. It's our 'special thing', she is going to have an amazing time with our friends – I am going to be alone for a week. I shall spend as much of it as I can in a skirt. Just to feel a little bit better. I am also going to see Kay on Friday; I am planning on going as me again. I will need to take some brave pills and show the world my true face. Note to self: I must remember to wear waterproof mascara this time.

The house is silent, I hate it when it is like this, it's too quiet. An eerie stillness and I am not comfortable. I'm sure I will be OK, but already I am uneasy.

I miss her.

I feel like I have shot myself in the foot. I am missing out on a brilliant trip. But how could I go? How could I go with her and not *be* with her? How could I watch her having a great time without me? To watch from afar, out of the circle, unable to join in on the conversation due to the language barrier? And to know, to <u>know</u> that if I tried to join in, although it would only be a minor inconvenience to my friends, my presence would not be wanted by the woman that I love? She would resent everyone having to speak English for me.

I've been in this position – it is utterly horrid. A miserable experience.

Much better to be alone at home, where I can make myself comfortable and do as I please – sure I am alone, but I would be

equally alone on holiday. Isolated from my love, welcomed by my friends, but in any conversation that we are both participating in, unwelcome by Eve. Her *"language learning experience"* means more to her than I do.

> A week in a skirt is much better than a ruined holiday – QED.

It is now seven am, I am getting up as I have to drop my daily driver off for a service...

There's still shed loads to do in the office, this particular client <u>still</u> hasn't fully bottomed out their two new concept designs. We are onsite in two weeks, and I am getting alterations to power, data, signage, and joinery on almost an hourly basis. With **ninety** drawings (10 drawings per site, 9 sites) to update, more than ever, this is an impossible task and trying to keep pace with it all is taking a huge amount of time. My colleague is back, but he's drowning too – he's trying to get Landlord's approval on seven of the nine sites so has a mountain of correspondence to deal with and drawings that are constantly in flux. It's not a good situation to be in to be honest – unnecessarily very stressful, caused by idiots who set ridiculous deadlines.

I spent a lovely evening dressed fully as myself though. Both to unwind and also to distract myself from my loneliness. I sent Eve a couple of WhatsApp messages during the day to make sure she arrived at Mark's place OK. She did thankfully, and now she is in the very best of hands for the rest of the trip. I am relieved. 600 miles in a 23-year-old car is not to be taken lightly and although we've been thorough with the preparations, due to expense, her car really should have been serviced ahead of her departure – so I was worried.

12½ hours today. I slept well too, although it took me longer than usual to drop off. I spent a little too much time on YouTube when I should have been sleeping.

I had a weird dream though – I lost my cars, one-by-one, making stupid bets with a crime boss over predicted mileage. I've no idea if this means anything, it possibly does, or it is just my brain dumping the day's worries and concerns.

I hope Eve is having a wonderful time – I'm sure she is. I also kinda hope she is missing me, even just a little. I'm on the fence on this, I am hoping I am still important enough to her to miss my company, but equally, I hope she is having such a great time she doesn't get 5 minutes to think about me not being there.

Either way, I miss her...

Thursday, September 16th

Day 2...

Usual routine – tired this morning – I am getting up shortly. My daily driver isn't ready yet, so I brought the company Golf home – I am not sure if I am picking up my nephew this morning, probably not.

The house is very quiet again – I *really* don't like it. But it looks to be a nice, sunny day today – I am grateful for some sunlight – this is hard enough without grey skies too.

It's strange looking out the window and not seeing either mine of Eve's cars on the drive...

Work happened – it was quite a nice day all in, I am drawing up shop fittings and it's quite a creative task, and, dare I say it, a little therapeutic. These will become the backbone of a toolkit to draw up future shops.

Went out for lunch today, found a Greek café and it was very yummy – I will have to return.

Home around 6pm, back in a skirt by half past. 13½ hours today, but I'll do better tomorrow – I have a session with Kay at 11am and I plan on attending as myself.

Bacon and egg rolls for dinner, I also had some cereal later on in front of the TV. I am nearly at the end of season one of my 'Angel' rewatch – it's been good to reacquaint myself with the series again. It's aged quite well all told, only the CRT monitors on desks and the lack of mobile phones date it a bit.

I spent some time tidying the house before bed – a big improvement and I feel good.

Night! xx

Friday, September 17th

Day 3...

9:15am, I have a day off work to see Kay, and later, pick up one of my neighbour's cars from Holborn. I am fully dressed appropriately and feel good about myself. I look like I feel inside and am very comfortable. I have also remembered to wear waterproof mascara this time!

I should be able to hit 20 hours today, I think. I only need to get changed to pick up the car. I am thinking that I could probably do all day tomorrow as well. We shall see... I am also planning to type up some more of Volume 2 today.

Kay was great, but I didn't go as myself in the end. One of my neighbours knocked on my door half an hour before my session and I began to worry about leaving the house. It was so stupid – lots of "What ifs?" and none of them really stacked up. I am so annoyed at myself, but I was rattled, and my plans were compromised. No make-up or jewellery, Adam's jeans, T-shirt, and shoes over my lingerie. It was only a flipping knock on my door! My subsequent look wouldn't pass close inspection, but from afar, I would look like I am expected to, instead of who I am. I was very disappointed and annoyed with myself. These opportunities come up so rarely and I blew it for no good reason. I discussed this with Kay and the more we spoke, the more I realised I had compromised myself for a social construct that was largely all in my head. I am a complete idiot!

We also talked about Eve being away and how much I am missing her. Photos are starting to appear on our friends' social media – these have brought home the feelings of me shooting myself in the foot. It looks (as usual) like it is an epic rally, and I so want to be there with them. But I also **know** that if I were there, I would be miserable. We talked through the reasons why I am sitting opposite her, when I could have been enjoying an

amazing tour – I am confident not going was the right decision. Sure, I am missing out, but I am OK. I am doing what I want to do, as myself, and I am not being rejected or stabbed in the heart by the woman I love. Yes, I have missed out on a fantastic trip, but I wouldn't have been able to enjoy it.

> But I am lonely.
>
>> And I hate it.
>
> Equally, I am Julia.
>
>> And I love it.

Eve gets to spend the week driving around Europe. I get to spend it in a skirt. It's not too bad you know? I'm trying to convince myself I made the right decision…

Home again, 10 minutes after walking through my front door, my neighbour knocked again – I hadn't gotten changed yet, so it was OK. She gave me some cakes for keeping an eye on their house while they were on holiday recently. It was very nice of her, although her timing couldn't have been much worse. But I am glad I didn't surprise her with my appearance after all. She was obviously keeping an eye out for my return, and I think she would have seen me in all my splendour. If only she knew what I was wearing underneath…

But shortly afterwards I was back in a skirt again. I need it today, Kay, as always, brought a lot of emotions to the surface.

I spent a lovely few hours, pottering around the house, but at 4:30pm, I began to disguise myself as Adam once again. I have to jump on a train with one of my other neighbours to pick up two of his cars. He knocked on my door at 5pm and I was ready – we set off to the station, chatting away and generally catching up. It was good, he's good company and we made our way to Stratford, as we walked through Westfield, I pointed out two of the shops we had worked on, and we bought him some Lego – he buys and sells on eBay and wanted to pick up a couple of UK exclusive box sets to hold onto and sell at a higher price in the future. Who would've thought that Lego could be an investment?

Stratford tube, then on to Waterloo, this was the first time I have been on a train since before the pandemic. It was OK. Lots of folks wearing masks still – I didn't feel unsafe or had taken any risks.

We walked to the venue, a theatre under some railway arches. Both of his cars were inside, iconic American vehicles. But the tunnel into the set was astonishingly narrow – he removed the wing mirrors from one car, and it came out first as it was narrower than the other one, a New York yellow cab. Wow! Was it ever a tight fit! Even with cardboard on the walls to protect the car, both wheel arches ended up being scraped a little. It was really stressful!

Wow, that's a tight fit...

I drove the other car back, we stopped for fuel, and again for a late McD's dinner. Driving these cars through London is an experience – they really turn heads! I can see why he likes them so much; they are good fun and very different to drive.

Back home around 11:30pm, I was in my nightie not long after – tired, but a good day all in, I think. I am going to relax tomorrow...

Saturday, September 18th

Day 4...

A nice, and well-earned lie in. Mogs done and showered by 10am, but today, I shaved my legs and re-painted my toes and then, after the shower, I did my make-up. I am going to be female **all day** and it began with a typical female bathroom routine.

I went to town a bit with my make-up, false lashes, and a primer for my eyeshadow. Lip gloss on top of my lipstick – good fun. Pencil skirt, satin blouse, matching lingerie, tights, jewellery, hair, and perfume – a full outfit – I look very nice, and I feel great. Today is going to be a good day, although I am not going to do very much.

More pictures of the rally on social media, but I am in my happy place, so I liked them, and it was great to see Eve so happy. The impact of her being gone was lessened today – it's amazing what a skirt can do!

I binge watched the end of season 1 of 'Angel' and am now 2 episodes into season 2. It's also very good. I had some toast for lunch and both mogs were out all day, so I wasn't disturbed.

Why am I so comfortable like this? After 50 years you would think I have all the answers by now, but I don't. Not even remotely. Everything just feels *"right"* – even though I am too big and not the correct shape, the clothes, the make-up, even the way I smell is spot on – it's a true expression of who I am and as such, it is so relaxing, and I love everything about it. I love being a woman.

And then, at 4:05pm, the phone rang. I didn't recognise the number, so I let it ring off. But they left a message... It was Gridserve asking if I was going to make my appointment to test drive a Polestar. Shit. I thought it was tomorrow! Erm, well, there was no way I was going to make it now. So I rang back and

apologised – it was an honest mistake and I was really looking forward to it. There will be another opportunity in October apparently.

I chilled for the rest of the day. A full 24 hours, not just dressed as a woman, but living as myself. It was lovely. But, like all women I suspect, I was glad to take my heels off at bedtime. Sore feet – the price of beauty I suppose.

Sunday, September 19th

Day 5...

Up around 10am, knickers only this morning, my disguise is needed as I have to go out for a bit. Mogs done, dishwasher stacked and switched on, Kitchen tidied, and the house hoovered, I can leave now. Socket set and battery in the car, first stop – car #3.

It's been 6 months since I started it up, and today was the day. Uncovered, bonnet open, battery connected, turned the key and vrrooom! The V6 sprang into life. No signs of vermin, fluids all good, belts good, the tyres could do with some air though. I should've brought a compressor. Ah well, next time... Also, the engine is making a ticking noise – hydraulic followers on the front bank maybe. Likely because it hasn't been run for such a long time. I will have it looked over when it goes back on the road. I ran the car for 20 minutes or so in the (well ventilated) barn, just to get it up to temperature and circulate all the fluids. I admit, it was very good to hear it running after all this time.

Tesco next, I bought some diet coke and a French stick for lunch. I consumed half and saved the rest for tomorrow.

More 'Angel' episodes. Thunderstorms this afternoon – it really fell down – I'm so glad I didn't do the laundry today – I was going to. I will have to wait until tomorrow. Tara cat shot into the house, she was a little wet, but had the sense to hide under a parked car when the heavens started to open. Larry cat was nowhere to be seen though.

I wrote up some more of Volume 2, wow, there's so much in there – this is taking some time and I'm getting very emotional re-reading it, it really wasn't that long ago... I also watched the rain for a bit.

Larry eventually returned home, completely soaked, poor thing. How cats can lick themselves dry is a mystery to me. But he did. And then I hoovered his mess up...

I ordered Chinese for dinner, just noodles and some char sui. After, I got changed again. Nightie tonight, I didn't go all out. A lazy day, so a lazy outfit.

I watched 'Black Widow' on Blu-Ray in bed – it was just as good as it was in the cinema. I also ordered a new Spectrum game. Hopefully my Spectrum Next will be here before Christmas... you never can tell with a Kickstarter campaign though. I am very much looking forward to re-living some of the very few fonder memories I have from this turbulent time in my youth.

More great photos of the rally on social media. They are having a wonderful time and are currently in the Mosel region.

I miss Eve.

Monday, September 20th

Day 6...

Day off. I am supposed to be on holiday right now, touring around Europe with Eve, but sadly, it hasn't happened. Nothing this year has worked out the way it was supposed to. Or rather, one gigantic thing has fallen apart, and this has fucked up everything else. So, instead of 6 days off work, I have only taken 2, Friday and Monday, today.

The lie in was appreciated, but I am at a loose end today. So, I have made a list, and actually, I have done quite well so far. Only the two big things remain, everything else has been ticked off as complete.

I started with the usual chores. Mogs, litter trays, clean the house and hoover. I then moved onto the laundry – all done, but as it has been a bit of a rainy day, the house now has clothes hanging up all over it. I bought some 'emergency' toilet rolls as we are getting a bit low, and I also visited the bottle bank. I put the bins out and did the same for my neighbour as they are also on holiday this week. Lastly, I wrote up some more of Volume 2. Phew!

Pleased with my work, I made lunch and settled in to watch some TV for a bit.

My new Spectrum game was delivered this afternoon. I have a small collection building up ahead of the new Spectrum Next arriving at some point, hopefully this year. Something to look forward to, although I backed the Kickstarter campaign last year. Still, no one could have predicted a global pandemic and now a chip-shortage in-between.

I kept busy because I am really missing Eve. She has been on my mind a lot today. The house is looking nice, and I am the only one here to appreciate it. She is due back on Thursday – it can't come soon enough.

The official rally ended yesterday, with the participants travelling to their respective homes today. Eve though, is travelling further east to Berlin, in convoy with Steve, Johan and Daphni – she has a couple of days in a hotel there – her favourite city. After which she has a *very* long drive to the Hoek of Holland and then a slow ferry back to Harwich. She'll be shattered, I hope she has her sea legs...

I am really struggling to let her go. I don't want to be possessive, or clingy, but it's plain I still love her – I can't help it. When she goes away on her own, not only do I miss her terribly, but I also feel left out. She has, to a large extent, surgically removed me from her life, and it hurts. We used to do everything together. I really miss those days. I miss the people we once were.

      She doesn't love me.

           The man I was is dead.

                  He had nothing left to live for.

I spent most of the day in disguise. But I am not him. What I wear makes no difference anymore, I am **always** Julia. Just showing my true face or hiding it. And if I am hiding it, just how much effort I put in to maintaining the illusion. Conversely, how much effort I put into my true self is also true.

Today, I hid my face, but put zero effort into it. I wore clothes to work around the house and to visit the bottle bank – That is all.

I was Julia 100% of the time as always, but today, I put my effort into the 'to do list', not my appearance. It made zero difference to who I am, but my nightie was very welcome around 6pm. Putting no effort into my appearance is **not** the same as relaxing as myself. It is a neutral state.

Back to work tomorrow.

      Eve comes home on Thursday.

Tuesday, September 21st

Day 7...

Back to work today, I am listening to the bin men outside and I am thinking about getting up shortly to deal with the mogs. Once the bin is emptied, I will have somewhere to put the cat litter, yuck, not my favourite job. Hopefully the downstairs isn't too wrecked. Tara cat wasn't very well last night, so I contained her on the hard surfaces downstairs overnight, thoroughly earning her distain, just to make whatever clean-up she may have left me easier to deal with. But I need the bin back first, so I am waiting.

I am also a bit out of sorts this morning. Some of it is because I am really missing Eve. I am missing some life in the house and most importantly of all, I am missing someone to talk to. The mogs don't count, although I do wonder if my future sees me turn into a crazy cat lady. I miss her company, even when she is being distant, her smile and just being close to her, even if I am no longer *allowed* to be close to her. Thursday can't come soon enough.

I am also thinking that I should have spent more time as me yesterday. The opportunity was there, but I chose to wear Adam's face for longer than I could have. It was OK, but I am not as relaxed this morning as I would've liked. I feel agitated and uncomfortable in my own skin, more so than usual. It's horrid, dysphoria is making me feel awkward once more. I will make up for it tonight. This is the other reason I am still in bed – I don't want to take my nightie off. But I am going to have to shortly – I need to go to work, so I need to make an effort, and it really feels like an effort today. But before I can leave the house, I am likely to have to clean it. Filthy mogs...

Right, seven forty am, enough procrastination, I am getting up...

Work, one of my colleagues is drowning, more work is coming in, I am helping, but I am drowning too. How the hell are we going to deal with our new client? Another long day. I arrived at work early and stayed late. It's not nice, we are all doing silly hours again.

I was glad to be home – it is looking tidy, or tidier anyway. The mogs haven't destroyed the place during the day for once! Pizza for dinner, changed by 7:30am, so 12 hours in a dress.

I am lonely.

        The house is empty without Eve.

                So is my heart.

Wednesday, September 22nd

Day 8...

Twenty minutes late getting up, I am in a bit of a rush – so a short entry this morning, I am about to go to work.

Important stuff:
- Looks like being a nice day.
- I am going to the Trafford Centre for a pre-start meeting tomorrow, it will be a long day.
- Mogs done.
- House is tidy.
- Eve comes home tomorrow!

Woo!!

Gotta go... Bye!

It was a long workday, but tomorrow will be longer still. I finished my drawing update. We are so busy; everyone is flat out – we need more staff.

On the plus side, I ordered a Mustang Mach-e today. I am not 100% sure I have done the right thing. I've not test driven one, or even seen one for real. But the car is at least a year away, so I needed to put things in place now. I like the car, but I am wondering if I should have gone for a Tesla Model Y like everyone else seems to be doing, the Y just doesn't excite me though. And anyway, since when have I been one to follow the herd? Never, I am unconventional at the best of times, and a LOT more unconventional than most folks will ever know...

Home late, around 6:30pm, mogs and a quick house tidy (the fun just never ends around here!) Nightie, TV and then bed.

Still, I managed 12 hours in a dress today, not sure how. Nice. Tomorrow will not be anywhere near as good.

Up at 5am, I need to be in Manchester for 10 o'clock…

Thursday, September 23rd

Eve comes home!!!!

Five am is a brutal time to get up, I was out of the front door by 5:40. It is still dark. I have a 465-mile round trip today to the Trafford Centre, Manchester for two site meetings. Four hours plus, each way, it is going to be a long day. But Eve comes home this evening – I am so looking forward to seeing her!

Breakfast at Norton Caines services on the M6 Toll. I met up with a colleague here and we continued our journey to the site in convoy.

The first meeting went well, lots to do though. We had an hours' interlude before the second one. The second meeting took three hours and there are a *lot* of design changes to be done with no time at all to complete them. I am visiting a site in Uxbridge tomorrow, so my colleague has had to change his diary to deal with it all. Again, the ramifications of others not doing things at the right time, creating a bottle neck further down the line. A bottle neck that we need to deal with to save their unappreciative arses.

Home at last around 6:30pm, as expected, a long day. Eve was on the ferry, I needed to swap the cars over on the drive as I am out tomorrow, so I waited for her. She arrived around ten past nine safe and sound, but understandably, very tired – we said our hellos – the hug was lovely. I'm sure we'll catch up tomorrow in detail.

I am knackered – my nightie is very welcome – I'm going to sleep now.

Eve, my love, is home!
Yay!

Friday, September 24th

Up at 6:30am, done in the bathroom, I am going to leave shortly for Uxbridge. Tara cat came to see me – super cute! Lots of kitty cuddles this morning. Larry cat is wandering around up here too – I suspect the door at the bottom of the stairs was left open, he sleeps downstairs and Tara sleeps up here – they like their own space.

Larry cat and Tara cat.

Eve is stirring next door – it's so nice to have a little background sound – I hate the house being so deathly silent.

OK, time to get up. The day awaits...

The drive to Uxbridge was OK, traffic was kind. Lots of police vans on the M25 bridges though – a response to the climate change protesters most likely. Also, on the radio news, there's a shortage of tanker delivery drivers and this means less fuel at the filling stations. I need to fill up to get home – hopefully there will be some fuel left when I get to a petrol station later.

The trip today was for a project handover – it went OK. The contractor is not quite done but will be complete by Tuesday. Back in the car, queueing for diesel, but they still had some thankfully, so I was OK.

The M25 was jammed at Potters Bar. An accident going the other way – bloody rubberneckers. I lost 40 minutes. Then a second accident at Junction 8 of the M11, I lost an hour this time. Some days you just can't catch a break…

I headed into the office. Put together some risk assessments for our new client and then sat down to fill in my time sheet – I was only 24 days behind!!! It took ages, I really must do better…

Finally, home around 6pm. Nando's for dinner. Eve wasn't very chatty, post-holiday blues, I think. She looks a bit down. I don't know what to do about it – but I don't like to see her like this.

A little TV afterwards, and then bed. I had a couple of hours fully dressed this evening, swapping into my nightie just after midnight. It was lovely, and very much needed.

Only 10 hours in a skirt today, but I loved every one of them.

Saturday, September 25th

A little lie-in – it is 9am as I write this. I slept in tights and make-up in addition to my usual nightie, undies, and earrings – nice to wake up a bit more girly than usual, plus the weather turned a little overnight – it's chilly this morning – the windows are a bit condensed up and it's misty.

I have some errands to run this morning, I am getting up now...

Errand #1, pick up a parcel from the Post Office. Completed. But more difficult than it should have been due to the queues of traffic at every petrol station between here and there.

Errand #2, drop dad's Will off at my financial advisors. Also successful. I parked up in the town and treated myself to a cheeky Gregg's breakfast.

Errand #3, visit car #3 and pump up the tyres – well, I got there OK, but it wasn't the battery in the car that was the problem, it was the battery in the key fob. I couldn't get the immobiliser to switch off – Mission: Fail. No engine = no compressor. I should've brought the foot pump...

I headed home and arrived around mid-day. Eve was out, I presume at the horses. I popped to Lidl and bought a French stick and some cold meats for lunch.

Eve came home around 2pm, we had a bit of a lazy afternoon – eventually she retired to her room to watch some Andre Rieu (not my favourite) – I watched some more 'Angel' on TV after I put my nightie on.

Eve picked up a small bedside cabinet from a charity shop today – she has moved some more of her clothes out of (our) my room. I am OK with this. I could do with the drawer space to

be honest. It's necessary as my wardrobe is expanding, lots of nice clothes now, very few prison uniforms…

I retired to bed around 10pm, 14 hours in a dress today.

I also emailed 3 months bank statement to the car lease company; I will do the utility bills tomorrow.

I am in bed listening to some dance music. It is coming from outside; someone has a party going on – it's quite loud. I may have to close my windows.

Sunday, September 26th

It's a misty morning so far – it feels like Autumn is almost upon us. September is a strange month, very changeable, unreliable. The last gasp of summer and the beginnings of autumn. I like it, keeps things interesting and autumn is my favourite season – truly spectacular.

It is twenty past nine, Eve is up, watching something in a different language downstairs. I am also up, ready for the day – not that I have anything planned. I may have to buy a new fridge freezer though… Being an adult is no fun sometimes.

I've done quite a lot of 'adulting' today. Eve walked out the front door to go to the horses and there was a waft of bacon – I suspect the party people from last night were BBQ'ing breakfast. So, while she was out, I visited the local supermarket and bought some bacon too and some soft rolls for lunch. I also found some bills with my name on them for the credit check on the Mustang Mach-e – I am now up to date, they have everything they need, I think.

Eve came home – the horses are all good. We had the bacon rolls for lunch and I set about fixing the shelf in my bedroom. Hmm, I need to get used to that, *my* bedroom. After, I replaced the dimmer switch in *her* room. Eve found a frog in the garden – really cute! I think this is the first wild frog I have ever seen. I have seen plenty of toads over the years, they used to be very common where I used to live and at certain times of the year they would be all over the country lanes. But up close and personal with a common frog (I looked it up on Wikipedia) was a treat. I think this one was a young one though – about 50mm nose to tail, er, rump – they can get bigger than this I believe. We caught it in a jar and moved it out of the raised flower bed and into our tiny pond.

I watched some TV while Eve went for an evening walk. And then, I bought a new fridge freezer online from John Lewis. Hopefully our old one will last until the 4th of October when it is due to be delivered. It cost close to £500.00 though – ouch!

We had a curry for dinner and then we both watched a bit more of 'House'- a nice evening. Eve had her usual bath and I got changed – 13 hours in a dress today.

A productive day, being adult wasn't too bad after all!

Monday, September 27th

I don't much care for these dark mornings. I am waking up typically half an hour later than usual – the sun is starting to rise as I am in the bathroom around 6:30am. It's throwing my morning routine out and I am getting less snooze time in bed.

Still, I am back in bed now. Tara cat has been in to see me already. I was clean, but now I am covered in cat fluff once more. It's a good job she is so cute...

I am going into work shortly. A new week is beginning – let's see what it has in store for me...

A quiet day in the office for once. I was home on time, more or less, I had to drop my nephew home, my brother was called into a meeting and, as they had shared a car this morning, I stepped in to drive him home.

Eve was out when I got in, but both of her cars were here, so I assumed she had gone for a walk. Actually, she had walked to Lidl for some stuff for her lunches, but the fridge is on its last legs – I am not convinced it will keep. Seven days until the new one arrives. Fingers crossed the old one lasts this long...

KFC for dinner, TV (House), and then bed. Nice to be dressed properly once more.

Two new blouses arrived today – both fit well. I like them very much. As I said, my wardrobe is expanding, in a very nice way.

Night. xx

Tuesday, September 28th

I don't want to get up. I am really cosy in my nightie. I'm feeling a bit lonely this morning. I realised that Eve has been home for five days and she hasn't told me about her holiday. At first, I thought it was post-holiday blues, but now I am thinking she just doesn't want to share any of it with me. Not even the stories from the event afterwards. I hope not, this is painful for me to consider. I do still think I was right not to go. The lesser of two evils – it was preferable to stay at home and be lonely than go with her, be resented, excluded and miserable. Neither, of course, is as good as going with her and being with her, but I think these days are sadly gone. I do know that they spent the entire time conversing in their own native languages. Me being there would definitely have changed the dynamic.

Anyway, I can't put it off any longer. Time to get up. Sigh. I look forward to being back in my nightie again later.

A busy day again, the 9 projects that I have been working on the drawings for (and <u>still</u> am) are going on site, so we divvied up the site meetings among us. I have Leeds and Trafford Centre to deal with. This means I am going to be out of the office on a weekly basis until November.

On a different subject, everyone in the office except me got fuel yesterday. With so much chaos surrounding fuel shortages currently, folks are having to take the opportunity when it arises, or risk running short. I have just over 200 miles in the tank, so I will need to get some over the weekend, I think. We followed a tanker into Sainsburys (in my brother's car) at lunch, he then put a call into the office and those who were low on fuel joined us in the queue.

I am planning on taking the office Golf to Leeds on Thursday, so I am OK for fuel for the time being.

Home around 6pm, 'two for Tuesdays' so pizza tonight. Eve was better this evening, we chatted more freely, but she is still a little aloof. I missed her so much whilst she was away, but I feel she is, in some ways, still over there.

She also dropped a bit of a bombshell this evening. She wants to go to her mum and dads with her sister this weekend. This is not about seats in cars, she is taking her daily driver. This is about wanting to spend time with her family, and by implication, meaning I am not part of it. As you can imagine, I found this upsetting. But I didn't show it. It's just another step in her cutting me out of her life I suppose...

The oh so familiar sting of her wielding the scalpel on my heart.

I am not sure what to do. I don't want to lose them; I enjoy their company enormously and consider them family. But it is clear she doesn't want me there. Do I just let it happen? Do I fight for them? Is this a lost battle? Do I even have a claim, or a say in this? Sadly, I don't think I do. My prediction that I was going to lose half of my family too a few months back is looking like it was bang on the money. Fuck.

Eve went to her room to watch some foreign TV around 7pm. I was in my nightie by eight. 11 hours today. Once she isolated herself in her room there was little point in maintaining the pretence anymore. This is happening most evenings. Just another example of how she has used her language skills to exclude me from her life. We used to share everything together. Sheesh, I miss those days...

Wednesday, September 29th

Seven thirty, I will get up soon. Eve is awake, but we have not spoken yet. I hate this. I need the common courtesy of a 'good morning', or just some conversation.

I am noticing a progression. Eve, it seems is not enjoying my company anymore and is spending more and more time apart from me. Mostly by taking a bath and then isolating herself in her room. We spend at most three hours together on most days of the week and this is over dinner. Furthermore, we don't really talk in those scant few hours. I try to make conversation, but she doesn't continue on from my opening gambits, just a few words to answer the question and then puts it to bed leaving me floundering, wondering how I can start a new topic.

Last night we chatted for a bit about her (finally!) sorting out the rust on her car, but with this done, she shut the conversation down and then followed it up with "I am going to see my mum and dad over the weekend with my sister and you are not invited". Or words to that effect. She was less direct, but this was the gist, and it came through loud and clear. How do I come back from that? Of course, it hurts. I don't think she cares much to be honest. In both senses of the word. I don't think she cares about me, or my feelings.

How did it all go so wrong?

Shit. I am crying.

It's been weeks, but I am not in a good place today.

I feel like I am living with ghosts. The ghost of who she used to be, and the ghost of who we were together. She is here, but not in any meaningful way. I am lonely *all the time.* Generally, I am OK now, but I still hate it. The woman I love is gone. Replaced by this stranger who delights in torturing me. She is here in body only and even then, only through necessity. She doesn't want to be here – this much is plain. Or rather, she

doesn't want to spend any time with me anymore. Nothing I do or say holds any interest for her. I miss her smile. Her touch. But most of all, I miss her company. When we are together, she is vacant. Detached. Clearly thinking about something else, not present, if you know what I mean. It's horrible. To reach out to her time and again, but not get to her. She isn't reaching back to me, and it is so painful.

I don't know how much longer I can keep doing this. I love her so much. That, fundamentally, is the problem.

> I love her, still.

> > Completely.

But she isn't really here. She doesn't enjoy my company and resents the time we spend together.

> It's astonishingly painful.

> > ...and she doesn't seem to care.

Pull yourself together Julia. Time to go to work.

Well, work was OK. Yet another conference call, but it was productive, it's just too late really. The projects are onsite, all these details should have been resolved weeks ago. Still, the drawings are as complete as they can be, and we are making it work. It's just much harder to achieve. At least we are working as a team and recognise that we are *all* wading through it as best we can.

Home around 6pm, we had a Nando's delivery tonight. Eve is working tomorrow, so has an early start, as do I. She'll be out of the door just as I am getting up at 5:30am, but she only needs to go to Potters Bar. I, however, am driving to Leeds and back.

Tomorrow's entry may well be a little brief consequently, we shall see...

I had a good chat with Eve tonight, she (finally) told me about her holiday. She had a great time, and a very welcome break thankfully. She certainly needed it. I am glad.

I decided to put on a full outfit tonight. Eve drew a bath, I put on a bra to match my knickers. Then added a skirt, blouse (one of my new ones), earrings, make-up, and heels – no hosiery. I want to see my painted toes tonight – my heels are older, but a 'peep-toe' style. I am very comfortable at last. I needed this and am feeling much better.

I will be driving the Golf tomorrow – it's not impressing me to be honest. Scratchy plastics and ill-fitting trim, how the hell has it got such a prestigious reputation? Bizarre, it's brand new!

Anyway, nightie night.

                Early start tomorrow...

Thursday, September 30th

Early rise today, I'm off to the White Rose Centre in Leeds for a site meeting. The first progress meeting here, I am going to be here weekly from now on and next week I have a meeting in the Trafford centre too on the same day. Out of the door at 6am, it's just over three hours to get there, but traffic is always unpredictable, and I like to be a little early onsite. My meeting is at 10:30am

Also, I am in the Golf. It's OK, not great (it's supposed to be, if you believe the reputation), but it's only OK. It also does far too much for you. The lane assist is intrusive and disconcerting. The computer on the cruise control isn't even remotely subtle, to the extent I am wondering if it is putting on the brake lights every other minute, annoying drivers behind. And lastly, the stopping distance it leaves by default is huge. Two to two and a half artic lorries length. Meaning that if you are in traffic overtaking a lorry, there is so much space between you and the car in front, other drivers are constantly undertaking you and nipping into the gap. This of course, slows you down again as the cruise control increases the gap once more. It's incredibly frustrating. On top of this, it keeps scaring the bejesus out of me, flashing up a red "collision alert" for no reason at all.

I also got quite upset in the car. There's lots of stuff going around in my head at the moment, not least of which was reviewing what has happened to me this year. By far the worst year of my life – nothing even remotely comes close. This is what Eve, my beloved, has done to me:

- She's cut me out of her life. This is about an 8 on the (1 to 10) pain scale and continues to hurt.
- She's broken my heart, this was an 11 on the pain scale, but has thankfully diminished to a steady 3 or 4 after time.

- She drove me to the very brink of suicide. Indeed, I went out to do it, I had a plan and frighteningly it felt rational at the time. It has taken me a while to realise and face, just how close I was. I did not come out of this unscathed. Adam went out to kill himself, and by some yardsticks, he was successful. Only Julia came back, hence 'J-Day'.
- She effectively killed the man I was, or at least revealed him to be a total sham. And left me with only the female side of my nature.
- In doing so, she turned me into a woman. I had to acknowledge who I truly am. For the first time in my life, in my mind, I am only one gender. But it is opposite to the gender of my body. But being a girl is great. I like it a lot.
- She stole my dreams and destroyed my future. My life is now on a **very** different trajectory to the one it was on before.
- She put me in therapy. Something I <u>never</u> thought I would do again.

She hurt me, more deeply and profoundly than I ever thought possible. I am still in pain today – it is diminished, but she continues to shut me out, so my pain also continues. She made me miserable, and I am lonely. And it was too much to bear, there have been long-lasting, life-changing consequences to her actions. Lastly, she didn't talk to me about any of it, she sat on this revelation for years and then at my lowest ebb, she dropped an atom bomb on us when it was far too late to salvage our relationship.

> And she did it for no tangible reason.
> We are both in a much worse place now, than before.

She is the one person in the world who was never supposed to hurt me. I would ***never*** have done this to her. It is an enormous betrayal.

Her reasons, such as they are...

- 01   *"I am not the person I once was".*

Well, whoopie-doo, people change. This doesn't justify what she did to me, not even close. It justifies a series of conversations, as it was happening, over time, to discuss it and give an opportunity to fix the relationship, or at least for me to catch up to where she is.

- 02   *"I can't deal with my boyfriend in a skirt".*

Nothing has changed here, yes, it is an unusual situation, but I have been 100% open and honest with her from before we got together. This is **not** my problem, it is hers. Suck it up.

- 03   *"I want to travel".*

So do I!! Let's go together like we used to? What? We can't anymore because you don't want to share your life with me? Well, good luck with that. Now that you are poor as a church mouse.

- 04   *"I am not attracted to you anymore".*

Love is not about attraction, that's lust. It's important, but I didn't shut this particular door, you did Eve. I kept making overtures and you rebuffed them, time and again. Crucially, this **didn't stop me loving you**. This is **<u>NOT</u>** a reason at all.

I think she got bored; I really do. This is the only thing I can think of that justifies her actions. And even then, it's a huge leap

from being bored, to screwing up both of our lives completely and driving me to the brink of suicide.

    She really has fucked up everything.

So, you can see why I was upset on my journey up to Leeds today, with all of this going around in my head.

The site meeting went well. I also popped in to see car #2 on the way back. It should be done in a month or two, I think. Springs are due next week, new front and rear bumpers ordered (the gel coat isn't taking the paint properly in a few places apparently). All in hand, so all is good.

I was home late-afternoon. I typed up my site notes and then settled in for the rest of the day in a skirt. 14 hours today, as you can see, I needed it.

Friday, October 1st

White rabbits, white rabbits, white rabbits...

Day off today, first Katie at 9:30am for session number 6 and then Kay later on.

The session with Katie went well, but it was a bit of a wash out of a day though. I am not sure if the IPL treatment is working – I think pretty much all the darker hairs on my chin are gone, but the blonde or white ones are not really affected by the laser light. I have sessions 7, 8 and 9 already booked up, but I am now sure that electrolysis is going to be necessary to get rid of the rest of it. It can't happen soon enough; I hate it all so much.

Afterwards, I went to see Kay – it was a bit of an emotional visit to be honest. I recapped some old ground – I am left wondering, if Eve is resenting spending time with me, why is she still here? I mean, I want her to stay, I miss her terribly when she is away and I treasure her company, even when she is not being very chatty. But lately, the impression I am getting is that she would rather be elsewhere. So, I am asking myself why she isn't?

As I was a little upset, I decided to treat myself this afternoon – I went to the cinema. Eve made it clear this morning that, as it is Friday, she intended to work, so I went on my own and watched James Bond (No Time To Die). I enjoyed it a lot, although I am a bit puzzled by the ending. "James Bond will return..."?

I was home around 5pm, Eve was in a good mood, and we had a pleasant evening. It is nights like this when I think this will work. It made me second guess my concerns from earlier in the day. But of course, tomorrow, she is going to her parent's place for the weekend – I am not invited. So, I suspect my concerns will return as I spend a (wet) weekend on my own (again).

We shall see...

13 hours today, I was changed around 8pm. Will be more tomorrow; I am very much looking forward to it.

Night. xx

Saturday, October 2nd

Eve left for the horses around 8am, she met up with her sister and then headed for their folks' house shortly after. I said my goodbyes as she walked out the front door and we had a nice hug. And then I was alone.

I work all week to spend the weekend with my true love and she leaves me on my own. How does a girl like me deal with such an upsetting situation? Comfy clothes, TV, takeaway, and a cuddly mog or two. But I was cosy in the house with the heating on and a nice warm blanket. A bit of a cliché I suppose – I even had some ice cream. I watched some more of 'Angel' – I should've watched a 'chick-flick' if I was really going to fit the stereotype. I was lonely and a bit rejected, but not pining – so I didn't go 'full Bridget Jones'. Thankfully. Actually, Bridget Jones' Diary would have been the perfect film to watch. More of the same tomorrow, I guess...

I had to pop out for something for lunch, so Lidl got the benefit of my Adam disguise – but other than this brief interlude, I've been in a skirt most of the day, around 19 hours, I think.

I miss Eve, but I've had a nice, chilled out, comfy day.

I hope she is having a nice time. I'm sure she is.

Sunday, October 3rd

16 hours in a skirt today – it's been really nice. I got up, showered etc, but dressed appropriately this morning and spent the first half of the day comfortably. I had enough food left over from yesterday for lunch, so I didn't need to go out until later. In the end, it was cat food and shampoo that resulted in me being shackled in trousers once more for a bit. It's annoying me that the minutia of daily life is getting in the way of me living as me full time – I need to sort this out.

Shopping done; I began work on emptying the old fridge freezer ahead of the new one's arrival tomorrow. I took the opportunity to throw out a lot of out-of-date items and it felt good to have a bit of a purge. What didn't feel good was taking down all the rally plaques from the outside of the fridge. I was reminded of all the good times Eve and I had had over the years and I was left wondering if we would ever have times like this again? I hope so, but I can't see how sadly. This upset me a lot more than I thought it would. I want the good times back again. I want them so much. I want Eve back... Here we go again... Sheesh, I'm pathetic.

Fridge emptied, drawers outside in the garden, I removed the plug and threaded the cable end out of the adjacent cupboard where the socket is. Hmmm... The new fridge is likely to have a moulded plug. The hole in the cupboard needs to be bigger. Out came my tools.

Eve arrived home around 5pm. She had indeed had a nice time with her folks. I am glad. We then moved the old fridge out into the garden together. Definitely a two-woman job. It's stuff like this where it really pays to live together. I couldn't have done this on my own.

We watched some more 'House' on the TV and had pizza for dinner before Eve retired to the bath and then her bedroom.

I am glad she is home. She appears to be in a good mood, so her weekend went well it seems.

Me? Well, I've had better weekends. But it was OK. Fairly productive, really relaxing, comfortable. But also, lonely, boring, and I am sick to death of the heartache.

I missed her a lot.
> She left me behind.
> > It hurt.
> > > But I am OK.

Monday, October 4th

6 months since 'J-Day'...

Work today, but it is going to be an odd one. We are getting new suits ahead of a charity dinner we have been invited to by one of our clients. Plus, the new fridge freezer arrives between 11am and 1pm, so my day will be broken up a bit. An interesting day beckons.

Because of the above, I was in the office a bit early and managed to get a good head start on the email backlog from the end of last week. A bit of drawing work and then I headed home around 11am for the fridge freezer delivery. They rang while I was enroute, and when I got to the estate there was a John Lewis van parked up, waiting to make the delivery. Eve was home too, and between us we moved our cars around so the van could unload next to the back gate. Soon enough the new fridge freezer was unloaded, and two very professional chaps took the old one away. They unpacked the new one and placed it in the kitchen. I had a quick look at the instruction manual, I am going to have to change the swing on the doors later on today. But first, back to the office and then off out with my brother, nephew, and colleague to get measured for our suits.

We headed to Epping in two cars, my colleague was going home afterwards, but my brother and nephew were going to swing by the office on the way home so they could drop me off to pick up my car.

I confess, I was a little nervous. Unusual underwear shaved legs and painted toes would not be what my colleagues would expect. A little paranoid – fitting rooms of course – Duh! But I was still nervous. The fitting room turned out to be a curtain in the corner of the sales floor, but it sufficed, and my chosen body hair and nail care routine remains something only Eve and I are aware of. Also, I loathe wearing a suit, it feels very much

like I am gilding the bars on my prison cell. I am not invested in it **at all.** And it'll feel worse when I see my female colleagues all dressed up to the nines in their beautiful gowns.

Suits ordered, we headed off, I collected the Golf and then drove it home.

Eve helped me lay the fridge on its back and I proceeded to switch the hinge pins over, so the doors open the other way. Quite a simple job really, I just needed to follow the instructions and be methodical. Eve left me to it while she popped out to get us a KFC for dinner. In the meantime, I finished the doors, stood the fridge upright, plugged it in through the newly widened cable port in the side of the adjacent cupboard and levered it up into its final position. Job done, I will let it settle and switch it on in the morning.

Eve is working tomorrow, so she dyed her hair and then had an early bath. We then both watched 'Silent Witness', me downstairs and her upstairs in her room with her hair wrapped up in a towel, drying off. I would've liked to have watched it with her, but she made herself comfy in her room instead. Oh well, I am not upset, I am used to this kind of anti-social behaviour from her these days – she just wants her own company is all. Plus, she has a bit of a cold coming – I don't want it! I haven't had a cold in months...

Silent Witness was good, but neither of us spotted Eve – she must be in episode 2 (tomorrow). I will watch it, but Eve could be late home. She can catch up on the iPlayer, I'm sure.

I hope she feels a bit better tomorrow. She has done a Covid test tonight, ahead of her workday (it's definitely a cold, it's in her nose, not her throat / lungs), but even so, it's not nice working whilst under the weather. I've no idea what she is doing, but I think I overheard her say it was in Surrey – quite a trek for her EV...

I was in my nightie by 8pm, so 11 hours in a dress today. Not bad.

Nightie night xx

Oh!

Dad and his lady flew to Portugal today for a holiday. But it nearly didn't happen. They made them both take a Covid test before the flight, by the time the (negative) results arrived, they had missed it! They had to re-book a later one (and alter the Passenger Locator Forms). Eventually they took off – what a palaver!

Tuesday, October 5ᵗʰ

Dad's birthday...

It's dad's birthday today, but he is in Portugal on holiday, so it should be good one for him.

Eve and I got up at the same time, she was done and out the front door first – she is working in Surrey today and had an earlier start than me. But I was also out earlier than I should've been – lots to do in the office today. But not before I'd fed the mogs and switched the new fridge freezer on.

In the office early and I worked late again. I have a really long day lined up tomorrow, so in addition to today's workload, I needed to be prepared for tomorrow as well. I also had a message from Eve, she has booked a local hotel for the night. I presume she had a long day ahead of her and felt it best to stay away rather than drive back tired. It's a good call, I'd much rather she was safe.

So, I had an unexpected night alone and spent it in my nightie, curled up on the sofa. I was comfy, although on my own once again.

The new fridge freezer is great and working well – it looks good in the kitchen, and I have re-stocked it and tidied up a little

I'm going to bed now. I am up at 5am for the drive up to Leeds, then, after the site progress meeting, I need to drive across to Manchester for another. Finally, I can drive home – it will be a long day, so I need to sleep now...

Wednesday, October 6th

It'll be a long day today, up at 5am, out the door and on the road to Leeds by 6. It was still dark when I left the house. Oops! I seem to have left the house dressed entirely in women's clothes! Hehe! I have 2 sites to visit today, so I decided I would make the trip as enjoyable as I could. Eve was away, I got up, fed the mogs, used the facilities, dressed myself head to toe in female attire, added some lipstick and jewellery, did my hair, and brought some of Adam's shoes, jeans, and a T-shirt to change into. Then I stepped out into the world in my high heels. Into the car and then off on a three hour plus drive up to Leeds.

It was lovely, I was *very* comfortable, and the miles clicked away as I took a leisurely drive up the A1(M). Ultimately, I found a lay-by just before the M62 and switched into something more socially acceptable, it's funny, lots of folks bring a pre-packed lunch, me? I brought a pre-packed disguise! I then drove the short hop to the first site. Meeting done, it was on to Manchester and the Trafford Centre via a lunch stop. Second meeting completed; it was time for the drive home. I pulled into services at the top of the M6 and used a WC cubicle to put my bra and tights back on under my jeans and T-Shirt. Then back to the car where I switched back into my skirt, blouse, and heels. Earrings, watch, hair let loose and some lipstick, with some false eyelashes, outfit completed, and this is how I drove home. M6, M6 Toll, M6 (again), A14, M11 etc. Really lovely, 4 hours of relaxed driving as the sun set, into the night.

I found a layby a few miles from home for the switch back, I didn't want to surprise Eve, but it was dark, so my neighbours likely wouldn't have seen, I think I could have stayed in these clothes if I wanted to. As it happens, Eve wasn't home yet, so I immediately switched back once I was inside. And this is how I spent my evening.

All in all, a great day. I made the best of 8 hours driving and a long work day. 17 hours in a skirt – bloody brilliant!

Thursday, October 7th

No entry

Friday, October 8th

Well, I've missed a day. In the seven months since I started this journal, this is the first day I have consciously missed. I am not sure if this is good or bad to be honest. But it feels significant. Writing in here just didn't happen yesterday. Some of the reason is that it was just a typical day, there wasn't much to write about, but mainly, because I didn't feel the need to. I suppose not feeling the need to write out all my emotions or try to make sense of my situation is a positive thing?

The other thing that is going on is my daily routine is exactly that, a routine. And so is mundane, and not worth repeating time and again in here. So, unless I am upset, or something happens, there isn't anything new to write about. What is the point of four volumes filled mostly with "I got up, went to work, watched TV and went to bed"? This is pretty much what happened yesterday. There wasn't anything worth recording in a diary. So, I didn't.

Today though, I went to see Kay. The session was after work (I didn't take the day off). It went well, although I was a bit teary at times. I am worried that Eve is putting even more distance between us. We are doing less and less together. It is her choice, but even though I have accepted this intellectually, emotionally it still bloody hurts. But it **is** her choice, maybe that's why it hurts?

Anyway, another good session, I think I am in a much better place than I was six months ago. Kay agrees, so we are going to try fortnightly sessions instead of weekly. Again, another positive step.

As a recap and summary of where I am now, I am still Julia, all the time. But looking though Adam's eyes is less hard work. I don't **have** to get changed as soon as I possibly can, but I do **want** to. This is a fundamental change to where I used to be.

Pretending to be Adam is still exhausting, and I cannot 'be' him anymore as I used to, it feels like an act, like I'm striving to convince people I am someone else. But it is more tolerable now and if I have to be in his shoes for an extended period of time, it takes me longer for the dysphoria to break through and my composure to falter.

Eve and I are "OK". We are not great, and it is nowhere near as good as it used to be, but we are muddling through a pretty awful situation as best we can. And although she is doing more and more without me, we are still friends. However, I am beginning to wonder about this. I am always going to want more from her though, I feel like I am going through a withdrawal, where the drugs I am being forced to give up are her time with me and love itself. I hate it completely, but, as I have said, it is sadly her choice.

Being Julia isn't an issue for me anymore, although I have no idea where this road will ultimately lead me. The fact is, I **<u>adore</u>** being Julia, I like it very much indeed. It's so good to be only one gender, true, it is the opposite gender to my physique, but being physically male and being both male and female inside is much more complex than being male in body and female in mind only. So, that is a huge plus in my book. Sure, it would be great to be all male, or all female, and indeed, being 100% female is very, *very* appealing to me now – I really want it badly. But I think I can live like this. And I think I can live at any of the points between here and full gender reassignment. I don't think I *have* to go all the way, although I desire to a great deal, and it doesn't scare me at all anymore. I long to be fully female, it is drawing me along the path. The imperative to do it all NOW is no longer there though, but this is who I am and should be ultimately. The thing is, in my mind, I am already there and furthermore I am good with this. I am going to continue to make changes, but I am no longer in a hurry, and I am going to enjoy

the journey. I feel like this is a train I could jump off at any time, I don't have to stay on it all the way to the end of the line, I really want to, and I have the one-way ticket in my hand, but if I don't get there, then I hope wherever I end up will be alright.

12 hours today. All is well.

Saturday, October 9th

Well, my optimism from yesterday was dashed right away this morning. Eve said she forgot to tell me, but she is going to spend the day with her sister. So, at the eleventh hour, my weekend with her was ruined. Still, we should have this evening and tomorrow I suppose.

With an unexpected day to myself, I really was at a loose end. I thought about going out, having some fun, but adopted a negative attitude despite my best intentions. "What's the point of having fun if I have no one to share it with?" A completely self-defeating argument, clearly, I was not in the right headspace following Eve's announcement. So, I made myself comfortable and had a lazy day. Effectively being a housewife. Laundry, tidying, hoovering, lunch, mogs, towels, bedding etc. Actually, a nice day after all - it's the simple things I suppose. I think I may have mentioned that I am very strange? Hearing the click of my heels on the floor as I push the hoover around whilst wearing a dress is not something many folks, of either gender, is supposed to enjoy!

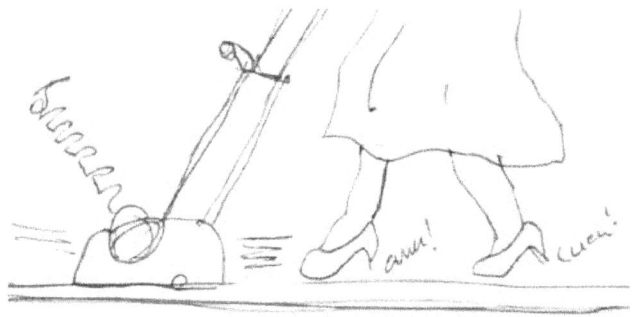

And then, my nice day went a bit sour...

I had a call from dad, literally a couple of minutes after I had placed an order for dinner. He is in Portugal at the moment and was trying to fill in the Passenger Locator Form. But he needed the unique reference numbers from his Day 2 Covid test, and

the boxes were delivered to the village shop in his absence. He asked me to drive there and pick them up, then send him the references. So, I had to get changed ahead of time, much to my annoyance and I also had to wait for my dinner before I could set off (and prevent the mogs from eating it whilst I was out). In the end it worked out OK. Dinner was stored in the oven to keep it warm and out of the fur babies' tummies (ravenous wee beasties!) With the drive to and from the shop completed, tests obtained, references photographed and texted to him and then the boxes posted to him through his letterbox.

My life can get very complicated at the drop of a hat sometimes...

While all this chaos was going on, Eve texted me to say she was going to be late home, so I had the evening to myself too.

Home, a nightie for the evening and then bed. Eve arrived around 10pm, she had had a nice day, so I was happy for her. Me? Well, with 18 hours in a skirt today, despite the errand, it was good all in. I got loads done too.

A good day.

Sunday, October 10th

Rudely awakened by dad at 8:30am. The hotel was still struggling to fill in the Passenger Locator Forms for him. Ok, now I was annoyed. Can I help? Will I fill them in for him? Of course, he's my dad, I love him, and he needs my assistance, but although I was civil and pleasant on the phone to him "no problem, I am on it for you, don't worry" – inside I was not happy. As it happens, 45 minutes later, he called back to say the hotel had done it after all. Phew, I was off the hook. But still not happy – how can he go away, after jumping through all the Covid hoops earlier in the year, and so knowing that there are a lot of additional steps, and still be this ill-prepared? Irritating.

I put it all behind me and had a very pleasant day with Eve. It was much needed (I missed her), and we had a nice time mooching around Chelmsford. A cream tea for lunch and I bought some new trainers. The sun was out, and although not hugely warm, we made the best of some of the last of the summer sunshine.

Home late afternoon, I bought some nibbles for dinner, and we settled into watch 'The Larkins' episode one together. It was really good! Much better than I could've hoped for.

Bed around 11pm, Tara cat is curled up on my bed in a cute little fuzzy cat ball. Only 11 hours today, but a good day never-the-less.

Monday, October 11th

My daily driver goes in this morning to have the driver's seat fixed. So, I am up a little early to be at the garage for 8:30am. I dropped the car off and waited outside to be collected by a colleague – sheez, it's cold this morning! I'm glad I remembered my fleece.

I was in the office by 9:15am and met a new member of staff. She's very nice, personable, and capable it seems. I think she will fit in well. A couple of glitches to sort out on her PC and she was up and running. All in all, a good productive workday, but the car wasn't ready, so I needed a lift home (and I will need one into the office tomorrow morning too). I hope it is done tomorrow; I need it for Wednesday.

Home around 5:45pm, curry for dinner and a couple more episodes of 'House' with Eve – I'm still very impressed by this series – it is great.

Eve had her usual bath and I got changed. I had a full outfit this evening, including one of my new blouses – it's lovely, so much so I ordered another one.

Bed around 10pm, but I didn't slip into my nightie until after midnight – I was enjoying my outfit too much to undress just yet. It was just the mood I was in, I suppose. Make-up stayed on all night, I also slept in a bra, along with my usual knickers and nightie.

Lovely.

13 hours.

Tuesday, October 12th

So nice to wake up in lingerie, a nightie, earrings, and make-up. I feel good and it is a great way to start the day. I am wearing one of my non-underwired bras, so I am comfortable, and my boobs weren't stabbed in the night.

I re-shaved my legs, chest, and underarms in the shower, just maintaining the smooth skin as best as I could. I am now back in bed but have added stockings to complete my underwear. Wearing stockings under a satin skirt on freshly shaved legs is a lovely, feminine feeling. Once of life's true pleasures. I love it so much.

I can't stay like this though, I am being picked up for work in the next half hour, so, as much as I don't want to, I need to get up and switch into my disguise for the day. Time for a bit of a rant first though…

I just can't get excited about my disguise. I have often been accused of being a scruffy sod. If only they knew… I am simply not invested in looking like Adam, his outfit, his appearance, his attitude, his mannerisms, the very skin I am trapped within, they are not, and have never been, *me*. They are the ultimate falsehood. A disguise I am physically locked inside, a cage I have tried to escape from my whole life – a permanent prison sentence. So, when folks call me scruffy, tell me I should dress better, or worst of all, cut my long hair. I am irritated, it's rubbing salt into some very tender wounds. I mean, they wouldn't dream of telling a woman to cut her long hair off? It's **exactly** the same! My hair defines me, it is one of the very few things I have that is actually *me*. And male pattern baldness is now slowly and insidiously robbing me of it. Why would any woman be invested in looking like a man, each and every day, for her entire life? Why would she spend time and money on this false face? Why would she not take offense by crass and ill-informed comments

from people who are ignorant and rude, or worse, really should know better? This kind of thing really pisses me off. Thankfully it doesn't happen too often, but I know what others think of my appearance, and it irritates me that they want to see me locked up even more securely.

Conversely, you can see given the above, why I crave validation as *me* so very, very much. It is incredibly important to me to be recognised for who I truly am. But hardly anyone can see me because I'm locked away in my purgatory. Only Eve has a clear view, and she doesn't care.

Work. It happens...

No Eve tonight, she left shortly after I arrived home – she is having dinner with her sister. Funnily enough, I am doing the same with dad on Thursday. I ordered a takeaway, got changed after and relaxed for the evening. Given my piece above, I was in need of a nice chilled out evening.

An early start again tomorrow, 500-mile roundtrip to Leeds and then Manchester. But 12 hours wearing a skirt today, so I'm feeling better.

Wednesday, October 13th

Out the door at 5:15am – Eve is asleep, and it is dark. So, I left the house in lingerie, stockings, skirt, and heels. I wore a T-Shirt though and brought shoes and jeans with me. From the waist up, other drivers just see Adam. But underneath, and from the waist down I am 100% Julia. I am going to spend as much time in a skirt as I can today – if I am going to do a 15½ hour workday, I am going to spend it as comfortably as I can. Before 'J-Day' I wouldn't have been able to do this, this mashup of genders. Opposite poles, they would have cancelled each other out. But Adam is gone, I am Julia all the time regardless of what I wear. So, although unconventional, I was comfortable, my lower half taking the edge off of my upper half.

The plan worked well, despite the one-hour traffic jam on the A1(M) at J37 (Doncaster). I arrived in Leeds and changed into a veneer of Adam to visit the site. Knickers of course, remain – I haven't worn anything else since March and they are all I own.

First meeting complete, I drove the M62 to Manchester – it's foggy today on the moors, kinda moody. I fuelled up enroute and grabbed a ham baguette for lunch. Diesel is mega-expensive!!! £1.75 a litre – daylight robbery!

I arrived at the Trafford Centre and commenced site visit number two. It was a bit stressful, but the thought of a trip back in a skirt and heels kept my spirits up. I couldn't wait to put them back on again, trousers are just wrong. Practical, but boring and uncomfortable and a constant reminder of my situation. In more ways than one, they just aren't me.

Meeting completed, then onto Lymm Services on the M6 south – I changed in the car, after finding a quiet part of the car park. I drove away but wasn't 100% happy with the way my skirt was sitting around my waist. So, I pulled into the next services (Knutsford) and once more, parked away from everyone else.

Stepping out the door I adjusted the fit of my skirt whilst standing up – all good, much comfier. Back on the road again, next stop: M6 Toll Plaza. I visited a McDs drive through on the A14 for dinner – no one noticed the oddly dressed lady – even during the face-to-face transactions – why would they? They served what they assumed was a man, but they never looked to see the skirt she was wearing! Finally, home around 8:30pm, but not before changing out of my skirt and heels in a lay-by close to home.

I walked in the door carrying a bundle of clothes – nothing obvious and I put them upstairs before saying my hellos to Eve.

It was a bloody long day – I'm shattered.

In my nightie by 9pm, 17½ hours today – tired but happy.

Thursday, October 14th

Well, I didn't sleep properly – not sure why, over-tired maybe? Either way I was still shattered this morning. In the end I texted the office to say I would be a little late in. I just needed another couple of hours in bed. And even then, it was a struggle to get up.

I was in work just before 11am, blimey I've worked enough extra hours recently, they owe me a one-off lie in. Even so, I worked through my lunch and stayed an hour late, so no real time lost.

After work, I headed over to see dad for dinner. He has a new canopy over part of his patio – it looks lovely, he also has a couple of space heaters to go up – it looks like a really nice place to sit regardless of the weather.

Dinner at a local pub – pie and mash, an Eastend favourite – it was very good (yum!)

We chatted about his holiday and the travelling debacle each way. Yes, it was overly complex, and the paperwork is really bad. But he was completely unprepared – sheesh...

Home around 9pm, in my nightie shortly after. 13 hours today.

I've not totted all the hours up, but I've spent close to seven months in mostly women's clothes, and I wear knickers every day. Bloody brilliant. Eve is away this weekend, so I'll be in a skirt all day, or as much as I can anyway – it's going to be great.

Friday, October 15th

The leaves on the tree, just outside my bedroom window, are yellowing. Autumn is definitely here. My favourite season – the autumn colours are so beautiful. But I am not looking forward to sweeping the wet leaves off my car every morning.

It was a bit of a stressful day at work today, four hours of back-to-back Teams meetings getting in the way of doing some actual work, work that I am being chased for. I was very much looking forward to putting a skirt on, so I made it happen as soon as I could when I got home.

Pizza for dinner, Eve and I watched some more episodes of 'House' and chatted a bit. She ran a bath and I, at last, slipped into something much more 'me'.

Full outfit tonight, skirt, blouse, heels, and make-up as well as the usual foundation garments and accessories. And relaaaxxxx...

It's been a long week.

12 hours of bliss...

Saturday, October 16th

I am at a bit of a lose end this weekend, Eve left for her parent's place early and I have a weekend to myself, again. To be honest, I am not liking this very much. I am not motivated to do anything, as I don't have anyone to share it with. It's kinda depressing and I can see this is a trap. I need to be busy or entertained and if I can't be, I need to feel good about myself. So, I am going to do all three today. At least, that's the plan anyway.

Chores first, laundry – work shirts, undies and all the lovely clothes I have worn in the evenings, er eveningwear? Erm, not really, I like to look nice, and I do lean towards formal instead of casual, but full blown 'eveningwear' is not really my thing. At least, I don't own anything this grand, I'd like to, but it's OTT without an event to attend. Anyway, I am more smart business attire, than sparkly ball gowns. All set, laundry all done as comfortably as I can be. I am going to hang them on the airer, so no need to go outside just yet. I tidied the house and hoovered too... A woman's work is never done... Only kidding of course, it'd all need doing regardless of my outfit, and I don't subscribe to the notion of different tasks divided by gender. A chore is a chore, I just chose to be comfortable is all.

Sadly, my levels of comfort were not to last – time to go out. I need to visit car #3 and remove some of the interior trim – it's going to take a while, so I shall split this task up over the two days. I spent a productive couple of hours, but in the end, I needed some tools to finish that I had forgotten to bring. I really need all my cars at home, so this kind of thing doesn't happen. The remainder of the work will happen tomorrow.

Home, via the supermarket for a bite to eat for lunch. Then, back into a skirt for the remainder of the day. I re-watched the 80's movie 'Fletch' and then the sequel, 'Fletch Lives' on DVD

into the evening – a very pleasant day in the end, circa 20 hours too – nice.

  Busy   - Check.
  Entertained   - Check.
  Felt good about myself - Check.

  Mission accomplished.

Sunday, October 17th

A little lie-in, the mogs got me up eventually. I am going to head back to the car and finish off today, then a bit more laundry (it never ends, two wardrobes to maintain...) and relaxation with a film before Eve comes home.

Correct tools in the car, I headed off around 11am. I managed to finish the work, but in the process, I got a sticky residue on my jeans and fleece – one of the jobs was to remove the headlining from the car as it was sagging, it turns out it's because the foam backing after all these years had perished into a fine, orange, sticky powder – yuck. I will need to pop them in the wash when I get home. All the trim out of one car and loaded up into the other, it was time for a trip to Southend to drop them off at a mate's place – he is organising a trimmer to restore the items back to their former glory. The journey took ages – they had closed the A12 entrance slip at Boreham, so I sat in a traffic jam with fellow confused drivers as we gridlocked Chelmsford heading for one of the other A12 entrances – it was utter chaos. Not impressed at all.

Parts dropped off and a McD's lunch on the way back. I was home around 3pm and in a dress shortly after. 'A Good Day to Die Hard' in the DVD player – it was OK, but not a patch on the original. John McClaine is supposed to be an everyman type character, not some super-human, indestructible hero. He's meant to be the wrong man, in the wrong place, a random chaotic factor that screws up the baddies meticulous plans. The spectacle vastly outweighed the minimal plot, so not a brilliant film and I lost interest around two thirds of the way through. Maybe I should've put a chick-flick on? I've not seen Steel Magnolias in ages and Miss Congeniality 1 and 2 are always good fun. Blimey, I really have changed...

Speaking of changed, an Amazon delivery was due, so I slipped back into jeans (clean ones, the others were in the wash), and this is how I was when Eve walked in.

We said our hellos, she had had a good weekend with her folks and was quite chatty. I told her about the success I had had with the trim removal and after I'd picked up a KFC for dinner, we settled in to watch episode 2 of 'The Larkins' – what a great show. Very entertaining.

In bed by 9:30pm, so around 16 hours today I reckon.

I kept busy, so not too lonely this weekend. It's been OK.

My legs are a bit scratchy though, note to self: shave them in the morning.

Night xx.

Monday, October 18th

A new week, Eve is working today (Covid test in Reading, of all places – what blooming long way to go for a test). So, I will be in work early again – it's going to be a long day, lots to do, Teams meeting too, on top of it all. I need to set up a potential new employee to survey and draw the office (a typical exercise for a new person to demonstrate their skills). But before all that, I still have 20 more minutes in my nightie before I need to get up, it's very welcome this morning.

The day panned out pretty much as expected. The candidate turned in probably the best survey of the office I have seen from a job interview. We do this test a lot, and her drawing rivals something I would do myself. It was very impressive.

Home around 6pm and I just beat Eve through the front door, but we then had to swap the cars around so I can go to work tomorrow first – flipping tandem driveway.

Nando's for dinner, and then we watched 'The Movies that made us – Robocop' together – we both love this film and found the documentary very entertaining.

I've been a little sad today about my situation with Eve, she's been on my mind a lot. Likely because I hardly saw her at the weekend, I suspect. I missed her, especially as it was the second weekend in a row. So, it was gratifying she was in a chatty mood tonight and we had a nice time before she retired for her usual bath. My usual routine followed suit, so around 11 hours today.

Tuesday, October 19th

No entry.

Wednesday, October 20th

Up, super early, I need to be in Manchester for 10:30am. So, I was up at 5am and bag packed for an overnight stay. Dressed in my half and half disguise, T-Shirt, lingerie, stockings, heels, and a skirt, then out the door for the long drive.

It was a miserable day, very heavy rain pretty much the whole way, but I was in no rush and was very comfortable driving steadily in my skirt.

I changed into something more acceptable in Keele services on the M6 north, and then completed my journey. The site meeting took some time but went well. I left just after midday and then drove to Wakefield for a meeting to take a brief and survey an existing industrial building. Thankfully there was a break in the weather for the couple of hours I was there.

Finally, off to a Travel Lodge in Leeds. A quick shower and then, at last, I could relax. I was tired, and I confess, that once I was changed, I lay on the bed and the next thing I knew it was 7pm – no dinner, too sleepy and unwilling to get changed again.

I watched some TV, I felt a bit lonely, and I wondered if I should message or call Eve, but didn't do so in the end and eventually, I slipped into my nightie and drifted off to a very welcome sleep.

280 miles driven.

2 sites visited.

16½ hours in a skirt.

A pretty successful day.

Thursday, October 21st

Handover of the project in Leeds today, after a remarkably restrained hotel breakfast, I headed to the site for 9am. It was full on in there! Contractors dealing with snags, retailers and VM people stocking up, and IT sorting out the tills. It's quite a small site, but there must have been a good 25 people in there, all beavering away.

I like handover day. It's totally chaotic, with the Contractor running around trying to finish off the last little bits and pieces whilst also making running repairs due to the staff and merchandisers bashing up the walls and door frames with all the new stock and packaging. I really feel for them, they put so much effort into the build over a very short space of time, only for it to be damaged before the first customers even walk through the door. And then you have me wandering around, picking up on the smallest of details for the snag list – it must be demoralising for them. Still, we are all there to do a job and the shop will never look as good as it does at handover again. Amidst the chaos, I like to try to find a brief moment to look around and think "I did this". Of course, it is always a huge team effort, but I am an essential part of this team. From pre-acquisition survey, through scheme design, sign off, approvals and working drawings. Tender action and project management right up to, and including, snagging and handover. We put a great deal into each project and the day of handover is when it all comes together. Retail is a transitory thing, each shop fit has a finite lifespan and in my professional capacity, nothing I do has any long-term meaning or impact. The results of my professional life are temporary at best – theatre, to display product and draw people in so our clients can make sales. A pleasant place to shop and it is all done at break-neck speed to get the tills ringing as fast as humanly possible. High pressure, but rewarding, especially at handover.

I liaised with Centre Management and resolved RD stage 4 (Consent to Trade) with them, snagging was already done, so my role became trouble shooting and PR mainly as two of the three-person client team were there. The signage company had let us down the night before, so I was involved in rectifications, working out what needed to be done and helping to organise the signage companies' return. Everyone else worked their socks off to hit their respective deadlines, so the signage company not doing the same was unacceptable.

I hit the road around 4pm and stopped at Greggs for a ham salad roll and some OJ, plus a diet coke for the journey home. I also picked up a doughnut as my energy levels were pretty low.

I slipped into my skirt just outside Leeds and drove home, into the night, arriving safely around seven o'clock. I flaked out on the sofa.

I'm really looking forward to a day off tomorrow.

260 miles.

Handover completed.

11 hours wearing a skirt.

It's good to be home... Zzzzz...

Friday, October 22nd

Eve was up early; this was the first I knew she was working today. I had a little lie-in, but I have things to do. Starting with Kay at 11am.

This was my first session in a fortnight, and it was quite emotional. I confess, I have found the two-week interval more difficult than I was expecting. I thought I was ready, and I still think I am, but it was harder than I thought it would be and my emotions were a bit pent up, so they all came flooding out today.

I began to realise just how little I have seen of Eve since my last session. And when we do spend time together, she is distant and there typically isn't much conversation. What chat there is, is nice though, and I am grateful for it, but equally, there are things we should discuss, but because these times are sporadic, I don't want to spoil the brief times we have, so I haven't rocked the boat.

We are living more and more like house mates. This is OK, it's not what I want of course, and I miss her company dreadfully, but even when we are together, we are not *together*. And, yes, this is still painful. I wish it wasn't, but even after all this time, it still is. The most painful thing she does though is when she chooses to spend her time without me, and this is happening so much now, it is by far the norm. I absolutely hate it.

When she crushed the man I once was, seven months ago now, wow. She introduced a ticking clock to our time left together. This makes every moment we have left astonishingly precious to me and therefore, her choosing to spend more and more time apart cuts me to the core. It is more painful than I can describe. It's like a stabbing emotional pain and it throws a blanket over anything good that happens – I have no motivation to do stuff other than feel comfortable. Why would I want to do

anything fun if I have no one to share it with? What is the point? So, I have all these things I'd like to do, but I likely won't do any of them without her. My life is dull and uninteresting now, so I 'self-medicate' by making myself look pretty and spend hours and hours just relaxing. Trying to feel as good about myself as I can. This is not a good way to spend my life. But Eve was my reason to live, without her, I simply exist. Nothing more. This categorically, *cannot* continue.

God, I miss her.

We had so very many wonderful times together. Life was so good; our love was unstoppable and the whole world was both wonderful and brimming with possibilities.

Now, I have nothing. Eve is still here, and I am so grateful that she is. But equally, she's not here at all, at least not in any meaningful way. We are not connecting on any level that means anything anymore. I hate it, we have both lost so much and I truly detest feeling like a victim.

I keep reviewing our relationship in my head. Sure, I made some mistakes, everyone does. But I don't think I did **anything** wrong, at least, nothing that couldn't have been fixed. I gave it my all and threw my entire self into being what she wanted. And in the process, I think I lost who I am. I became literally, *'Eve's boyfriend'*. Nothing more, this was who I was. And when she took that away, I had nothing left. I had given it all away to her and she hadn't given anything back to me in return.

I am 50 years old. I was 35 when we got together. Eve categorically doesn't want kids; I am ambivalent on the subject. If it had happened, I would have loved being a father, I am sure, but I chose not to have children so I could be with Eve. I found my true love and sacrificed this possibility to be with her.

Now, 15 years later, she has ended our relationship. I still love her completely, but I realise that I have lost my chance to

be a father. If I have a child now, I will be 68 years old by the time they are 18. So, it's not going to happen. And this sacrifice would have been worth it if we were still together. But we are not. I want to be, but she doesn't. So, I am not going to be a dad; I gave this up for Eve. And I don't have her anymore, so this was a sacrifice that was far too much, given the outcome of our relationship. She asked this of me, and I gave it willingly, only for her to pull the rug out from under me. The curse of hindsight I suppose. It felt like the right decision at the time...

And now, I am not a man at all anymore. My chance to be a father has gone, not just due to age, but also due to gender. I would love to be a mum, but biologically, this is just not possible. And someone approaching their older years is not a good adoption prospect – an elderly, single parent with gender issues? Yeah, that's never going to happen...

Eve and I need to talk. But I don't want to ruin the few good moments we may have left. I don't know how many of them remain...

As I said, my session with Kay was emotional.

From here, traffic jam on the A120 notwithstanding, I headed off to see Katie and I am thinking that after session number 9 (this is session 7), I will likely need electrolysis to get rid of the rest of my beard. But I have asked her to move onto my torso – and this is going to be expensive, there is a **lot** of acreage to cover, but even a small reduction will be worth it. I hate my body hair. I have always disliked it, but now it not only reminds me of the man I no longer am, but it also ruins every outfit. It's an insidious thing, a sickening and pernicious reminder that my body hates me. Well, the feeling's mutual.

Home, and after a Teams meeting, I got changed. Eve came home around 7:30 and pretty much went straight for a bath, followed by her shutting herself in her room with a foreign language TV show.

I retired around 8:30pm, I'm not really tired, just bored, and lonely.

It's been a day...

Saturday, October 23rd

I wrote in this journal up to 9am, a bit of a catch up for yesterday. I am not sure what I/we are doing this weekend, but Eve has had a bit of a lie-in this morning, so I am surmising that she is not planning on visiting her folks (without me) this weekend. At last!

It looks like a reasonable day out there too, dry, a bit overcast, but it is not raining. Let's see what it has in store, shall we?

The day started off OK, Eve looks tired though, under-the-weather, this is very disappointing. I've not really spent any time with her in ages. We get together in the evenings, have dinner, and watch a little TV. But conversation is light and, I guess, the word is stilted. I keep broaching subjects, or asking questions and she gives one-word answers or loses herself in her laptop. So, when she chooses to spend the whole weekend at her parents' place without me, the time I was expecting to spend with her is taken away from me. I look forward to our time together, it is the only thing I have left of what used to be "us". It is what gets me through the week and enables me to give her time in the evenings when she is tired. I am not even getting changed so early, just to make whatever time we have together as pleasant for her as it can be. I also don't want to upset the apple cart – the time we have left is astonishingly precious to me, I don't want to ruin even a second of it. This is why I haven't spoken directly to her yet. But I think it must happen.

Anyway, I was really looking forward to this weekend. She has spent the past two weekends away from me at her parent's place – she made it clear; she didn't want me there too. I found this **very** hard to deal with. So, this weekend, finally, I get to see my love.

But.

She wasn't really here.

We went out for a cream tea lunch; she brought a magazine with her and read it at the table instead of talking with me. I might as well have not been there. It was astonishingly rude. When we came home, she went straight to her room – and that was it. She is working tomorrow, so my entire weekend consisted of an unwell Eve ignoring me over lunch and then shutting herself away in her room.

I went to bed early, around 8 o'clock, feeling very upset.

What a horrible day.

Sunday, October 24th

I didn't sleep well.

I spent an hour or so around 6am crying. This hasn't happened in months. I feel like this is a huge set back. I was doing so well, but Eve continues to withdraw from me. It's gone beyond "not being a couple" – I get the impression more and more that she actively resents the time we spend together. She would rather be anywhere other than in my company. This is the most painful thing yet. The woman I love can't stand to spend any time with me.

It is not overwhelming, like her breaking my heart, but it is a stabbing pain – it hits me hard and sharply but fades quickly. Until her actions / behaviour reminds me all over again. It's a repeating cycle of pain. She is doing this a **LOT**.

It's one thing that my soul mate doesn't love me anymore, but my best friend not valuing my company is absolutely awful.

> If this is true, then I can't see us being able to stay together.
>
> Why the hell is she still living here?

We are supposed to be friends – where is the friendship?

I sat on the end of the bed, upset, and watching Eve busy herself ready to go to work. In the end, she asked what I was doing. That's something, I suppose. At least she noticed me. In tears, I said we need to talk, not now, but we do. And then she left.

I think I just ruined her day. I feel terrible.

So, I got changed, fully expecting to spend yet another day doing very little other than trying to feel a little better about myself. But this didn't happen either.

A message from one of our neighbours – can I pop over to help him with is cat? The cat had lost some fur but wouldn't

sit still long enough for him to see if it needed a vet. A friend in need.

I got changed into something less comfortable / comforting and wandered over to his house. The cat had indeed lost a line of fur – it's probably tender, but no blood – at least, we didn't find any. We had a good chat and afterwards I went back home where I booked a (single) ticket to the cinema.

I watched the new 'Dune' movie – wow, blooming brilliant (although the sound was almost painfully loud). I lost myself for a couple of hours in an epic sci-fi fantasy. It was really good and just what I needed. But it would've been better if Eve had been with me though.

> **What is the point in doing stuff if I don't have anyone to share it with?**

This is sadly, the truth of my life at the moment. I am not motivated to do anything for myself – every time I do something good, I am struck by the thought that "Eve would've liked this." It takes a big effort on my part to actually do something, anything, as I know that no matter how good it is, it would have been better with her. It's a vicious circle, one I **have** to break.

Home again after the cinema, I waited around for an Amazon parcel, then slipped into my nightie, and watched "Dr Becky" on YouTube for a bit. She's great.

I messaged Eve around 8:30pm with an apology and to say we do need to talk at some point this week. She messaged back to say she had just finished, so I wished her a safe journey back.

And that was my day, a bit of a roller-coaster in the end.

I miss Eve.

Even when she is here, she isn't really here.

I miss her so much.

Monday, October 25th

Not a good day today, or at least, I've had better ones. Eve is on my mind a lot. So, I decided to try to try to lose myself in work. Up early, in the office before anyone else and I left for home late too.

Eve though, she is genuinely ill. She has put a brave face on it but has flu-like symptoms. She is tested for Covid all the time for work, so we know it isn't this, plus she is sneezing too, not just a cough and she is having hot and cold flushes as well. She has had it for over a week it seems and has been managing her symptoms with pills. I was thinking she was being distant, but all the while, she has been feeling rough. It's no wonder she has been stand-off-ish.

In the past, I would have caught this straight away (in both senses of the word). But she has put so much distance between us, and I am totally self-absorbed as a consequence. I jumped to the wrong conclusion, and now, I don't know what I can do to help her. She doesn't want me to. I think she is trying to prove a point. Self-reliance and all that. Stupid. Without permission, there is little I can do, and I hate seeing her under the weather.

I've said it before, and I'll likely keep on banging this same drum. We are both worse off.

An early night for us both, I am comfy in my nightie again.

11 hours.

Tuesday, October 26th

- Eve is still not well.
- Pretty standard day.
- Early night, I have a long day tomorrow.

12 hours.

Wednesday, October 27th

Out the door at 5:30am, for the drive up to Manchester. I wasn't *'feeling it'* this morning, so I am in Adam's disguise, and I haven't brought anything nice to wear, other than my usual everyday knickers. It's a bit of an experiment – let's see what the day brings and how I feel at the end...

...Very tired!

It turned out to be a **very** long day. 515 miles driven, I arrived back home and walked in through the front door circa 8:30pm.

And my experiment? Well, it turned out to be OK. Yes, I missed all that time in a skirt, and although I was kicking myself a little, I really wanted to be in one, but I don't feel like I **needed** it. Wearing a skirt for this length of time feels like an opportunity rather than a necessity. As I said, I *wanted* to wear a skirt and so, I missed it. But it wasn't *necessary*, it would have been a treat.

So, I'll most likely wear a skirt on my travels again, often even. But if it doesn't happen every time, it's not a problem.

This has got to be a good thing.

Eve is still ill.

I miss her company.

Thursday, October 28th

Not much to report. I woke up, work happened, came home, Eve is not well, didn't see much of her, watched some TV and then went to bed. 11½ hours.

Night!

Friday, October 29th

Usual stuff happened. The tree outside my bedroom window is starting to lose its leaves – it looks spectacular, all yellow, especially when lit up by the streetlight. But my car is covered in leaves every morning. I'm going to have to wash it soon, I don't like a filthy car.

Life is boring...

I am in a bit of a rut and have no motivation to get out of it. There is no point in... No, I'm not going to say it again. Besides, she would rather do stuff on her own – this is where I need to be. Having no impetus to do anything other than make myself comfortable is not a good way to live.

This **HAS** to change.

But I don't know how?

It's a vicious circle and no mistake. I need to make the effort to do something, anything, but have zero motivation to do it.

I am going to work on this, but not this weekend. I have a meeting with my financial advisors on Saturday and Eve is working on Sunday.

12½ hours.

Saturday, October 30th

Eve went to the horses and then took herself off to Chelmsford. I did my laundry (oh! My life is sooo exciting! Not). And then headed over to see my financial advisors.

It was a good meeting (at last!) I was there for a couple of hours all in. I signed some documents, my pensions are now combined and invested more wisely. Good. Also, dad's Will checks out, they have looked it over and it seems like I don't need to do anything, at least not in the immediate future at any rate.

I spent the day comfortably, watching TV. It hammered it down with rain overnight and into the morning. Halloween tomorrow and lots of folks have decorated their houses. We haven't, but it is fun seeing what others have done. I hope it isn't a wash-out for the kiddies…

Sunday, October 31st

All hallows eve...

Eve went to work, most likely her last day on 'Holby City'. The long-running show has been cancelled. It's such a shame, all those people out of a regular job. I know Eve will miss it.

Me? Well, torrential rain and no Eve = dress comfortably and chill out for Julia. So, I did!

I spoiled the cats, had a light lunch, Star Wars Episodes II and III – it was a pleasant, if totally unproductive day.

Eve was home around 7pm, she went straight for a bath and then watched the telly in her room.

I've hardly seen her at all this weekend.

But at least she seems to be on the mend at last.

Monday, November 1st

White Rabbits, ahh – you know the drill!

Usual Monday stuff, work mainly. Not much to report really. I am unsure about this journal though. Who am I writing it for? I started it because I had so much grief going around in my head it was too much to contain. So, it spilled out, warts and all, into these pages. A literal stream of consciousness on occasions and it was astonishingly good for me – to just brain dump all the poison and all the emotional highs and lows. The act of writing it all down made me put it all into some semblance of a rational order. Piece-by-piece I began to deal with an overwhelming tide of change and sadness. I've said it before, but these words and pages literally saved my life. And this journal, along with Kay, allowed me to put some of the shattered pieces of my life back together again. The jigsaw of who I am is smaller, and still doesn't fit together as well as it did. There are a lot of damaged pieces left over that, like me, are broken. I am substantially less than I was. But what I have left, the pieces that remain, are incomplete - there is room for *so much more*. So, after going on eight months now, I see that despite everything – there is still hope for me. I am on a new path, the road is rocky and full of hazards, the view isn't as good, and I have no idea where it leads. But at least I am on a path and at least I am still moving. Away, in the distance, is another path. I can see it, Eve is on it but it is paralleling mine, it doesn't intersect. She pushed me off her path, into the deep chasm that lies between them. The fall did a lot of damage, but thankfully, I managed to climb out of it. The only problem is, I am on the other side. On a different path to Eve. I want so badly to join her, I keep calling across the chasm, but she doesn't hear me most of the time, or doesn't want to hear...

This path is my own. Eve, through her own choices, now has a path to walk alone too. I miss her company; it is an arduous walk at times, and it was a lot easier when we could help each

other along. God, I miss those days. Our shared path was wide, and the views were spectacular. We worked as a team and overcame all the bumps in the road together. We confidently strode towards the horizon, safe in the knowledge that we had each other's backs and that whatever lay ahead, we would face it with our combined strength.

Why did she push me off the path into the chasm?

I still don't really know. Why would anyone do that to their teammate?

The hope of something better? How is this more achievable without the help of your partner?

I just don't understand how anyone could turn on their partner, crush their heart and push them screaming into the chasm below?

I mean, what kind of person does this? Who chooses to throw away a willing and loyal partner, one who loves them beyond measure and only wants to make their lives better and happier? One who would've done anything to help them along life's journey and was 100% supportive of everything she wanted to do?

Who does this? This random act of sabotage, not just to me, but to herself to?

There is no logic here.

We are both stumbling along on separate rocky paths and don't have each other to help anymore.

We are both in a worse place.

And for no reason at all.

So, I wrote. I wrote it *all* down. It was all I could do – the hurt and the sadness were weighing me down, keeping me in the chasm, I needed to jettison the load, so I dropped it all in here. If it wasn't for these pages, I would still be down there in

the chasm, broken and hurting, or worse. My path is narrow and dangerous, I feel in real danger that I could fall back into the chasm, so I keep on writing. I have to be nimble and sure-footed to carry on. So, I travel light, discarding my burdens into this diary to keep me focused on the path ahead.

I look across the chasm and see Eve, my love, struggling too. But I can't reach her anymore to help. She doesn't want me to. I want to re-join her. I want to help her stride confidently forward as we used to – we were much stronger together, more so than our separate parts. She gave me purpose and our future together was worth the effort to get there.

I keep trying to build a bridge to her, but she keeps tearing my work down.

I have no idea now what my future holds. I had a loose plan, before. The plan revolved around working together to make the best possible future for each other. But now, my future is for me. But I am not accustomed to being selfish, and the journey to get there is much harder.

So, I travel light, and I jettison excess baggage. But I have lost my purpose, so all I see, is the struggle of the path, right in front of me - I am completely focused on not falling back into the chasm. I can't see the vista, the horizon. I can't appreciate the view, the sunshine, or the flowers and the trees. I am looking at the trip hazards in front of my feet and having seen what is down there, the threat of the chasm is all consuming. I can't fall back in; I mustn't it'll kill me...

And I miss my love. My teammate, my partner.

Life is a journey.

My journey is much harder than it was, and it looks to be a lonely one.

But I am still moving. And I am still writing.

At least, for now...

Tuesday, November 2nd

Not much to write about today, epic piece yesterday. Eve is feeling a little better today, it seems, but she was working yesterday and then stayed overnight at her sister's place – it is local to the set. I've not seen her and although she is back home tonight, I have my usual Wednesday trip to Manchester coming up, so I'll likely be in bed – an early night to help with the following early morning.

This is probably why I wrote what I did yesterday – I had a lot on my mind, and I am lonely. Plus, the monthly 'J-Day' anniversary is looming again.

I have spent a lot of time comfortably though – 15 hours today and 14 hours yesterday. I am planning on bringing my stockings, skirt, and heels with me tomorrow – I am going to drive in them, just as any other woman might.

Wednesday, November 3rd

Up early, out the front door by 6am, on the road north-west to Manchester. Eve arrived back yesterday evening and we chatted a little. She is on the mend at last and seemed in better spirits than recently. I hope it lasts. But I had to retire early as today is going to be another long one.

The journey to Manchester was good, although I didn't put my skirt on – I was a couple of minutes late out of the front door and this, combined with the slow north bound traffic on the M11 just beyond Junction 8 meant I didn't want to lose any time. Annoyingly, I arrived with time to spare, so I could've spent the journey more comfortably attired if I had known.

The site meeting today took a while, I hit the road back towards home around 3pm. No messing around this time – Knutsford services – stockings, skirt, and heels on – 4½ hours driving in a skirt – I turned a chore into a pleasant experience.

Home around 7:30 – I stopped in a local lay-by to change back – no idea why – Eve likely wouldn't care, and I was back in a skirt a short while after. It was dark already, so I could've walked the short distance between the car and the front door unobserved, I think. It just felt like the right thing to do.

We said our hellos – she was not interested in my day, as usual. So, conversation was brief. Eve had a bath, I got changed (fully) and we both had a relaxing, if separate, evening.

14 hours.

Thursday, November 4th

8 months

I've nothing to say. This is not an anniversary I should be commemorating. So, I won't.

Friday, November 5th

Day off today, I have a session with Kay at 11am, but despite my day off, I also have a Teams call an hour beforehand. New client, a 'put faces to names' kind of thing. Important, but also nice, not onerous. So, I was up at the usual time, I visited the cash point for Kay's money and then spent some time setting up a phone mount in the car and getting some paperwork in order, for the meeting. I was well prepared, and so the meeting went equally well.

I knocked on Kay's door at 11am, and the session began...

THE END

?

Tuesday, October 4th 2022

A conclusion, of sorts...

I've not written in here for a **very** long time. Not because things have changed much, but because they haven't really. What has changed, is my need to write it all out. This is an astonishingly good thing, at least for me, maybe not so much for you, dear reader. Additionally, a couple of months after the last entry, I brought my sessions with Kay to an end. Also a good thing, I was over the worst.

My situation remains the same, Eve and I still share the house, but I don't see her much. She spends nearly every evening in her room and most weekends away, typically at her mum and dad's house. Me? Well, car #2 is back, and I have done a few car shows through the summer. Baby steps you know? The big problem remains for me, I just don't want to do anything on my own. And as Eve doesn't want to spend any time with me, I can't do anything. Q.E.D.

I have not had a holiday this year, and I am not expecting to. I've no one to share it with, so it is pointless.

I don't go to any of the local car meets anymore, again, with no one to share it, there is no point.

I am not expecting to drive car #1 again. This car's purpose is EU touring with Eve. As much as this car is an integral part of my life, it will always be associated with Eve. Just thinking about it breaks my heart all over again. I can't bear to look at the empty passenger seat. That part of my life, I think, is in all likelihood, over.

Car #2 though is my own and carries far fewer associations with Eve, especially after all the recent works on it. I have been visiting shows that are not associated with my old haunts or clubs – this has, for the most part, been OK. But of course, the old adage is still true, they would have been much more

enjoyable with Eve's company. However, this is a thing for *me*, I can do this on my own.

Eve has sold her EV and is working on buying a van. She wants to fit it out and live in it. Go travelling and stay on set over night as needed. I think, when she does this, I am unlikely to see her again. I am dreading this day. But she is very enthusiastic and wants to do this on her own. I get it. This is her thing, and she is literally making her own home. She is so prideful, and although I would love to help, or even be involved in a small way, I won't ask, or mention it as I already know her answer. Dad is being a complete arse about it. He wants it to happen yesterday, he's even offered (me, not Eve) to pay for it! What a git! I love him for caring but hate him for hating her and wanting her out of my life. He also, just doesn't get it. Eve **has** to do this for herself – I can't get involved, it would be *very* unwelcome, and actually, him even more so. But I do think it's odd that she has done all of this to us and to me, just so she can go and live as a gypsy. I always thought this was a lifestyle you were born into and if you wanted, struggled to escape from, rather than something to be aspired to. Very strange. Again, there is no logic to her actions. Who is this woman? I don't recognise her at all anymore.

Given the above, the house is more and more, just feeling like a house. Not a home. I look around me and see Eve **everywhere**. All the good times, and the bad (not that there many of these, well, not until she broke my heart anyway).

When she goes off on her travels, I will sell the house. I am not invested in it anymore and I can't live here alone for long or build a new life for myself in these rooms.

Despite all this, more and more I am convinced that Eve is the person I am supposed to spend my life with. This sounds bizarre, given what she has done, and when I say 'Eve', I mean the person she was, not the stranger she now is. I still find her

decision to bring our lives together crashing down baffling. But she did it, and she did so definitively and irreversibly. Love conquers all, and I still love her with what is left of my shattered heart. But love has to be mutual. And she doesn't feel this way about me. Without love on both sides, we are doomed. In particular, I can't move on, and after this time, I still have feelings for her. All that has really changed is that I am in a *lot* less pain. And so, I am much better equipped to deal with the situation. It's horrible, especially as she is still living here. I want to be with her, she doesn't want to be with me. But without the intense pain of a broken heart, I can compartmentalise and deal with things more logically.

My trans nature is also much more manageable. I am still Julia, not Adam. My prediction, back when I first started writing, has sadly proven to be true. Without Eve, Adam has lost his reason to exist – he wasn't truly real to begin with, so there wasn't anything of substance there. I may not have physically killed myself on that night, so long ago now, but one thing is for certain – only Julia came home.

I am <u>bloody good</u> at hiding this. And now, as I am not in so much pain, my daily charade continues, at least professionally…

But, when I look inside, a huge part of my heart, my soul, is missing. The part that existed to be the best possible boyfriend I possibly could be for Eve, was murdered. My ability to fully inhabit Adam's countenance and choose my gender identity was destroyed. And the male side of who I was has become nothing more than a shadow, a façade the world demands to look at, but ultimately, something without any tangible substance.

I have accepted this, and embraced who I now am. What choice did I have?

I am Julia.

As sure as night and day, without Eve, Adam does not exist. He is a pointless construct. A face to hide my heartbreak behind.

But being Julia is great. More than great in fact, I adore being her. Actually, I like **everything** about her, well, other than she is not acceptable to the world. But I, Julia, am a good person and I absolutely have value. I am a positive force in the world and whether people see me, or just Adam's face, people in general, like me. And, with the exception of Eve, want to spend time with me – my company is valued. My professional abilities are highly valued. And I am (I hope) good company.

I will say this again:

My life has value.

For so very long, I just couldn't see past the pain to this unassailable fact.

I may not leave much of a legacy ultimately, but I know that if I wasn't here, I would be missed, and my presence is a positive influence on the world.

I love Eve.

I am Julia.

I am valued.

I am a good person.

I am OK.

I am OK.

Epilogue

Friday, May 10th 2024

The future... Woo!

We are back in the future as I write this, well relative to the main body of these pages anyway. Actually, now that I think about it, by the time you read this, it will be the past again! I'm so confused right now...

And so, we come to the very end, congratulations, you have made it! More importantly, so did I.

I am not sure how I should try to wrap this all up, for me, the journey is still continuing, but I suppose I should start with where I am at this point in time, and I should explain why I am writing this now.

My new friend, Tanya, has been reading these volumes and I have been typing them up, ostensibly for her, but also, as I worked my way through them all again, for me. I have come a VERY long way since 'J-Day', all those many months ago now. And typing these volumes up has let me see just how far along the road I have travelled. I've really enjoyed, well, enjoyed is probably not the right word; re-visiting the momentous events in 2021, the not so highs, and the very lows – I confess, I have been in tears on lots of occasions whilst typing. I have also seen between the lines and have drawn some new conclusions about some of the events that happened, just joined some dots that were more obvious with hindsight but hidden from me at the time. For example, I am now pretty sure that Eve crossed the final 'Red Line' at the end of her solo Euro rally. I've no evidence *at all* other than circumstantial – but given her mindset at the time and the opportunity, plus the change in her demeanour after she returned, I believe it happened. This point in time was the beginning of the slow downward spiral to her leaving, and I think this was the catalyst that ultimately prevented us from

carrying on as housemates. Betrayal, it changes people, but none more so than the betrayer. And she just wasn't the same after the rally.

I dedicated Volume 2 to Tanya, it is very true that without her, these volumes would not exist in a format that could be read by anyone other than me (my handwriting is truly awful), so you would not be reading this now if it were not for her enthusiasm and encouragement for the words that saved me. Thank you, Tanya. Thank you for being in my corner and for knowing me, not just the shell I display to the world. And most importantly of all, thank you for being my friend.

So, what has happened and where am I now?

Well, the most important thing you should know is – I am Julia – this is the reason for the title of this very volume. Adam did not return, I am who I have always been, but now I am fully accepting of this fact and have, and still am, embracing it as fully as I can. My life is about authenticity these days, I feel I am ready to take more steps, small ones, but significant ones to me. Sometimes I try to run, and some may say, I go a little too far on occasions – for instance, I recently had my ears pierced again. I can now wear two pairs of earrings, like a lot of women, but equally, unlike almost all men. This was noticed, but everyone bar one (important) person, has reacted positively. I am also visiting a salon for regular eyebrow shaping and a pedicure. Kayleigh is my beautician, and she is also doing my electrolysis (I have a double session today, ouch – it is not something I would recommend to anyone, but the results are exactly what I need to complete what Katie and her IPL treatment started). Kay, to this day, has still only read Volume 1, I may well print off a full set and drop it off at her house. It seems like a long time ago when I last saw her, but she may well be interested to see the journey so far and for me, it will feel like closure. I am ready to close this chapter of my life and move onto the next one.

Next, in the list of most important things that have happened, is Eve left home towards the end of 2022. She finished her van, largely at her parent's house, over weekends and then one day, she said she was going on her travels, but she never returned. I was fully expecting her to after a couple of weeks or so, but she never did. There was no goodbye, or poignant hug, no tears, just a throw away comment and then she was gone. It was a massive anti-climax after all the emotional build up. I look across the chasm that divides us now and it is so wide, I can no longer see her. I am confidently walking my own path and I can at last appreciate the majesty and splendour of the view, instead of trying desperately to avoid falling back into the depths below. I am alone, well, other than Tara cat. But I am not really lonely. I was *far* lonelier when she was still living here…

Speaking of cats, shortly before Eve left, we sadly lost Larry. He was off of his food, and we eventually took him to the vet, only to find he was riddled with cancer. Poor mite. We were both there when he was sadly put to sleep – this is the last time I really cried my heart out. I miss the little fluff ball, his antics, and his attitude. Tara cat though, well she's stepped up her game, now that she has my undivided attention. She's much more interactive (sometimes a right pest), but cute as a button and I would hate to be without her – I really am turning into a crazy cat lady…

My favourite picture of Larry cat. Sleep well my little furry man.

After Eve left, my weight ballooned. At the beginning of this year, I was pretty much 26 stone – none of my clothes fit me and I was beginning to see some health issues. So, I resolved to do something about it, once and for all. I joined a local slimming club, and I am really happy to say, I have lost 4 stone in 5 months. I am motivated and 'in the zone' for the first time in my life. I am currently 21 stone 11½lbs, my interim target is 20 stone, but I will be happy if I am less than 18 stone (so I am over halfway there. Still heavy, but as mentioned, I am a big frame (6'-2"). Ideally, I would be closer to 16 stone, but we shall see what I feel like when I get there. One thing is for certain though, if running two wardrobes is expensive, you should try doing it whilst on a crash diet!

Another tangent... Back on topic Julia... Why, after all this time, am I writing this up now?

Simply because my friend Tanya wants to read them. She came into my life because of one thing – **the house is up for sale**. As a consequence, I have put a lot of things in place and carried out a number of essential home repairs etc. Tanya became my cleaner, but we hit it off on a personal level immediately. She is quite brilliant at her job, but is so much more than this to me now, we just clicked, you know? Some of this I think is because she only really knows me as Julia. Sure, she has seen me in my prison clothes, but, as someone who knows the house inside and out, there was no way I was going to be able to hide who I am from her. There are clues all over the place if you know where to look. So, when we very first met, I started off by saying that she needed to know that I am trans, because she would work it out pretty much straight away anyway. Open book, from the very beginning. Even if I am attired in something horribly male when we see each other (although we usually meet with me dressed correctly), I am able to let the mask slip, and we chat as women do, as good friends do. My demeanour changes

and regardless of how I am dressed, Julia shines through. This is **very** precious to me. To have people in my life who actually know *me*. Rachel, her daughter, and my lash technician, actually **only** knows me as Julia so far. My first appointment with her, I attended dressed correctly. She likely would walk past Adam in the street. This fact blows my mind. I would very much like this state of affairs to continue and there is no reason for it not to. I have been to see Kayleigh as me too, twice now, but I want to visit her authentically all the time if I can – leaving the house in broad daylight is still very nerve-wracking for me (I have a badge in my handbag that says: "Scared shitless but doing it anyway". It's kinda crude but seems to sum things up perfectly!) Driving the car and even walking down the high street is no problem, but my neighbours – I don't want them to be surprised or shocked by my appearance (even though I am sure they would be OK with it. I am properly attired after all, dressed smartly as a regular woman, not for any kind of effect). It's weird that I should care about this, they are very good neighbours, but I am moving house. I guess, after all this time living in such close proximity, I still want them to have a good opinion of me... So I am nervous, and I am careful. But it feels wrong, skulking around like I have something to hide. I absolutely do not.

Selling the house is the **very last** thing that ties Eve and I together – the time feels right, I want to have my own place. Somewhere just for me, somewhere I can come and go as I please, and somewhere I can build a new life for myself. I am looking, but I've not found a new home for me just yet, a few possibles, but nothing that feels right so far.

Doing things for me – this was the biggest hurdle I have overcome recently. And I have done it by doing things **for me**. Not for Adam. Buying clothes, make-up, a dressing table, electrolysis, pedicures, eyebrows and of course lashes as well as the weight loss. These are things that definitely would not

be – *"Better if I shared them with Eve"* – they are for me, and me alone. And I am <u>very</u> motivated to do them, not least of which because they are really lovely things to do. Well, maybe not the electrolysis, but the results absolutely are. My beard is finally, being beaten into submission – I have clear patches!! I can't express just how important this is to me. Thank you Katie, for giving me a head start and thank you so very much Kayleigh, for shocking each and every remaining hair into oblivion (as well as giving me pretty toes!) You two are my heroes.

I still don't know if this could be published – I suppose if you are reading this now, then I have my answer. I am not living openly as me and am unlikely to be for some time yet. It's not that I don't want to, I do, very much indeed. That bitch Dysphoria is never far from my side, but I am not in a hurry anymore – in general, I am doing things for me because I want to, not because I need to. Authenticity and validation – these are two words I try to live by these days. I am striving for both, but at this point in my life, there are still limits on what I can do, mainly professionally, sadly. I am doing things now that will help later, when I hope to be in a position to go much further. I have been editing out names as I have been typing these pages up. At the moment, there are still quite a few names left, especially in the earlier volumes, and of course, the names Eve and Adam are everywhere, even in some of the sketches making them harder to alter. There is also general location information and information on my professional life, as well as our pets, hobbies, and passions. So, I think those folk that know us personally would be able to identify us very easily, assuming they ever read this of course. Is that an issue? Well, for me, kind of. These pages are **very** personal indeed, there are things in here that I wouldn't want to be common knowledge, they are just too intimate. I think that Eve in particular would absolutely not want these pages published, although I have asked her, even offered to

share them with her, she declined to read them and just asked for names to be altered, hence "Adam and Eve", generic man/woman names (Julia though is absolutely the real me). If she knew what I've written, I don't think Eve would want them out there, largely for the same reasons, but also because, although I tried to be fair, I was in a *very* dark place, and consequently I have not always painted a rosy picture of her. I do not bear her any ill-will, as you know, I just want her to be happy – and I am pretty sure publishing these pages would likely have the opposite result. *But although I have her permission and offered to share, she has still not read them* – the opportunity was there back in 2021 too, when the handwritten journals were available to her all the time at home. But I'm pretty sure she never read them. If she had, I think her actions and attitude towards me would have been noticeably different. If she truly knew how far she had pushed me, how close to the brink I was... Then there's a whole section in Vol3 relating to our good friend Mark that was told to me in strict confidence – I have sadly had to edit this out (it's the *only* substantial edit). Betraying the details of this confidence to a wider audience is not something I would ever do. And lastly, both my dad and brother were incredibly supportive, all-be-it not in the way I needed at the time, largely because, through their own denial of who I am, they were not in the full picture. These pages are not very complimentary because of the mindset I had at the time – this journal is an honest account, warts and all, of how I was feeling and what was going through my mind. Even though I love them both dearly and in hindsight, really appreciate their support, when it was given however, I only saw the negatives, not the positives because they were attacking my love – as with any relationship, attacking a partner will elicit a very negative response, even if the attack is justified. My relationship with both my dad and my brother has improved enormously since, not that they were

aware back then that I was struggling with this, they were trying to help in the only way they knew how, and once Eve was gone, this particular brand of 'help' dried up, and so my issues with them hating her also petered out.

But, if these pages help just one person, one person in a similarly dark place, then maybe, just maybe they are worth publishing...

This is what keeps me thinking about publication.

Yep, 2024 is shaping up to be a very big year for me. A year of transformation.

I have been on hormones for a good number of months now. Blockers (anti-androgens), as well as oestrogen. This time around, they have been a revelation to me. Yes, I have taken hormones in the past, enough to develop breast tissue, but never for this long and I've never been on blockers before. I originally decided to go back on them because I am sadly, experiencing some male pattern baldness. I just can't lose my hair; or at least, I can't lose any more of it. I need to have some when I finally retire and reach the decision point to transition fully.

The hormones are damage control mainly, but of course, I am loving the other effects too. I have seen a lot of small changes, nothing hugely significant, and some odd things as well as the more expected things like subtle changes to my body shape and my skin becoming softer. An example of one of the more unexpected things was my body smell isn't the same. I am using a woman's antiperspirant, not because I want to (although of course I do), but because it is much more effective for me now than a men's deodorant.

The elephant in the room: *Eve. Do I still love her?*

Yes. I suspect I always will. But I haven't seen her in any real sense for months now. Just correspondence mainly whilst the house sells. I am now used to living on my own and my love for her is nowhere near as fierce as it was. But, when I think of her, I still only want her to be happy and I would still like her back in my life, even if only in a small way. The difference now is I am OK if this doesn't happen, a nice to have, instead of an all-consuming need. And I feel ready at last to move onto the next chapter in my life.

The biggest change though has been in the way I view the world. A little of this is hormonal I think, but this doesn't explain it all, far from it. My emotions are heightened and as such, everything I experience has a new, more meaningful emotional attachment. It all carries much more weight. The grass is more vivid, the sky is bluer, the flowers are prettier, smells are more intense, sounds are more tuneful, and my clothes feel softer and much more fulfilling. It is like a fog has been lifted on my interface with the world. Everything has been dialled up to 11. I can't go back to living such a dull, muted existence. I just can't. It's no wonder I have spent my life feeling like I am locked in a horrid male prison. All the old cliches about seeing beauty everywhere, in a drop of rain, or the smile on someone's face, are true, and most importantly, it all feels 'right'. It gives me a renewed passion for life, in every sense.

I want to see what comes next, I am sure it will be beautiful and wonderous.

I am Julia. Long live the Queen.

www.ingramcontent.com/pod-product-compliance
Lightning Source LLC
Chambersburg PA
CBHW051521020426
42333CB00016B/1728

Sadly this is the end for you dear reader,
my life story continues…